Innovation, Complexity and Economic Evolution

If evolutionary economics is to compete with neoclassical economics as a general-purpose economic theory, it needs to incorporate new aspects of socioeconomic reality, such as institutions of all types, including technical, scientific and political. Furthermore, evolutionary economics needs to be able to provide policy implications at least as interesting as those of neoclassical economics. Thus, as this book argues, evolutionary economics must become evolutionary political economy. Innovation plays a central role in the book, but not in the sense of providing a technologically determinist interpretation. Rather, the book argues that innovations do not emerge in isolation from other components of socioeconomic systems but coevolve with institutions, infrastructures and organizational forms. This concept of coevolution is absolutely central in the book and provides a link with theories of complexity. In addition to providing an epistemological basis for evolutionary economics, the link with complexity and coevolution offers the connection with evolutionary political economy. Innovations and technologies do not emerge and develop in an institutional vacuum, but interact with existing institutions and reshape them, in addition to inducing the formation of new institutions. In this process, technologies and institutions reinforce each other, providing a potential mechanism to transform socioeconomic systems. The book also explores the policy implications of these innovative societies, where wealth is created but unequally distributed. The book is addressed to open-minded economists, social scientists who are dissatisfied with the approach of neoclassical economics, technologists and policy makers.

Pier Paolo Saviotti has been Research Professor in the Grenoble unit of INRA (now INRAE), the National Institute of Agricultural Research of France, and in GREDEG CNRS in Sophia Antipolis. He taught in the Departments of Science and Technology Policy and of Economics of Manchester University (1980–1994) and in Universidad del Zulia, Venezuela. He was Visiting Professor in the University of Jena in 2002–2003, in Rand Afrikaans University (now University of Johannesburg) in 2004, in the University of Hohenheim in 2010–2011, in the Technological University of Eindhoven in 2012–2013 and in the Utrecht University in 2015–2017. In

2012 he was research fellow in the Institute of Advanced Studies of Durham University. Between January 2015 and December 2017, he has been visiting Professor in Innovation Studies, Copernicus Institute, Utrecht University. He is now Affiliate Professor at Department of Economics, St Anna School of Advanced Studies, Pisa, and associate researcher in GREDEG CNRS, Sophia Antipolis. Between July 2008 and July 2012, he has been vice-president of the International Schumpeter Society.

Saviotti is the author of several publications about the economics of innovation, development and knowledge.

Routledge Frontiers of Political Economy

Marx and *Le Capital*
Evaluation, History, Reception
Edited by Marcello Musto

Permanent Economic Disorder
Shahzavar Karimzadi

Temporary Economic Crises
Shahzavar Karimzadi

Money and Capital
A Critique of Monetary Thought, the Dollar and Post-Capitalism
Laurent Baronian

Modern Money and the Rise and Fall of Capitalist Finance
The Institutionalization of Trusts, Personae, and Indebtedness
Jongchul Kim

Innovation, Complexity and Economic Evolution
From Theory to Policy
Pier Paolo Saviotti

Economic Growth and Inequality
The Economist's Dilemma
Laurent Dobuzinskis

Wellbeing, Nature and Moral Values in Economics
How Modern Economic Analysis Faces the Challenges Ahead
Heinz Welsch

For more information about this series, please visit: www.routledge.com/Routledge-Frontiers-of-Political-Economy/book-series/SE0345

Innovation, Complexity and Economic Evolution

From Theory to Policy

Pier Paolo Saviotti

Routledge
Taylor & Francis Group
LONDON AND NEW YORK

First published 2023
by Routledge
4 Park Square, Milton Park, Abingdon, Oxon OX14 4RN

and by Routledge
605 Third Avenue, New York, NY 10158

Routledge is an imprint of the Taylor & Francis Group, an informa business

British Library Cataloguing-in-Publication Data
A catalogue record for this book is available from the British Library

Library of Congress Cataloging-in-Publication Data
Names: Saviotti, Paolo, author.
Title: Innovation, complexity and economic evolution : from theory to policy / Pier Paolo Saviotti.
Description: 1 Edition. | New York, NY : Routledge, 2023. | Series: Routledge frontiers of political economy | Includes bibliographical references and index. |
Identifiers: LCCN 2022043661 (print) | LCCN 2022043662 (ebook) | ISBN 9781032278148 (hardback) | ISBN 9781032278186 (paperback) | ISBN 9781003294221 (ebook)
Subjects: LCSH: Evolutionary economics. | Neoclassical school of economics. | Organizational change—Economic aspects. | Technological innovations—Economic aspects.
Classification: LCC HB97.3 .S278 2023 (print) | LCC HB97.3 (ebook) | DDC 330.1—dc23/eng/20221223
LC record available at https://lccn.loc.gov/2022043661
LC ebook record available at https://lccn.loc.gov/2022043662

ISBN: 978-1-032-27814-8 (hbk)
ISBN: 978-1-032-27818-6 (pbk)
ISBN: 978-1-003-29422-1 (ebk)

DOI: 10.4324/9781003294221

Typeset in Bembo
by codeMantra

Access the Support Material: www.routledge.com/9781032278186

This book is dedicated to my wife, Laura, without whose constant support, faithful companionship and tender love it would not have seen the light

Contents

Preface

This book started as an exploration of the present state of evolutionary economics and its future development. In particular, the main question underlying the book consisted of asking what evolutionary economics would need to do to compete with neoclassical economics in order to become a general-purpose theory of socioeconomic behaviour and be capable of providing equally relevant policy implications. In what is here called the modern revival of evolutionary economics, which began in the 1970s and was officially inaugurated by the 1982 book by Nelson and Winter, the theme in which most progress was made was innovation. Whereas this undoubted success must be applauded, it raises the risk of locking evolutionary economics into the role of a subset of economics specialized in the study of innovation. The strategy required to pursue the previous objective cannot consist simply of the addition of other topics to innovation, but needs to include such topics within an intellectual framework in which they are interpreted on the basis of assumptions, hypotheses and concepts different from those of neoclassical economics.

The main components of the alternative view of evolutionary economics are linked to the interactivity and instability of modern socioeconomic systems (SESs). While for neoclassical economics an economic system should normally be stable and any eventual disturbances could be expected to disappear, for evolutionary economics an economic system can be expected to be permanently dynamic, always undergoing some form of change. This shifts the focus of the discipline from equilibrium to the relationship between stability and change. Furthermore, while neoclassical economics assumes the separability of economic behaviour from other types of behaviour, as implied in the concept of homo oeconomicus, for evolutionary economics a social system is highly interactive and not separable into its different components. It is this high interactivity that justifies the choice of talking about socioeconomic systems (SESs), rather than about economic systems, and the very important role accorded to coevolution in this book. In turn, this same interactivity justifies the importance of complexity as an intellectual framework contributing to the development of modern evolutionary theories and to the conclusion that to become a general-purpose theory of socioeconomic behaviour evolutionary economics needs to become evolutionary political economics.

It is quite clear to me that this project cannot be completed by just one person. I know that some of my colleagues are working along similar lines and I hope I can contribute to what needs to be a collective effort to construct the evolutionary economics of the future.

At the end of this book, I wish to express my enormous gratitude to the community of evolutionary economists within which I have been working during most of my career. The list of people to whom I owe this gratitude needs to begin with those whom we all consider our intellectual fathers, Chris Freeman, Dick Nelson and Sidney Winter. Also, at a personal level, I can hardly imagine what my intellectual development would have been if Stan Metcalfe had not moved back to Manchester at about the same time I was appointed as a lecturer there. The collaboration we had during that period has been fundamental in determining my conception of evolutionary economics. Since the early 1980s, evolutionary economists formed a community in which we all shared a great diffidence towards neoclassical economics, a relatively unstructured conceptual basis with which to compete with it and a perceived need to construct an intellectual alternative to it. Amongst the many colleagues who influenced me, I had the most frequent interactions with Giovanni Dosi, Cristiano Antonelli, Franco Malerba, Luigi Orsenigo, Ulrich Witt, Horst Hanusch, John Foster, Kurt Dopfer, Bengt Ake Lundvall, Esben Andersen, Peter Allen, Bart Verspagen, Gerry Silverberg. To the many others who were less visible but who made my experience of evolutionary economics both agreeable and fruitful, I owe an equal debt of gratitude. Then there were those I would call travel companions, because we shared work, publications or events: they ranged from previous PhD students and colleagues from Manchester, Grenoble and Sophia Antipolis: Koen Frenken, Lionel Nesta, Marie Angele de Looze, Jean-Luc Gaffard; younger colleagues such as Andreas Pyka, Bogang Jun, Jackie Krafft, Francesco Quatraro, Sandro Montresor and Antonio Musolesi; and more experienced ones who organized lively and interesting events such as José Cassiolato, Helena Lastres, Alenka Guzman, Gabriel Yoguel, Veronica Roberts, Francisco Fatas-Villafranca and Isabel Almudi. Last but not least, Morris Teubal, with whom we published little but discussed a lot. The knowledge we can develop has always partly collective character. I do not know what I would have become without all these people.

1 Economics, qualitative change, and discontinuities

1 Introduction

The process of economic growth changed substantially starting from the industrial revolution. Whereas before that time any period of growth had always been followed by a recession and no permanent improvement in individual wealth had been possible, in the following two centuries GDP per capita increased by a factor of about ten (Figure 1.1). At least since Adam Smith, economists and economic historians tried to understand how this change in growth mechanisms took place. Although no definite and consensually accepted interpretation of the mechanisms that led to the present economic systems exists, several factors are closely associated with them. Innovation is today generally recognized as one of the main factors that contributed to make the modern world what it is. Steam engines, textile machinery, railways and steel are examples of the long series of innovations that contributed to transform advanced SES into what they are today. These innovations and the products they allowed to produce are examples of Man-Made Artefacts (MMAs).

However important, innovations were not the only factor that contributed to the economic development that has been observed in the last 200 years. Many important changes in institutions and organizational forms took place simultaneously. Examples of such changes are the emergence of a capitalist society, of the factory system, of labour unions, and later of the modern firm, of R&D, of a service society and of welfare states. All these institutional and organizational changes did not occur simultaneously with a growing stream of innovations by chance, but coevolved with them by providing rules that defined the ways in which innovations could be used in a socioeconomic system (SES). Thus, in this book I will focus our attention on the types of innovations that emerged, on the institutional and organizational changes that accompanied them and on their interactions in an overall process of coevolution. I am thus regarding the phenomenon of innovation in a general sense, including technological, organizational and

institutional innovations. In other words, I focus my attention on the differences between a non-innovative and an innovative society.

DOI: 10.4324/9781003294221-1

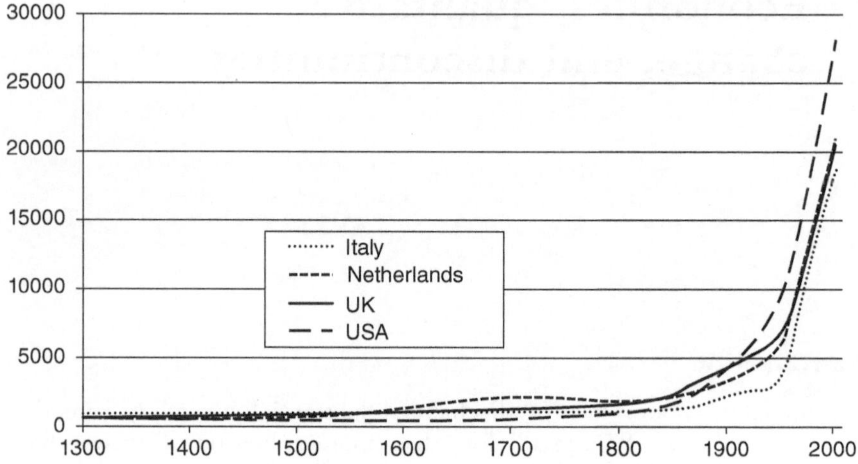

Figure 1.1 GDP per capita for the leading industrial countries.
Source: Maddison (2004).

In human history there have been innovations before the industrial revolution. Examples of such innovations are tools, water and windmills, and the wheelbarrow (Mokyr, 1990). Although extremely significant, these innovations did not have the power to change the external environment of human beings in the way that those that came after the industrial revolution did. The reasons for this enhanced effect of technological innovations on SESs which started towards the end of the XVIIIth century are likely to be related to the scientific revolution which started about 200 years before (Lipsey et al., 2005; Mokyr, 1990). Although economic historians generally agree that the early innovations of the industrial revolution were not explicitly science based until about the 1850s (Khan, 2016; Landes, 1969; Mokyr, 2005), the science of the time had already improved to the point of being able to suggest interesting experiments and to rule out worthless ones (Mokyr, 2005). These changed conditions allowed innovations to be created with a much higher frequency than in the past, thus laying the ground for the beginning of a cumulative economic development. In this sense the period before the industrial revolution can be called Malthusian and the following period post-Malthusian (Galor, Weil, 2000).

2 Man-made artefacts and structural change in socioeconomic systems

I can start our analysis with the need to represent a socioeconomic system (SES). Land, Labour (L) and capital (K) have traditionally been considered very important by economists. Land and labour are important throughout the course of human history. However, capital acquired its importance only since the beginning of the industrial revolution. This could be an understatement since capital goods can be considered exosomatic instruments (Georgescu Roegen, 1971) which expand human capabilities. The first exosomatic instruments are the stone tools that primeval human beings created. If capital goods had been the successors of stone tools, then their emergence would have occurred at the same time as land and labour. The surge in growth rates at the beginning of the industrial revolution seems to indicate that something new and different started happening then. Although capital goods can be described as exosomatic extensions of human capabilities, the scale and diversity with which they emerged since the industrial revolution makes it very difficult to compare them to primitive stone tools. Capital goods are so greatly different from primeval tools that they could only emerge and diffuse in a radically different SES, the capitalist system. The fundamental role played by capital goods increased their importance relative to that of land to the point where land has virtually disappeared from production functions (Gowdy, 1994; Daly, 2007; Georgescu Roegen, 1971). While neglecting land could in the past have been understandable in view of the rapidly falling share of agriculture in overall output, the same assumption is increasingly questionable as the impact of human activities on our physical environment makes the present model of economic development unsustainable. The exclusion of land prevents us from considering the finiteness of resources and the impact of human activities on the external environment. The reinsertion of land is required to develop models of sustainable economic development. I will come back to this topic in Chapter 4. For the time being I concentrate on the effect of the heterogeneity of capital on economic development.

The representation of labour (L) and capital (K) suffers from the problem that neither of them is homogeneous. In fact, for a very long time both labour and capital have been represented as if they are homogeneous. In this book I will consider capital goods and many types of consumer goods as MMAs and I will analyse innovation by means of a general representation of a very important category of MMAs, that of product technology.

The core of this representation will consist of distinguishing two dimensions of MMAs, one corresponding to their physical nature (the way in which different bits of matter are combined in them) and the other one to the services supplied to their users and consumers. Such a representation, which is extensible to both process technology and services, bears some similarity to the way biological species are represented by means of their traits. The similarity between biological species and MMAs lies in both being heterogeneous and qualitatively different from one another. The difference between qualitative and quantitative change will be one of the main themes underlying this book. Qualitative change has radically different implications from quantitative change for variety and knowledge. The role of heterogeneity will be studied by separating it into simpler components. In what follows I will use almost interchangeably the terms Man-Made Artefacts (MMAs), physical technologies (Beinhocker, 2007) and material products, specifying when some differences amongst them are likely to matter.

The existence of qualitative differences is not limited to MMAs but occurs also for institutions or organizational forms. For example, education and health care are two qualitatively different institutional components of an SES. In fact, MMAs and institutions or organizational forms are not independent but complementary. During economic development, they have coevolved, with new MMAs requiring new institutions or organizational forms, which in turn shaped the subsequent development of MMAs.

I begin by calling all the new goods and services which emerged during economic development new Man-Made Artefacts (MMAs). I think that the creation of these MMAs is one of the most important sources of structural change and that, although it does not exhaust the problem of economic development, it connects many of its most important aspects. Consequently, I will use the origin of MMAs as a lens through which to observe and analyse economic development.

One of the fundamental questions underlying this book is: how and why are new MMAs created? And, 'are the MMAs I can observe the only ones that could have been generated?' The tentative answer that can be formulated in the book includes by definition innovation. In fact, I will define both production and innovation based on the nature of MMAs. In this book I intend to analyse the mechanisms by means of which innovation contributed to economic development within a time horizon comparable to the one from the industrial revolution to the present. During this period such mechanisms underwent considerable changes. The choice of such a time period follows from our conviction that economics needs to be able to explain long-run processes. Economic history should be both a field of observation and a testing ground for economic theories.

2.1 MMAs and the twin characteristic representation

What is common to all MMAs is their degree of novelty, or their qualitative difference with respect to anything that preceded them. This feature is common to both MMAs and biological species. A car is different from a telephone in the same way as an elephant is different from an ant. In both cases it is generally clear to what species a given entity belongs, although there may be entities which seem to fall in between two existing and well-defined species. The other feature common to all MMAs, as well as to all biological species, is that they are all highly internally differentiated, or heterogeneous. There are thousands of car models or portable computers.

In order to define MMAs adequately, I start focusing on goods and services, and on material goods. Any material good is the meeting point of human needs and wants and of human knowledge about our physical environment. The production of material goods designed to satisfy human needs and wants requires the ability to manipulate and transform matter. Such ability has improved enormously in human history due the increase in our knowledge of the physical environment. The designer of a new physical good needs to identify an unsatisfied need or want and some materials which, when adequately treated and combined, can satisfy the need, or want. The transformation of the materials from their initial state into the finished good gives rise to the internal structure of the good. This process of transformation starts with scientific and technological knowledge, and ends with services provided for the users of the products. Scientific and technological knowledge are embodied in the technical characteristics of the technology. These are the only characteristics that can be modified *directly* by the producers. Thus, a motor car manufacturer can only design the engine and the shape of the car body in order to produce a required speed of transport, but it cannot directly produce that speed of transport. Seen from the view point of a producer, technical characteristics are like buttons that, when pushed, produce required services.

The production of all physical goods has an impact on the natural environment, by drawing from it materials and energy and by returning to it the wastes we create. Consequently, all the processes producing physical goods are subject to the second law of thermodynamics, which is concerned with the direction of natural processes. According to this law, natural processes run only in one sense, and are not reversible. In the case of isolated systems, the direction in which natural processes evolve inevitably entails an increase in entropy, which for our purposes means an increase in the *disorder* of the system. This may seem strange in the case of physical goods, which are quite ordered structures, and are certainly much more ordered than the raw materials from which they are made. This apparent contradiction is explained by the fact that the transformations occurring in a non-isolated, open system can give rise to final states more ordered than the initial ones (Prigogine, Stengers, 1985; Hidalgo, 2015, Prigogine, 1996). However, such behaviour is not incompatible with the second law of thermodynamics, which is valid for an isolated system. In fact, such exception to the second law of thermodynamics would only be 'local' confined within an open system. However, all open systems are part of larger, isolated systems, and in order to satisfy the second law of thermodynamics, the entropy generated by the wastes accompanying the production of any given MMA needs to be greater than the negative entropy corresponding to the artefact itself. Thus, the production of any material artefact (MMA) gives rise to wastes and pollution that are incompatible with the finiteness of our physical environment. This theme will be discussed again in Chapters 7 and 8. Here it is already important to note that the neoclassical production function, by including as inputs only labour and capital at the exclusion of energy and raw materials, denies itself the possibility to consider the environmental impact of human activities. For the time being I go back to the discussion of MMAs, and to those that are material goods, and stress that this discussion is of central importance for a theory of production and for a theory of production that links directly the manipulations of matter, the satisfaction of human needs and wants, and the impact on the natural environment.

A given internal structure is used to supply services that in turn satisfy human needs and wants. I can then represent a physical good of this type by means of two sets of characteristics, corresponding to the internal structure and to the services supplied to users and consumers respectively (Figure 1.2). The services correspond to human needs and wants and can be used to represent demand. Biological species have a genotype and a phenotype, the former determined by their genetic heritage and the latter by their traits. Man-made artefacts do not have a phenotype but can be represented by means of a dichotomy between their internal structure and the services they perform for their consumers or users. This representation has been proposed by Saviotti and Metcalfe (1984) (Saviotti, 1996).

Furthermore, MMAs can be considered as interfaces between an *inner environment*, 'the substance and organization of the artifact itself', and an *outer environment*, the surroundings in which it operates (Simon, 1969, 1981). One can clearly think of the internal structure as the inner environment and of the service characteristics as the interface (Saviotti, 1986). Finally, MMAs based on a material product correspond to what Beinhocker (2007) called physical technologies. It is interesting to note that the reordering of matter in the production of material goods had already been noted by Marshall (1961) and Daly (2007).

In this representation, two different MMAs have qualitatively different technical and/or service characteristics. The emergence of a new MMA occurs when a completely new internal structure or a new set of services or both are created by means of a radical innovation. An example can help to understand this aspect of the problem. An aircraft and a train can be considered two different 'technologies' which supply transport services. Their services are not entirely equivalent, but there is a degree of substitutability between them. However, their internal structures are completely different and require *qualitatively* different concepts and variables to be represented. Two different

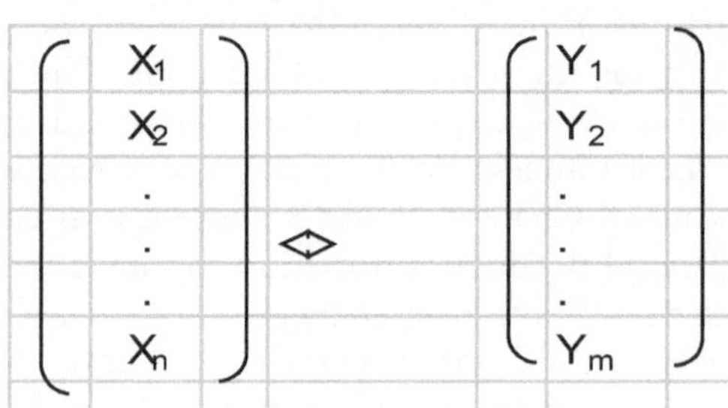

Figure 1.2 Twin characteristic representation.

technologies differ at least for their internal structure. A change in technology implies a change in internal structure. The case in which both internal structure and services are new is probably rare. I think that many innovations give rise to new internal structures which satisfy existing needs and wants in new or improved ways. For example, cars, trains, and airplanes supply transport services, which correspond to an ever-existing want for mobility. Similarly, telephones, e-mail and Skype correspond to a want for communication. These different product technologies supply similar but not identical services. We could say that the initial want for mobility which existed in mankind since the beginning of history becomes differentiated into a set of component services representing different aspects of mobility. We use an airplane when we go from Europe to America but we can choose to fly, go by train, or go by bus when we go from Paris to London. Various means of transport are potential substitutes in some trips but not in others since they differ for their speed, payload, and the range of distances they can cover. Thus, in the process of economic and technological evolution, new wants are created and existing wants become more and more differentiated.

The internal structures of new MMAs are initially created, based on intuition and simple forms of learning by doing. Examples of such artefacts could be tools, simple clothing, etc. Gradually, during human evolution, a form of technological knowledge, which was sometimes referred to as 'the industrial arts' was created. Until quite recently such technological knowledge was separate from scientific knowledge. It is only since the XVIIIth century that technology became closer to science, although the two types of knowledge remained quite distinct (Mokyr, 2005). The main point I want to stress here is that the evolution of MMAs required human knowledge of the natural environment to transform matter and energy into services which could then be supplied to human beings in order to satisfy their wants and needs. Of course, the types of knowledge which led to the creation of man-made artefacts have changed enormously in the course of human history and more so since the scientific and industrial revolutions.

We can think of all these needs, wants and functions as giving rise to human activities consisting of the transformation of inputs into outputs. These inputs and outputs can be both material and immaterial. In most cases, human labour, either raw or augmented as human capital, and knowledge are two of the inputs. Other inputs can be physical capital, materials, energy, etc. Amongst these inputs, knowledge occupies a particular place because without the changes it underwent in the course of human history, the economic development which occurred since the industrial revolution would not have been possible. I am not referring here only to scientific knowledge but to all types of knowledge human beings can use to improve their adaptation to the external environment (EE). Thus, craft knowledge and the knowledge engineers use to build airplanes, bridges or tools are parts of it. In Chapter 5 I will discuss the nature of knowledge, which can be of the EE or, increasingly, of human societies. The former can help us to transform material inputs into material outputs, thus creating very large number of MMAs. Incidentally, natural resources become resources only when human knowledge finds ways to create value for them. The sticky black stuff which sits in underground reservoirs from which it can be extracted with variable difficulty would never have acquired the economic weight it has today unless human knowledge found ways to transform it into energy, plastics, rubber, fertilizers, etc. We could then say that human knowledge is embodied in man-made artefacts. In the meantime, man-made artefacts are created to satisfy some human needs or wants by transforming materials and energy into services.

In principle, there is no necessity for the laws of nature and the world of human needs and wants to be connected. It is just human knowledge which gave rise to MMAs by creating a bridge between laws of nature and human needs and wants. It is knowledge of the external environment (EE) which allows us to detect the combinations of inputs which can give rise to outputs which in turn can satisfy human needs and wants, a point which will be explored in Chapter 3. The general point I would like to stress here is that the satisfaction of all these needs and wants is obtained by the 'consumption' of goods or services, goods or services which are themselves produced by transforming some inputs into outputs. For example, a watch, a portable telephone, or a holiday package, which supply time measurement, communication, or leisure services, are produced by combining human capital, materials, energy and knowledge. Human knowledge allows us to detect combinations of matter and energy which can supply useful (welfare-enhancing) services to their consumers and users. The number of such combinations increased enormously with the progress of human knowledge.

The previous general representation of product technology is applicable to both consumers and capital goods. In principle, it is also applicable to process technology, since a process can be considered a sequence of activities, each using capital goods. An extension to chemical or pharmaceutical technologies is possible. In summary, the twin characteristic representation is in principle applicable to a very wide range of technologies.

2.2 Generalized production of services

So far in our analysis of MMAs, I have focused exclusively on physical products, represented as having an internal structure, of a physical nature and a set of services which they supplied to users and consumers. I had stated at the beginning that MMAs should include both goods and services. Here I extend our representation of MMAs to pure services, that is, to services which are directly supplied by human beings, either individually or as members of an organization. Such an extension has been proposed by Gallouj and Weinstein (1997). I opt for an even simpler one, based on the generalization that all human activities produce services of some nature, intended to satisfy some wants. There can thus be two paths through which these services can be supplied, one in which they are supplied indirectly by embodying them in material artefacts, and the other one in which they are supplied directly by human beings. I will call the former type *indirect* or *embodied* services and the latter type *direct* or *disembodied* services (Figure 1.3).

Of course, what is here called disembodied is in fact supplied by human labour supplied by individuals or organizations. Most of these services can be supplied in both an embodied form and a disembodied form. In other words, the embodied and disembodied forms can compete. Of course, even disembodied services increasingly require the use of capital equipment. However, in this case consumers and users purchase only the services and not the associated capital goods, as they would do in the embodied case. A relevant example of this substitutability is given by the possible substitution of cinemas by television coupled with recording or streaming devices for showing films (Table 1.1). In the former case the service would be supplied in a direct or disembodied form while in the latter it would be supplied in an indirect or embodied form. In fact, the latter case would correspond to what Gershuny (1978) called self-services. Other examples of the substitutability of embodied and of disembodied services are given in Table 1.1.

Here we can observe that the substitution of disembodied by embodied services has been an extremely important trend since the industrial revolution. For example, the services supplied by spinners and weavers were embodied in machines in the textile industry. An extremely important example of this substitution will be given in Chapter 5, where the transition to SESs in which employment is predominantly concentrated in service activities will be discussed.

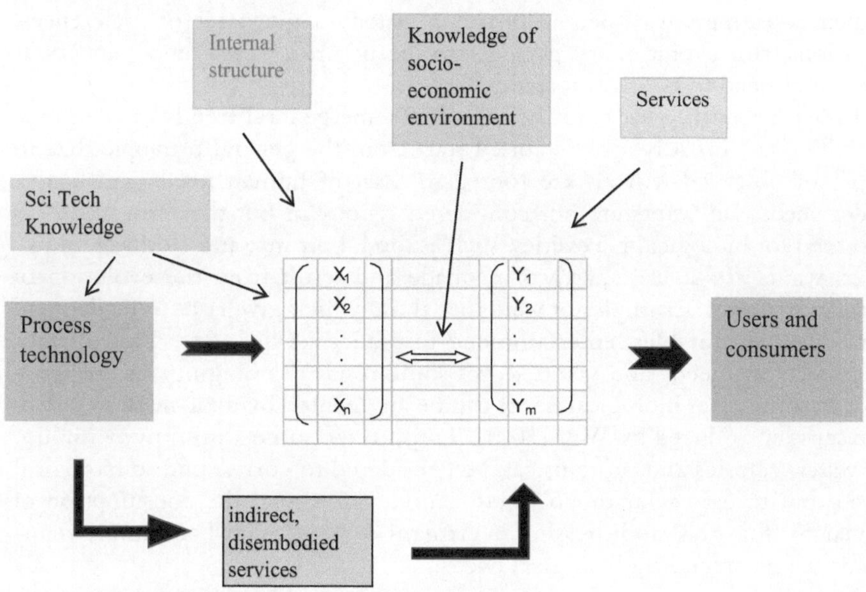

Figure 1.3 Embodied and disembodied services.

Table 1.1 Examples of embodied and disembodied services

Embodied	*Disembodied*
Photographic camera	Professional photographer or shop
Medical self-testing device	Physician
Television + DVD	Cinema
Car	Buses, trains, taxis
Booking trips on computer or portable telephone	Travel agency
Bread making machine	Baker

2.3 MMAs, wants, needs and basic human functions

If we are interested in the analysis of long-run economic development, we need to face several questions related to the evolution of both the internal structure and the services of MMAs. For example, 'How did different types of needs and wants arise and give rise to the supply of services either pure or embodied in MMAs?' and 'Are they always present in a constant set and are they only gradually satisfied as the required technical capabilities are developed?' Or, 'Are some of them inherent in the biological nature of human beings while others are created by the process of economic development?' Thus, theories of the *content* of demand, rather than only of the quantity demanded, are required for the analysis of long-run economic development. A central point in this respect is occupied by a theory of preferences. While in mainstream economics the only relevant problem is considered the way in which consumers use their resources to satisfy a given set of preferences, in a long-run evolutionary perspective the nature of preferences and their dynamics need to be investigated.[1]

I start by putting forward the idea that some general trends in economic activities are 'broadly' predictable. I start from the general principle that all types of observed MMAs are rooted in a set of human needs and wants. Here needs and wants are not considered synonyms but the term 'needs' is reserved for biological necessities, such as food, housing, and clothing. However, wants are at least partly man-made and result from the evolution of human societies. Examples of wants are those which give rise to the demand for consumer durables, entertainment, insurance services, etc. This distinction between needs and wants leaves some residual ambiguity in the sense that in some cases biological needs can be augmented by man-made wants in the sense introduced by Witt (2001). Thus, to consume a minimum amount of water, calories and proteins can be considered to correspond to biological needs but to eat caviar or 'fois gras' cannot. However, the consumption of caviar or 'fois gras' and dressing in Armani or Yves Saint Laurent are man-made wants extending biological needs.

Not all wants arise from biological necessities. Many wants correspond to what could be considered basic human functions. These functions are customarily carried out as part of the life of human groups, or communities, and contribute to the survival and adaptation of such groups. Examples of these functions are travel, transport, and communications. These functions, while not being biological necessities, can provide given communities with competitive advantage in their access to vital resources, such as food, which are biological necessities. Functions such as travel, transport and communications can then be considered group or social necessities, and they are at the origin of large and growing numbers of human wants. For example, the need for communication was at the origin of language. In turn, the usefulness of language was greatly enhanced by means of storing food. Printing first and ITC later constituted revolutionary developments in the storage and transmission of written information. These function related wants do not correspond to biological necessities but to social or group necessities and they evolve in the course of time because of changes in human knowledge and technology. For example, the transport function gave rise first to the domestication of animals (horses, mules, etc.) and later to the creation of MMAs (cars, buses, trains, airplanes, ships, etc.). The evolution of the wants and services supplied by MMAs to satisfy these wants could be placed in this general context. The mechanisms giving rise to human wants and needs which emerged during economic development can then be summarized in Table 1.2.

A question that has always escaped the attention of economists and which probably cannot have a complete answer is: what is the nature, or content, of innovations? I can certainly notice that some of the most important innovations of the XXth century are about means of transport, chemical processes or telecommunications, but could we have predicted that innovations were going to emerge in these fields rather than in other ones? Or, for that matter, could we now predict what the innovations of the XXIst century are going to be? Quite likely a complete answer to these questions is impossible to obtain for what concerns radical innovations, otherwise we could produce innovations at will by an algorithm in the same way as routines.

We can expect that to be successful innovations will have to supply services corresponding to biological necessities, or to basic human functions and induced functions and wants (Table 1.2). What is more difficult to predict is the internal structure that innovations corresponding to the functions and

Table 1.2 Human needs, wants and functions

1. **Satisfaction of biological necessities (innovations in agriculture, textiles, house building, etc.)**
2. **Enhanced satisfaction of biological necessities (high-quality differentiated goods and services, tools)**
3. **The productive processes required to produce 1 and 2**
4. **Basic human functions (transport, communications, etc.)**
5. **Induced functions and wants (substitution of human labour, health care, education, insurance financial services, etc.)**
6. **Leisure activities**

wants will have. As we have seen, the internal structure of a product innovation is a combination of different types of matter and energy that can supply particular services. The progress of science and technology has been essential to conceive and realize these internal structures (Saviotti, 1996; Lipsey et al., 2005). Furthermore, comparable types of services can be produced by different types of internal structure, as electrical or internal combustion engine cars show. In summary, the types of services that successful innovations will need to supply are likely to fall within one of the classes of Table 1.2, while no such regularity is likely to occur for internal structures.

3 Qualitative change and economic development

The distinction between qualitative and quantitative change is by no means trivial and it occupied the mind of philosophers at least since Greek times. However, qualitative change is much more difficult to study than quantitative change. Qualitatively different entities are not commensurable and we cannot apply to them any mathematical operations. During the development of modern science, qualitative change was eliminated by focusing on what Galileo and Descartes called primary qualities (Losee, 1977, pp. 71–73), such as shape, size, number, and position, which they considered objective properties of bodies, to be distinguished from secondary qualities, such as colours, tastes, odours, and sounds, which in their view existed only in the mind of the perceiving subject. In the subsequent development of physics, only changes of quantity or position were considered. The same happened with economics, although the presence and importance of qualitative change is likely to be more relevant than in physics, or at least of the physics that was developed until the beginning of the XXth century. As Georgescu Roegen said:

> ...the prevalent temper in economics is to ignore qualitative change and even to belittle all preoccupations with it despite the fact that in the economic domain change is even more the soul of what happens than in astrophysics.
>
> (1971, p. 62)

To stress the importance of qualitative change does not mean that quantitative change is unimportant. In fact, the boundaries between qualitative and quantitative change are sometimes both fuzzy and shifting. The emergence of a new product created by a radical innovation is an example of qualitative change, but it is usually followed by several incremental innovations that improve its performance without transforming its nature, as it happens, for example, in product and industry life cycles (Klepper, 1996; Jovanovic MacDonald, 1994). However, at what time in the life cycle does the emergence end and the initial qualitative change is transformed into a gradual quantitative change? And, is the entity that originated the new sector the same throughout the long series of incremental innovations?

The distinction and representation of qualitative and quantitative change is easy to establish in general but there can be some ambiguities in cases that seem intermediate between the previous two. For example, *Ornithorhynchus anatinus* is a mammal laying eggs and having other characteristics intermediate between mammals and birds. Also, are amphibious cars, cars, or planes? Furthermore, the distinction between inter-sector variety and intra-sector quality is a relevant example, and constitutes a very important stylized fact about economic development: since the beginning of the XXth century, there has been a considerable increase in product quality and intra-sector diversification (see Chapter 5). Such increase in quality has been 'measured' by means of the characteristics of the different product models supplied by producers and sellers. The idea of measuring the change in quality of different product models may seem a contradiction in terms since qualitatively different objects are by definition non-comparable. The apparent contradiction can in fact be overcome by decomposing differences in quality into common components: then the different quantities, or levels, of each in product models measure the differences in quality (Box 1.2). Despite its problems, such measures of quality have been used in several economic problems in addition to the measurement of variety. For example, they have been used in explaining the price of product models by means of the hedonic price method (Rosen, 1974), which is used in the construction of price indexes, in the analysis of demand and in that of productivity.

One of the most important implications of qualitative change is that it gives rise to discontinuities. Discontinuities are breaks, sudden and drastic changes which, when they occur, completely transform the nature of existing systems. For example, the industrial revolution represented a discontinuity in those human activities which transformed matter and energy. The concept of discontinuity is closely related to that of revolution. The types of discontinuities that we will be mostly concerned with in this chapter are discontinuities in technology and industry, discontinuities in knowledge and discontinuities in institutions and organizations. Discontinuities in technology and industry occur when a new MMA emerges. Examples of this situation are the emergence of trains, cars, and computers. Nothing like them existed before in human history. The converse of a discontinuity is a process of continuous and quantitative change in which an existing entity undergoes modifications which somehow improve the 'performance' of the given entity while leaving the entity recognizably the same. For example, motor cars after their initial invention at the end of the XIXth century have enormously evolved in those properties that define their performance while remaining motor cars. The distinction between discontinuity and continuous change corresponds to that between qualitative and quantitative change or between radical and incremental innovations: the emergence of motor cars was a radical innovation, the result of qualitative change and giving rise to a discontinuity, while the subsequent evolution of motor cars consisted mostly of incremental innovations which enormously improved the performance of motor cars.

The existence of discontinuities is not limited to MMAs. Discontinuities can occur for institutions, organizations, or whole economic systems. The industrial revolution gave rise to a discontinuity in the process of growth of human societies. Such a discontinuity is revealed by the sudden (in historical times) change of slope of the curve for the output of several economic systems (Maddison, 1982, 2001, 2004) (Figure 1.1). Starting from the industrial revolution, the rate of growth of output became enormously higher than at any previous times. Amongst the possible factors underlying such a discontinuity, there are the innovations which allowed human beings to generate non-animal energy, to develop machinery capable of enhancing and substituting human labour, and to organize human labour in ways which are substantially different from the past.

3.1 The evolution of MMAs

As pointed out, an important example of qualitative change is provided by the evolution of MMAs. Not only MMAs are qualitatively different from one another but they are heterogeneous. Each MMA is defined by the presence of several technical characteristics, corresponding to a given internal structure of the technology, and by some services provided to its users. Therefore, each MMA is represented by a population of different models, each having different values, or levels, of the same technical characteristics. The properties of each MMA and the role it plays in the economic development of an SES depend both on the 'average' properties of an MMA and on their distribution in the population. Thus, in the whole SES there are several distinguishable populations of MMAs, each containing many members with different values, or levels, of the common characteristics defining the MMA. The whole SES is differentiated at the level of aggregation of the MMA and of its members.

I can recall here that one of the main differences between neoclassical and evolutionary economics is the heterogeneity of agents (Dosi, Nelson, 1994; Nelson, 1995). Such heterogeneity implies that the objects of choice of consumers and users of MMAs are equivalently heterogeneous. From the heterogeneity of demand follows logically the heterogeneity of generalized services and of the capital goods required to produce all MMAs. This stresses that another very important difference between neoclassical and evolutionary economics is not just the presence of dynamics but that of the *dynamics of qualitative change* in the latter: neoclassical economics never attempted to study qualitative change, following in this the approach adopted by physics until the end of the XIXth century.

3.2 Capital goods

Capital goods are qualitatively different, and cannot be compared directly in terms of their physical characteristics, but become comparable when measured in terms of their price.[2] While this might seem a solution to the problem of qualitative change, it is only a partial solution. If capital intensity in each economy increased very rapidly, but if in the meantime the efficiency with which capital goods are produced increased even faster, the total value of capital goods could fall while the quantity used in the economy increased. Furthermore, the nature of capital goods could change during the process considered above. In this case the effect of the same quantity of capital goods could increase even if their price were to fall in the meantime. Computers have provided recently quite a spectacular example of this situation. In fact, the concept of capital as it has been used in economics implicitly assumes that the aggregation of capital units can give us a homogeneous whole that can be used to study economic development. While this can be a useful approximation for some purposes, it hides the nature of the processes by means of which capital is created and used (Endres, Harper, 2012, 2013). Such a process involves the creation of new types of MMAs and their combination with other types of MMAs and institutions in a coevolutionary process. The qualitative change occurring when two technologies differing at least in their internal structure compete and one of them replaces the other is at the centre of the so-called technological transitions (Geels, 2002a, 2002b, 2004). Of course, such transitions do not occur in an institutional vacuum but are a primary example of the coevolution of technologies, institutions, organizational forms, infrastructures, and complementary technologies. This approach follows from the research tradition on sociotechnical systems (Pinch, Bijker, 1984; Rip Kemp, 1998), but, apart from the terminology and the interdisciplinary mixture used, involves the coevolution of different components of an SES.

3.3 Variety vs differentiation

When an MMA has members sharing the same characteristics but differing in the levels of these characteristics, the MMA is internally differentiated. This is an example of intra-sector diversification. The variety of a system is affected by the number of its distinguishable MMAs and by the extent of their internal diversification. Thus, variety depends on qualitative differences while internal differentiation depends on quantitative differences.

To decompose two apparently qualitatively different entities into common components, often used in different disciplines, allows us to perform measurements of the relative properties of qualitatively different entities. Examples of this procedure are the reduction of complex objects, such as biological cells, physical objects, or goods, to combinations of entities at a lower level of aggregation, such as atoms, molecules, or product characteristics (Saviotti, 2007).

According to our definition, MMAs need to be distinguishable. For example, a car and a computer are clearly distinguishable. However, sometimes there may be doubts about how different two potential MMAs are. For example, are a Rolls Royce and a Renault Twingo two different MMAs or different members of the same MMA? As there are different types of elephants there can be different types of cars or computers. In order to deal with this point,

I assume that two MMAs are different if they are *qualitatively* different from each other while the different members of the same MMA differ only *quantitatively*. For example, as in the biological case, the different members of the same MMA could have different values of the same traits. Even this distinction is not free from criticisms since extremely different biological species, such as an elephant and an ant, could have been derived from common antecedents by the accumulation of very small modifications. However, in this and similar cases the populations of two MMAs would be clearly separated in characteristic space. Summarizing, I consider that two MMAs are different if they are *qualitatively* different either when they share no characteristics (inter-sector differentiation) or when an MMA is internally diversified, but when its members differ enough for the level of their characteristics for their populations not to overlap in characteristics space. In the latter case I can even measure a distance between the populations, two MMAs, and such a distance can be considered an index of dissimilarity of the two MMAs.

The previous discussion shows that despite difficulties sometimes inherent in it, the distinction between qualitative and quantitative change is very important and that it can be used analytically.

3.4 Efficiency and creativity

The distinction between qualitative and quantitative change finds a counterpart in that between *efficiency* and *creativity*. The concept of efficiency follows from the ratio between the outputs and the inputs of a given process.[3] I can say that the efficiency of a process increases when the quantity of inputs required to produce one unit of a qualitatively constant type of output falls. For example, the efficiency of shoe production increases if the amount of leather, glues, rubber, labour, etc. used to produce one pair of shoes falls. However, this definition of efficiency makes sense only if the type of shoes produced is qualitatively constant. If the shoes produced change from very basic to luxurious ones and we find that the quantities of inputs required to produce the more luxurious type of shoes is greater than the one required for the more basic type, we cannot by that say the efficiency of the process has fallen since we have now combined a change of efficiency with a change of quality, and correspondingly of value. In other words, a change in the efficiency of a given process can only be measured at constant output quality. In Chapter 4 it will be shown that the economic development observed since the industrial revolution cannot be explained by increases in efficiency alone, but requires a combination of efficiency and creativity, the latter being the capacity to give rise to qualitative change.

4 Analytical implications of the twin characteristic representation

The previous representation has important analytical implications for the substitution or specialization of technologies, for competition and for demand.

All such implications follow from (i) the *heterogeneity* of all MMAs and (ii) the completely different nature of the dimensions in which the two sets of characteristics exist. Let us begin with heterogeneity. Each of the characteristics corresponding to a given MMA can have a range of values. Thus, there can be small or large, fast or slow cars or aircraft as well as simple or extremely sophisticated cameras or portable telephones. Each MMA is constituted by a 'population' of members which have different values of common characteristics. The common characteristics define the MMA while their values define their members. The population of each MMA contains a distribution of the defining characteristics' values. The existence of such heterogeneous populations depends on the existence of corresponding distributions of preferences and purchasing power amongst consumers or users of the MMAs. Let us observe here that one of the most important differences between mainstream and evolutionary theories is the heterogeneity of agents in the latter (Nelson, 1995; Dosi, Nelson, 1994). Each consumer or user can be expected to buy a member of an MMA, or a model, corresponding to his/her preferences and purchasing power. The difference between mainstream and evolutionary theories corresponds to that between a typological and a population approach (see Saviotti, 1996, Metcalfe, 1998), where the former focuses on the representative individual (the means) while the latter considers both the means and the distribution of the population. A given MMA is represented by two populations of models: one in technical characteristics, corresponding to its internal structure, and one in service characteristics space, corresponding to the services performed by the MMA. In both technical and service characteristics spaces, the population representing the MMA is constituted by a distribution of points, each point corresponding to a model. Thus, the population of an MMA is represented by a cloud of points, of variable shape and density. In the course of time, we can expect the population of an MMA to change position, number of models included and extent of segmentation. All these features of the population acquire increased significance in the long run, since the distribution of models does not remain constant as the means changes.

In the presence of heterogeneity, there can be several types of substitution and specialization. Both processes are affected uniquely by service characteristics. In pure substitution, a new technology (T2) with a different internal structure supplies the same services as an old technology (T1) but at a lower cost.[4] In partial substitution, the new technology supplies a different range of services, some of which coincide with those of the old technology and some of which are different. In an extreme case, the new technology T2 can supply all the services of the old one plus some additional ones. This difference in substitutability can have an impact on the substitution process and economic development. In pure substitution, the old technology T1 is completely replaced by T2 and the substitution process is driven uniquely by their relative prices; in partial substitution, a technological specialization with market segmentation is likely to occur, with each of the two technologies acquiring a share corresponding to its advantage in cost or performance. In the case of partial substitution, in which T2 supplies all the services of T1 and some additional ones, the substitution can even be complete.[5] Examples of different types of technological substitution and technological specialization are given in Box 1.1 and eResources (Chapter 1).

Box 1.1 Examples of different types of substitution

Watches: (i) mechanical vs (ii) digital. They have radically different internal structures. (ii) supplies most of the services of (i) at a lower cost, plus new services, but does not supply the 'status' service. Outcome: market segmentation – (ii) dominates the low-price segment, while (i) dominates the high-price segment.

Cameras: (i) chemical vs (ii) digital. They have radically different internal structures. (ii) supplies all the services of (i) at a lower cost, plus new services. Outcome: complete substitution of (i) by (ii).

Cars: (i) internal combustion cars vs (ii) electric cars. They have radically different internal structures. (ii) supplies cleaner and cheaper transport services than (i) but (ii) has a lower autonomy and a higher fixed cost, plus lacks infrastructures. Outcome: substitution of (i) by (ii) just beginning. To become complete, higher autonomy (improved batteries) and better infrastructures (charging stations) required.

4.1 Competition

The concept of perfect, or pure, competition used in mainstream economics has been criticized by several economists – Morgenstern (1972), Georgescu Roegen (1971, p. 32), McNulty (1968), Hayek (1947, 1978), Marshall (8th ed., p. 355) including recently evolutionary ones (Metcalfe, 1998) – stressing that it involves neither interaction or rivalry nor the presence of increasing returns. Underlying their different criticisms there are two tensions:

i The tension between competing by doing what others are doing as well or better than them, and competing by being the first one to do what no one else is doing.
ii The tension between the allocation of existing resources and the creation of new ones. This tension between competition as a coordinator of existing human activities and as a promoter of economic development had already been recognized by Adam Smith (Metcalfe, 1998).

These tensions are clearly perceived by Schumpeter (1942), who pointed out that competition is based not only on price but also on 'the new commodity, the new technology, the new source of supply, the new type of organization' (p. 84).

Following the previous considerations, we can distinguish two types of competition: one called Schumpeterian competition, which consists of being the first one to do what no one else is doing and stresses the creation of new resources; and another one called classical competition, which consists of doing what all competitors are doing, but more efficiently, and stresses the allocation of existing resources. However, even within Schumpeterian competition a further distinction is possible between the creation of a qualitatively new product or service and the intra-sector diversification of an existing product or service.

The locus of competition between firms is their output, be that a physical product or an immaterial service. Both physical products and immaterial services exist as diversified populations of models. Competition is a form of selection in which consumers or users select differentially firms' output. The outputs which are selected more often reinforce firms and conversely. Thus, firms are selected differentially based on their output. In fact, only mono-product firms would correspond to this description. Large firms produce highly differentiated outputs addressing different markets. In this sense the actual unit of selection is the business unit (Metcalfe, 1998; Beinhocker, 2007), if it produces only one homogeneous product. Business units are indirectly selected.

Each product is represented by a population of models, a set of points in characteristics space. Here I assume that competition occurs mostly in service characteristics space. Technical characteristics, representing the internal structure of a product technology, are generally not known to most consumers and they are unlikely to affect their choices. Products supplying qualitatively different services will be in completely different regions of characteristics space and will not be competing. In order to compete, different products need to have at least some common service characteristics. Here the case of products supplying the same types of services will be discussed and the situation will be simplified by using a bidimensional characteristics space. A relevant example is that of different transport technologies, such as cars, trains, and planes. If we represent them in the space of speed and range, we will find that the populations of cars and trains overlap to a limited extent while those of cars and planes overlap much less (Figure 1.4). Now, we can expect different products to compete to the extent that their populations overlap. Furthermore, the intensity of competition can be expected to vary also within the same product. In general, we can expect the intensity of competition to be directly proportional to the similarity of product models or, conversely, inversely proportional to their distance in service characteristics space (Figure 1.5). Thus, we can calculate the pairwise intensity of competition between two product models within a given product population (Eq. 1.2) and the relative intensity of competition of different product populations (Eq. 1.2):

$$IC_{ij} \propto \frac{1}{D_{ij}} \tag{1.1}$$

$$IC_j \propto \frac{1}{D_j} \tag{1.2}$$

Schumpeterian and classical competition have different implications for economic development. Whereas the Schumpeterian entrepreneurs creating a qualitatively new product or service increase the variety of the SES and give rise to an expansionary effect, different firms interacting through classical competition increase production efficiency but at best increase the quantity of output without changing output variety. However, intra-sector differentiation can contribute to monopolistic competition and raise variety but at a lower level of aggregation than Schumpeterian competition. In this sense, monopolistic competition can be an intermediate case between classical and Schumpeterian competition. To better understand this point, I will need to stress our difference with another of the basic conditions of perfect competition, that of product uniqueness and homogeneity of firms. This point will be better explained if I examine a further concept of competition, the one used in biology.

Biological species compete for resources, which in this case could be food, water, or shelter. By definition in this case competition is an interaction in which if one competitor gains the other one loses. In other words, biological competition is a zero-sum game. Another feature of the biological concept of competition is that species compete with other species which use the same or a very similar resource. For example, birds compete only with other birds eating seeds of the same size. Thus, an eagle will not compete with a sparrow. Furthermore, competition is an interaction which occurs when the quantity of resources (food or services supplied satisfying a given want) is inferior to the quantity demanded, or, in other words, when there is *scarcity* of the resource. If the quantity of services supplied were larger than the demand for them, there would be no need for competition. An excess supply can exist during periods both in biological environments and in real economic systems. However, when this happens either an increase in the biological population or a decrease in the supply of the wanted services is induced, thus

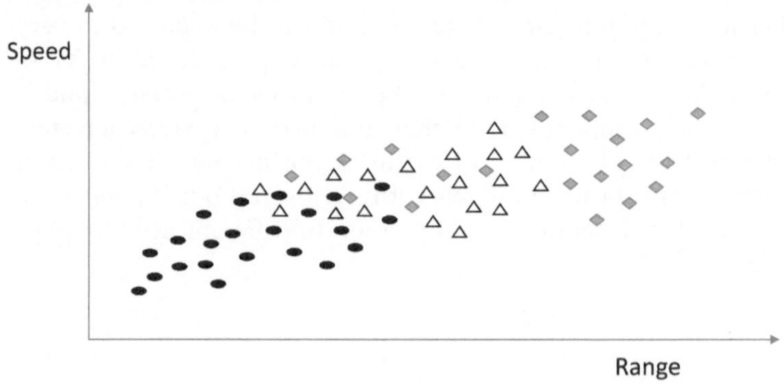

Figure 1.4 Semiquantitative representation of the populations of product models of different transport technologies (cars ●, trains ▲ and planes ◆ in the space of the two service characteristics, speed, and range.

leading the system back to a local equilibrium. The intensity of competition is related to the balance between demand and supply.

Finally, it is to be observed that in biology competition is only one of the possible forms of interaction, the other ones being commensalism and predation (Maynard Smith, 1974, p. 5). Commensalism, which is defined as an interaction in which each species has an accelerating effect on the growth of the other, is a form of cooperation related to complementarity. Economics' excessive emphasis on competition neglects the fact that complementarity can have a role in economic development as important as competition. For example, the emergence of complementary sectors and activities can be expected to exert a different, and possibly greater, effect on economic development than the emergence of independent and non-interacting sectors.

In Figure 1.5 product models are unevenly distributed in service characteristics space: some are very close and some are very far apart, or, in other words, the density of product models in service characteristics space is uneven. Furthermore, Y_1 and Y_2 are assumed to measure required services, with higher values of Y_1 and Y_2 indicating higher and more desirable, if more costly, product quality. Finally, the population of models in Figure 1.5 has regions of relatively high density near the origin and lower density further away from the origin. In the region near the origin of the axes, where the level of services is low, the density and the intensity of competition are very high. Simple product models in the low-quality region near the origin of the axes compete intensely amongst themselves but they are unlikely to compete with those which are furthest away from the origin and which represent high-quality products. The former could be a very cheap type of car while the latter could be luxury cars. The general principle that can be derived from this figure is that the intensity of competition between product models is inversely proportional to their distance, or equivalently, directly proportional to their similarity in service characteristics space. Therefore, a producer who can produce a unique combination of service characteristics within a given

Figure 1.5 Distribution of the product models of a given technology in service characteristics space.

population can be expected to have some degree of 'local' monopoly depending on how the product models of other competitors are placed. Let us bear in mind that the situations represented in Figures 1.4 and 1.5 correspond uniquely to the differentiation of already existing products or services but cannot represent the emergence of a qualitatively new product or service. Such emergence would need to be represented in new dimensions of characteristics space.

The above heterogeneity of product populations emerged after the industrial revolution and during the XXth century, in what Saviotti and Pyka (2013) called the transition from 'necessities to imaginary worlds' and in what some commentators call the consumer revolution (Saviotti, 2018). In this transition, together with the emergence of new goods and services, existing goods and services became of increasingly higher quality and increasing intra-sector differentiation.

This historically created heterogeneity has important implications for the theory of competition. Amongst the conditions required for the existence of perfect competition, there is the homogeneity of products or outputs. It was previously pointed out that the vast majority of goods and services traded today are not homogeneous. Consequently, perfect competition does not exist in the corresponding markets. However, an equivalent of perfect competition can exist when two or more product models of different business units have identical service characteristics. In this case a population of product models would be represented by a unique point in a multi-characteristics service space, given that all the models would have the same service characteristics. In this case there could not be monopolistic competition but only classical competition based uniquely on efficiency and price. Except for the previous case, we can expect (i) competition to be monopolistic rather than perfect and to allow each producer to have a region of 'local' monopoly in service characteristics space, (ii) the intensity of monopolistic competition to increase as the density of the product population in service characteristics space falls, (iii) the extent of monopolistic competition to be higher in regions of low density than in regions of high density.

So far, I have been discussing the implications for competition of differentiation occurring within a given product population and thus within a given sector. Competition is also affected by the emergence of new product populations. This is the most typical example of Schumpeterian competition which consists of doing something that no one else can do to reap the advantages of a temporary monopoly. The new product populations arising in this way can be (i) new products with internal structures and services qualitatively different from any existing ones, or (ii) new products with new internal structures supplying services like existing ones. Case (ii) could be, for example, an electric car as opposed to an internal combustion car. In case (ii) the new product could be a partial or complete substitute of an existing one (see Box 1.1). The representation of case (i) would involve the creation of new dimensions in service characteristics space and a discontinuity. Thus, the new product would not compete at all with any existing one. On the contrary, case (ii) would involve the creation of a new population which would overlap partially or completely with, and thus compete with, an existing one in the service characteristics space. For example, if a new product with an internal structure qualitatively different from a pre-existing one (Figure 1.6) supplied some similar and some different services, they would be partial substitutes of existing ones and they could in principle compete. The intensity of competition possible is determined by the extent of overlap of the two populations. In Figure 1.6, the degree of overlap is limited and the two populations are not competing very intensely. However, many situations are possible, ranging from two populations having a high degree of overlap, thus approaching the multidimensional analogue of perfect competition, to a complete absence of overlap, giving rise to market segmentation (Figure 1.7). The possibility that product technologies having qualitatively different internal structures can supply similar services can give rise to inter-technology competition and, to the extent that different product technologies are produced in different industries, to inter-industry competition. This is one of the mechanisms which can give rise to market contestability (Baumol, 1982).

The dynamics of competition following the emergence of a discontinuity in technology and/or knowledge leads to windows of opportunity for entry by new entrants having learned the new knowledge. This occurs, for example, when a new technology capable of generating a new internal structure emerges. If this MMA has a new internal structure and can supply qualitatively new services, its emergence can lead to the creation of a new sector. This affects competition by (i) allowing early entrants to enjoy a period of temporary monopoly in a typical example of Schumpeterian competition, to be followed by a period of increasing intensity of competition due to the entry of a bandwagon of imitators (Figure 1.8). The emergence of the new sector can be expected to (ii) raise the average intensity of competition in the economic system to the extent that it affects inter-technology and inter-industry competition. By creating a temporary monopoly, the former effect (i) would reduce the intensity of classical competition within the new sector, while the latter effect (ii) would raise the intensity of classical competition at the higher level of aggregation of the whole economic system. A second type of discontinuity can occur when a new MMA with a new internal structure supplies services similar to those of an existing technology. In this case entrant technologies and firms compete with incumbents. To be successful entrants need to have an advantage in a niche of an existing market or a complete superiority that allows them to replace incumbent technologies and firms. The outcome of competition in these cases can vary between increasing Schumpeterian and increasing classical competition.

Creative destruction is probably the best-known Schumpeterian concept. Although innovation is the most important driving force for economic development, it does not produce only benefits. As a result of innovation, there are both winners and losers. The former are the entrepreneurs who manage to

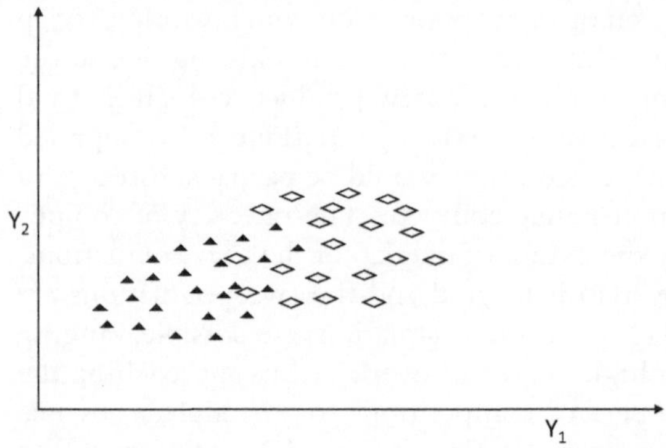

Figure 1.6 Two product populations arising from different internal structures but supplying similar services. The intensity of competition is proportional to the degree of overlap and the two populations.

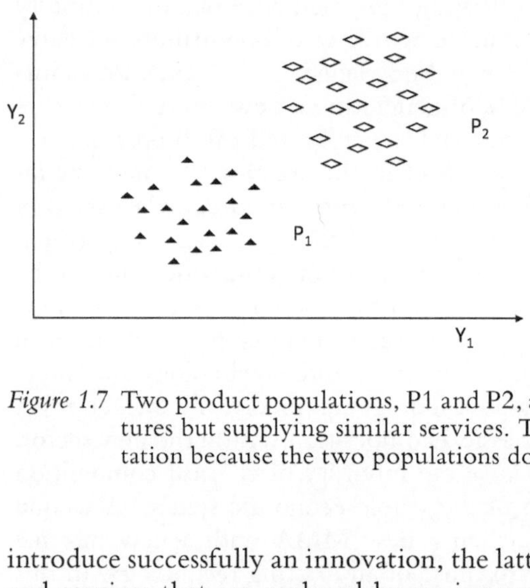

Figure 1.7 Two product populations, P1 and P2, arising from different internal structures but supplying similar services. This corresponds to market segmentation because the two populations do not show any degree of overlap.

introduce successfully an innovation, the latter are the producers of the goods and services that are replaced by an innovation. In its most extreme form, creative destruction involves the complete destruction of the old by the new. While there are several cases in which this happened, it is probably not the only or even the most frequent example of creative destruction. The complete disappearance of an old technology or industry can only happen in the case of pure substitution (Box 1.1), when the new technology produces the same services as the old one but at a lower price. In most cases the new technology produces new services not comparable to those of any pre-existing one, or a mixture of services new and common to the old technology. In the former case the new technology does not compete with any pre-existing ones, in the latter the intensity of competition depends on the degree of similarity between the new and the old technologies. This can give rise to inter-technology competition and, to the extent that different product technologies are produced in different industries, to inter-industry competition, which can have important implications for the theory of competition and for economic development, as we will see in Chapter 5.

The consequences of qualitative change and output heterogeneity discussed in the previous paragraphs imply that the intensity of competition cannot be measured only by the number of competitors but needs to consider the nature of the output such competitors produce. Thus, the outputs of different firms can be (i) qualitatively different and not competing, (ii) sharing some service characteristics and competing with an intensity proportional to the similarity of their common service characteristics, (iii) producing identical outputs and competing with the multidimensional analogue of perfect competition. Case (i), which corresponds to Schumpeterian competition, and case (iii), corresponding to classical competition, are the extremes of a range of possible types of competition, with case (ii), corresponding to monopolistic competition, representing all the intermediate cases. It follows that to calculate the intensity of competition based only on the number of competitors is not enough because the same number of competitors could give rise to different output types. Furthermore, the possibility that technologies with different internal structures can produce the same type of services can give rise to inter-industry competition if these technologies are classified in different industries.

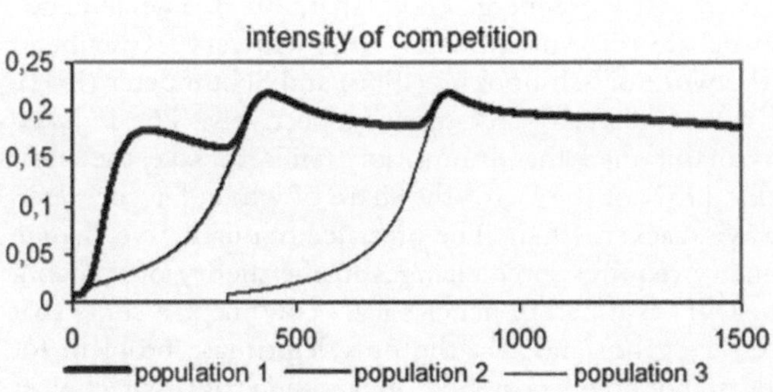

Figure 1.8 At the emergence of a new sector the intensity of competition is zero, corresponding to a temporary monopoly, then it increases as a bandwagon of imitators enters the sector, until the sector reaches a condition of shake-out with exits predominating over entries. The populations are populations of firms in each sector.

Box 1.2 Inter-technology competition and market contestability

Planes and airlines outcompeted trains and railway companies in some countries and periods, but not in others. In this case inter-industry competition between airlines and railway companies was based on inter-technology competition between planes and trains. In the USA, Canada and Australia, trains became almost a niche but the same thing did not happen in Europe or Japan. The different outcomes of this competitive process can be explained by major factors such as country size and population density. Trains have a differential advantage on relatively short distances and planes on longer distances (see Figure 1.4). Furthermore, the average inter-city distance is inversely proportional to population density. This is also an example of market contestability because the market for transport, which was almost monopolized by trains in the first half of the XXth century, was largely taken over by planes and airlines and more evenly shared with trains depending on local factors. The set of factors and circumstances that can affect a competitive process is called a 'selection environment'. In addition to country size and population density, other components of the selection environments that can potentially affect competition are regulations, income per capita, labour unions, etc.

4.2 Demand theory

The priority of demand or of innovation and supply as factors affecting growth has been a frequent subject of discussion in the economics literature (Kaldor, 1957; Gualerzi, 2001; Mowery, Rosenberg, 1979; Chai, 2017). The demand-pull, technology-push debate (Freeman, Soete, 1997; Mowery, Rosenberg, 1979) followed from the work of Schmookler (1966) and Schumpeter (1911), who had stressed the role of demand and supply respectively. The induced innovation hypothesis maintained that innovation tends to save the most expensive factor (Hicks, 1932) or the factor the share of which has increased (Kennedy, 1964; Von Weitzacker, 1966). The presence of qualitative change and product heterogeneity requires some changes in the theory of demand. First, can we, as it is usually assumed in neoclassical economics, assume that consumers' preferences are given and that the only legitimate problem for economists is to understand how consumers make their optimal choices based on their preferences and resources? Whereas for short-run problems this assumption could be useful, if one is interested in long-run processes of economic development the same assumption implies the existence of omniscient consumers capable of predicting the emergence and properties of all future objects of consumption. Preferences for new objects of consumption are likely to be gradually formed, beginning with an initially fuzzy form, and becoming gradually more precise, by an interaction of entrepreneurs and consumers, similarly to Schumpeter, who maintained that it is producers who must educate consumers to use innovations (1911, 1934, p. 65). Even the huge growth in advertising that started occurring in the early part of the XXth century (Saviotti, 2018) was at least partly intended to supply consumers with the information they needed in their purchasing decisions. Of course, not all scholars agree that the function of advertising was not exclusively to allow consumers to fully enjoy their consumption freedom. Others point out that the true role of advertising was to impose upon consumers' preferences that they would not spontaneously have had (Galbraith, 1969). I will discuss later this interesting aspect of the political economy of consumption. Here we just need to point out that there were mechanisms that helped consumers to form preferences for new objects of consumption. Thus, consumer preferences could be expected to be at least partly endogenous.

I have previously discussed how preferences for new MMAs have qualitatively new internal structures but supply services corresponding to general human functions. Then the process of formation could be expected to show a greater continuity than the knowledge of new internal structures. Then we could expect preferences for new MMAs to be initially fuzzy and to gradually become more precise by a form of learning by doing.

Here I will recall some stylized facts about the evolution of consumption. For most people during most of human history consumption consisted essentially of trying to satisfy basic necessities, which can be summarized as food, clothing, and housing. Only rich people could afford a more varied range of consumption items. This continued to be true in the XIXth century despite considerable increases in productive efficiency caused by the industrial revolution. It was only during the XXth century that in industrialized countries a growing share of the population started to be able to consume a wider range of goods and services beyond necessities (Hobsbawm, 1968). This transition has been called by Saviotti and Pyka (2013) 'from necessities to imaginary worlds. This transition is part of the overall process of differentiation of the economic system. In connection with long-run growth and development, this raises three important questions: (i) the formation of preferences, (ii) the mechanisms by which the composition of consumption changed endogenously, (iii) the modifications required in demand theory to accommodate heterogeneous consumers and heterogeneous goods and services.

The trend towards rising product quality and differentiation is also likely to affect demand curves. Such growing quality and differentiation can only occur if consumers have a disposable income allowing them to purchase the corresponding products which can be created by the combination of growing productive efficiency in incumbent sectors and by the employment effect accompanying the emergence of new sectors. We can then expect that as societies become richer a growing share of their income will be spent on (i) new products and services and on (ii) higher quality and more differentiated products and services. Consequently, the distribution of product quality and prices within the offered range could change with the average (or median) product moving from the cheapest to higher priced ones. This hypothesis is confirmed by experiments in which the extent to which product quality and differentiation are increased by search activities was varied. By studying the effect of different parameters affecting product quality and product differentiation, Saviotti and Pyka (2017) calculated quasi demand curves for extended periods of time of variable length. In Figure 1.9, we can see that when search activities can lead to high rates of growth of product quality and product differentiation demand curves are not uniformly downward sloping as price rises, but contain a section in which demand rises as price rises. A similar behaviour is empirically found for many types of differentiated goods, such as cars, watches, television sets and washing machines.

The section in which demand and price rise together could correspond also to the behaviour observed by Veblen (1899) (Trigg, 2001) and called conspicuous consumption, according to which consumers do not buy what they need in a functional sense but to impress other people and to establish their social status. While before the industrial revolution this used to be true only for very rich and powerful people with the growing wealth generated, in industrialized countries such a form of consumption has become very common. Indeed, the cheapest goods in each sector are not those which sell the most. Figure 1.9 shows that the possibility of conspicuous consumption increases when innovation can generate high rates of growth of product quality and product differentiation of goods and services. Given the extent to which this phenomenon has become widespread, it is doubtful whether the

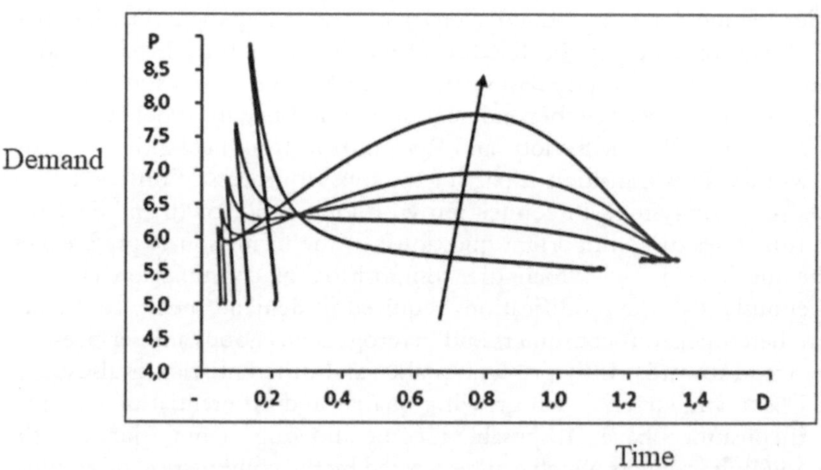

Figure 1.9 Effect of changing the parameters affecting product quality and product differentiation on the shape of demand curves. As product quality and product differentiation increase, demand curves change from the typical downward sloping shape to one in which the curve is initially upward sloping. The slope of the initial part keeps increasing with increasing product quality and product differentiation.

term 'conspicuous consumption' should be used for the whole range in which demand rises with rising price or just for extremely expensive products. Further experiments are required to clarify this type of behaviour.

The previous aspects of demand are intrinsically linked to the presence of qualitative change and to its relationship to quantitative change. Thus, the radical uncertainty accompanying the emergence of a new product technology depends on it being qualitatively different from any incumbent product technology. However, the subsequent parts of the life cycle of the technology and of the corresponding industrial sector are based on more incremental innovations, that is on quantitative change. Furthermore, the existence of the process of differentiation of the economic system, which constitutes one of the most important stylized facts of economic development since the industrial revolution, depends on the output of each sector being qualitatively different from those of all the other ones. The dynamics of qualitative change is more difficult to study than that of quantitative change. Its study is one of the frontiers that evolutionary economics and the science of complexity need to progress towards.

Notes

1 Here see Beinhocker (2007, pp. 308–310).
2 This problem was at the basis of the so-called Cambridge capital controversy from the 1950s (Saviotti, Pyka, Jun, 2020).
3 This corresponds to choosing one of the four definitions of technology given in Rip and Kemp (1998).
4 Pure substitution is an example of increased efficiency, as it will be defined later, since the type of output remains constant. However, the qualitative change of internal structure requires creativity (see Chapter 3).
5 A graphic representation of these types of substitution can be found in Saviotti (1996) and eResources (Chapter 1).

References

Baumol W.J. (March 1982) Contestable markets: an uprising in the theory of industry structure, *American Economic Review*, 72(1): 1–15.

Beinhocker E.D. (2007) *The Origin of Wealth, The Radical Remaking of Economics and What It Means for Business and Society*, Boston, MA, Harvard Business School Press.

Chai A. (2017) Tackling Keynes' question: a look back on 15 years of learning to consume. *Journal of Evolutionary Economics*, 27: 251–271. https://doi.org/10.1007/s00191-016-0455-7

Daly H.E. (2007) *Ecological Economics and Sustainable Development: Selected Essays of Herman Daly*. Cheltenham, Edward Elgar.

Dosi G., Nelson R.R. (1994) An introduction to evolutionary theories in economics. *Journal of Evolutionary Economics*, 4: 153–172.

Endres A.M., Harper D.A. (2012) The kinetics of capital formation and economic organization. *Cambridge Journal of Economics*, 36(4): 963–980.

Endres A.M., Harper D.A. (2013) Wresting meaning from the market': a reassessment of Ludwig Lachmann's entrepreneur. *Journal of Institutional Economics*, 9(3): 303–328.

Freeman C., Soete L. (1997) *The Economics of Industrial Innovation*, London: Pinter.

Galbraith J.K. (1969) *The New Industrial State*, Harmondsworth, Middlesex, Penguin Books.

Gallouj F., Weinstein O. (1997). Innovation in services. *Research Policy*, 26(4–5): 537–556.

Galor O., Weil D.N. (2000) Population, technology, and growth: from Malthusian stagnation to the demographic transition and beyond. *American Economic Review*, 90(4): 806–828.

Geels F.W. (2002a). Technological transitions as evolutionary reconfiguration processes: a multi-level perspective and a case-study, *Research Policy*, 31 (8–9): 1257–1274.

Geels F. (2002b). *Understanding the Dynamics of Technological Transitions: A Co-evolutionary and Socio-technical Analysis*, Twente, Twente University Press.

Geels, Frank W. (2004) From sectoral systems of innovation to socio-technical systems: insights about dynamics and change from sociology and institutional theory. *Research Policy*, 33 (6–7): 897–920.

Georgescu Roegen N. (1971) *The Entropy Law and the Economic Process*, Cambridge, MA, Harvard University Press.

Gershuny J. (1978) *After Industrial Society: The Emerging Self-service Economy*, London, MacMillan.

Gowdy J. (1994) *Co-evolutionary Economics: The Economy, Society and the Environment*, Dordrecht, KluIr Academics.

Gualerzi D. (2001) *Consumption and Growth, Recovery and Structural Change in the US Economy*, Cheltenham, Edward Elgar.

Hayek N. (1947) The use of knowledge in society, Chapter 4 in *Individualism and Economic Order*, Chicago, IL, The University of Chicago Press, 77–91.

Hayek N. (1978) *New Studies in Philosophy, Politics, Economics the History of Ideas*, London, Routledge, 184.

Hicks J.R. (1932) *The Theory of Wages*, London, MacMillan.

Hidalgo C. (2015) *Why Information Grows, The Evolution of Order, from Atoms to Economies*, London, Penguin Random House.

Hobsbawm E.J. (1968) *Industry and Empire*, Harmondsworth, Penguin Books.

Jovanovic B., MacDonald G. (1994) The life cycle of a competitive industry. *Journal of Political Economy*, 102: 322–347.

Kaldor N. (1957) A model of economic growth. *The Economic Journal*, 67(268): 591–624.

Kennedy C. (1964) Induced bias in innovation and the theory of distribution. *Economic Journal*, 74: 541–547.

Khan B.Z. (2016) Knowledge, human capital and economic development: evidence from the British Industrial Revolution, 1750–1930, The London School of Economics and Political Science, Economic History Working Papers No: 249/2016.

Klepper S. (1996) Entry, exit, growth and innovation over the product life cycle. *American Economic Review*, 86: 562–583.

Landes D.S. (1969) *The Unbound Prometheus: Technological Change and Industrial Development in Eastern Europe from 1750 to the Present*, Cambridge, Cambridge University Press

Lipsey R.G., Carlaw K.I., Beckar C.T. (2005) *Economic Transformations*, Oxford, Oxford University Press.

Losee J. (1977) *A Historical Introduction to the Philosophy of Science*, Oxford, Oxford University Press, 104–105.

Maddison A. (2001) *The World Economy - A Millennial Perspective*. Paris, OECD Development Centre.

Maddison A. (2004) *The World Economy: Historical Statistics*. Paris, OECD Development Centre.

Maddison A. (1982). *Phases of Capitalist Development*. Oxford, Oxford University Press.

Marshall A. (1961) *Principles of Economics*, 9th edition, originally 1920, New York, MacMillan.

Marshall A. (1890) *Principles of Economics*, London, MacMillan, 8th edition (1949).

Maynard Smith J. (1974) *Models in Ecology*, Cambridge, Cambridge University Press.

McNulty P.J. (1968) Economic theory and the meaning of competition, *Quarterly Journal of Economics*, 82: 639–656.

Metcalfe J.S. (1998) *Evolutionary Economics and Creative Destruction*, London, Routledge.

MoIry D., Rosenberg N. (1979) Market demand and innovation. *Research Policy*, 8: 103–153.

Mokyr J. (1990) *The Lever of Riches: Technological Creativity and Economic Progress*, New York, Oxford University Press.

Mokyr J. (2005) *The Gifts of Athena: Historical Origins of the Knowledge Economy*, Princeton, NJ, Princeton University Press.

Morgenstern O. (1972) Descriptive, predictive and normative theory, *Kyklos*, 25(4): 699–714. https://doi.org/10.1111/j.1467-6435.1972.tb01077.x

Nelson R. (1995) Recent evolutionary theorizing about economic change. *Journal of Economic Literature*, 33: 48–90.

Pinch T.J., Bijker W.E. (August 1984) The Social construction of facts and artefacts: or how the sociology of science and the sociology of technology might benefit each other. *Social Studies of Science*, 14: 399–441. https://doi.org/10.1177/030631284014003004

Prigogine I. (1996) *La Fin des Certitudes*, Paris, Odile Jacob.

Prigogine I., Stengers I. (1985) *Order Out of Chaos: Man's New Dialogue with Nature*, London, Fontana Paperbacks.

Rip A., Kemp R. (1998) Technological change, in Rayner S., Malone E.L. (Eds) *Human Choice and Climate Change*, Columbus, OH, Battelle Press, Volume 2, Resources and technology, 327–399.

Saviotti P.P. (1986) Systems theory and technological change, *Futures*, 18: 773–786.

Saviotti P.P. (1996) *Technological Evolution, Variety and the Economy*, Cheltenham, Edward Elgar.

Saviotti P.P. (2007) Qualitative change and economic development, in Hanusch H., Pyka A. (Eds) *Elgar Companion to Neo-Schumpeterian Economics*, Cheltenham, Edward Elgar, 820–839.

Saviotti P.P, (2018) Innovation and Consumption in the Evolution of Capitalist Societies, in Spinozzi P., Mazzanti M. (Eds) *Cultures of Sustainability and Wellbeing. Theories, Histories and Policies*, London, Routledge

Saviotti P.P., Metcalfe J.S. (1984) A theoretical approach to the construction of technological output indicators. *Research Policy*, 13: 141–151.

Saviotti P.P., Pyka A. (2013) From necessities to imaginary worlds: structural change, product quality and economic development. *Technological Forecasting & Social Change*, 80: 1499–1512.

Saviotti P.P. Pyka A., Jun B., (2020) Diversification, structural change, and economic development, Journal of Evolutionary Economics, 30(5), 1301-1335, DOI 10.1007/s00191-020-00672-w

Saviotti P.P., Pyka A. (2017) Innovation, structural change and demand evolution: does demand saturate? *Journal of Evolutionary Economics*, 27: 337–358. https://doi.org/10.1007/s00191-015-0428-2.

Schumpeter J. (1911) *The Theory of Economic Development*, Cambridge, MA, Harvard University Press (1934, original edition 1911).

Schumpeter J. (1942, 5th Edition 1976) *Capitalism, Socialism and Democracy*, London, George Allen and Unwin.

Schmookler J. (1966) *Invention and Economic Growth*, Cambridge, MA, Harvard University Press.

Simon H.A. (1969) The natural and the artificial world, in Simon H.A. (Ed.) *The Sciences of the Artificial*, Cambridge, MA, MIT Press (1969), new edition (1981).

Trigg A.B. (2001) Veblen, Bourdieu, and conspicuous consumption. *Journal of Economic Issues*, 35(1): 99–115.

Veblen T.B. (1899) *The Theory of the Leisure Class: An Economic Study in the Evolution of Institutions*. New York, Macmillan.

Witt U. (2001) Learning to consume: a theory of wants and the growth of demand. *Journal of Evolutionary Economics*, 11: 23–26.

2 The coevolution of innovation, technologies and institutions

We started this book by saying that evolutionary theory needed to go beyond innovation as its exclusive focus if it wanted to compete with neoclassical economics as a general theory of economic behaviour and development. In Chapter 1 we discussed the nature of the MMAs produced by most firms as interfaces between the laws of nature, as interpreted by human knowledge, and human needs and wants. In spite of the importance of these artefacts, we could never understand long-term economic development without taking into account institutions and the organizations that operate within them. However, institutions and organizations are not just the unchanging background against which a moving picture evolves, but are themselves actors that interact with technologies and innovations. Thus, institutions and organizations can induce the emergence of technologies and innovations as well as amplify their subsequent diffusion. In other words, institutions and organizations coevolve with technologies and innovations. In biology, coevolution occurs when two or more species reciprocally affect each other's evolution through the process of natural selection. Coevolution is a part of complexity theory, a new way of interpreting reality which emerged after the Second World War and is increasingly applied to physics, chemistry and biology and is making its way to the social sciences (Allen, 2001, 2007). Complexity is not a complete and well-defined theory but a set of ideas which aims to overcome some important limitations of human knowledge in several disciplines. One of the most important features of complex systems is the interactivity of their components. This interactivity leads to non-linearity since the dynamics of interacting subsystems needs to be represented by products or higher powers of their concentration. In turn, some problems involving complex systems are difficult or impossible to solve analytically and often can only be approximately solved by simulation, requiring a computing capability which has only recently become available (Arthur, 2007a, 2007b).

Complexity will play a very important role in this book. However, rather than starting with a complete definition of complexity and then proceeding to apply it to specific problems, we will introduce it gradually in connection with aspects of the dynamics of innovation and institutions. The coevolution of technologies and institutions is fundamental both to acquire an adequate

DOI: 10.4324/9781003294221-2

understanding of the dynamics of modern SOEs and to incorporate broader aspects of SOEs into evolutionary theories.

The approach to coevolution adopted here is similar to the work on gene–culture coevolution, also called dual inheritance theory (DIT) (Boyd, Richerson, 1985), developed from the 1960s to the early 1980s to explain how human behaviour is a product of two different and interacting evolutionary processes: genetic evolution and cultural evolution. However, the concept of culture adopted there is far too simplified to enable us to discuss meaningfully the coevolution of technologies and institutions. Rather than referring to culture, we prefer to focus on institutions, although we recognize that the two terms overlap to a certain extent. Like culture institutions can have many possible definitions (Boyd, Richerson, 1985, Chapter 3). Here we will consider institutions as sets of rules and adopt North's (1990) distinction between institutions and organizations: institutions are the rules of the game and organizations are its players. In what follows, we will first discuss separately technologies and institutions and then their coevolution.

1 Technologies and innovation

Modern technologies can be considered the descendants of the tools used by early human beings, which Lotka (1925) and Georgescu Roegen (1971) called exosomatic instruments. Like all subsequent technologies, these tools improved the adaptation of human beings to their external environment. Of course, to consider that primeval tools, aircraft, and computers are all technologies can seem to stretch the definition of technology too far. However, quite aside from the different shapes and functions of individual technologies, modern technologies differ from primeval tools because they not only improved human beings' adaptation to a *given* external environment, but could also help human beings to modify their external environment. In Chapter 3 we will introduce the concept of adaptive behaviour and distinguish between adaptation *to* a given EE and adaptation *of* a given EE, stressing the point that the capacity to create extensive modifications of the EE was specific to human beings as opposed to other biological organisms.

Innovation creates qualitatively new technologies, distinguishable from pre-existing ones, and modifies existing technologies. For a long time, innovations were very infrequent and technologies, once created, remained almost unchanged during long periods. Innovation has for a long time been considered a component of economic development (Rosenberg, 1976; Nelson, 1959; Mokyr, 1990, 2002; Freeman Soete, 1997) but its frequency and impact have considerably accelerated since the beginning of the industrial revolution. In this book, we maintain that innovation entails the presence of qualitative change and that qualitative change requires the use of knowledge processes and decision-making procedures different from those adopted for the analysis of quantitative change.

Some of the most important concepts introduced in the economics of innovation, such as dominant designs (Abernathy, Utterback, 1975) and technological paradigms (Dosi, 1982), are implicitly based on the existence of qualitative differences. We have seen that physical product technologies are different if they have no common characteristics describing their internal structures. However, once a new physical product technology has been created, its subsequent versions, or models, are quantitatively different from the founding one. This twin characteristic representation helps in studying the structure of an economic system and phenomena like competition. For example, to the extent that industrial sectors are defined by the type of output they produce, the variety of the socioeconomic system (SES) is determined both by the number of distinguishable (i.e., qualitatively different) physical product technologies and by their internal differentiation.

Despite the central importance played by qualitative change in Schumpeter's work, the term 'qualitative change' is, with few exceptions (Georgescu Roegen, 1971), virtually absent in the economics literature. Qualitative change has been far more present in the economics literature, and particularly in the work of neo-Schumpeterian economists, than the results of a search for the term itself would indicate. Furthermore, there is a rich literature dealing with the closely related though non-identical problem of quality change. In this literature the quality of a given MMA is defined by a combination of its product characteristics, without making any distinction between technical and service characteristics. Following the work of Lancaster (1966, 1971) and based on the hedonic price method (Rosen, 1974), it is possible to determine implicit prices for product characteristics. The hedonic price method is used also to calculate consumer price indexes (CPIs). This literature is focused on a much lower level of aggregation, that of a product group, with respect to Schumpeter's analysis of economic development. Nevertheless, some results of the analysis of quality change are useful in a generalized analysis of qualitative change.

Amongst the earliest contributions of scholars of innovation, there was the distinction between radical and incremental innovation (Freeman, 1982; Freeman, Soete, 1997). A radical innovation is so completely different from an incremental one that it is to be considered a form of qualitative change. A radical innovation represents a discontinuity in the evolution of a technology while an incremental innovation represents only a continuous, quantitative improvement in an existing technology. Furthermore, a radical innovation can be considered a revolution, and it is radical innovations which give rise to new technological paradigms (Dosi, 1982). In a similar way, concepts like technological guideposts (Sahal, 1975), dominant designs (Abernathy, Utterback, 1975) and technological regimes (Nelson and Winter, 1977, 1982) involve the existence of qualitative change during certain stages of their economic development. The emergence of a new, later to become dominant, design or of a technological regime creates a discontinuity in technological and possibly economic development, although the subsequent trajectories of improvement are likely to be based mostly on incremental innovations.

The existence of qualitative change has both taxonomic and dynamic implications. Essentially, the taxonomic implications involve the ability to distinguish radical from incremental innovation. However, dynamic implications are related to the ways in which qualitative change affects economic development. In other words, in general, we can expect radical innovations to have a different impact on economic development than incremental innovations. The dynamic component was very central to Schumpeter's work, while the taxonomic component was virtually absent. Important changes in economic development, such as the recovery of an economy from a recession or a depression, could only be due to clusters of radical innovations.

Summarizing this section, we could say that although the concept of qualitative change is used very rarely in neo-Schumpeterian economics, many concepts, some of which are currently used by these economists, bear a very close relationship to the distinction between qualitative and quantitative change. Qualitative change can be considered a unifying concept, bringing unity to distinctions such as the one between radical and incremental innovation, continuous and discontinuous development, and to concepts such as technological paradigms, dominant designs, technological regimes, and technological guideposts.

1.1 Innovation concepts and the twin characteristic representation

The existence of MMAs has several important analytical implications which the twin characteristic representation allows us to appreciate. Such implications follow from (i) the *heterogeneity* of all MMAs and from (ii) the completely different nature of the dimensions in which the two sets of characteristics exist. Let us begin with heterogeneity. Each of the characteristics corresponding to a given MMA can have a range of values. Thus, there can be small or large, fast or slow cars or aircraft as well as simple or extremely sophisticated cameras or portable telephones. Each MMA is constituted by a 'population' of members which have different values of common characteristics. The common characteristics define the MMA while their values define their individual members. The population of each MMA contains a distribution of the defining characteristics' values. The existence of such heterogeneous populations depends on the existence of corresponding distributions of preferences and purchasing power amongst consumers or users of the MMAs. Let us observe here that one of the most important differences between mainstream and evolutionary theories is the heterogeneity of agents in the latter (Nelson, 1995; Dosi, Nelson, 1994). Each consumer or user can be expected to buy a member of an MMA, or a model, corresponding to his/her preferences and purchasing power. The difference between mainstream and evolutionary theories corresponds to that between a typological and a population approach (Saviotti, 1996; Metcalfe, 1998; Kirman, 2011), where the former focuses on the representative individual (the means) while the latter considers both the means and the distribution of the population.

The representation of product technology illustrated in Chapter 1 helps to put the distinction between radical and incremental innovation on a more logical basis. Thus, radical will be an innovation which leads to a qualitatively new internal structure and possibly to new services, while incremental will be an innovation which improves quantitatively services without any qualitative change in internal structure and/or technical characteristics. A radical innovation is one that gives rise to entirely new technical characteristics, which need to be represented by different variables. For example, power to an aircraft can be supplied either by a piston engine and propellers or by a jet engine. The two technologies have qualitatively different internal structures and require different variables to be represented. The transition between the two has evidently been a radical innovation. At least for what concerns material goods, the emergence of a new MMA involves a radical innovation which gives rise to a new internal structure. Let us notice that, as in the example of piston engine and propellers and of jet engine, the two qualitatively different technologies constitute a subsystem of the whole aircraft. However, what could at first sight be conceived as a modular replacement of piston by jet engines while the rest of the aircraft remains unchanged turns out to be incorrect. Strengthening of the aircraft body, improved aerodynamics and cabin pressurization are examples of complementary innovations which are required to exploit the greater potential of the new motive power technology. The aircraft is a system in which modifications of one component require other related modifications.

This example shows that MMAs can exist at different levels of aggregation (subcomponent, component, the whole system) and that an innovation introduced in one component is likely to require other related, architectural (Henderson, Clark, 1990), innovations at higher levels of aggregation, including that of the whole system. These considerations raise the need for a hierarchical classification of MMAs similar in principle to the one which has been developed for biological species. This is clearly not the objective of this chapter or of this book. Here we wish only to introduce the concept of MMAs and to stress (i) the importance of qualitative change and discontinuities, and (ii) the role that the interactions and coevolution of different ESs can play in economic development.

Some of the most important concepts in the economics of innovation are those of dominant designs (Abernathy, Utterback, 1975), technological regimes (Nelson, Winter, 1977), technological guideposts (Sahal, 1975), technological paradigms, technological trajectories (Dosi, 1982; Dosi, Nelson, 2018), etc. These concepts are somewhat different, but here we do wish to focus on their similarities rather than discuss their differences. They all imply the existence of a life cycle of innovation and a sequence of periods dominated by qualitative or quantitative change. All these concepts bear a close similarity to those of scientific paradigms and of scientific revolutions (Kuhn,

1962). According to Kuhn, science progresses by a combination of scientific revolutions, in which a new scientific paradigm emerges as a new world view incompatible with the previous paradigm, and of 'normal science', during which the new paradigm becomes better articulated and extended to new situations. In a similar way, the life cycle of an innovation would begin with a qualitative change and a discontinuity, for example, at the transition between two technological paradigms, and would be followed by the convergence of all the participants in a given technology on a set of technical solutions (internal characteristics) narrower than the one that could in principle be available. During such convergence, a degree of self-regulation of the technological systems thus created is achieved (Saviotti, 1986). Thus, the multiplicity of technological designs which emerged initially would subsequently be replaced by a dominant design. In this process the radical innovations which had given rise to a new technological design, regime or paradigm would be followed by a stream of much more numerous incremental innovations, which would gradually enhance the services that the given technology can supply to its users and consumers.

All the above concepts involve a break or a discontinuity in the internal structure of MMAs and in the knowledge base of the firms and organizations that produce and use them. It is during the initial phases of the life cycle of a new technological paradigm that the impact of discontinuities is the greatest. It is during these phases that any assumption of perfect knowledge becomes completely unsuitable. New MMAs are created in a situation of highly imperfect knowledge and radical uncertainty. As the new technological paradigm advances in its life cycle, the underlying knowledge becomes better articulated and radical uncertainty is replaced by calculable risk. In these later, more mature, phases of their life cycles, the predictability of the outcomes of innovation increases and assumptions of rational optimizing behaviour become more plausible. Thus, the types of knowledge used can change during the life cycle of technologies and innovations. This can have an important impact on the behaviour of firms and organizations. For example, when a new technological paradigm emerges and is perceived as potentially profitable to exploit it, a firm may need to replace a large share of its competencies.

It is then possible to relate these concepts to the previous twin characteristic representation of goods and services (Chapter 1). For example, a dominant design (Abernathy, Utterback, 1975, 1978) or a technological regime (Nelson, Winter, 1977) can be conceptualized as the presence of a constant set of technical characteristics the *levels* of which could change in the course of time. During the evolution of the design/regime, only changes in characteristics *levels*, that is, incremental innovations, take place until a new design emerges. The automobile gives a very good example of a dominant design and technological paradigm: some components of a modern automobile, such as four wheels and an internal combustion engine, have been constantly present in the internal structure of the automobile during the whole XXth century and until the present. It has to be noticed that these components were not all necessarily present in the initial form of the automobile, which included several designs, and became a standard component of the automobile with the emergence of a dominant design (Arthur,1996). Likewise, photographic cameras underwent a complete change of dominant design and technological paradigm when their internal structure changed from a chemically based one to an electronically based one (Table 2.1). A similar change occurred in the technology of watches, although in this case the new electronically based design coexists with the pre-existing mechanical design. Some of these examples have already been used in Chapter 1 in relation to processes of substitution and specialization.

As we can see from the previous examples, there are technologies in which a complete change of internal structure leads to a complete change of dominant design and technological paradigm while in other technologies new and pre-existing ones can coexist. We have already discussed how internal structures affect processes of substitution and specialization of technologies: complete substitution occurs when the new internal structure supplies the same services as the old one but at lower cost; coexistence of different internal structures occurs when each of them supplies particularly well a subset

Table 2.1 Designs, dominant designs and transitions

Technology	*Internal structure vs dominant design*	*Other designs*	*Transitions*
Cars	Internal combustion engine, four wheels, transmission by gears	Three wheels, electrical and steam engines	i. Multiple designs →dominant design ii. Electrical, hybrid and hydrogen cars (?) iii. Self-driving cars (?)
Agricultural tractors	Internal combustion engine, four wheels, transmission by gears	Steam tractors	
Photographic cameras	Chemical vs ITC-based		2000s Chemical → ITC-based
Watches	Mechanical vs electronic	Co-existence	
Jet engines	(a) Piston and propellers vs (b) jet engine	Almost complete substitution of (a) by (b)	Piston and propellers → jet engine
Pharmaceuticals	Organic chemistry vs (b) biotechnology	Growing adoption of (b) but always in combination with some (a)	(a) → (b)

of the common services they all supply. Here we simply wish to point out that all these forms of substitution or coexistence occur by means of qualitative change in the internal structure of the corresponding technologies. The reasons for which an old design, regime or paradigm is superseded by or coexists with a new one depends both on the progress of science and technology and on changes in the external environment. For example, the substitution of vacuum tubes by semiconductors occurred as a result of the progress of science and technology. However, the growing emphasis placed on the reduction of environmental impact is induced by the saturation of our physical environment.

1.2 Institutions and organizational forms

New technologies can emerge in an a-institutional economic environment, but their subsequent diffusion and the creation of the corresponding industries and markets could never have occurred without the formation of general and technology-specific institutions. Institutions, organizational forms and infrastructures are components of a socioeconomic system (SES), which has an external economic environment (EE) to which it needs to adapt, but which it can also modify. Examples of general institutions are language and the law, which are used in any type of human activity. Examples of specific institutions are the international air transport association (IATA), ministries of environment, health, specialized research, or teaching institutions, etc. Both general and specific institutions need to adapt to the presence of new technologies. For example, both language and the law need to incorporate new words or new laws to describe or define the use of new MMAs. In other words, infrastructures, institutions, and organizational forms coevolve with MMAs.[1] Coevolution occurs when some institutions allow the diffusion of new technologies and the construction of relevant markets to proceed far beyond the level that would have been possible without them. Coevolution can involve more than two components. For example, cars could never have reached their present diffusion without roads, driving laws and complementary inputs such as petrol and tyres (Geels, 2002a, 2004; Saviotti, 2005).

We can expect both technology-specific institutions and general institutions to affect economic development by creating an economic environment appropriate for the technologies or innovative activity in general. Consequently, we can include in the description of a National Innovation System (NIS) only institutions which we consider specific, thus adopting a narrow conception of the NIS, or include a broader range of institutions, thus adopting a broad conception of the NIS (Freeman, 1987; Nelson, 1993; Lundvall, 1992). Both approaches have been used. It needs to be pointed out that even general-purpose institutions can heavily affect economic development. For example, Acemoglu and Robinson (2012) stressed the interesting distinction between *inclusive* and *extractive* institutions and maintained that only countries capable of creating inclusive institutions can successfully develop.

General institutions emerged much earlier than innovative societies. Language and the law were required in any type of human community. However, innovations started to become frequent and widespread only since the industrial revolution. Thus, even institutions which today seem quite general, such as the firm or R&D, are historically quite recent. Both date from the second half of the XIXth century (Rosenberg, Birdzell, 1986) and their origin is closely related to the progress of science and technology (Saviotti, 2012). Furthermore, it needs to be observed that sometimes general institutions require the creation of specialized subsets. For example, the legislation on air traffic control was introduced because of air transport.

The distinction between institutions and organizations has never been completely clear cut. In this book we will follow North's (1990) definition according to which institutions are the rules of the game and organizations are the players. The residual ambiguity derives from the fact that when new rules are created, they need to be implemented and monitored by organizations. Institutions are, so to say, 'embodied' in organizations. Thus, the university is an institution and individual universities are organizations. The industrial firm, which for economists has been the most important type of organization, is also an institution.

The defining general feature of both institutions and organizations is that they are *rule-based entities*. In a very general sense, rules are statements connecting events, concepts, behaviours, etc. Physical laws can be considered an example of rules. The first law of mechanics establishes a relationship between force, mass and acceleration which is valid in a wide range of conditions. This type of rules will be discussed in the context of human knowledge in Chapter 4. We will distinguish this type from those rules affecting human behaviour which can be defined as prescribing, prohibiting or constraining particular types of behaviour. In this context, institutions can be conceived as sets of rules connected by a common objective. In a general sense, institutions are required in the life of groups and communities in order to *coordinate* (Hodgson, 2014) the behaviours and activities of individual members. Groups and communities owe their existence to the evolutionary advantage they have with respect to sets of unrelated individuals. In turn, this evolutionary advantage is rooted in the possibility to use division of labour, thus greatly enhancing the efficiency with which the community can use existing resources and develop new ones.[2] Here it needs to be pointed out that we refer to a conception of division of labour which is not only internal to productive activities, as in Adam Smith, but which applies to all human activities and functions. An example will help.

1.2.1 The modern firm

Organizations constituted by a group of people and operating to achieve objectives which were at least partly economic have existed for a very long time. Important examples of such organizations are the medieval guilds and the chartered corporations, such as the East India Company. However, these organizations differed from the modern corporation in that they required a special permission to operate, or sometimes a monopoly, issued by the state (Rosenberg, Birdzell, 1986). The concept of a corporation, which could be formed by a group of individuals to trade or manufacture and which could hold property rights, acts as a moral person, and accept liability, only emerged in the second half of the XIXth century, mostly in the UK and the USA (ibid). It is quite likely that such joint stock corporations became a permissible legal form during the second part of the industrial revolution when they represented the most appropriate form to exploit the productive potential such revolution had unlocked.

The evolution of the modern firm is in many ways closely linked to technological evolution. Before the industrial revolution, the scale of most manufacturing firms was small and essentially family based. For example, the textile industry was dominated by the so-called cottage industry (Landes, 1969; Hobsbawm, 1968). The large machines and the consequent capital requirements of the factory system started the growth in size of the manufacturing firms, growth which was to accelerate considerably towards the end of the XIXth century (Chandler 1962, 1977; Hannah, 1976). Such further spurt of growth in firm size was due to a combination of new technologies and the resultant process of market expansion. The new technologies which contributed to the emergence of large corporations were of two types: first, there were new technologies which led to the creation of new sectors, thus providing new productive opportunities. Examples of these could be found in the chemical and electrical industries. Second, other technologies were enabling in the sense that they allow the transport and communication required for the geographical enlargement of markets. Examples of such technologies were the railways, refrigeration and the telegraph. According to Chandler (1977, pp. 287–289), the modern corporation was created by the integration of mass production with mass distribution.

Thus, technology has shaped and accompanied the evolution of the modern firm since the industrial revolution. However, the mechanisms whereby technology affected industry and the firm changed substantially with the institutionalization of R&D (Saviotti, 2012).

To discuss the coevolution of technologies and institutions,[3] we need to define clearly the boundaries between economic and non-economic activities. The concept of *homo economicus* assumes that one can precisely circumscribe and clearly separate economic from non-economic activities. If we are interested in the analysis of long-run economic development, such an assumption is illegitimate. Let us, for example, think about science, an activity which until the XIXth century was almost completely separate from the economy but which from the XXth century has become closely interconnected with it. Today when observing the huge investments in science and industrial R&D who can say where the economic system ends and where science begins? In an even more telling way, although the welfare state emerged in advanced industrialized countries mostly for political reasons, it has acquired very important economic dimensions (see Chapter 5). This close interaction can be appreciated by imagining what consequences a drastic reduction in holiday times or health care would have on tourism or the sectors supplying inputs to the medical system (e.g., pharmaceuticals). This very close interaction between strictly economic activities and apparently non-economic ones is often one of complementarity. This implies that the strict separability of economic from non-economic activities required for the existence of homo economicus is an inadequate assumption for the analysis of long-run phenomena. It follows that the boundaries between those which can be considered strictly economic activities and other activities which, although not strictly economic, can interact with economic activities are not fixed but they are likely to change endogenously in the course of time.

The transition from a society of hunters and gatherers to settled agriculture (see Diamond, 1997; Gowdy, 1994) by reducing the search costs required to locate food and by allowing greater independence from seasons combined with the ability to store durable crops (e.g., grains) contributed heavily to increase the efficiency of food production. Together with the emergence of urbanization (Jacobs, 1969), this made possible for some members of the population to carry out activities other than food production. For example, there could be traders, priests, administrators, and warriors. This was the first example of the differentiation of human activities and it increased the extent of division of labour in human communities. Of course, together with this enhanced division of labour, new types of coordination problems requiring new rules emerged. For example, it was necessary to decide how to allocate individuals to these new activities and how to reward each of them. These were the bases of new institutions. Settled agriculture has been considered by Lipsey et al. (2005) as a general-purpose technology which has made a fundamental contribution to long-run human development.

Firms and other organizations do not behave according to optimizing rationality but use routines, which can be defined as repetitive patterns of interdependent actions in the organization. The use of routine-based rather than optimizing behaviour is explained by the enhanced cognitive efficiency and by the decreased complexity that routines allow. However, routines can be usefully repeated only if relevant environmental variables remain within given ranges. For example, firm routines are usually repeated until a threat or a failure challenges them (Nelson, Winter, 1982, pp. 128–134). In parallel with their routines, firms carry out search activities, a general analogue of R&D, by means of which they scan the external environment looking for potential alternatives to their present routines. Whenever they are associated with a failure, present routines are replaced by new ones derived from search activities. All human activities are a combination of routines and search activities. The adoption of new routines by a firm is an innovation induced by threat or failure. This combination of routines and search activities is part of a theory of innovation.

Furthermore, all organizations have a structure designed to make them adapt well to their external environment. Such structure changes when changes in the external environment occur. A particularly interesting example of adaptation is that of industrial firms at the end of the XIXth century. The process is interpreted by making use of the Chandlerian distinction between *strategy* and *structure* (Chandler, 1962, 1977). The need to adopt a more efficient structure, which started to emerge as industrial firms grew very rapidly at the end of the XIXth century first in the USA and then in some European countries, gave rise initially to the U and then to the M form organization of the firm. Growing industrial firms found that they could not manage a much-enlarged organization while preserving their previous type of organizational structure. The transition to the U form firm involved a growing specialization of functions, for example, the separation of financial, production and sales activities into different departments or functional units. Amongst these functions a historically new one was R&D, which began to be internalized in large firms (Hounshell, Smith, 1988; Reich, 1985). As the economy grew in size it also became more differentiated, due to both the emergence of completely new markets and the growing internal differentiation of each one of them, corresponding to the transition that Saviotti and Pyka (2013) called 'from necessities to imaginary worlds. Firm structure adapted changing from U (multifunctional) to M (multidivisional) form, changing from the pursuit of efficiency in a market of constant composition to the exploitation of market differentiation. In this sense, changes in firm structure consisted in an adaptation to (i) two of the most important trajectories of economic development, those of increasing variety and of increasing quality (see Chapter 4), and to (ii) the institutionalization of industrial R&D.

Changes in firm structure were accompanied by, or perhaps induced by, the emergence and the subsequent changes in firm strategy. With the creation of the general office, the day-to-day running of the firm was separated from the scanning of the external environment to detect opportunities and threats. The general office was created with the task of formulating firm strategy. Perceived changes in the external environment were reflected in changes in firm strategy which then led to structure (Chandler, 1962). An interesting example of the different capabilities to detect changes in the external environment comes from a comparison of Ford and General Motors in the 1920s: while the former insisted with the uniformity of the model T up to the point of risking the ruin, the latter opted for the differentiation of its car models thus becoming the most important US and world producer.

The enlargement of the markets which led to changing firm strategy and structure was not just the result of growing consumer wealth but relied also on a number of technologies which drastically reduced the transport and coordination costs involved in serving markets very far away from production sites. Amongst these technologies, the most important ones are the railways, telegraph, telephone and refrigeration (Chandler, 1977). By allowing the centralization of production on few sites, these technologies induced scale economies and the increased throughput which, according to Chandler, led to the adoption of the U form (Chandler, 1962, 1977, p. 241).

Railways, telegraph, telephone and refrigeration are technologies complementary to most industries. Thus, if they grow, they contribute to the growth of those industries with respect to which they are complementary. The same can be said for infrastructures, which are man-made for artefacts that involve such huge investments that no individual investor can afford but that generate payoffs for very large numbers of actors and users. Roads, bridges, and airports are examples of infrastructures which enable the performance of economic activities which would be impossible without them. Other technologies are complementary not to the whole economic system but to specific industries. For example, tyres are complementary with respect to cars. These examples show the general importance of complementarity, a further type of interaction in addition to competition. When two or more technologies or activities are complementary to each other, the growth of one lead to the growth of the others, giving rise to positive feedback amongst all the interacting activities. This constitutes coevolution, a mechanism that we have already mentioned but to which we will keep referring in the rest of the book for its general importance in economic development. The main purpose of introducing here infrastructures, institutions and organizational forms is to study their interactions with MMAs within an overall system-/complexity-based approach. Within such an approach, which will be discussed in Chapters 5 and 7, interactions are not in general local, pair wise and limited in time but part of the extended interactivity of a complex system. This approach will be considered by us as one of the main components of a modern evolutionary theory of economic behaviour. Here we wish to give some examples of the interaction and coevolution of MMAs and of infrastructures, institutions, and organizational forms.

1.3 Transformations and transitions

So far, the difference between qualitative and quantitative change has been examined mostly for man-made artefacts (MMAs), be they products or services. However, the previous observations about the importance of coevolution imply that the emergence of important new technologies cannot occur without major changes in the structure of SESs whereas the following stages in the life cycles of the same technologies are likely to proceed within the institutional framework defined at the emergence stage. This is certainly an oversimplified representation of the evolution of technologies and social structures, but has the advantage of stressing the difference between qualitative and quantitative change at the level of aggregation of an SES. Thus, we could say that a transition occurs between two different states of an SES characterized by important qualitative differences in technologies, institutions, infrastructures, patterns of consumption, etc. Conversely, a transformation would occur within the framework of existing technologies, institutions, infrastructures, and patterns of consumption and it would be a predominantly quantitative change. Thus, a transition would involve a discontinuity while a transformation would entail more predictable changes. A meaning like the one proposed here is used in Geels' work on technological transitions (2002a, 2002b, 2004). Transitions in transport, such as those of horse-trams, bicycles, automobiles, electric trams, propeller or jet aircraft, and steamships, involve major changes in patterns of urbanization, for example, allowing the existence of larger and more decentralized cities, or increasing the scope of intentional trade transport. The study of technological transitions follows from the literature on sociology of science and technology (Pinch, Bijker, 1984; Rip, Kemp, 1998), although the term 'coevolution' is not always mentioned in it.

Notes

1 Further analysis of the interactions within the SES and of the SES with its EE will be carried out in Chapters 3 and 6.
2 More about rules and communities in Chapter 3.
3 We will often refer to the coevolution of technologies and institutions even when discussing more general types of coevolution, including other types of components of an SES, such as health care or education.

References

Abernathy W.J., Utterback, J.M. (1975) A dynamic model of process and product innovation. *Omega*, 3(6): 639–656.

Abernathy W.J., Utterback, J.M. (June/July 1978) Patterns of industrial innovation. *Technology Review*, 41–47.

Acemoglu D., Robinson J.A. (2012) *Why Nations Fail: the Origins of Power, Prosperity and Poverty*, New York, Crown Publishing.

Allen P. (2001) Knowledge, ignorance and the evolution of complex systems, in Foster J., Metcalfe J.S. (Eds), *Frontiers of Evolutionary Economics*, Cheltenham, Edward Elgar, 313–350.

Allen P. (2007) Self-organization in economic systems, in Hanusch H., Pyka A. (Eds), *Elgar Companion to Neo-Schumpeterian Economics*, Cheltenham, Edward Elgar, 1111–1148.

Arthur W.B. (1996) Increasing returns and the new world of business. *Harvard Business Review*, 74(4): 100–109.

Arthur W.B. (2007a) Complexity and the economy, in Hanusch H., Pyka A. (Eds), *Elgar Companion to Neo-Schumpeterian Economics*, Cheltenham, Edward Elgar, 1102–1110.

Arthur W.B. (2007b) *Complexity and the Economy*, Oxford, Oxford University Press.

Boyd R., Richerson P.J. (1985) *Culture and the Evolutionary Process*, Chicago, Chicago University Press.

Chandler A.D. (1962) *Strategy and Structure*, Cambridge, MA, MIT Press.

Chandler A.D. (1977) *The Visible Hand*, Cambridge, MA, Harvard University Press.

Diamond J. (1997) *Guns, Germs, and Steel, The Fates of Human Societies*, New York, Norton.

Dosi G. (1982) Technological paradigms and technological trajectories: a suggested interpretation of the determinants and directions of technical change. *Research Policy*, 11: 147–162.

Dosi G., Nelson R.R. (2018) Technological advance as an evolutionary process, in Nelson R.R., Dosi G., Helfat C., Pyka A., Saviotti P.P., Lee K, Dopfer K., Malerba F. Winter S., *Modern Evolutionary Economics: An Overview*, Cambridge, Cambridge University Press, 35–84.

Freeman C. (1982) *The Economics of Industrial Innovation*, London, Pinter (2nd ed).

Freeman C. (1987) *Technology Policy and Economic Performance*, London, Pinter.

Freeman C., Soete L. (1997), *The Economics of Industrial Innovation*, London, Pinter.

Geels F.W. (2002a) Technological transitions as evolutionary reconfiguration processes: a multi-level perspective and a case-study, *Research Policy*, 31: 8–9, pp. 1257–1274, 17 p.

Geels F.W. (2002b) *Understanding the Dynamics of Technological Transitions: A Co-evolutionary and Socio-Technical Analysis*, Twente, Twente University Press.

Geels F.W. (2004) From sectoral systems of innovation to socio-technical systems: insights about dynamics and change from sociology and institutional theory. *Research Policy*, 33(6–7): 897–920.

Georgescu Roegen N. (1971) *The Entropy Law and the Economic Process*, Cambridge, MA, Harvard University Press.

Gowdy J. (1994) *Co-evolutionary Economics: The Economy, Society and the Environment*, Dordrecht, Kluwer Academics.

Hannah L. (1976, 1983) *The Rise of the Corporate Economy*, London, Methuen.

Henderson R.M., Clark Kim B. (1990) Architectural innovation: the reconfiguration of existing product technologies and the failure of established firms. *Administrative Science Quarterly*, 35(1), Special Issue: Technology, Organizations, and Innovation (Mar., 1990): 9–30.

Hobsbawm E.J. (1968) *Industry and Empire*, Harmondsworth, Penguin Books.

Hodgson G.M. (2014) *Conceptualizing Capitalism, Institutions, Evolution, Future*, Chicago, Chicago University Press.

Hounshell D.A., Smith J.K. (1988) *Science and Corporate Strategy: Du Pont R and D, 1902–1980*, Cambridge, Cambridge University Press.

Jacobs J. (1969) *The Economy of Cities*, New York, Vintage Books.

Kirman A. (2011) *Complex Economics: Individual and Collective Rationality*, London, Rutledge.

Kuhn T.S. (1962) *The Structure of Scientific Revolutions*, Chicago: The University of Chicago Press.

Lancaster K.J. (1966) A new approach to consumer theory. *Journal of Political Economy*, 14: 133–156.

Lancaster K.J. (1971) *Consumer Demand: A New Approach*, New York, Columbia University Press.

Landes D.S. (1969) *The Unbound Prometheus: Technological Change and Industrial Development in Western Europe from 1750 to the Present*, Cambridge, Cambridge University Press.

Lipsey R., Carlaw K.J., Bekhar C.T. (2005) *Economic Transformations: General Purpose Technologies and Long-Term Economic Growth*. Oxford, Oxford University Press.

Lotka A. (1925) *Elements of Mathematical Biology*, Dover (1956, 2nd edition).

Lundvall B.A. (1992) *National Systems of Innovation*, London, Pinter.

Metcalfe J.S. (1998) *Evolutionary Economics and Creative Destruction*, London, Routledge.

Mokyr J. (1990) *The Lever of Riches: Technological Creativity and Economic Progress*, New York, Oxford University Press.

Mokyr J. (2002) *The Gifts of Athena: Historical Origins of the Knowledge Economy*, Princeton, NJ, Princeton University Press.

Nelson R. (1959) The simple economics of basic scientific research, *Journal of Political Economy*, 67: 297–306.

Nelson R.R. (1993) *National Innovation Systems: A Comparative Analysis*, Oxford, Oxford University Press.

Nelson, R. (1995) Recent evolutionary theorizing about economic change, *Journal of Economic Literature*, 33: 48-90.

Nelson R., Winter S. (1977) In search of useful theory of innovation. *Research Policy*, 6: 36–76.

Nelson, R., Winter, S. (1982) *An Evolutionary Theory of Economic Change*, Cambridge, MA, Harvard University Press.

North D.C. (1990) *Institutions, Institutional Change and Economic Performance*, Cambridge, Cambridge University Press.

Pinch T.J., Bijker W.E. (1984) The social construction of facts and artefacts: or how the sociology of science and the sociology of technology might benefit each other. *Social Studies of Science* 14: 399–441. https://doi.org/10.1177/030631284014003004

Reich L.S. (1985) *The Making of American Industrial Research*, Cambridge, MA, MIT Press.

Rip A., Kemp R. (1998) Technological change, in Rayner S., Malone E.L. (Eds) *Human Choice and Climate Change*, Columbus, Ohio, Battelle Press, Volume 2, Resources and Technology, 327–399.

Rosen S. (1974) Hedonic prices and implicit markets: product differentiation in pure competition. *Journal of Political Economy*, 82 (1): 34–55.

Rosenberg N. (1976) Science, invention, and economic growth, in *Perspectives on Technology*, Cambridge, Cambridge University Press.

Rosenberg N., Birdzell L.E. (1986) *How the West Grew Rich*, New York, Basic Books.

Sahal D. (1975) Technology guide posts and innovation avenues. *Research Policy*, 14: 61–82.

Saviotti P.P. (1986) Systems theory and technological change, *Futures*, 18: 773–786.

Saviotti P.P. (2005) On the co-evolution of technologies and institutions, in Weber M., Hemmelskamp J. (Eds) *Towards Environmental Innovation Systems*, Berlin, Heidelberg, New York, Springer.

Saviotti P.P. (1996) *Technological Evolution, Variety and the Economy*, Cheltenham, Edward Elgar.

Saviotti P.P. (2012) R&D and the firm, in Dietrich M., Krafft J., (Eds) *Handbook on the Economics and Theory of the Firm*, Cheltenham, Edward Elgar, 405–423.

Saviotti, P.P., Pyka, A. (2013) From necessities to imaginary worlds: structural change, product quality and economic development, *Technological Forecasting & Social Change*, 80: 1499–1512.

3 Adaptive behaviour as the most general form of socioeconomic behaviour

1 Introduction

In the first two chapters of this book, we point out that the existence of qualitative change in economic development leads to discontinuities and radical uncertainty. As a consequence, optimizing rationality is unlikely to have been usable during most of economic development, although that may be less true for some phases dominated by incremental innovations. As we previously pointed out, we think that neoclassical economics is based upon a series of foundations which, although useful to provide coherence to a highly formalized theory, make it unsuitable to analyse very complex situations and in particular the emergence of new man-made artefacts (MMAs). We wish to avoid the confrontational attitude that rejects in its totality neoclassical economics and to adopt the point of view that its admirable elegance and deductive structure are achieved at the expense of excluding a large range of phenomena from its pursuit. In particular, we think that all phenomena involving qualitative change, foremost amongst which is the emergence of new MMAs, are excluded from neoclassical economics by the same assumptions which make its edifice logically elegant and apparently all powerful. We will develop a general comparison of neoclassical and evolutionary economics as knowledge structures in Chapter 6. Here we wish to compare two types of behaviour, adaptive and optimizing, which correspond to evolutionary and orthodox economic theories respectively. As already pointed out, our objective is not to outcompete a rival theory but to contribute to the development of a general economic theory able to encompass both 'traditional' economic phenomena on the basis of which economic theories have been constructed, and the innovation-related phenomena which have been the basis for the construction of evolutionary theories. Here we will describe adaptive behaviour and show that it is the most general type of the two and that it includes optimizing behaviour as a special case.

In this chapter we discuss the nature and the limitations of adaptive behaviour and its applications to economic policies. In order to discuss adaptive behaviour, we introduce some general concepts of systems theory that will be of use in this and in the following chapters. The readers of this book may

DOI: 10.4324/9781003294221-3

think that the introduction of adaptive behaviour does not help us to understand economic behaviour more than optimizing rationality. It is relatively easy to state in a simple way the nature of these two types of behaviour but it becomes much more difficult to analyse real-life situations of greater complexity. Even in the case of 'complex adaptive systems' (Miller, Page, 2007), no general definition of adaptation is given. Rather, 'complex adaptive systems' is a modelling approach to complex social systems that stresses the interdependence of different components of such systems. However, in biology, adaptive behaviour is extensively used, and in the coevolution of genetics and culture (Boyd, Richerson, 1985). In this book we are more interested in the coevolution of technologies, institutions, organizations, infrastructures and complementary technologies. We think that providing some definitions of adaptive behaviour can allow us to move towards a general evolutionary approach to economic behaviour. Of course, this can only be considered the beginning of an exploration and not a complete treatment of adaptive behaviour.

2 Adaptation and systems

Adaptive behaviour can be defined as a change of behaviour adopted when individuals or groups experience a change in their external environment which either worsens their situation or holds the promise of an improvement. For example, students obtaining bad marks at school can decide to change their behaviour by studying more to improve their marks. At a more aggregate level, a country which relied on a given type of economic policies and obtained very disappointing results can decide to change policies in order to improve its economic performance. This would be especially the case if other countries adopting different policies turned out to be much more successful. Adaptive behaviour would make sense if (i) it was easy to realize that the results obtained are disappointing, and if (ii) the change in behaviour required to improve the disappointing results was easily understood and unique. A further condition for the usefulness of the concept of adaptive behaviour in the case of a group is that (iii) the change of behaviour must be adopted by a large enough percentage of the population of the group.

Any theory of system adaptation must start by defining the nature of the system. It must then proceed by identifying its components and subcomponents and finally by understanding the laws of interaction of these components. Such laws of interaction when applied to the components and subcomponents should explain why and how we observe particular patterns of development over the period we intend to study. The systems we will study are generally complex, including a variable number of interacting components, or subsystems, and are separated by an interface from their external environment (EE). The definition of the system itself and its boundary with the EE is somewhat arbitrary and depends on the objective of our analysis. The most fundamental components of economic systems are human beings and a series of their aggregates, such as households, firms, hospitals, schools and governments. In this book the most common systems we will study are individual human beings and communities. By the term 'community' we will here mean a group of individuals that have a shared set of, formal or informal, rules of behaviour and a defined boundary with the rest of the EE. When there is a change in the EE of a system in equilibrium with it, defined as a state in which neither the system as a whole nor any of its components have an incentive to change, we can expect the system itself to change in order to re-establish the equilibrium. We can say that the system in equilibrium was well adapted to its EE, that the change in the EE involved a loss of adaptation and that such a loss was likely to induce a change in the system's internal structure.

The system itself is generally complex, including a variable number of interacting components, or subsystems. The organization of the internal structure of the system consists of the pattern of interaction of its subsystems, which in turn determines overall system stability. Such stability is not indefinite and it is challenged by any change that occurs in the EE. Adaptation to such a change can sometimes occur by small and quantitative modifications of the system's internal structure, but in other cases more drastic changes are required. As already pointed out (Chapter 1), the boundary between qualitative and quantitative change is not always clear-cut, and sometimes over long periods the accumulation of small incremental changes within a given system can give rise to a new state of it which is clearly distinguishable from the initial one and which can be considered qualitatively different from it. Although this entails some ambiguity in the definition of MMAs and makes more difficult to distinguish between transformations and transitions (Geels, 2002) (Chapter 2), the twin characteristic representation (Chapter 1) can help us to understand this difference.

The EE in principle includes all the rest of the universe outside the system. In most circumstances, only a small minority of the components of the EE affect our system. In most cases, it is enough to include in our representation of the EE only its most important components, some of which are other systems. An important distinction is that between the natural environment and the socioeconomic environment.

In some cases, the interface between system and EE is discrete and clearly defined, in other cases it is fuzzy and possibly shifting in the course of time. For example, the legal boundaries of a city may be very clearly defined, but the real boundaries keep changing as new inhabitants arrive from elsewhere and settle in places not formerly within the city. Thus, in describing a system we must pay attention to the nature of its interface with the EE. We can then define the interface as the locus of change of the properties of the system, a change that can be discrete or gradual.

2.1 System stability and change

A system comprising several interacting subsystems tends to acquire a *structure*, or a form of *order*, defined as a combination of its most elementary subsystems, which tends to be stable over relatively long periods of time. Some ambiguity in this idea stems from the fact that even the components are never identical to themselves at two different times. The whole system is continuously changing, although the various subsystems can with a degree of approximation be recognized to be the same across time. For example, the automobile industry is considered the same system from the beginning of the XXth century to the present, although many important changes occurred within it. We can only maintain that the system remains the same in the course of time by differentiating the fundamental aspects of the system from its secondary ones. We can then say that the system is the same at two different times if its fundamental subsystems are qualitatively unchanged. Thus, both quantitative changes in the fundamental aspects of the system and the emergence or extinction of some secondary aspects do not alter its nature (see the box on the automobile industry). In this case we can say that the system changes its state, represented by numerical values of its components, while the structure remains constant. Obviously, there is some arbitrariness in this procedure, but it allows us to study the evolution of systems and subsystems with a reasonable approximation.

The stability of the system has been analysed by means of several concepts, such as self-organization, homeostasis and self-regulation. Self-organization can occur at different levels of aggregation. Individuals self-organize into families, firms, associations and groups; firms self-organize into sectors and industrial associations; cities self-organize into regions, regions into countries and countries into the international socioeconomic system. Amongst these levels of aggregation, we can distinguish the lowest, or micro, the highest, or macro and a series of intermediate, or meso (Dopfer et al., 2004) levels of aggregation. In principle, there can be an almost infinite number of meso levels, but most of them are not meaningful. Thus, although ten or twenty people constitute levels of aggregation higher than one person, they are not a meaningful level of aggregation unless they are organized into a whole having a shared set of objectives, an internal division of labour and a clearly defined boundary/interface between the group and its EE. In other words, a meso level of aggregation is meaningful if it corresponds to the existence of a subsystem having a definite boundary with the other subsystems within its overall system. Thus, 10,000 biological macromolecules or 1,000 cells are not a meaningful level of aggregation unless the former are organized in cells and the latter in organs. A system is more than the sum of its parts, this more being supplied by the nontrivial pattern of interactions amongst its components. Thus, it is quite clear that the number and types of meso levels of aggregation are crucial in determining the overall, or macro, properties of the system.

Box 3.1 System sameness and the automobile industry

The automobile industry was born at the end of the XIXth century to produce a modified mail coach in which the horse was substituted by an engine. In other words, the innovation consisted of a change in the mode of production of energy, previously supplied by an animal (horse) and now by a chemical reaction. The first automobiles looked more like mail coaches than like the modern ones. Modern automobiles share with the early ones some components but contain many new ones. Whether modern and early automobiles are the same entity depends on the importance we attach to the different components. If the definition is based only on the shared components, then modern and early automobiles are the same entity; otherwise, they are two different entities. Alternatively, we can define automobiles as artefacts that supply transport services (Chapter 1) without the intervention of an animal source of energy. However, in this case automobiles would be part of a more general category, including trains, buses and airplanes. Thus, whether today's automobiles are different from the early ones and whether the automobile industry is still the same depend on our classification criteria. This situation is not specific to the automobile industry: most industries and presumably most human activities keep changing in the course of time in ways that are not purely quantitative, but whether an industry remains the same or changes into a different one depends on the extent to which we consider the changes qualitative changes leading to the formation of different industries or activities or quantitative, affecting only the 'size' of the industry.[1] Thus, we could consider that the automobile industry is still the same but that it has been undergoing important transformations or that within it there have been important transitions and that it is no longer the same industry. Once more, the distinctions between qualitative and quantitative change or between transformation and transition depend on the aspects of the SES that we are predominantly focusing upon.

2.2 System dynamics

An SES is never static and keeps changing. This can be due to exogenous or endogenous factors. An example of the former is the formation of the Sahara Desert from the fertile region that seems to have existed at some time in the same part of Africa. Endogenous transformations in general entail some innovation. One of the earliest examples of an endogenous change is the advent of settled agriculture from the society of hunters and gatherers (Gowdy, 1994, Harari, 2011). This was based on a long learning process by means of which some groups of human beings discovered that some plants could be cultivated and some animals could be domesticated (Diamond, 1997; Gowdy, 1994; Harari, 2011). Such a discovery allowed human communities to overcome the seasonal character of some fruits and vegetables and to use domesticated animals as source of food and energy. Such a transition allowed human beings to increase their efficiency of food production, thus liberating some of their human resources for other uses. This was the beginning of the differentiation of human societies. This transition was endogenous in the sense that it came from within the SES and it was not forced upon it from outside the system. We could say that this transition was based on a form of 'learning by doing'. Changes arising within modern SESs can occur in a more consciously purposeful way.

A different and historically more recent form of learning is constituted by R&D, or its generalized analogue, search activities (Nelson, Winter, 1982). In principle, all human activities can be reduced either to *routines* or to *search activities*, where the former are standardized types of behaviour adopted by individuals or organizations in response to demands coming from components of their same system or from their EE. Routines are changed infrequently and only when a change in the EE renders them unusable. However, search activities scan the EE about a given subject trying to understand the laws governing our natural environment and using this knowledge to (i) reduce the quantity of resources required to achieve some productive objectives or (ii) suggest ideas for new products, processes, or organizational forms. As opposed to learning by doing, search activities can be considered a form of *learning by not doing*. This form of learning is relatively modern since it became institutionalized only in the second half of the XIXth century and it diffused generally only after the Second World War.

Innovation occurs when some changes are introduced into existing ways of doing things, be they physical processes or organizational arrangements, or when completely new goods or services are created. Innovations can affect in different ways the *stability* of a system. They can improve the efficiency of existing processes or give rise to new goods and services. They can then contribute to the growth of the system and its changing structure. The detailed ways in which this occurs will be analysed in Chapter 5. Here it suffices to say that the effect of innovations is to change the 'size' and the nature of the system. The nature of the system changes as new sectors, qualitatively different from pre-existing ones, emerge. Growth in the 'size' of system can occur both because new sectors add new markets to pre-existing ones and because increases in productive efficiency can allow pre-existing sectors to grow either in volume and/or in value. These mechanisms will be explored in a more detailed way in Chapter 5.

Innovation is one of the most powerful forces moving the system away from any position of equilibrium it might have attained (Schumpeter, 1911, 1934). Once an SES starts using innovation, it has condemned itself to be in a state of permanent instability (Metcalfe, 1998; Ramlogan, Metcalfe, 2006). If the technology life cycle identified in the previous chapter, starting with a radical innovation, and gradually moving to a more predictable stream of incremental innovations, is followed, we can expect instability to go through different phases, ranging from the construction of new system components (e.g., new training, education, complementary institutions) to a gradual increase in their productive efficiency. As the most innovative system in history, 'restless capitalism' (Metcalfe, 1998, 2006) creates permanent instability. An aspect that we will stress heavily in Chapter 5 is the differential rate of change of different components of the SES that will give rise to a change in the structure of the same SES.

2.3 Closed and open systems

A distinction of the greatest importance for biological and socioeconomic systems is that between closed and open systems (Prigogine, 1947; Prigogine, Stengers, 1984; Von Bertalanffy1950; Hidalgo, 2015; Beinhocker, 2007, Haken, 1983; Allen, 2007, 2001). The former systems are separated from their EE by an interface that does not allow the passage of matter, energy, or information. A closed system tends to achieve an internal equilibrium characterized by the maximum possible disorder of its components. On the contrary, an open system has boundaries that allow the passage of matter, energy, and information. Open systems can differ for the rate of flow of matter, energy, and information across their boundaries. In fact, this rate of flow constitutes a measure of the *distance of the system from equilibrium.* Contrary to closed systems, open systems have the remarkable property that they not only do not tend to give rise to states of maximum disorder but can create states of increasing order. This property was crucial in demonstrating that the existence and nature of biological systems could be explained by the same concepts and laws used to explain chemical and physical systems. Furthermore, the evolution of SESs does not give rise to continuously increasing disorder but to more ordered, if more complex, structures. The order characterizing both biological and socioeconomic systems can be explained by their nature of open systems.

Like biological systems, SESs are characterized by a high degree of order and complexity, which is likely to have increased in the course of human history. Components of SESs, such as firms or organizations, are open and have continuous flows of matter, energy and information crossing their boundaries. An interesting example of this open nature is given by the work of Alfred Chandler (1962, 1977) who suggested that changes in the structure of a corporation could be induced by the increasing throughput crossing its boundary. The increasing labour force required to use such a rising throughput needs to be organized hierarchically with a growing number of levels. The same principle can be expected to apply to hospitals, schools, and other types of organization. Without going into greater details, the existence of open systems is crucial to explain the observed pattern of economic development.

3 Adaptive behaviour

The concept of adaptation is used in several disciplines and research areas, such as biology, ecology, psychology, computer science and climatology. Although the definitions used in the different fields vary, they have something in common. For example, in behavioural ecology adaptive behaviour contributes directly or indirectly to an individual's survival or reproductive success and is thus subject to the forces of natural selection. Conversely, a non-adaptive behaviour is counterproductive to an individual's survival or reproductive success. In a more general sense, we can define adaptation as a change of behaviour of an entity living/operating in each external environment (EE) aimed at improving the survival or some other objective of the entity. The entity itself can be a biological organism, a human being, an algorithm, or a community at different levels of aggregation.

We can extend this concept to the study of economic development by introducing some modifications. The definition of adaptive behaviour requires a system, its EE and an interface between the two. Let us start with a system in a state of equilibrium with its EE, in such a way that there is no 'force' or tendency leading the system to change. Then, if a change, which for the time being we can regard as exogenous, occurs in the EE, such equilibrium will be destroyed. We can then expect the system to try to re-establish a state of equilibrium by changing something within itself. Consequently, we can expect that when the new equilibrium is eventually attained the state of the system will be different from its initial pre-perturbation state. If the system is a human being or an organization, we can expect it to change its behaviour to re-establish a state of equilibrium. For example, if it starts raining, we can expect human beings to take refuge in a dry place or to use an umbrella. Likewise, if the price of a particular input rises, we can expect firms to reduce the quantity of it they use. If the change in the EE is just a shock, that for the moment we consider exogenous, then after the adaptation of the system the equilibrium is re-established. Things would be different if the perturbation instead of being a discrete shock acted continuously in the course of time at a given speed. In this case the process of adaptation would be more complex, with the outcome depending on the relative speeds of system perturbation and system adaptation. We will shortly come back to this dynamical problem in discussing the existence of a general equilibrium. Before doing that, we need to articulate better the concept of adaptation.

3.1 ADTO and ADOF

In the previous examples, adaptation was defined as a change of behaviour of the system required to re-establish equilibrium with its EE after a perturbation occurred in the latter. In human communities, a second type of adaptation is constituted by the deliberate introduction of changes in the EE intended to improve the future adaptation of the community to the modified EE. A few examples of such adaption include the construction of roads, houses, bridges, and airports. This form of adaptation occurs also for some biological species, such as termites, ants, and bees, but at a much lower scale than for human communities. In fact, this second type of adaptation has become so widespread that its impact on the EE became of the same order of magnitude as that of natural phenomena, giving rise to what is now called the 'Anthropocene' (Steffen et al., 2011). In what follows, to avoid repetitions we will distinguish between the adaptation to a given EE (ADTO) and the adaptation of a given EE (ADOF).

Summarizing, we can distinguish two types of adaptive behaviour:

i Adaptation *to* a given EE [ADTO]
ii Adaptation *of* a given EE = transformation of EE [ADOF]

where (ii) involves the modification of EE and its transformation into $EE' \neq EE$.

The fundamental difference between ADTO and ADOF is that the former only involves a change in the system while the latter involves a change in the EE which needs to be followed by an ADTO to the modified EE. Any form of ADOF involves some type of innovation. Innovations were very infrequent in ancient SESs but have become the norm in modern ones. Change is then endogenous to the extent that it requires the decisions made to be internal to the system. In the course of time innovations are accompanied by a process of learning and of accumulation of knowledge that can lead to more and larger scale innovations.

When the EE is changed by ADOF the system will not be immediately adapted to the new EE (EE'). The process of ADOF can be represented as a human community operating on a given EE and transforming it into a different one:

$$HC(EE) \rightarrow EE'$$

The human community will now need to adapt to (ADTO) the new EE (EE'). This will have very important implications for the dynamics of our system.

In principle, both ADTO and ADOF can exist for both biological and human populations, but ADOF is much more developed in socioeconomic systems than in biological ones. The types of nests that some animals (e.g., bees, ants) can construct are indeed very elaborate and can qualify as ADOF *of* a given EE. However, their scale and variety does not match that of human artefacts and infrastructures. The term 'Anthropocene' has recently been introduced to describe an era in which the scale of the impact of human activities on the EE matches that of natural phenomena (Steffen et al., 2011). A similar scale had never been achieved by any biological system. However, it is not just the scale of the type of adaptation that differs between socioeconomic and biological systems. The objective of adaptation is much more narrowly defined for biological than for socioeconomic systems. Whereas for the former the objective of adaptation is survival or reproductive success, such objective can be far more varied in socioeconomic systems. For example, the fall in the rate of population growth in modern industrialized societies cannot be interpreted as an increasing maladjustment of these socioeconomic systems to their EE. Although this fall in the rate of reproduction seems to be in stark contrast to the observed behaviour of all biological systems in the course of history, it is in fact the result of a change in the objective of adaptation. In a modern, industrialized society, it is preferable to have fewer children and to give them a better education than to have many children endowed with a very poor capability to adapt to such a socioeconomic system. The required education cannot be given to any number of children because it is very costly. Furthermore, the need for large families is less pressing in a modern industrialized society due to the presence of various forms of social assistance, ranging from health care to the care of the elders. These new forms of social assistance transformed the objective of adaptation. In other words, the previous evolution of the socioeconomic system gave rise to new institutions (education, health care, pensions) which induced a change in the objective of adaptation. These new institutions were endogenous to the socioeconomic system because their emergence was induced by previous changes in the same system. The objective of adaptation is likely to have remained substantially constant for biological systems, or if any changes in the EE occurred, they would have been exogenous to such systems. Summarizing, we could say that for socioeconomic systems the objective of adaptation is likely to have undergone changes due to the endogenous evolution of such systems, while for biological systems the objective of adaptation is likely to have remained substantially constant except for exogenous changes in their EE. This difference reflects the growing importance of the man-made component of their EE for socioeconomic systems. The emergence of new types of MMAs is one of the most important forms of ADOF. As we will see in Chapter 5, new MMAs never exist in an otherwise unmodified system and EE. As we will see in Chapter 5, in order to grow and diffuse, they need the construction of complementary infrastructures and institutions in a coevolutionary process.

3.2 Collective and individual adaptation

Another very important difference between biological and human evolution is the much greater collective nature of human adaptation. Forms of collaboration occur also amongst biological species but they never reach the organizational complexity existing in human societies. Group behaviour is observed amongst animals but such groups are much smaller and less complex than those observed in human societies. The fact that societies of large size and great complexity exist is a proof that collective adaptation is superior to individual adaptation. Robinson Crusoe could never compete with any kind of modern organized society. Such superiority of collective adaptation is due to the possibility to develop within a group *division of labour* and *coordination*. Here the division of labour is not limited to production activities but it is extended to all functions in the community, including judges, doctors, lawyers, traders, teachers, etc. Specialization in particular tasks, which was initially mostly related to the procurement of vital resources, increases their efficiency, thus freeing a part of human labour which could then be applied to other functions. Thus, the transition to settled agriculture enhanced the efficiency of food production and contributed to the differentiation of human societies (Diamond, 1997; Lipsey et al., 2005). Although most of the population was still engaged in food production, new activities could be introduced: priests, traders and warriors became recognized functions in human societies. We can start here observing what will turn out to be a general point in economic evolution: the growing efficiency of existing activities can free resources, in this case labour, and induce the emergence of new activities.

For all its power to enhance the efficiency of human activities, division of labour could not improve collective adaptation alone. To do that it needs to be combined with coordination. In the same way as in a productive process, if the outcome of a given stage is not coordinated with the other ones, the overall process does not produce any desirable outcome. If some workers in an assembly line do not do their job, the process cannot proceed. If teachers stopped teaching, social life as we know it could not continue. Consequently, collective adaptation is superior to individual adaptation only if it is accompanied by an appropriate coordination. Furthermore, societies which have a 'better' system of division of labour and coordination tend to outperform other societies which have less advanced systems. This implies that group selection operates at the level of human communities and societies.

The overall organization of division of labour and coordination in a society is not explicitly decided by any individual but slowly created in the course of history. Individuals in a community differ in several aspects. For example, they can differ for their strength, intelligence, education, competencies, wealth, etc. In a modern society, inter-individual differences are also heavily influenced by education and training. Furthermore, these differences determine and are determined by the place in the overall division of labour that individual members occupy in the community. The coordination of the behaviour of individuals is largely determined by institutions, themselves defined as sets of rules. In the meantime, inter-individual coordination in a community involves the mutual adaptation of individual members to one another, leading to a form of self-organization. Individuals choose, or are 'assigned' to, some form of division of labour based on their condition and place of birth or on their competencies. For example, often people born in families of farmers or miners tended to be themselves farmers or miners. The types of division of labour, and consequently of coordination, vary in the course of history and between different societies. New types of division of labour are often created by innovation and the relevant competencies are diffused by education.

The heterogeneity of the capabilities and the tasks carried out by individual members contains the roots of the distribution of wealth and power in a community. Such tasks can be expected to vary in importance and therefore in the value which is attached to them in the community. In every society there is a different allocation of resources to the different members, including the rewards they receive in exchange for their labour. Decisions about these different allocations depend on existing institutions, human activities and the choices made by individuals and organizations. Innovation creates new human activities, new forms of division of labour, and requires new forms of coordination. The existing set of institutions is likely to reflect to different extents the existing distribution of wealth and power in a community. Typically, in all real socioeconomic systems, there are elites which concentrate a much larger share of wealth and power than the less privileged members of the same systems and have a greater influence on the construction and maintenance of institutions. For example, salaries and wages are determined mostly by industrialists and labour unions in addition to the state of the economic system. Communities can differ for the extent to which institutions are designed to take care of the general interest of all the members or those of elites. The distinction between extractive and inclusive institutions (Acemoglu, Robinson, 2012) reflects the extent to which institutions allow the entry or the upward mobility of less privileged strata of society.

In general, there is no society in which everyone is happy with all the institutions and rules existing at a given time. Even if such a state of general happiness existed at a given time, it would be very unlikely to persist forever or even for a very long period. Both perturbations in the EE of the SES or innovations arising endogenously within the SES would potentially affect differentially the welfare of different members of the SES. A very important example of such differential effect of innovation on the members of an SES is that of the industrial revolution on the tasks to be carried out and on the welfare of workers and industrial capitalists. Such example will be discussed in greater detail later. The stability of each community or society depends on their ability to find an acceptable compromise between the tasks and competencies carried out and the rewards offered to their different members.

Thus, coordination completes division of labour and allows human societies to enjoy their capacity to give rise to growing efficiency and creativity. We will discover later that even growing efficiency alone is not always advantageous.

The advantages of communities come at a price. Communities never included all possible human beings but were groups of limited size, although such size tended to increase in the course of history. By definition, any community needed criteria of *inclusion* and *exclusion*. It was important to know who was a proper member and who was an enemy. These criteria could be

Box 3.2 Community and migrations

Any community needed criteria of *inclusion* and *exclusion*. These criteria are translated into rules that define who is a proper member of a community. When the community considered is a nation state, the concept of citizenship defines who is a proper member of a community. Only a citizen enjoys all the rights available in principle to the members of the community. There are also concepts of partial inclusion, such as temporary or visiting residents. These other criteria give only some rights, for example, the right to work but not to vote. People foreign to the community do not have any automatic right to enter it or to work in it. The existence of these criteria is essential to the existence and the survival of the community. Without exclusion criteria, enemies could enter it and threaten it by robbing, maiming, or killing the existing members. Borders, passports, and frontier police are examples of exclusion criteria or means to implement them.

Migrations have occurred all throughout the life of mankind. In general, people tended to migrate from resource-poor to resource-rich places. This is still the case today and probably will be the same in any foreseeable future. Thus, the existence of great economic and political differences is likely to remain an important inducement to the migration of people between nation states and regions. Furthermore, such migrations have become easier with the improvement of transport technologies. Even though very large-scale migrations contributed heavily to create countries such as the USA, Canada, Australia, Brazil or Argentina, they are still resisted even in countries that benefited from them. Climate-induced migration has already become and it is increasingly going to be an important factor leading to migrations (World Bank, 2020). This is a further reason to reduce as much as possible the impact of human activities on the EE.

The present geopolitical situation provides examples that migrations can be resisted as well as tolerated or even welcome. In turn, the effect of migrations on a receiving country or community depends on a few factors, including the activities and resource endowment of the receiving country or community and the difference between the cultures of the migrants and the host country. For example, large differences in resources allocated to science, technology, and innovation and in the relevant institutions can lead to the so-called 'brain-drain', the migration of scientists and engineers from poor to very rich countries. In general, migrations are a very important factor affecting the stability of both countries originating or receiving them.

based on language, religion, or physical features such as skin colour. Furthermore, rules were intended to encourage collaborative behaviour within the same community and rivalrous behaviour between the members of different communities. Modern conceptions of intolerance find their antecedents in the exclusion criteria required for the formation of ancient communities. Hence people are not intolerant or racist because they are bad but because the ability to exclude members of different, enemy, communities has always been a part of inter-communal life. These considerations cannot be interpreted as an attempt to legitimate intolerance or racism, but they amount to considering the exclusion of strangers or enemies as an extension of attitudes which up to a point were considered legitimate or even to be praised (see the hate for enemies taught to soldiers and even to athletes in some sports and its extension to the hate of the 'other' in intolerant or racist movements). Tolerance and human rights are human inventions which go against millennia of intolerant behaviour rooted in the life of communities.

3.3 Adaptation, stability, and change

The previous considerations could be interpreted as implying that once a society has achieved a 'good' adaptation to its EE and of its component members to one another, nothing more would happen unless the external environment (EE) changed. We could say that a state of equilibrium would have been attained in which there would be no inducement to change coming endogenously from within the same society. However, such extreme stability is unlikely to be ever attained. No existing society is without internal tensions and contradictions. Innovation is a destabilizing force which could shake up any equilibrium that was temporarily attained. Of course, innovation is by no means the only factor that could create instability and lead to change. Other factors can be a source of frustration and suffering for some members and groups in society who feel that they have been unfairly treated. For example, the distribution of income and power has been or is being perceived as unjust in the industrial societies of the XIXth century or in the post-industrial societies of the XXIst century. Even when there are no grudges about injustices or sources of suffering, there is always a general tendency of human beings to improve that had already been observed by Adam Smith who wrote that 'the desire of bettering our condition comes to us from the womb, and never leaves us until we go into the grave' (1776, p. xx, cited in Friedman, 2010). We could then consider human beings *adaptive improvers*. It could be argued that adaptive behaviour is not specific to human beings but that it occurs also amongst animals and plants. However, the extent of adaptation *of* a given EE is likely to be much greater for human beings than for any other animal species. Consequently, we will consider that human actors, or agents, are adaptive improvers. This does not imply that all human beings are continuously searching for improvements in their situation. In fact, many people are rather averse to change. The statement that people are adaptive improvers needs to be applied to the level of the community. Communities differ as to the percentage of their members who are searching for improvements in their situation and are prepared to take the risks that this involves. Such a percentage is not constant but varies with the institutions and the knowledge base of a community. Schumpeterian entrepreneurs are perhaps the best example of adaptive improvers and we do not expect to find them with the same probability in different communities: Silicon Valleys are not uniformly distributed all over the world. The existence of adaptive improvers depends on the inducements, resources, and rewards that a community can provide for them. In the end the probability of finding adaptive improvers depends on the institutions of a given society.

In modern societies adaptive improvements come largely from innovation. Most innovations lead to changes in our EE, either in its physical or in its social component. Thus, innovation leads to ADOF. Whenever an innovation changes the EE of a society to a different one EE¢, the society is not immediately well adapted to the new EE¢. The process of adaptation to the EE¢ (ADTO) can in some cases take a very long time. Innovations like railways, cars, electricity, or computing were introduced and adopted fully during periods of tens or hundreds of years covering several generations. During these periods, SESs are subject to inducements to changes, leading to the further incorporation of innovations into society. These periods cannot in any sense be considered as being of equilibrium intended as a complete absence of change. At best we can think about them as periods in which the future development of the system (SES) corresponds broadly to *expectations* that have been formed in the initial phases of an innovation. We will refer to the complete life cycle of an innovation, called technology life cycle (TLC), as the period going from the *emergence* of the innovation to its complete diffusion, corresponding to the *saturation* of the SES. We realize that such definition is oversimplified since some life cycles can be more complex than that. We will initially use this simplified form to describe our viewpoint and add later more complex situations. As was pointed out in Chapter 2, the life cycle of subsequently changing technologies adds further complexity. In general, pervasive (Freeman, 1982) innovations begin with an initial period characterized by radical uncertainty and proceed with a subsequent phase of more predictable incremental innovations. The latter phase of the life cycle can correspond to periods of high and stable growth. However, balanced growth does not correspond to an equilibrium in which nothing changes but to a situation in which things can grow according to expectations, or change occurs mostly quantitatively.

The dynamics of an SES can then be analysed at a more aggregate level, as that of the whole system, or by considering the interactions of its different components. If we first consider the whole system, the emergence of an innovation creates a future hypothetical state of the system which can become the source of investment, planning and action. This hypothetical state of the system acts as an attractor towards which the system tends to move. The transformation of an SES from its real state to the hypothetical one defined by the innovation can take a long time. Then, in the presence of innovations, the dynamics of human development will be constituted by a sequence of ADOF and ADTO, in which the creation of a new EE by means of ADOF will always be followed by the process of adaptation to this new EE by means of ADTO. The corresponding processes occur at *finite* speeds and the outcome depends on the relative speeds of different component processes.

We can now place the previous considerations in a more analytical format to show that in a system which is continuously innovating a general equilibrium can exist only in special circumstances. Let us start with a system S that is initially in equilibrium with its external environment EE. We can consider this a general equilibrium and represent it as $(S_0, EE_0)^*$, where S_0 and EE_0 respectively represent the states of the system and its external environment in the equilibrium situation. Let us now assume that an important, radical innovation emerges within the system S. This innovation can be expected to create a new product or process technology, a new organizational form, or a new market, and to modify the external environment EE transforming it into a different one. At its emergence the new technology is just a broad and not perfectly defined idea, at best accompanied by few prototypes. This starts a coevolutionary life cycle in which the new technology is produced in an initial form, the required investment is obtained, complementary institutions and infrastructures are constructed and the technology itself is gradually modified. The previous changes modify the EE. Both the extraction of new materials and the building of infrastructures modify the natural environment. Moreover, new institutions need to be created and existing institutions to be modified. Clearly, the effect of the innovation cannot be instantaneous. The transition necessarily occurs at a finite speed in a finite period. Thus, the innovation has destroyed the equilibrium represented by the state (S_0, EE_0) since the system S in its state S_0 is no longer adapted to the new state of the external environment. The innovation destroyed the initial state of equilibrium and created an imbalance between the present state of the system and the hypothetical state that would be adapted to the new state of the external environment. The greater the difference between the 'real' state of the system and its hypothetical adapted state, the greater the imbalance.

As the innovation goes through its life cycle, the state of the EE keeps changing gradually. Meanwhile, the system is subject to a continuing imbalance depending on the relative rates of change of the system S and its EE. Let us try to describe some simplified cases:

Case 1: An innovation is created perturbing the initial state of equilibrium (S_0, EE_0) and inducing transformation of EE_0 into EE_1. In this case the innovation once created remains unchanged (Figure 3.1), where S_1 is the state of the system adapted to the new state of the external environment EE_1, and R_S and R_{EE} are the speeds at which the states of the system and the external environment move towards the final state (S_1, EE_1). Such a state could be considered a new general equilibrium. Even in this oversimplified case, the time required for the system and its EE to go from the initial to the final equilibrium state could be extremely long. All the intermediate positions and times correspond to non-equilibrium states of the system and of its EE.

The previous case was clearly oversimplified since no important innovation ever remained unchanged in the form in which it was initially introduced. Clear examples are the train, the car, the airplane, the computer, etc. In this case the final state (S_1, EE_1) might simply not exist, except as an attractor. Then all the subsequent states would be non-equilibrium states characterized by different degrees of imbalance.

Case 2: In this case the initial emergence of the radical innovation giving rise to one or more new sectors is followed by a stream of incremental innovations that will modify the innovation itself and the EE. Then the combined state of the system and its external environment is likely to change continuously with different degrees of imbalance, where imbalance is a measure of ill adaptation, or distance from the equilibrium (Figure 3.2).[2]

In this case the combination of the system and its external environment never reaches an equilibrium except in the special case in which the speed R_S of adaptation of the system is much greater than the speed of change R_{EE} of the external environment. Based on historical examples, this situation seems to be very rare.

Based on the previous considerations, we can conclude that SESs are never at general equilibrium but that they are always undergoing some type of change. However, while it seems clear that countries which are not undergoing any change are unlikely to benefit from economic development, we cannot conclude that the more a country or region changes, the better off the

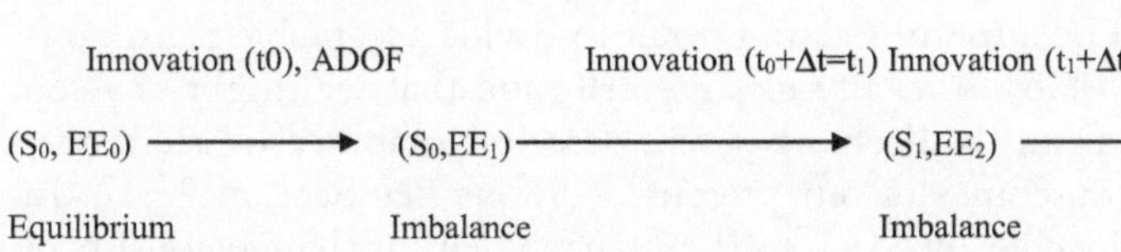

Figure 3.1 Effect of an isolated innovation on a system at equilibrium.

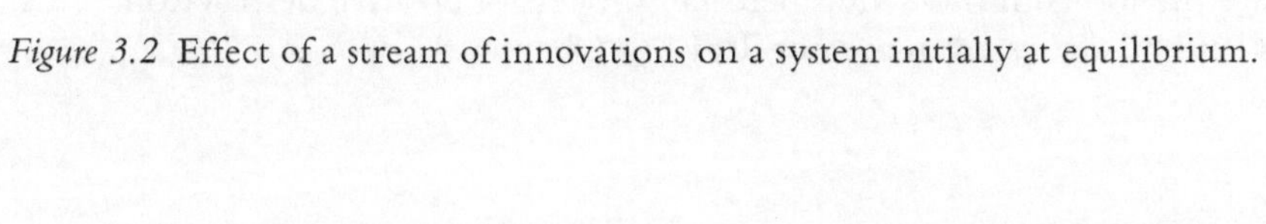

Figure 3.2 Effect of a stream of innovations on a system initially at equilibrium.

country will be. Change can be and often is disruptive. This is certainly true of innovation. Even when most people benefit from an innovation, some or many others suffer from it. Thus, the question 'is there a "good" relationship between stability and change?' becomes of central importance. When asking this question, we need to bear in mind that the factors leading to stability and change are distributed unevenly in the world system. Stability can mean the absence of change, as shown by constant values of the variables that 'measure' the state of the SES considered, or by the general happiness of all the members of the SES, in which case nobody desires any change. In the former case stability could coincide with the unhappiness of a large share of the population, as it would happen in an SES perceived as corrupt and unjust by most of its members. However, the latter case is likely to be extremely rare. We can reasonably expect that in most SESs there will be a distribution of degrees of happiness amongst its members, for example with some people being very happy, others neutral and others averse to its present state. Change will then occur either to eliminate present sources of unhappiness or to introduce sources of novelty expected to improve the state of the SES. An example of the former would be a policy reducing inequality in an SES having a very unequal distribution of income and wealth; examples of the latter would be innovations providing new forms of mobility or new leisure activities, such as the car or the cinema.

Not all forms of stability are desirable. Some types of change and some degrees of change are desirable but even change can be dangerous or present in excessive degrees. For example, the adoption of ITC in public administration can greatly simplify life for the people who can use it, but be very difficult for those who cannot learn ITC. The problem is not that of finding a general equilibrium as defined by neoclassical economics, but that of finding a reasonable balance between stability and change. The outcomes of change are distributed unevenly in the world SES. The policies adopted in individual countries depend on what happens in other countries.

The very high priority given to growth in present economic policies implies that a static SES is not considered desirable. However, nobody would consider that a situation of civil war in a region or a country, although causing an enormous amount of change, is desirable. On the contrary, such a situation would likely be considered highly destabilizing. Perhaps the criterion of Pareto progress, stating that to be acceptable a change would need to involve an improvement for some while leaving everyone else at least as well off as before, could be a useful starting point to divide acceptable from non-acceptable change.[3] However, any ex-ante criterion that we might develop to separate 'good' from 'bad' changes will face our inability to accurately predict the future outcomes of our present decisions (see Section 3.5.6). In the end, the only possible approach to the management of change consists of a commitment of society to favour exploration and innovation, but to compensate the losers in the Schumpeterian process of creative destruction. This point will be discussed in greater detail in Chapter 8.

3.4 Fitness

The previous considerations can be expressed in terms of fitness. Fitness is a measure of the adaptation of organisms, species, individuals, communities, or technologies to the environment in which they live. Fitness is specific both to a given EE and to a given objective function. Thus, an organism that is very fit in each EE can be very unfit in a different one. Likewise, an organism or a community which is very fit with a given objective function can become very unfit if the objective function changes. As we have seen for the example of the falling rates of reproduction, the objective function of fitness can change from making many children to making a few and educating them due to endogenous transformations of the same industrialized socioeconomic systems. Thus, an important difference between socioeconomic and biological systems is the much greater range of endogenous changes which can occur in the objective function of fitness of the former as compared to the more limited and exogenous changes for the latter.

The concept of fitness is intimately related to that of natural selection (Sober, 2001). For biological systems, genetic heritage favours some individuals or species which tend to become relatively more abundant in the course of time. For socioeconomic systems, there is no precise analogue of genetic heritage, but learning and knowledge become progressively more important during human development. Thus, the fitness of modern socioeconomic systems can be expected to depend on their knowledge, which in turn depends on their mechanisms of learning. Although forms of learning by doing are not unknown for other biological species, they have never achieved the importance and the scope that they have for socioeconomic systems. Thus, a very important difference between the evolution of biological and socioeconomic systems consists of the much greater relative extent of ADOF with respect to ADTO for the latter with respect to the former. In turn, the higher ratio of ADOF/ADTO depends on the role that knowledge and institutions played in the evolution of socioeconomic systems.

3.5 Barriers to adaptation

Part of the previous discussion could have given the impression that the change in behaviour required for adaptation is self-evident and that the only problem consists of carrying it out. That is not the case in general. Many countries remain in a state which is not the best possible one, in the sense that other countries are generally considered to be in a 'better' situation. An example of this occurs with economic development. Although opinions might differ about the best form of economic development, it would be logical for all the countries that are less developed to move towards higher levels of development. Such a move would require the adaptation (ADTO) of many institutions and forms of behaviour of the countries considered. Generally, such adaptation would involve the imitation of the institutions and forms of behaviour of the leading countries. However, adaptation to the industrial revolution, which started in the UK in the late XVIIIth century, took 100 years for other European countries and almost 200 years for non-European countries. Why did it take so long for this adaptation to occur? In the following, we will try to find an answer to this question.

3.5.1 Imperfect or partial adaptation

Several barriers can delay or make impossible the process of adaptation. First, in a complex system constituted by subsystems at different hierarchical levels the process of adaptation can involve changes in all subsystems at many hierarchical levels. Such process can be called *complete adaptation*. However, less complete forms of adaptation can sometimes occur and improve the adaptation of the system without making it perfect. This occurs because complete adaptation is likely to require more costly and less probable modifications of system structure than partial ones. In general, we can expect simpler, even if less complete, forms of adaptation to be faster than more complete ones. Thus, simpler partial adaptation processes would be more probable than complete ones and dominate observed adaptation paths. In this case a system could be permanently ill-adapted and conserve parts or components that were adapted to a previous EE.

3.5.2 Imperfection in biological evolution

We can hardly find examples of perfect adaptation biology. In most cases forms of animals or plants retain organs or parts that were created in previous states of their external environment or in species that preceded them in biological evolution. Examples of these imperfections can be found at the level of organs, DNA or the brain.

After the discovery of DNA, a large part of the genes in the human genome seemed to have no function in the production of proteins. These apparently useless genes were called 'junk DNA'. It was subsequently discovered that these genes were not useless but that they had been inherited from different species that preceded humans in biological evolution. Such genes were simply switched off, but they could be switched on again for their initial function or for a modified one. Thus, natural selection can contribute to the formation of new genes but it does not necessarily clean up the old genes. Some of these genes survive even when they are not used. Sometimes these genes can be reactivated for a function different from their initial one.

In a similar way some biological species retain organs that were developed for species or previous states of the external environment. For example, whales and snakes have very small legs that are completely useless to them (Pievani, 2019, Chapter 3). Other times organs that were developed for a given function are used for different one. For example, the ostrich and the kakapo use their wings to achieve balance when running rather than to fly

(Pievani, 2019, p. 79). The retention of genetically determined structures or attributes that have lost some or all the ancestral function in each species is called 'Vestigiality'. Vestigiality had already been observed by Aristotle, Lamarck, and Darwin himself.

Even the human brain contains different parts that were formed at different stages of its evolution, parts that carry out different and sometimes contrasting functions. For example, the subcortical areas, and above all the amygdala, can detect threats in external events such as people who look 'different' and potentially dangerous. However, the upper cortical areas tend to suggest interpretation of the same external events, suggesting more 'reasonable' and potentially cooperative strategies. These parts of the brain were formed at different stages of human evolution and were adapted to different environment: the amygdala provided a signal useful for members of small and tightly knit communities to compete for vital resources with other similar communities; the upper cortical areas, which developed later together with the increasing complexification of human societies, suggest a strategy more useful in such situations and including cooperative components (Pievani, 2019, p. 127). Here different parts of the brain provide signals that focus on a more varied range of social interactions rather than just on the exclusion of 'strangers.

While some organs or traits can survive even when they seem to be no longer useful, other organs can acquire new functions that allow them to adapt to a wider range of external environments. An example of this phenomenon, called *exaptation* (Gould, Vrba, 1982), is given by bird feathers: initially they may have evolved for temperature regulation, but later were adapted for flight. Even in the evolution of technology there are cases of exaptation: a classic example is the innovation of the microwave oven from the technology previously used for the development of radar.

The previous examples show that natural selection is not a perfect algorithm that wipes out all imperfectly adapted forms of life but that it acts on the relative fitness of different forms and species. On the contrary, adaptation to changes in the environment or the emergence of new species occurs by generating new organs but without necessarily destroying older ones. In biological evolution there is no great plan to optimize the adaptation of organs or systems but opportunistic use and reuse of existing organs and parts to achieve an improvement in fitness. Thus, in a population containing different mutations of a given species, natural selection leads to the survival of the *relatively* better adapted mutation, even if this is far from perfectly adapted (Darwin, 1859, Chapter 6).

3.5.3 Statics vs dynamics

The prevalence of imperfect, or partial, adaptation is not unique to biological systems but is shown also by socioeconomic systems (SESs) and it can be explained by general considerations about complex systems. The possibility that forms of partial adaptation are more frequent than complete adaptation arises from the tension between statics and dynamics. Any change in the EE of a system can induce different extents of adaptation, ranging from complete adaptation, in which all the components of the system and all their interactions would change, to incomplete or partial adaptation, in which only some of the components and their interactions would change. Let us assume (i) the cost of partial adaptation to be higher than that of complete adaptation, (ii) the probability of partial adaptation to be higher than that of complete adaptation and (iii) the speed of partial adaptation to be higher than that of complete adaptation. In this case, we could expect transitions involving partial adaptation from a system structure S_0, corresponding to a state of the environment EE_0, to a final system structure S_1, corresponding to a state of the environment EE_1, to be faster and more frequent than transitions involving complete adaptation between the same states:

$$(S_0, EE_0) \rightarrow (S_1, EE_1)$$

To explain the previous point better, we can imagine to start with a system perfectly adapted to its external environment EE_0. When the external environment changes to EE_1 the structure of the system needs to be modified from S_0 to S_1 in order to adapt. Several types of modifications are possible, ranging from the best adapted (optimal) one $S_1{}^{\star}$ to one ($S_{1,min}$) that is only marginally better adapted than S_0. We expect $S_1{}^{\star}$ to be more stable than $S_{1,min}$, but also to require greater amount of resources, including time, to be generated. Thus, the change in EE could lead to the emergence of a range of system structurers, such as $S_1{}^{\star}$, $S_{1,min}$ and several others with intermediate fitness $S_{1,2}$,$S_{1,3}$, $S_{1,4}$, ... $S_{1,n}$, each requiring different quantities of resources and occurring at different speeds. If we assume that the generation of better adapted structures requires more resources and time than that of less well-adapted ones, during many periods following the change of EE the population of a given system could be dominated by imperfectly adapted structures. Furthermore, at any time, the observed distribution of structures of different fitness for a given system S is likely to vary, depending on the relative speed with which the EE changes and each structure can be generated: structures that can be generated quickly are likely to dominate for a fast-changing EE while structures that need a longer time to be generated are likely to increase their participation in the presence of slow changing EEs. Thus, the type of structure S_1 dominating after the transition from S_0 to S_1 following the change in the EE from EE_0 to EE_1 from S_0 to S_1 depends on the relative speeds of change in the EE and adaptation of the system S to this change. A highly innovative system that can rapidly change its EE by means of ADOF is likely to create a sequence of imperfectly adapted system structures. For example, in the presence of small changes in the EE, firms introducing limited modifications of their products could increase their market share more than firms introducing greater but slower and more costly modifications.

Following the change in EE, the population of new structures of our system could be dominated for a long time by imperfectly adapted ones. In fact, the generation of the perfectly adapted structure S* could require such a long time that it would never be observed. This seems to be the situation in biological evolution.

The previous considerations are quite general and could be applicable to both biological and social systems. However, we have already seen that the objective of adaptation is much more complex and possibly changing endogenously in the course of time for socioeconomic systems (SES) than for biological systems. Furthermore, in many cases, the change in behaviour required to adapt is not known at all or we know only the aspects of the system we want to change but we do not know with what conditions to replace them or how to do it. For example, if some phenomena indicate that human activities are starting to affect our natural EE in a non-sustainable way, then we need to reduce their impact. Even if everyone shares this objective, there are a very large number of ways of attaining it, each imperfectly known. Furthermore, even if the costs and benefits of one adaptation strategy were perfectly known, its advantages and disadvantages would likely be unevenly distributed across the world SES. A general feature common to this and many other examples is that we tend to react to a situation that we find unjust or dangerous, and thus in need of change, but that we do not know how to change or cannot collectively do it. In other words, any adaptation strategy faces at least two types of a barrier, a cognitive and a political one. The former arises because sometimes the changes in the EE are not adequately perceived or understood. For example, more than 50 years after the impact of human activities on the EE started to be perceived (e.g., Commoner, 1971; Club of Rome, 1972), there still are conflicting interpretations of how that is occurring or of what can be done to avert its inherent dangers. As already pointed out, such limited understanding is an inevitable feature of the emergence of important and radical innovations.

In addition to the cognitive barriers, the adaptation to some changes in the EE can be opposed by existing vested interests, or it is likely to follow a different path depending on the nature of the institutions existing in a particular society. For example, groups carrying out activities with a high impact of the natural EE from which they were deriving their wealth and power are likely to resist or slow down attempts to limit such impact. Furthermore, even when a general agreement exists within a given society about the need to change some rules in order to adapt to changes in the natural EE, the outcome of these rule changes is likely to differ depending on the institutions pre-existing in such a society. The stability of an existing subsystem (e.g., a country in the world system) is likely to be supported by those groups who derive benefits from an existing social structure and opposed by other groups who see their interests neglected. Generally, the former groups tend to be more powerful than the latter and to dominate the country. Thus, what could be considered the 'best' adaptation to the evolution of the world system can be resisted by the former and to be favoured by the latter. This competition between different social groups stabilizes existing social structures and can be considered an example of path dependence (Arthur, 1989, 2007; David, 1985, 2007; Castaldi et al., 2011; OECD, 2017) in social evolution.

3.5.4 Structural barriers

Some barriers to the adaptation by follower countries are created by the development of leading countries. For example, the creation of a new technology in a leading country is generally followed by the establishment of barriers to its imitation by follower countries. These barriers can be (i) internal to the technology and due to learning by doing or to search activities, or (ii) due to the insufficient development of complementary institutions, infrastructures and organizational arrangements that coevolve with the new technologies (Saviotti, Pyka, 2010). All these changes were introduced gradually in leading countries. Thus, the longer the delay between the emergence of a new technology and its imitation by follower countries, the higher the barrier to imitation becomes. In the end such barriers can become so great as to make imitation by follower countries impossible. This same mechanism can even operate if a follower country has the financial resources to acquire a new technology but lacks the complementary human capital and institutions required to use it. This type of barrier is due to the coevolutionary nature of economic development in SESs.

This type of barrier can also be explained by the relative stability of different structures in SESs. For example, when the structure of an existing SES is dominated by a given social group, the changes required to adopt new technologies or new institutions may be judged by such group likely to damage its interests and resisted rather than adopted. In other words, adaption to new technologies or new institutions is unlikely to occur when it is considered contrary to the stability[4] of an SES. Furthermore, a different type of adaptation can be based on supplying countries with inputs required by new technologies and derived from natural resources. However, this type of adaptation strategy is far from universally successful and, when it is not combined with appropriate technologies and institutions, can give rise to the so-called curse of natural resources (Sachs, Warner, 1995, 2001).

3.5.5 Cognitive barriers

The previous type of barriers is typically faced by less developed countries attempting to catch up with leading ones. A different type of barrier, called cognitive, exists because important innovations are always created in a state of incomplete knowledge. In fact, we expect entrepreneurs to conceive an innovation having only a broad idea of the innovation itself but to be generally incapable of defining with any accuracy the actual form the innovation will take. That can be true at different levels of aggregation, ranging from an

MMA to that of a whole SES, or even of a long-term trend such as industrialization. Uncertainty about a given MMA arises both in a technical sense, as early innovators in cars or telephones could not conceive the precise form these artefacts would take, or in broader sense as such MMA did not develop in a vacuum but needed many complementary infrastructures or institutions. Furthermore, uncertainty arises about broader trends, such as the relationship between human activities and the natural environment. In fact, we have already referred to the incomplete knowledge based on which entrepreneurs create major innovations as entrepreneurial knowledge. As already pointed out, entrepreneurs create innovations in an initial form which is subsequently improved by a string of incremental innovations, which advance both the services supplied by the innovation (Chapter 1) and the knowledge surrounding it. The uncertainty surrounding major long-term trends is likely to be even higher than that referring to individual innovations. Examples of these trends could be industrialization or the impact of human activities on the natural environment.

3.5.6 Political barriers

In a general sense, political barriers are linked to system configurations that have been created within SESs in the past.[5] The ownership of land or the differential access to military power have from the very beginning constituted the basis for the domination of society by groups. Since the beginning of the industrial revolution, the new social classes of the industrial bourgeoisie and of the proletariat have emerged. The combination of these groups, the activities they carry out and the new or modified institutions that accompany their emergence define a configuration of the SES that can be stable for long periods of time. Any social group trying to improve its share of resources and its status is likely to face a barrier due to the possible attempt by previous dominating groups to protect their status and power. We can expect resistances of this type to be stronger in a society in which the resources available are fixed and in which consequently competition from emerging groups occurs according to a zero-sum game. However, an SES which can create new resources, thus leading to an increasing sum game, or that is politically inclusive (Acemoglu, Robinson, 2012), can provide an easier entry for emerging social groups. The variety of situations in which such political barriers can arise and impede adaptation is very large.

In addition to the previous barriers, the nature of existing institutions or the culture of a country could act as an obstacle to innovation. These types of barriers may sometimes be difficult to distinguish from political barriers in the sense that existing institutions could constitute obstacles of different magnitudes to the same reforms in different countries. What is important here is not to list all possible types of barriers but to identify the main ones and to point out that such barriers can prevent the economic or social development of countries or regions. The existence of barriers of these types explains why sometimes particular social groups, regions or countries do not adapt to changes in the EE which seem to require adaptation. In general, an adaptation strategy is likely to emerge by a process of decision-making involving a series of stages, going from the perception and understanding of the change, to the formulation and implementation of the strategy itself. Processes of human decision-making are in general based on incomplete knowledge and affected by existing structures of SESs. Furthermore, even when adaptation strategies are implemented and are successful in attaining their initial objective, they may transform the EE in ways that replace the previous problem with new ones. In the following boxes, we will analyse some examples that will make more concrete the previous general considerations.

Box 3.3 Pensions

The achievement of pensions during the XXth century was a progressive institutional change. Recently, because of changes occurring in related aspects of the SESs of most industrialized countries, the funding of pensions has become a growing problem. Increasing life expectancy, itself due to improvements in nutrition, hygiene and health care, and a falling birth rate have both prolonged the period that the average individual spends in retirement and reduced the ratio of people of working age to that of retirees. Furthermore, people tend to be relatively healthy and capable of carrying out purposeful activities beyond retirement age (Economist, 2017). Consequently, a combination of raising costs, falling resources and poor utilization of human capital has been created.

During the period since its creation, there has been a transformation of the meaning of retirement as well as of the meaning of work. What was perceived as a form of justice to eliminate old age poverty became contested terrain due to changes occurring simultaneously in other aspects of the SES. As previously pointed out, such changes are increasing life expectancy and reducing birth rate. Their combination has increased the costs of pensions (people spend a larger share of their lives in retirement) and reduced the resources required to fund pensions (the ratio of the number of working people supporting pensioners to that of pensioners tends to fall). Furthermore, the health and human capital of the average retiree has improved due to progress in education and health care. Although heavy and potentially dangerous occupations still exist for which early retirement would be appropriate and well deserved, many retired people are capable of carrying out complex functions (Economist, 2017). Furthermore, work provides income and identity, both of which could be enhanced for retired people by their continued involvement with purposeful organized activities. Such involvement would not necessarily be full time but it could be modulated to combine income from work and income from pension, with shares varying in the course of time to suit individuals' preferences and capabilities. For example, working time could be gradually reduced and the falling income stream could be supplemented by an increasing pension share. A solution of this type, consisting of a three-pillar system, has been proposed by the Geneva Society (2005). The first pillar is a pension of the present type, the second is additional personal savings and the third pillar is an income stream from working activities.

Although Increasing life expectancy and falling birth rates have been operating at least since the 1970s, reforms of the pension system aimed at reducing its potential imbalances have been introduced only since the late 1990s. Such a situation can be interpreted as a lack of institutional adaptation. Increasing life expectancy and falling birth rate can be easily observed, and an adaptation of pension regimes could have consisted of raising pensionable age in parallel with life expectancy. Furthermore, the advantage of better health after retirement can be exploited by defining working conditions appropriate to the corresponding age. Although increasing life expectancy and falling birth rates have been operating at least since the 1970s, reforms of the pension system aimed at reducing its potential imbalances have been introduced only since the late 1990s. Furthermore, reforms of the pension system going in these directions are now underway in several countries, but they encounter different barriers. For example, raising the pensionable age has proved to be more controversial in France than in other European countries. Thus, the need for adaptation is perceived relatively slowly everywhere and it elicits adaptive responses which can differ markedly amongst different countries. In a long-term perspective, pensions, which were introduced to reduce old age poverty, have at least partly attained this objective (see OECD, 2015) but have created new contradictions and problems.

Such a situation is by no means unique for pensions but shows some common features with other types of human decision-making. First, the knowledge used in human decision-making is generally incomplete and our ability to predict the future impact of such decisions is extremely limited. Second, part of the reason for our inability to predict future outcomes of present decisions is linked to the high interactivity of complex SESs. Such interactivity gives rise to the coevolution of different components of the SES (see Chapter 2). Third, many of the objectives of policies arise from the perception of existing problems. Considering our inability to predict future outcomes of present policies, we can understand how, even when such policies can solve the problem for which then were created, they give rise to new ones.

Box 3.4 Environment

It is now quite clear that human activities affect our natural environment in multiple ways. Although the scale of human activities started to increase significantly since the industrial revolution, their potential impact on the environment did not raise any objections until after the Second World War. By that time the impact of human activities was about to become of the same scale as that of natural phenomena. No prediction that this impact would have reached this point was made in advance. Until quite recently economists dismissed the possibility that the exhaustion of natural resources and the increasing pollution generated by human activities could substantially harm our natural environment and lead to a crisis if not to a catastrophic collapse (Georgescu Roegen, 1971; Daly, 2007). The earliest cries of alarm were in fact raised by naturalists (e.g., Commoner, 1971) and by interdisciplinary studies and reports (e.g., Club of Rome, 1972). Although such initial forecasts were sometimes considered exaggerated, there is now a growing consensus that we must change the way we produce and interact with the natural environment. However, when it comes to deciding what strategies to adopt to make our development sustainable opinions still diverge considerably.

We now face both a cognitive barrier, constituted by our limited ability to predict the outcome of different decisions about present and future human activities, and a political barrier, constituted by the opposition of groups in both developed and developing countries about who should pay or invest to reduce environmental impact. Thus, LDCs maintain that to reduce environmental impact is the task of developed countries (DCs) since they created the technologies that pollute our environment. Even in DCs there is no consensus about the timing and the path to be followed to reduce environmental impact and make our SESs more sustainable. The transition towards more sustainable types of production is likely to be a combination of major innovations, most of which are going to harm the firms and the workers in industries linked to past and polluting sources of energy and materials. This is a clear example of Schumpeterian creative destruction in which opportunities will be created for new technologies and industries while reductions in size and employment will occur for older industries. The opposition coming from the representatives of the oil and coal industries to the implementation of strategies aimed at reducing environmental impact (Paris agreement, 2015) is an example of how vested interests based on incumbent and polluting industries oppose changes aimed at making our SESs more sustainable.

Adaptation to the natural environment is required at a world level, with different strategies used for countries at different levels of economic development. For example, countries that are suppliers of raw materials or energy inputs will need to change their development strategies. DCs will need to develop new methods of production and styles of consumption that make our SESs sustainable.

While the problem of the environment shares with most other types of decision-making the two barriers to adaptation, in this case the world dimension and the longer time scale magnify the impact of such barriers.

3.5.7 Decision-making

All our decisions regarding adaptation are based on a limited knowledge and involve uncertainty, often of the radical type. We perceive past problems in a partial way, without a full understanding of all the factors that can have contributed to them and that keep affecting them. We are even more limited in our predictions of future outcomes of present decisions (see parts of Chapters 6 and 7). Essentially, we neglect the systemic nature of our SESs and focus separately on one or few factors neglecting their interactions. Furthermore, and this is a relatively more important point in the social sciences than in the physical sciences, our human knowledge helps us change the external environment (EE), thus requiring a new knowledge of the modified external environment (EE¢). As a result of this limited knowledge, we end up at best solving past problems while creating new ones. Furthermore, we keep applying to some problems the same policies based on the way they were observed initially while such problems are undergoing important transformations (here see transformations vs transitions in Chapter 2). A simple example of this can be given by the changing objective of healthcare systems. When they were created their mission consisted of supplying basic health care to everyone. Recently their objective has shifted from supplying basic health care to everyone to improving the quality of life by using a series of new but increasingly expensive medical technologies. Combined with an ageing population, this leads to an extremely fast and economically unsustainable rise in medical expenditures.

Thus, in general, our inability to predict the outcomes of our initial adaptive decisions combined with the changing nature of the problems we intend to solve implies that, even when we succeed in solving past problems, we end up creating new ones. We could express this situation by saying that the solution to a past problem based on an incomplete knowledge generally leads to the emergence in the SES of contradictions which in turn will demand more, although always incomplete, solutions. In turn, the new solutions will at best solve the new contradictions and lead later to further ones. Thus, there is no final state of history in which all problems have been solved, and the SES is in a sort of Nash equilibrium where there are no tensions or desires to change. On the contrary, our SESs are in persistent dynamical condition determined by a succession of different states.

4 Adaptive behaviour vs optimizing rationality

Generally, our knowledge is so limited that it is impossible to use optimizing rationality. However, there are cases in which adaptation and optimization coincide. For example, if we had to make a choice which is very simple and in a constant environment, such as the choice of a product under the constraint of financial resources, we could say that our best adaptation strategy is the optimum. This is not possible in general since our choice problems are so complex that not only calculating the optimum but even conceiving it is impossible. Let us imagine a choice problem in which a person or a group needs to make a choice amongst some possible alternatives. Only if the person has a clearly established set of preferences and a given set of resources, the solution is the choice that maximizes utility, or satisfaction, within the existing resource constraint.

The possibility to find the above-mentioned optimum depends on several assumptions which are rarely satisfied. First, the preference systems of different individuals must be independent (see Georgescu Roegen, 1971). Second, even if the calculation is in principle possible, the cost of computation could be extremely high or infinite (Simon, 1969, 1981; Beinhocker, 2007). Third, the calculation could be in principle be impossible if we do not know what factors are likely to affect the outcome of our choice problem. This is going to be the case during discontinuities when qualitative change and radical uncertainty prevail.

We can analyse the possibility of describing economic behaviour as rationally optimizing behaviour by referring to Friedman's metaphor. According to Friedman (Hodgson, 1988), although firms do not attempt to maximize profits, it is as if they were doing so because the firms that get closest to the optimum survive while those that remain further away from it go bankrupt. This implies that firms have at least some knowledge, however imperfect. Then firms that have the best knowledge base (KB), the one that most closely approximates the KB required to optimize, survive while the other ones go bankrupt. If we were to admit that firms had zero knowledge and that their behaviour differed in a purely stochastic way, we could still state that the firms whose performance most closely approximates the optimum would survive while the other ones with further from the optimum performance would go bankrupt. However, in this case, firm performance would be determined purely by luck and no advice could be given to firms on how to improve their performance, quite a damning indictment for an economic theory. Thus, Friedman's metaphor needs to be reduced to differences in firms' KB so that firms having the KB closest to the optimum will survive while the other ones go bankrupt. Or, in other words, to attain optimum performance a firm will need an optimum knowledge base. Now, to decide what is an optimum knowledge base (KB), we would need to know what is the optimum. In this context, if we accept that firms cannot have such an optimum knowledge base, Friedman's metaphor implies that getting as close as possible to the optimum is likely to require a non-negligible amount of luck. Presumably a policy prescription recommending firms to be lucky would not be received very favourably by entrepreneurs and managers. The problem then turns to the nature of firm knowledge and to how it can be improved. In a simplified neoclassical view, this knowledge would consist of an optimizing algorithm which, if fed the right information, can easily and at zero cost calculate the optimum behaviour.

If such algorithm were costless and easily available to all firms then all of them would use it and their performance would be identical. An even casual observation of firm behaviour reveals that (i) no such algorithm is easily available; (ii) when optimizing algorithms are available, they are designed for specialized purposes and can only deal with very simplified and static environments; (iii) in general, the amount of information required is not available; (iv) even when such information were available, the computational costs could be unbearably high; and (v) even more importantly, the conception of any optimizing algorithm needs to be based on a solid knowledge of the underlying SES. As has been repeatedly pointed out so far, such knowledge is in general absent, particularly so in periods of radical and discontinuous change. Then, although we can identify some simplified and static environments in which it is possible to conceive and use an optimizing algorithm, this is not possible in general.

A situation in which only highly incomplete knowledge would be available is the beginning of a transition (Geels, 2002). The introduction of a new MMA is dominated by entrepreneurial knowledge, that is, by knowledge which is sufficiently articulated to allow the formulation of broadly defined objectives but not to predict with any accuracy the future evolution of the SES, and in particular the structure of the subsystem constructed around the new MMA. Sometimes a choice must be made amongst a set of discrete options, such as the multiplicity of designs existing at the beginning of technology life cycle (TLC) (Abernathy, Utterback, 1975; Nelson, Winter, 1977; Dosi, 1982). At this stage the knowledge present in the community related to the new MMA is insufficient to conceive any model which could be the basis of an optimizing algorithm. The development of the new MMA and its complementary institutions is guided by heuristics. Furthermore, the development of the subsystem built around the new MMA is highly path-dependent, with decisions made at this stage affecting the subsequent development of all the subsystems. Often, the initial multiplicity of designs is followed by the convergence on a dominant design (Abernathy, Utterback,

1975; Nelson, Winter, 1977, Dosi, 1982). This does not end the differentiation of the MMA, but realizes it by combining in a modular way the components of the design. In other words, each of the different product models to which differentiation gives rise is obtained by combining a small number of common components. As the technology of the new MMA matures, the knowledge present in the corresponding community becomes much more detailed, even if only within the existing regime/design/paradigm. This knowledge is not necessarily scientific, in the sense of being deductively derivable from scientific theories, but, as compared to the knowledge present in the initial stages, it has an enhanced capability to explain, improve and make limited predictions about the evolution of the MMA and its subsystem. Within these limits, the knowledge related to an MMA can allow the construction of *locally limited* (see Chapter 5) models, which can in principle be used to derive quasi optimizing algorithms. Of course, in no case such algorithms are going to be costless or easy to use. Thus, although Friedman's metaphor would be completely irrelevant in the initial phases of the TLC, it could become increasingly meaningful as a broad approximation as the technology matures and becomes more predictable.

Even in these phases the advantage of having an optimizing algorithm would depend on its cost and how it can help technologists to reduce the distance from the optimum, that is, from the frontier of the KB. Firms could not be classified as good or bad ones just based on their distance from the optimum. Then the shorter their distance from the optimum, the better their knowledge base and the more advanced their performance would be. We can expect the cost of moving towards the optimum to increase more than linearly as the distance from the optimum falls. In this case a firm reducing quickly and by a limited amount its distance could increase its market share more than a firm attempting to go as close as possible to the frontier but more slowly and at a higher cost.[6] The extent to which Friedman's metaphor is an appropriate representation of firm behaviour is a mooted point.

In summary, we can say that the possibility for economic actors (firms, entrepreneurs) to make optimal choices regarding the evolution of technologies is in general very limited and can only be approximated in situations in which the MMA technology, its community and its complementary institutions have become stable and locally well understood. Outside these situations, knowledge can only develop by heuristics and learning by doing. Even within the mature phases of a TLC, the cost and time of application of a potential optimizing algorithm are such that the best performing firm(s) is not necessarily the one that gets closest to the optimum. However, although quasi-optimizing algorithms can be and are used in economics, the physical sciences and technology, they are highly specialized and only 'locally' applicable.

In a population of firms, we can expect to find a distribution of firms having KBs at different distances from their frontier, thus having different levels of performance and profitability. Even the concept of frontier cannot fully represent the distribution of competencies and capabilities of existing firms. There may be firms that are leading their sectors, thus apparently being very close to the frontier, and other firms which are exploring avenues for future that could lead them to become future leaders. Thus, the frontier is being constantly redefined and measuring the distance from it can be problematic. In summary, Friedman's metaphor not only would be largely inapplicable to the emergence of new MMAs and important transitions but would be very problematic even in a more stable situation in the maturing phase of a new MMA and the corresponding subsystem configuration.

Thus, optimizing rationality can be an approximate representation of the behaviour of economic actors in a limited number of cases, although such cases may tend to occur with very high frequency, but far from transitions. In these cases, the balance between the benefits and costs of using an optimizing algorithm could even be positive.

Notes

1 On the distinction between qualitative and quantitative change, see Chapters 1 and 2.

2 The concept of distance from equilibrium will be discussed more specifically in Chapter 6 about complexity.

3 At this point we leave aside the question of whether the Pareto criterion is complete or whether it needs to be complemented by further conditions. Likewise, we do not discuss the related point of how many real-life changes do in fact respect the Pareto criterion. These points will be discussed in Chapter 8.

4 The concept of stability used here does not imply that a stable society is just or optimal, but that such society can survive long periods without important changes of structure.

5 They can be considered a subclass of structural barriers but given their importance they deserve to be analysed separately.

6 The previous description (Section 3.5.2) of how some biological species can retain organs created at previous stages of evolution to adapt to a different external environment can be quite relevant here. A technology that constitutes a limited improvement with respect to existing ones but can be produced more quickly than more perfect ones can dominate during given periods. Here as well is the survival of the relatively better adapted, not of the perfectly adapted.

References

Abernathy W.J., Utterback J.M. (1975) A dynamic model of process and product innovation. *Omega*, 3(6): 639–656.

Acemoglu D., Robinson J.A. (2012) *Why Nations Fail: The Origins of Power, Prosperity and Poverty*, New York, Crown Publishing.

Allen P. (2001) Knowledge, ignorance and the evolution of complex systems, in Foster J., Metcalfe J.S. (Eds), *Frontiers of Evolutionary Economics*, Cheltenham, Edward Elgar, 313–350.

Allen P. (2007) Self-organization in economic systems, in Hanusch H., Pyka A. (Eds), *Elgar Companion to neo-Schumpeterian Economics*, Cheltenham, Edward Elgar, 1111–1148.

Arthur, W.B. (1989) Competing technologies, increasing returns, and lockin by historical events. *The Economic Journal*, 99: 116–131.
Arthur W.B. (2007) *Complexity and the Economy*, Oxford, Oxford University Press.
Beinhocker E.D. (2007) *The Origin of Wealth, The Radical Remaking of Economics and What It Means for Business and Society*, Boston, MA, Harvard Business School Press.
Boyd R., Richerson P.J. (1985) *Culture and the Evolutionary Process*, Chicago, Chicago University Press.
Castaldi C., Dosi, G., Paraskevopoulou, E. (2011) Path dependence in technologies and organizations: a concise guide, Working Paper N° 11.04, Eindhoven Centre for Innovation Studies (ECIS), School of Innovation Sciences, Eindhoven University of Technology, The Netherlands.
Chandler A.D. (1962) *Strategy and Structure*, Cambridge, MA, MIT Press.
Chandler A.D. (1977) *The Visible Hand*, Cambridge, MA, Harvard University Press.
Club of Rome, Donella H. Meadows, Gary. Meadows, Jorgen Randers, and William W. Behrens III. (1972) *The Limits to Growth*, New York, Universe Books. ISBN 0-87663-165-0
Commoner B. (1971) *The Closing Circle: Nature, Man, and Technology*, New York, Knopf.
Daly H.E., (2007) *Ecological Economics and Sustainable Development: Selected Essays of Herman Daly*, Cheltenham, Edward Elgar.
Darwin C. (1859). *On the Origin of Species* (1st ed.), London, John Murray.
David P. (1985) Clio and the economics of QWERTY, *The American Economic Review*, 75(2), Papers and Proceedings of the Ninety-Seventh Annual Meeting of the American Economic Association: 332–337.
David P.A. (2007) Path dependence – a foundational concept for historical social science *Cliometrica, The Journal of Historical Economics and Econometric History*, 1 (2): 91–114.
Diamond J. (1997) *Guns, Germs, and Steel, The Fates of Human Societies*, New York, Norton.
Dopfer K., Foster J., Potts J. (2004) Micro–meso–macro, *Journal of Evolutionary Economics* 14: 263–279, http://dx.doi.org/10.1007/s00191-004-0193-0
Dosi, G. (1982) Technological paradigms and technological trajectories: a suggested interpretation of the determinants and directions of technical change. *Research Policy*, 11: 147–162.
Economist (2017) The New Old: the Economics of Longevity, Special Report, July 8th 2017
Freeman C. (1982) *The Economics of Industrial Innovation*, London, Pinter (2nd ed.).
Friedman B.L. (2010) Economic well-being in a historical context, in Pecchi L., Piga G. (Eds) *Revisiting Keynes: Economic Possibilities for our Grandchildren*, Cambridge MA, MIT Press, 125–134.
Geels, F. W., (2002) Technological transitions as evolutionary reconfiguration processes: A multi-level perspective and a case-study, *Research Policy*. 31, 8-9, p. 1257-1274 17 p.
Geneva Association, (2005) *The Geneva Papers on Risk and Insurance—Issues and Practice* 30: 4, October 2005 Special issue on 'The future of pensions and retirement income'.
Georgescu Roegen N. (1971) *The Entropy Law and the Economic Process*, Cambridge, MA, Harvard University Press.
Gould S.J., Vrba E.S. (1982). Exaptation — a missing term in the science of form. *Paleobiology*, 8(1): 4–15. http://dx.doi.org/10.1017/S0094837300004310.JSTOR2400563.
Gowdy J. (1994) *Co-evolutionary Economics: The Economy, Society and the Environment*, Dordrecht, Kluwer Academics.

Haken H. (1983) *Synergetics*, Berlin, Springer Verlag.
Harari Y.N. (2011) *Sapiens: A Brief History of Humankind*, London, Penguin Random House.
Hidalgo C. (2015) *Why Information Grows, The Evolution of Order, from Atoms to Economies*, Penguin Random House.
Hodgson G.M. (1988) *Economics and Institutions*, Cambridge, Polity Press.
Lipsey R., Carlaw K.J., Bekhar C.T. (2005) *Economic Transformations: General Purpose Technologies and Long-Term Economic Growth*. Oxford, Oxford University Press.
Metcalfe J.S. (1998) *Evolutionary Economics and Creative Destruction*, London, Routledge.
Miller J.H., Page S.E. (2007) *An Introduction to Computational Models of Social Life*, Princeton, NJ, Princeton University Press.
Nelson R., Winter S. (1977) In search of useful theory of innovation. *Research Policy*, 6: 36–76.
Nelson, R. Winter, S. (1982) *An Evolutionary Theory of Economic Change*, Cambridge, MA, Harvard University Press.
OECD (2017) *Debate the Issues: Complexity and policy making*, OECD Insights, OECD Publishing, Paris, http://dx.doi.org/10.1787/9789264271531-en.
OECD (2015) *Pensions at a glance 2015: OECD and G20 indicators*, OECD Publishing, Paris. http://dx.doi.org/10.1787/pension_2015.en
Paris agreement (2015) https://www.nrdc.org/stories/paris-climate-agreement-everything-you-need-know HYPERLINK "https://unfccc.int/process-and-meetings/the-paris-agreement/the-paris-agreement"Paris Agreement on climate change (UNFCCC)
Pievani T. (2019) *Imperfezione: una Storia Naturale*, Milano, Raffaello Cortina.
Prigogine I., Stengers I. (1984) *Order out of Chaos*, London, Fontana.
Prigogine Y. (1947) *Etude Thermodynamique des Phénomènes Irréversibles*, Paris, Dunod.
Ramlogan R., Metcalfe J.S. (2006) Restless capitalism: a complexity perspective on modern capitalist economies, in Garnsey E., McGlade J. (Eds) *Complexity and Co-evolution*, Cheltenham, Edward Elgar, 115–146.
Sachs J.D., Warner A. (1995) *Economic Reform and the Process of Global Integration*, Brookings Papers on Economic Activity, 1.
Sachs J.D., Warner A.M. (2001) Natural resources and economic development, The curse of natural resources. *European Economic Review*, 45(4–6): 827–838.
Saviotti P.P., Pyka A. (2010) Generalized barriers to entry and economic development, *Journal of Evolutionary Economics*, 21: 29–52.
Schumpeter, J. (1911) *The Theory of Economic Development*, Cambridge, MA, Harvard University Press (1934, original edition 1911).
Simon H.A. (1969, 1981) *The Sciences of the Artificial*, Cambridge, MA, MIT Press.
Sober, E. (2001). The Two Faces of Fitness. In R. Singh, D. Paul, C. Krimbas, and J. Beatty (Eds.), *Thinking about Evolution: Historical, Philosophical, and Political Perspectives*. Cambridge University Press, pp. 309–321.
Steffen W., Jacques Grinevald J., Crutzen P. McNeill J. (2011) The Anthropocene: conceptual and historical perspectives, *Phil. Trans. R. Soc. A*, 2011 369: 842-867, doi: 10.1098/rsta.2010.0327
Von Bertalanffy L. (1950) The theory of open systems in physics and biology, *Science*, https://en.wikipedia.org/wiki/Elliott_Sober"Sober, E. (2001). The Two Faces of Fitness. In R. Singh, D. Paul, C. Krimbas, and J. Beatty (Eds.), *Thinking about Evolution: Historical, Philosophical, and Political Perspectives*. Cambridge University Press, pp. 309–321 111: 23–29.
World Bank 2020, (2020) Groundswell: Preparing for Internal Climate Migration' World Bank Report 2020.

4 Knowledge and economics

1 Introduction

The present state of development of modern industrialized societies seems to involve an increasing knowledge intensity, a phenomenon described as the emergence of the knowledge-based society. Although the intensity of knowledge utilization increased after the Second World War, this is not a new phenomenon. In a sense some form of knowledge has always been used in communities of human beings. Recipes to hunt for animals, light fires, pick fruits or vegetables, and feed infants have always been used and transferred from one generation to the next. However, the types of knowledge used in the early periods of human history seem radically different from those used today. Amongst the main factors contributing to these changes in the production and utilization of knowledge, there were the scientific and the industrial revolutions. The former, which occurred between the XVIth and XVIIth centuries, gave rise to a new mode of generating knowledge, the latter, which started in the XVIIIth century, radically enhanced the capability of human beings to modify their external environment (EE). Although these two revolutions occurred in different periods, and although for a long time they were quite separate, their development has since become increasingly linked. The development and success of both science and technology since the two revolutions did not consist only of new recipes to understand and modify our external environment, EE, but also of constructing new institutions which were specialized in the creation and diffusion of knowledge.

The origin of the knowledge-based society can be found in the second half of the XIXth century with the advent of the modern university system and with the institutionalization of industrial R&D (Murmann, 2003; Freeman, Soete, 1997). Despite the growing importance of knowledge for economic development, we still have a very limited understanding of processes of knowledge creation and utilization. This is not to deny that many valuable contributions to this theme have been made. On the contrary, such contributions exist, starting from the pioneering work of Hayek (1947, 1978), Machlup (1962), Simon (1965), Griliches (1979, 1988) and Mansfield (1980). Furthermore, most of the literature on innovation covers the same subject

DOI: 10.4324/9781003294221-4

although under a different name. The point to be made here is that in economics knowledge has rarely been studied *directly*. Usually, some phenomena involving or requiring knowledge, such as innovation, have been studied, giving us very important insights about knowledge itself. We can consider the entities and phenomena that we associate with knowledge, such as publications, patents or innovations, just *traces* of an underlying activity that we call knowledge. Thus, previous studies have somehow remained without proper foundations since an adequate characterization of processes of knowledge generation and utilization was missing. The objective of this chapter is precisely to start defining such a characterization. We can notice right away that this characterization must be applicable both to fundamental, or basic, knowledge and to the most applied types of industrial knowledge. In other words, it cannot be a characterization of knowledge that satisfies only the historian of science and the epistemologist, or alternatively the economist and the historian of business. Not only is it becoming increasingly clear that advances in industrial applications require advances in basic knowledge, but the degree of interaction between the two is becoming more intense and frequent, thus making these very distinctions increasingly irrelevant. Scholars of innovation have even started defining a second mode of knowledge generation and utilization, called Mode 2, in which fundamental and applied knowledge would continuously interact, thus becoming difficult to separate both chronologically and institutionally (Gibbons et al., 1994). Without entering this problem, we can simply notice here that an adequate theoretical representation of processes of knowledge generation and utilization must be applicable to both fundamental and applied types of knowledge.

The earliest studies of knowledge in economics consisted mostly of attempts to extend the existing approaches to production by considering knowledge a stock and introducing it into a knowledge production function (see, for example, Griliches, 1979, 1988). This approach is briefly reviewed in Krafft and Quatraro (2011). The approach adopted in this book consists of considering knowledge a structure having components and interactions. This approach is now adopted by a growing number of scholars and constitutes a good basis for the development of an economics of knowledge.

2 Some considerations on the nature of knowledge

2.1 Knowledge as adaptation

Human beings have always been searching for some explanation of the universe in which we live. In the early phases of human history, religions and myths supplied this type of explanation. This is not to say that the knowledge created in these forms was perfect. According to our present knowledge today, we know that these types of explanation were not correct. However, the 'goodness' of these explanations in the sense in which we would conceive it today was not important. What mattered was the existence of mechanisms that ensured the credibility of the narratives accompanying these explanations. Typically, this occurred when the explanations were backed by the authority of some institutions and individuals that lent the narratives the required credibility. We can then consider that understanding of the EE in which we live was a primary need of human beings. Such need existed in two related senses: these explanations (i) provided happiness and psychological equilibrium to human communities, and (ii) improved their capacity of adaptation to the external environment (EE) in which they lived, which we previously called ADTO (Chapter 3).

Today the credibility of the different religions and myths created in the course of human history has been substantially challenged, although not destroyed. Starting with the scientific revolution in the XVIth century, science raised serious doubts about the truthfulness of the explanations of particular phenomena supplied by religions and myths and provided alternative, more convincing, explanations. In this context, we do not wish to discuss whether science is superior to religion or the reverse, but simply to say that (i) religions, myths and science have a cognitive dimension and that such a dimension allowed them to satisfy the human need to understand our EE; (ii) after the XVIth century, science started competing with religions and myths to satisfy this need.

A second sense in which knowledge contributes to human adaptation is in the modification of our EE, which we previously called ADOF (Chapter 3). Such a modification, which is the objective of technology, requires knowledge, but the knowledge required can be of two different types:

1 Knowledge created to understand the entities and processes that constitute our EE. This type is an end in itself, is driven by human curiosity and has been in existence for a very long time. Early examples of mathematics and astronomy have been found in very ancient civilizations (Joseph, 1991).
2 Knowledge developed with the specific objective to modify in some sense our EE, for example, by building roads, bridges and houses.

Types (1) and (2) correspond approximately to science and technology, although the boundaries between the two are always fuzzy. They are in principle separable and have been separate during long periods of human history. However, they have a common root because they are both based on observations carried out by human beings based either on their senses or on the enhanced senses constituted by scientific instruments (Brooks, 1994). It is clear that in principle a well-developed knowledge of the EE can help to modify it (ADOF). The laws of mechanics can greatly help in the construction of buildings and biology can enhance the power of medicine. However, a positive interaction between the two only occurred after the scientific revolution. Science needed to achieve a threshold in its capability to understand at least some parts of the EE in order to be useful. A technological knowledge existed before that but it was not derived from existing science. Wind and water mills could be invented based on observations that winds or water flow could move objects by designing mechanisms that used this motion to modify the EE, for example, by grinding grains or pumping water. Even today technological knowledge is developed making a much greater use of science, but it is not a simple mechanical application of scientific theories (Layton, 1974).

An essential difference between science and technology is that science looks for generalizations while technology works on *specific* systems. Scientific generalizations help technology by suggesting the artefacts that would be very difficult or impossible to imagine without science. Furthermore, scientific generalizations can show that particular types of artefacts are impossible to develop because they are incompatible with scientific laws. For example, an artefact that required the violation of the principle of conservation of energy would be impossible to create. In this sense knowledge narrows the range of searches and experiments required to develop new MMAs.

However, artefacts that can be used in human activities, such as a screwdriver, a plough, a typing machine or a car, are constituted by specific materials moulded and combined in a specific way. As pointed out in Chapter 1, different materials are shaped and combined to supply useful services to human beings. In turn, these services allow human beings to adapt to the *local* EE. The way the materials are shaped and combined depends on the types of needs and wants that the artefact is intends to satisfy. Such shapes and combinations are not suggested directly by science, but derived from human experience. Science considerably enhances the power of technology to develop artefacts that supply useful services to human beings. In turn, such services are useful to the extent that they allow human beings to adapt to ADTO to their EE. Science provides an epistemic basis (Mokyr, 2002) for the development of technology, and on this basis new technologies can be created and existing technologies can be improved.

In fact, science and technology are not as separable as the previous considerations implied. Not only are most technological artefacts not completely designed by science alone, but often new avenues of scientific research are suggested by problems and observations encountered in the development of new technological artefacts. The classic example is the development of thermodynamics that was induced by the steam engine.[1]

2.2 Two properties of knowledge

In this section, two properties of knowledge that are very general and applicable to any type of knowledge, from scientific to more empirical and craft-based, are described. These two properties do not constitute a complete representation of knowledge, but, as it will be seen, they provide a surprisingly powerful basis to analyse processes of knowledge creation and utilization. The two properties are given as follows:

(P1) Knowledge is a co-relational structure.
(P2) Knowledge is a retrieval or interpretative structure.

2.2.1 Knowledge as a co-relational structure

In this book it is assumed that a reality independent of human observers exists in the sense that there are several entities constituting the external environment which cannot be modified at will. However, what follows is compatible with a wide variety of different positions. The observables and variables that will be the objects of co-relations are not assumed to be 'true' entities, but only our mental representations. Depending on the basic assumptions of different scholars such observables and variables may be real objects in themselves or simply intellectual constructs useful to create theories, but which can find no counterpart in nature. In other words, the representation of knowledge described in this chapter is compatible with basic assumptions ranging from those of Berkeley (Losee, pp. 165–167) who maintained that 'material substances do not exist', of Mach (Losee, pp. 168–170) who shared Berkeley's conviction that it is a mistake to assume that the concepts and relations of science correspond to that which exists in nature, or with the most naïve realist assumption that observables and variables are real entities. The focus of this chapter is on the production of knowledge as a collective enterprise and this focus is compatible with the conception of observables and variables both as real entities and as mental representations. In fact, these different positions relate more to what we could call variation, the production of new ideas, than to selection, the testing of these ideas. However, selection will eliminate several potential observables, variables and connections. Whatever assumption one makes about the ontological character of observables and variables it is impossible to formulate mental representations of the external environment at will. The external environment constitutes both a set of resources and a set of constraints for the activity of human beings. Such constraints mean that the ability of human beings to modify it in order to survive is in principle considerable, but limited. No magic wand that allows us to obtain particular outcomes at will exists.

Recent theories of science and technology challenged the objective status of reality and its independence from human knowledge. In a movement called the *social construction of technology* (SCOT) (Pinch, Bijker, 1984), sociologists pointed out that technology does not determine human action, but rather human action shapes technology. They also argued that evolution cannot be obtained without considering its social context. SCOT is a response to technological determinism, the belief that technology develops according to its own internal laws. This is sometimes known as *technological constructivism*. However, a philosophical movement called *critical realism*, initiated by Roy

Bhaskar (1975), distinguished between two levels of knowledge, its epistemological or 'transitive' side *and* its objective, ontological or 'intransitive' side. Critical realism attempts to combine the reality of the objects of science, and their knowability, with the insights of the 'sociology of knowledge' movement, which emphasized the theory-laden, historically contingent and socially situated nature of knowledge.

Despite their differences, these research traditions have firmly established that technology cannot be properly understood without considering their social context, although such social context does not fully explain the evolution of science and technology. Lawson (1997) shares the approach of critical realism but stresses the importance of structure and choice, as opposed to event regularities, and discusses the differences between the physical and the social sciences. In particular, he criticizes the excessively deductive approach of economics. We do not fully rely on either SCOT or critical realism, but find both very valuable because they allow us take into account both the influence of society on science and technology and the independence of natural objects from human enquiry and human attempts to modify them. Also, we already made and are going to make extended use of the concept of structure, although we derive it more from complexity science. Furthermore, we fully agree with the criticism of the (hyper) deductive character of economics: it is not possible to derive all or even most of economics as a deduction from a limited set of axioms and assumptions. In Chapter 6 we will stress that (i) in evolutionary economics, the use of induction or abduction is equally, if not more, important; (ii) economic history should be used as a field of observation and testing by evolutionary economists; and (iii) appreciative theorizing should precede attempts to develop more formally sophisticated approaches such as modelling or formulation of theorems. This is not to deny the importance of generalization in the advancement of knowledge, but generalizations should be regarded as arising from previous knowledge, as such, temporary, valid only in a limited range of circumstances, subject to some conditions, and always modifiable and expandable. The conception of knowledge as a network, to be presented later, only requires that the nodes of the network correspond to observables and variables and that in some cases the nodes are connected.

Human beings interact with this external environment by means of their sense organs and by means of a series of enhanced sense organs and tools. Initially human beings had to rely only on their sense organs for any observations on the external environment. During human evolution, they developed enhanced sense organs (e.g., telescopes, measuring devices, scanners) that allowed them to access parts of the external environment not directly accessible through their primary sense organs. Furthermore, they developed a series of tools (e.g., axes, hammers) that allowed them to modify purposefully their external environment, tools that Georgescu-Roegen (1971) called *exosomatic organs*. We find here already the basic distinction, described in the previous section, between two distinguishable but intimately interconnected activities. On the one hand, there is a need to observe and to know; on the other hand, there is a need to modify the external environment (EE). The activities corresponding to the two needs are clearly separable, at least conceptually, but closely related because it is easier to modify the external environment if we know its structure and properties. In fact, as already pointed out, these two needs and the related activities correspond to what we currently call science and technology. Science is the activity that understands and knows our external environment and technology is the activity that modifies the same environment. Examples of the relatedness of these two activities can be found from very ancient times, for example, in the field of navigation. However, until the second half of the XIXth century, such relationships were more occasional than systematic. In this sense they are separable although their institutional separation is a relatively modern phenomenon dating to the period after the scientific revolution. This relationship has become more intense recently today in the societies characterized by a high intensity of R&D, although they are still separate bodies of knowledge.

The relationship between science and technology will be discussed in greater detail in Section 2.2.5. For the time being let us proceed to explain what is meant by co-relational structure. We can identify in our external environment several observables, that is, of entities which can be responsible for observed phenomena. To each observable, we can associate one or more variables that represent and measure different aspects of the observable. As previously pointed out, in this chapter no particular assumption is made about the truthfulness of the observables and of the variables representing them. In other words, we are not assuming the observables to be real entities that can be observed in an unbiased way by human observers. Observables and variables are mental representations (Loasby, 1999) that allow us to explore the external environment and to establish in it a series of constituting entities and structures. All theories are conceived in the space of mental representations. Of course, our mental representations and the theories that are based on them can be generated at will but not all of them can pass the required tests: correspondence with experimental results selects 'good' from 'bad' theories. In other words, the variety of mental representations that can be constructed is much greater than that of the mental representations surviving empirical tests.

The presence of co-relation, or connexion, between two variables means that, at least for a number of the properties of the systems of which they represent the observables, their behaviour is not independent but linked. It is to be observed that if variables were not linked our knowledge of the external environment (EE) would be far more costly to acquire. If all the entities which constitute EE were completely independent, our knowledge would be the sum of what we knew about each entity. The presence of co-relations, or connexions, allows us to calculate values of unknown variables from those of known and related ones. Thus, the existence of connexions reduces our information costs. Typically, we detect co-relations by detecting correlations in the behaviour of different variables. The two terms 'co-relation' and 'correlation' are not synonyms: the former indicates a link between two variables within the structure of EE while the latter describes the statistical correlation between the properties of the same two variables. In a sense co-relation, or connection, is the more fundamental of the two terms, because it pertains to the structure of the EE, but the existence of a co-relation is usually detected by the presence of correlation.

Let us now consider an example of knowledge as a co-relational structure.

Example 1 The law of ideal gases

$$PV = nRT \tag{4.1}$$

If P is the pressure of a gas, V is the volume of a gas, n is the number of moles of the gas and T is the temperature of the gas, with R being a general constant, Eq. (4.1) tells us that all these variables are correlated in such a way that if we raise the temperature, the volume and the pressure of the gas must increase for Eq. (4.1) to keep being satisfied. In other words, Eq. (4.1) represents the co-relation of the behaviour of several variables of the gas. Eq. (4.1) is part of a theoretical model, that of ideal gases, in which the atoms or molecules of the gas are considered points occupying zero volume and behaving independently of one another. Such a model is part of a wider theory of gases, and contributes to theories such as thermodynamics or kinetics.

In this case the co-relation takes on a very accurate and quantitative character. In many cases the co-relation provided by a theory can be qualitative and loose, while still being a co-relation. Examples of accurate and quantitative correlations are found mainly in the physical sciences, although they can also be found in the biological and social sciences, even if with a lower frequency.[2]

Any scientific law that can be expressed under the form of one or more equations provides examples of an accurate and quantitative co-relation between variables. Despite the great number of these laws and equations that can be found, they do not represent most of our knowledge, except for a few fields. Many theories of the EE must be content with much looser and less accurate co-relations. For example, the so-called Engel's law (Hirshleifer, 1988, pp. 98–100) states that the share of income spent on basic commodities, such as food and housing, falls as the average income per head increases. Here the co-relation between income per head and expenditures in particular categories of commodities can be detected empirically and measured, but there is no complete theory of Engel's law. A co-relation (leading to a correlation) is established, but in a less accurate and quantitative way.

An even looser, even if very interesting, type of co-relation can be found in Max Weber's theory linking the *Protestant Ethic and the Spirit of Capitalism* (Weber, 1968). The co-relation can be stated in the following form: countries/societies/groups adhering to a protestant religion have a higher probability to give rise to a capitalist economic system than non-protestant ones. It is of no consequence for the objective of this chapter that today many scholars criticize this theory. The point to be made here is not the truthfulness of the theory, but the form in which it is created, and this form is that of a co-relation. The theory correlates in a loose and non-quantitative way religious and cultural beliefs and economic performance.

A particular place in this context must be reserved for econometric analysis. Econometric equations provide an example of very accurate correlations, but they do not necessarily allow us to detect co-relations as we can with so-called analytical models. In analytical models of given systems, co-relations, or connexions, between entities and variables are assumed as initial hypotheses in order to calculate system properties. The correspondence between calculated and measured values of system properties confirms the existence of the co-relations hypothesized. In econometric models, however, we find out that some variables are correlated, but we do not attempt to determine the precise nature of the interaction of the basic variables. Thus, econometric analysis establishes the *presence* of a correlation, rather than its precise form (co-relation) as it could be done in an analytical model.

In summary, the property of being a co-relational structure can be considered a general property of knowledge. This has both limits and many interesting implications.

2.2.2 Knowledge as a retrieval or interpretative structure

According to information theory (Shannon, Weaver, 1949), information does not have meaning, it is purely factual. In this sense information is different from knowledge. Based on the previous characterization, we could say that knowledge detects co-relations between different variables while information is constituted by the numerical values of the variables. However, while information does not in itself carry any meaning, its use requires knowledge of the context in which information was created (see also Cowan et al., 2000). Thus, data sets on atomic transition frequencies or on the distribution of some biological populations would not be interpretable by an observer who does not know the relevant theoretical framework. Thus, information is not generally interpretable by a non-knowledgeable agent/actor, but any information set requires the knowledge of one or more subsets of EE. In this sense knowledge can be considered a retrieval/interpretative structure.

The idea of information as totally devoid of meaning is more plausible in cases where the required underlying knowledge is widely available and taken for granted by all members of a community. For example, a train timetable with a list of times of arrival to and departure from particular places is generally interpretable by most of the members of a reasonably well-educated society. However, the smaller the community knowing a particular subset S(EE), the more non-members of that community will be unable to interpret an information set generated within that community.

One of the properties commonly attributed to knowledge is its cumulative character. Human beings cannot learn more advanced parts of knowledge within a given discipline unless they have previously learned the most basic parts of the same discipline. The previous knowledge held by an individual or organization determines the capacity of the same individual or organization to learn any further and more advanced piece of knowledge within the same discipline. Thus, knowledge is a retrieval/interpretative structure both for information sets corresponding to a given discipline and for other more advanced pieces of knowledge within the same discipline. The concept of knowledge as a retrieval/interpretative structure bears a considerable resemblance to that of absorptive capacity (Cohen, Levinthal, 1989, 1990) although the latter was formulated with reference to R&D. R&D is not only useful for creating new knowledge but it can also help a firm to learn (absorb) some external knowledge created by another firm or research institution, or simply stored in the scientific and technical literature. The probability that a firm having performed a given type of R&D can absorb some external knowledge depends on the *similarity* of the internal R&D and of the external knowledge. In turn, the similarity of two pieces of knowledge is the inverse of their cognitive distance (Nooteboom, 1999, 2000).

2.2.3 Knowledge as a network

The property of knowledge as a co-relational structure implies that (i) the subsets of EE studied are systems with components given by observables and their interactions, and that (ii) we can represent the knowledge of such systems by means of a network in which variables constitute nodes and co-relations/connections constitute links. A network representation of knowledge has a static and a dynamic aspect. The dynamic aspect is captured by the variety and the density, or connectivity, of the network. The former is defined as the number of nodes while the latter is defined as the ratio of the number of actual links to that of possible links for a given number of nodes. In general, for any type of network we can expect both the number of links and the number of nodes to vary in the course of time. In the case of knowledge, the number of nodes can vary, and typically tends to increase, with the discovery of new observables or variables while the number of links can vary with the number of co-relations, or connections, between variables. We can expect network variety to rise during scientific and technological development while network density can be expected to rise when the number of nodes grows faster than the number of links and to fall when the reverse happens. Thus, network variety can be expected to rise following a trajectory like that described in Chapter 4 for sectoral output while network density is more likely to oscillate around a trend line that could either rise or fall in the course of time. The dynamics of network variety and network density will be further discussed in the subsequent section on knowledge production.

We can expect that observables will be discovered and relevant variables will be defined by a gradual process. Once new variables have been defined, they will not immediately be connected to all the pre-existing variables. Using a network analogy, we can expect that the process of creation of new nodes/variables will be faster than the process of establishing links/correlations between existing nodes/variables. Thus, in periods in which many new variables are introduced we can expect the average density of linkages in the network of knowledge to fall. Conversely, when no new variables are introduced, we can expect the density of linkages/correlations in the network of knowledge to increase (Saviotti, 2005, 2007).

This dynamic representation of knowledge is compatible with Kuhn's (1962) analysis of the evolution of science. New observables and variables are likely to be created when new paradigms emerge. In this early phase we can expect new variables to be poorly connected to those existing in the previous network of knowledge. Thus, the emergence, or revolutionary, phase of a new paradigm is likely to be accompanied by a falling connectivity of the network of knowledge. However, we can expect the subsequent phase of normal science to be characterized by a growing number of links and thus by a growing network connectivity.

2.2.4 The local character of knowledge

The concept of local, or localized, knowledge can be understood by reference to a knowledge space, a space in which all human knowledge is contained, and which is subdivided into parcels each of which corresponds to a discipline, a sub-discipline or a specialty. If there are a very large number of these parcels, the share of knowledge contained in each of them is likely to be very small. Furthermore, if each of these disciplines employs large number of people the share of knowledge understood by everyone is likely to be much smaller than that of their discipline. In other words, the production of knowledge is highly specialized and the share of knowledge held by each individual or even discipline is going to be highly localized in knowledge space (Antonelli, 2008). A further meaning of the local character of knowledge follows immediately from the properties described in the previous sections. Even when co-relations can be represented by analytical equations, such equations can contain a very limited number of variables and are generally valid in a limited range of the same variables. If we consider Example 1, the law of ideal gases, the relationship of pressure, volume, temperature and the number of moles of an ideal gas is valid only at very low pressures and very high temperatures. However, at very high pressures and very low temperatures, Eq. (4.1) becomes gradually inadequate to predict the behaviour of real gases. Thus, we can expect that the validity of most models will be limited to some ranges of the values of the variables and interactions of the subset S_i (EE) investigated.

There is a further way in which knowledge can be considered local. Learning requires to retrieve knowledge from an existing stock. However, the difficulty of learning is inversely proportional to the dissimilarity between the internal knowledge of the learner and the external knowledge to be learned. Such dissimilarity corresponds to a *cognitive distance* (Nooteboom, 1999, 2000, 2007) in knowledge space. The more similar the internal and external knowledge of the learner, the easier learning is going to be and the higher the probability of learning. Here the local character of knowledge implies that to absorb a type of knowledge that has been created by R&D the learner needs to carry out R&D in the same or a similar field.

A discontinuity in technology occurs at the emergence of a new MMA because the variables required to represent its internal structure are different from those of any pre-existing one. However, when a new type of man-made artefact (MMA) emerges, another related type of discontinuity in human knowledge occurs. Typically, the types of knowledge used to produce two different types of MMA differ considerably in the sense that they cannot be easily transferred or updated. This is another example of the *local* character of knowledge, which means that each type of knowledge is specific to a narrow set of phenomena and not particularly useful elsewhere. Furthermore, in the very early stages of the life cycle of a new MMA, the knowledge about it will be very limited and the uncertainty about it radical.

It is this radical uncertainty that prevents any form of accurate planning and constitutes the defining feature of entrepreneurial activity. We cannot accurately predict the emergence of new MMAs since they are by definition qualitatively different from pre-existing ones. This is an example of radical uncertainty (Knight, 1921, Ormerod, 2015). If the emergence of new MMAs could be accurately predicted then there would be no innovations and the new MMAs would immediately become part of the Schumpeterian circular flow. Schumpeterian entrepreneurs operate in a situation of radical uncertainty in which they can at best predict the broad contours of a new MMA or a technological transition, but not the precise features of its future evolution. Past attempts to do that were not completely wrong as the work of Jules Verne and of Leonardo da Vinci show, but did not produce accurate results. Thus, it is precisely the radical uncertainty surrounding the emergence of new MMAs which defines the potential and the limitations of entrepreneurial activity: if there were no such uncertainty, the first entrepreneur to produce a new MMA could build a plant capable of satisfying the whole market.

As the life cycle of the new MMA proceeds beyond emergence, we can expect the knowledge about it to improve and the corresponding radical uncertainty to become calculable risk. Typically, the improvements in the production of a new MMA involve both increases in efficiency, which reduce costs, and increases in the quality and internal differentiation of the new MMAs. All these improvements are achieved by means of incremental innovations. Thus, we can expect the life cycle of an MMA to consist typically of a founding radical innovation, leading to the emergence, followed by a long string of incremental innovations. The importance of radical innovations, and thus of qualitative change, is not diminished by the fact that the number of incremental innovations in the life cycle of an MMA is likely to be much larger than that of radical innovations: the former would not have been possible without the existence of the latter.

Firms, organizations and countries have knowledge bases, the combination of the elements of knowledge accumulated in their labour force. The emergence of a discontinuity in the form of a completely new technology outside the firm with the potential to improve the services supplied by the firm's products is likely to require a profound modification of the firm's knowledge base. If the new technology is radically different from the pre-existing one, in the sense that the two have no common knowledge concepts, observables and theories, then a retraining of the labour force will be extremely difficult or impossible. More often a new labour force with new competencies will be required. While these new competencies will substitute some of the pre-existing ones, they will also need to be combined with some pre-existing ones in the organizational structure of the firm. The emergence of a knowledge discontinuity is likely to be for firms a more difficult learning process and a more complex organizational adaptation than the management of an incremental innovation of the corresponding calculable risk. This situation is recognized in the literature with the distinction between competence-destroying and competence-enhancing technological change (Tushman, Anderson, 1986; Rosenbloom, Christensen, 1994). The effect of discontinuities on the knowledge bases of firms and other organizations will be treated again later in this chapter and Chapter 5.

The possibility to represent knowledge as a network reinforces the existence of the local character of knowledge. We can expect to find highly connected variables within the same discipline or a narrow subset of the same discipline and to find much lower densities of connection between very far apart disciplines or subsets of knowledge. An example of this phenomenon can be found in the evolution of physics, chemistry, and medicine in the last 200 years. During this period, the connections between organs, cells, molecules and atoms became gradually elucidated. In other words, the observables of medicine (organs, cells) were gradually interpreted and explained based on the observables of physics and chemistry. As previously pointed out, although an important objective of knowledge is to create a fully connected network, the connectivity/density of the real network of knowledge is likely to keep fluctuating because of the balance between the rate of creation of nodes and the rate of creation of links (Saviotti, 2005, 2007).

Let us observe here that the local character of knowledge has some explicit and implicit precedents (Antonelli, 2008), although they are far less general than the version of the concept presented here. Atkinson and Stiglitz (1969) introduced a production function in which only a limited number of techniques is feasible. Improvements in technology do not concern the whole production function, but affect only one or few techniques. Innovations are concentrated in the technology that is currently in use, while other technologies remain largely unaffected. Thus, only a limited number of choices is available to a firm at a moment in time. Nelson and Winter (1982) talked about the local character of search in a similar sense. In their model each firm at a given time can be represented in input factor coefficient space by a point, corresponding to the technique used by the firm (pp. 180–183). According to their model, the probability that as a result of an innovative process a firm ends up with a different ratio of input factor coefficients is inversely proportional to the difference between the initial and the final ratios, or equivalently, to their distance in input factor space. This of course implies that local search involves incremental modifications of existing techniques, and that ratios near the initial one are most probable. It has been shown that search is generally more local than global, and based predominantly on the recombination of existing knowledge (Fleming, 2001; Fleming, Sorenson, 2001; Sorenson et al., 2006). More distant search in less familiar regions of the knowledge space is more difficult to manage, and requires appropriate competences (Antonelli, 2008). In the meantime, it is also more likely to lead to the creation of radical new technological knowledge, giving rise to discontinuities in evolutionary patterns (Nightingale, 1998; Katila and Ahuja, 2002).

Summarizing, we can say that knowledge has a local character because:

Knowledge can provide co-relations/connexions only over a small number of variables at a time.
It can provide co-relations only over a limited range of values of the variables considered.
The probability that a human actor holding a given internal knowledge K_i learns some piece of external knowledge K_e is inversely proportional to the distance between K_i and K_e in the observable space O(EE).

The creation of new nodes can be expected to precede the creation of links within the new nodes and between the new and the old ones.

2.2.5 Science and technology

According to the previous definitions, both science and technology are forms of knowledge (Layton, 1974). Both identify observables and try to connect them to other observables, but for different objectives: technology uses observables to provide services that satisfy human needs and wants. Science uses observations and observables to explain our EE. Thus, the distinction between science and technology corresponds roughly to that between *to know-what* and *to know-how* (Loasby, 1999). To know-how allows us to modify our external environment. To know-how can be made easier by knowing what happens in the subset of the external environment that we intend to modify. However, the knowledge of *what* of the subset is not always available, thus sometimes knowledge of *how* has to be developed without the knowledge of *what* of the subset considered. In the extreme case in which no knowledge of *what* was available the search for appropriate forms of modification of the EE could follow a trial-and-error method. Such a method would be very costly in search activities. However, the number of trials required to design appropriate strategies for the modification of EE could be drastically reduced if we had a sound knowledge of the nature of EE. Johnson et al. (2002) use a more sophisticated classification of knowledge types, including know-why and know-who. In this book the distinction between know-what and know-how is considered more fundamental than the other two. Know-why and know-who are two categories which, while very useful, are in principle derivable from know-what and know-how. This close connection between science and technology is considerably enhanced by the truth criterion we normally use. A theory is 'temporarily' correct if its predictions correspond to empirical observations of the EE. This close connection between the nature of theories and the structure of EE lies at the roots of our ability to use theoretical knowledge to modify our EE.

The progress of both science and technology and technology depended greatly on the types of means of observation existing at each time. The earliest means of observation were the senses of human beings. Then, at any time, the types of observables that could be detected depended on the limits of human senses. For example, if stars could be observed only by eyesight they appeared to be points in the sky. When more powerful means of observation became available, such as lenses, binoculars and telescopes, it was realized that stars were not simple objects but complex systems having a structure constituted by subsystems and their interactions. Thus, instruments of observation expanded the range of observables accessible to human beings. This affected science by requiring it to describe the new observables and to connect them to the pre-existing ones and by offering technology the possibility to create new technological artefacts. In turn, the instruments of observation were a product of technology which affected the progress of science. The introduction of more powerful means of observation allowed us to detect observables that were either 'smaller' or 'bigger' than the ones accessible to our senses. The former observables were at lower and the later at higher levels of aggregation of the universe. Examples of the former are atoms, molecules, or cells while examples of the latter are constellations, extragalactic nebula and black holes.

The invention of new types of scientific instruments allowed science to connect not only different macroscopic properties but also macroscopic and microscopic properties of objects/systems, thus connecting different levels of aggregation. Correspondingly the range of observables, variables and connections available to technologists to create human services widened considerably.

The relationships between science and technology were very limited until the industrial revolution. Most historians tend to agree that there were no *direct* effects of science in the early phases of the industrial revolution (Mokyr, 2002; Musson, Robinson, 1969). By *direct* effects we mean, for example, scientific discoveries that induced the creation of new technological artefacts.

However, even in the early phases of the industrial revolution, science could affect industry indirectly. For example, if useful knowledge had to be used widely in society, it was not just the amount of it created that mattered. The general availability of this knowledge was equally important. What Mokyr called Industrial Enlightenment (Mokyr, 2002, Ch 2), that is, the presence of learned societies capable of transmitting the new knowledge and of a public interested both in learning it and in exploiting its practical aspects, played an essential role in the industrial revolution (ibid).

Science started to have a direct effect on technology only in the second half of the XIXth century when the development of organic chemistry became closely linked to the chemical and pharmaceutical industries (Murmann, 2003). The relationships between science and technology became even more intense after the Second World War. Examples are developments in electronics and molecular biology and their impact on ITC and biotechnology. However, in spite of this increasingly close relationship, technology did not become a passive and mechanical application of science. The source of this persisting difference is that science produces *general* statements by abstracting from the specific properties of individual systems while technological artefacts are *specific* systems. Thus, the knowledge required to create and transform technological artefacts can never come only from science. Furthermore, technology needs to know not only the properties of different materials and of their combinations but also how these properties can produce services that can satisfy human wants and needs. In summary, although relationships between science and technology are becoming increasingly intense, technology remains a separate body of knowledge. Science does not directly determine technology but provides an epistemic basis (Mokyr, 2002) for it.

2.2.6 Theories of knowledge

The representation of knowledge described so far does not constitute a complete theory of knowledge. However, it is compatible with widely accepted epistemological theories. First, the creation of new observables and variables constitutes conjectures, to be tested by their correspondence to empirical observations. As Popper (1934) demonstrated, existing observables, variables and connections can never be proved to be true or correct. Their validity can only be corroborated by new experiments, but it is limited to the set of experiments carried out up to that point. Even in this limited sense knowledge can be very useful to modify our EE in the subsets of EE where the theory has been adequately tested.

In a broader sense the representation of knowledge as a co-relational and as retrieval/interpretative structure is compatible with the idea of knowledge as an organized structure, to which both Kuhn's and Lakatos' theories belong (Chalmers, 1980). In particular, the representation of knowledge described in this chapter is compatible with some recent structuralist theories of science (Balzer et al., 1987; Franck, 1999), according to which the collection of all empirical science forms a theoretical *holon*, composed of constellations of elementary theories, theories that would be *connected* by inter-theoretical links of different types, such as equivalence, specialization, and connection. Furthermore, as Polanyi pointed out (1958), the process of creating new knowledge cannot by its own internal rules lead inevitably to true knowledge. There is no such thing as a so-called scientific method. Science does not develop through an algorithmic machine in which such a method is embodied, but requires intuition and imagination. Important generalizations are put forward long before they can be supported or corroborated, and sometimes they are adhered to even in the presence of falsifying evidence. Objective knowledge can be created, but only by the critical analysis and the comparison of the ideas of different researchers and groups. Objective features of knowledge emerge in the context of verification and not in that of theory or concept formulation. Thus, new knowledge is not created by the combination of individual scientists and the scientific method but by the collective effort of scientists working in institutions where they formulate new ideas, compare and contrast them to those of their peers until a collectively acceptable theory emerges. The collective character of knowledge production is thus one of its most important aspects. One can then talk of knowledge embedded in social networks (Nightingale, 1998, p. 692).

Finally, the representation of knowledge as a co-relational and as a retrieval/interpretative structure can be used for both true and false theories. Different networks of knowledge, consisting of different variables and connections, will exist at different times. The evolution of knowledge will be represented by the transition between these different networks. The nodes and links of a theory which are proposed at a given time and at later times turn out to be false or incorrect will be replaced by new nodes and links.

Recently the idea proposed by Schumpeter that innovation is the outcome of a recombination process has been rediscovered by number of scholars (Weitzmann, 1998; Fleming, 2001; Fleming, Sorenson, 2001; Krafft, Quatraro, 2011). Most incremental innovations are generated by the combination of existing innovations in new and previously untried ways. Radical innovations stem from the combination of existing components with brand new ones. While the existence of recombination as an innovation generating mechanism cannot be placed in doubt, the questions arise: (i) where do the brand-new ones which are not due to recombination come from? (ii) Do we have recipes or routines by means of which we can combine existing innovations to obtain a desired one? These questions show that the existence of recombination-based mechanisms does not provide us with a complete explanation of the generation of innovation. In fact, the possible ways in which different innovations or, more fundamentally, different types of knowledge are created cannot be limited to the simple recombination of existing ideas. There are many examples of institutionally driven recombination, as in the formation of so-called interdisciplinary fields (biochemistry, molecular biology, bioinformatics, astrophysics), or by innovations such as numerically controlled machine tools and robots. However, the process of creation of new knowledge or new innovations cannot be reduced to a trivial combination of existing pieces of knowledge or innovations, but contains a component of genuine creativity. As a consequence, although to create new theories or innovations usually requires the knowledge of previous theories or technologies in similar or proximate fields, the mechanisms by which new theories or innovation emerge are unpredictable and they are not explicitly known even to discoverers and inventors. In this sense to say that the creation of new types of knowledge or new innovations requires the recombination of existing knowledge or innovations is little more than saying that knowledge is cumulative.

In the previous representation of knowledge, the emergence of new observables, concepts and variables is shown by the creation of new nodes in the knowledge network, while the recombination of pre-existing variables is shown by the emergence of new links between previously unconnected nodes. Thus, our proposed representation of knowledge can encompass both the creation of new concepts and the recombination of existing ones. Of course, our representation can only map the structure of existing knowledge and not predict what types of knowledge and innovations will emerge in future. However, our representation is compatible with existing epistemological theories. For example, the creation of new nodes is the result of bold conjectures which survive the selection of the scientific profession. Furthermore, not all new nodes have the same impact on the knowledge network. Some new concepts and variables open new fields, which will become new disciplines, and can induce the formation of new nodes, corresponding to new concepts and variables. The nodes generating new concepts and disciplines give rise to new paradigmatic structures and are likely to be accompanied by radical uncertainty. However, the creation of the nodes that articulate the new fields and disciplines represents the equivalent of normal science (Kuhn, 1962) and is likely to be accompanied by lower uncertainty. Thus, the structure of the network of knowledge is likely to proceed by the formation of clusters and to give rise to science and technology life cycles. Furthermore, we can expect the network of knowledge to differentiate during its evolution in a way similar to the one described in Chapter 5 for economic systems. The concepts that give rise to new fields can be expected to raise unrelated variety while the subsequent concepts that differentiate the new field can be expected to raise preferentially related variety. These predictions have been at least partly confirmed by a study of the evolution of biotechnology and telecommunications (Krafft et al., 2014).

3 Knowledge in socioeconomic systems

3.1 The production of knowledge

The term 'knowledge production' is deliberately used here to stress the possible similarities with processes of material production. Of course, *a priori* the production of knowledge cannot be considered identical to that of shoes or semiconductors. However, there is a level of generality at which some similarities can be identified. Thus, we can say that the production of knowledge requires resources and inputs. Furthermore, these inputs are transformed into outputs, consisting of various types of knowledge. Using the concepts previously developed in this chapter, we could say that the detection of observables, the creation of variables and connexions are the required outputs. Several economists have used production functions to analyse the production of knowledge (Griliches, 1988; Audretsch, 1998). Like any form of material production, the production of knowledge occurs in specialized institutions, although generally they are not firms (Murmann, 2003; Mokyr, 2002). Thus, it seems that some established economic concepts are in principle applicable to the production of knowledge. In this section we proceed to outline a series of other economic concepts that are in principle applicable to the production of knowledge.

3.1.1 Division of labour

Since Adam Smith (1776), division of labour has been recognized as an important determinant of economic growth. By reducing the size of the task each worker has to carry out and by specializing in it a growing efficiency can be achieved. A finer division of labour is obtained by increasing the number of steps into which each process is subdivided. A growing division of labour can improve efficiency but it is limited by the extent of the market and by coordination costs. The production of knowledge started to grow so much in the period preceding the industrial revolution that no individual could learn it all (Mokyr, 2002, p. 57). The division of labour became progressively more important with the creation of scientific disciplines, learned societies, etc. Furthermore, to obtain economic advantages from a growing division of labour, coordination costs must not rise simultaneously.

While these concepts have been predominantly discussed in the contexts of firms and markets, they are equally applicable to the production of knowledge. According to the previous sections, knowledge can be created by discovering new observables, defining appropriate variables, and finding co-relations between these variables. A logical local way in which the production of knowledge could be subdivided would be to partition the EE into a variable number of subsets and to assign to each of these subsets an organization that we will call discipline. Each discipline would then have a different observable space. The number of disciplines could be expected to increase in the course of time as the number of observables and variables increases. Furthermore, an extensive division of labour is likely to take place within each discipline leading to sub-disciplines, specialities, etc. Bearing in mind that knowledge creation can provide two distinct routes to the adaptation of human beings to their EE, two alternative processes of discipline formation can be identified: (a) select a subset of EE, identify within it observables and variables and establish correlations between these variables; (b) select a particularly important human need, such as nutrition and housing, and define it as the task of a particular discipline. Processes of type (a) correspond to our desire to know, or to general knowledge or basic research, while processes of type (b) correspond to the modification of our EE, or to technology.[3] We can call *cognitive*, or scientific, the disciplines corresponding to our desire to know what and *technological* those corresponding to our desire to modify the EE. These processes can be separated in principle, but, as we saw in the previous section about science and technology, they will inevitably be mixed in real knowledge creating organizations. The reason for this inseparability is the advantage given to technological disciplines by the existence of cognitive ones having overlapping observables spaces. We can expect technological disciplines to have an observable space partly overlapping that of one or more cognitive disciplines and partly constituted by variables that are unique to them. For example, civil engineering requires knowledge of mechanics, materials chemistry and geology amongst others, while having some variables and concepts that are unique to it. Engineering or applied disciplines provide a better way to modify EE if they are based on a sound knowledge of the subset S_i(EE) of EE which they intend to modify.

The previous considerations suggested a functional explanation for the origin of existing disciplines. However, although some correspondence between the observation space and the organization of disciplines is likely to exist, other factors can be expected to shape the way modern disciplines are organized. Modern disciplines were invented starting at the end of the XVIIIth century (Stichweh, 1992). Although some antecedents of disciplines can be identified since the Middle Ages, they differed in several ways. First, the overarching objective of modern disciplines shifted from the preservation of truth to the creation of novelty. Second, disciplines are not organized according to exclusively functional criteria but are social systems with their means of communication, shared values, etc. Third, the possible subdivisions of the EE vary as our knowledge develops. Thus, physics would not have been a discipline until the end of the XVIIIth century. Before that time fields of science corresponded to the established subdivisions of nature. Thus, zoology, botany and mineralogy corresponded to the animal, plant, and mineral subdivisions of nature. In this context physics would not have had an objective of its own.

An important question, to which only a partial answer will be given during this chapter, concerns the criteria used to define the boundaries of different disciplines, specialities, theories, models, etc. Is there only one possible way of defining those boundaries? No complete answer will be attempted here, although part of the answer will come from the following discussion. The partitions within the overall activity of knowledge generation can be defined at different levels of aggregation. Thus, sub-disciplines are subsets of disciplines, specialities subsets of sub-disciplines, theories subsets of specialities, models subsets of theories, etc. This classification could be developed further, but what has previously been introduced suffices for the purposes of this chapter. The main conclusion of this discussion is that the production of

analysis, etc., and quite often those of two disciplines are of difficult compatibility. A clear example of these specificities is given by the different value attached to quantitative analysis and modelling in economics and sociology, two disciplines that have partly overlapping observable spaces. Of course, one way of overcoming this problem involves defining disciplines whose variables match exactly those of the subset of EE that one wants to modify. This is the solution consisting of creating engineering, applied science disciplines, medicine, etc., that is disciplines not defined by the choice of a subset of the EE to be explained, but based on the choice of a subset of EE to be modified. In fact, if we examine existing disciplines, we can realize that there is a mixture of those defined by knowledge objectives and those defined by modification/technological objectives. Even within the disciplines that seem to be primarily oriented towards knowledge generation per se an important motivation to the creation of knowledge often came from practical problems. For example, both in astronomy and in physics, several important developments were due to very practical problems: navigation, the measurement of time and the development of the steam engine are but some of the examples of practical problems providing powerful inducements for scientific development. According to Popper (1972, p. 258), practical problems are very often the sources of new theories. Nelson (1994) and Nelson and Rosenberg (1993) maintain that the creation of technology-based disciplines is by no means the exception, but it is likely to be a very general phenomenon.

3.1.3 Competition

The relationship of different theories depends on the similarity of their observation spaces and the variables that correspond to them. When two theories have *identical* observation spaces, corresponding to a given subset S_i (EE), they *compete* for the explanation of that subset S_i (EE) (Saviotti, 1996). Competition would here occur by means of: (i) the identification of observables and variables within S_i (EE) and (ii) the establishment of connexions between the relevant variables. Theories can then differ for the timing of both (i) and (ii). Success in this competition would depend on the differential ability to establish connections leading to accurate predictions of experimental results. In this case, which we expect to be very rare, the 'better' theory will be able to establish more or 'better' connexions and to predict more accurately experimental results. The opposite case is that of two theories covering separate subsets of EE and *specializing* within each of them. This is the case of theories belonging to different disciplines. An intermediate case is that of two theories covering partly overlapping subsets of EE. This case corresponds to a situation of *imperfect competition*, in which each theory competes for the explanation of the shared parts of EE, but has a local monopoly in the parts of EE which are unique to it. All these cases can be represented graphically in terms of set theory (Saviotti, 2004).

Let us analyse in greater detail the situation. First, competition occurs when two theories Th1 and Th2 have identical observation spaces. They are then competing because they must provide competing explanations of the same phenomena. A phenomenon is here defined as an event or a set of events which can be explained by means of its connexions between underlying observables and variables. However, when the two theories Th1 and Th2 have separate observable spaces, the phenomena that they try to explain are different. In this case Th1 and Th2 do not compete but specialize each in explaining a different subset of EE. The relationship of Th1 and Th2 can be either of independence or of complementarity. For example, if the two theories were jointly required to explain some more general phenomena at the level of the whole discipline or to perform a modification of EE, then they would play a complementary role.

Summarizing, we can expect the relationship between different theories, and consequently their patterns of interaction, to depend on the relationship of their observation spaces. Thus, a relationship of competition between Th1 and Th2 will exist if they have the same observation space and if they attempt to explain the same phenomena. The use of competition made here can be reconciled with the one commonly found in economics textbooks by referring to the equivalent biological situation. In biology competition is only one of the possible forms of interaction between species. Two species are competing when they attempt to make use of the same resource, for example, two types of birds feeding on the same seeds. In economics firms try to sell goods and services that consumers want to buy. Consumers are the firms' resources. Perfect competition requires identical and homogeneous goods because firms try to beat their competitors in selling to a homogeneous population of consumers. In the present case theories, Th1 and Th2 use as resources their identical observation spaces. Thus, competition in any case involves identity of the resources used. Of course, in these cases the meaning of resources must be given a very general interpretation. The intermediate case in which Th1 and Th2 have only partly overlapping observation spaces corresponds to imperfect or monopolistic competition. Th1 and Th2 compete in the shared parts of their observation spaces, but there can still be some form of competition in the parts of EE which are not common to both theories depending on the degree of similarity of the relevant observables. Let us here recall the case of imperfect competition in economics. In this case firms produce non-identical but limitedly substitutable outputs. It is possible to imagine that if the degree of substitutability could be measured, for example, by means of the distance of different outputs in service characteristics space, competition would be more intense the closer the products are to service characteristics space. We can similarly say that the intensity of competition between theories will be more intense the more similar their observation spaces are. Of course, both in the case of products and services and in that of theories, when the resources are not identical, there is a degree of local monopoly, as in monopolistic competition. In this context theories that have separate observation spaces may either be independent or complementary, depending on whether their outputs have to be used jointly to produce further scientific explanations or to achieve a modification of EE or not. This would typically be the case when different scientific disciplines are jointly required to explain complex phenomena which are not represented in the observation space of any discipline. Examples of such phenomena could be climate change, the expected development of the bioeconomy or the impact of AI on human societies. The creation within each discipline of concepts and mental representations that are not easily compatible with those of other disciplines tends to raise coordination costs.

In summary, we can see that those processes such as the creation of different disciplines, the setting of their boundaries, the joint use of disciplines in treating a complex problem and the interactions of different disciplines can be analysed by means of very well-established economic concepts, such as division of labour, coordination, and competition, although these concepts might have to be redefined in a slightly more general sense than the one in which they have been used in the past.[5]

3.1.4 Knowledge and the firm

In the previous part of this chapter, a framework for the analysis of processes of knowledge generation and utilization was discussed. As was pointed out, the objective of this framework is to enable us to understand how these processes contribute to the economic performance of firms, industries and countries. In this section the analysis will be extended from knowledge generation in general to how knowledge is generated and used in the firm. The creation and utilization of knowledge is of central importance in an evolutionary theory of the firm. A firm is a bundle of resources, where resources include physical capital, workers, management and knowledge base (KB). The firm needs to transform resources into productive services, which in turn give rise to products[6] (Penrose, 1959, 1995). Although firms tend to use a given set of routines (Nelson, Winter, 1982) over long periods of time, they constantly carry out search activities, whether in a formal (R&D) or informal way, even if the results of these may only infrequently be used. The management of a successful firm constantly strives to improve the productive services it can extract from the existing set of resources. If firms are successful, they are naturally going to create a 'surplus' of productive services (Penrose, 1959, 1995), some of which can give rise to new products. It is by this mechanism that a dynamic and successful firm tends naturally to diversify its output (Penrose, 1959, 1995). This aspect of firm behaviour is the microeconomic counterpart of the macroeconomic trajectory towards growing variety discussed in Chapter 5.

In a firm knowledge is generated in a number of ways and in different subsets of the firm. The subset that receives the greatest attention in the literature is R&D. As will be seen in the subsequent section on knowledge and institutions, industrial R&D is a relatively modern activity, although one without which any successful firm could hardly survive today. However, while R&D is probably the most important contributor to knowledge generation in firms, it is not necessarily the only contributor. In a general way, we can divide all economic activities into *routines* and *search activities* (Nelson, Winter, 1982). In this context, search activities are all those activities which scan the EE looking for suitable alternatives or additions to existing routines. Search activities include R&D but also other activities, such as parts of industrial design or marketing. In fact, we can imagine routines and search activities to be the extremes of a range including all other possible economic activities.

Within the firm, knowledge is generated in different subsets of the organization. Internal division of labour determines the knowledge-generating activities carried out by each individual or department. However, the final objective of the firm is not knowledge generation per se but the creation of new products and services with which the firm is going to compete. In other words, we need to understand (i) processes of knowledge generation, and (ii) how these processes contribute to the economic performance of the firm.

Given what was said in the previous paragraph, we can expect knowledge generation within the firm to be a collective process, involving both division of labour and coordination. The outcomes of individual research projects need to be combined in order to lead to marketable outputs. Thus, the dynamics of knowledge generation and utilization can be expected to depend greatly on firm organization. A key concept in this analysis is that of the knowledge base (KB) of the firm, similar to Penrose's (p118) technological base, defined as the *collective* knowledge that the firm can use to achieve its productive objectives. The term 'collective' is due to the fact that the process of knowledge creation in the firm is based on division of labour and coordination. Many individuals, departments, subsidiaries, etc. of the firm contribute to the creation of new knowledge, each carrying out a small subset of the whole process. The production of the resultant knowledge necessarily involves the coordination of all these activities. The collective nature of this knowledge is due to the fact that the production of new knowledge is intrinsically dependent on the interactions of individuals within organizations. Such interactions are highly organization specific and we cannot expect the same knowledge to be produced by two organizations even if at a previous time they hired people with the same competencies. The knowledge base is itself a structure, the components of which are the types of knowledge used by the firm or organization and the interactions of which are determined by their joint utilization. We can understand that an objective of a good firm is to coordinate the activities of its members so that the overall knowledge base is greater than the sum of the pieces of knowledge held by individual members. In Section 4 the mapping and measurement of relevant properties of the KB will be discussed, as well as the impact of the same properties on firm performance. Furthermore, this type of analysis will be shown to be in principle compatible with the general framework previously described. According to this framework, knowledge can be represented as a network of variables and their connexions.

3.2 Knowledge and institutions

In the previous sections we discussed the 'content' of knowledge and its evolution in the course of economic development. The changes which occurred in the content of science and technology since the industrial revolution did not occur and could not have occurred without important institutional changes. New institutions were required, such as a new university system, which emerged in Germany in the mid-XIXth century; R&D as a new function in the economic system and the firm; and the creation of a system of intellectual property rights. Perhaps the most fundamental of these changes was the creation of the modern firm. In this section we will briefly review some of these institutional changes.

3.2.1 Technology and the firm

Organizations constituted by a group of people and operating to achieve objectives which were at least partly economic have existed for a very long time. Antecedents of such organizations can even be located at roman times (Rosenberg, Birdzell, 1986). Important examples of such organizations are the medieval guilds and the chartered corporations, such as the East India Company. However, these organizations differed from the modern corporation in that they required a special permission to operate, or sometimes a monopoly, issued by the state (ibid). The concept of a corporation, which could be formed by a group of individuals to trade or manufacture and which could hold property rights, acts as a moral person and accept liability, as opposed to its individual members, only emerged in the second half of the XIXth century, mostly in the UK and the USA (ibid). It is probably no coincidence that such joint stock corporations became a permissible legal form during the second part of the industrial revolution when they represented the most appropriate form to exploit the productive potential such revolution had unlocked.

The evolution of the modern firm is in many ways closely linked to technological evolution. Before the industrial revolution, the scale of most manufacturing firms was small and essentially family based. For example, the textile industry was dominated by the so-called cottage industry (Landes, 1969; Mokyr, 1990). The large machines and the consequent capital requirements of the factory system started the growth in size of the manufacturing firms, growth which was to accelerate considerably towards the end of the XIXth century (Chandler 1962, 1977; Hannah, 1976). Such further spurt of growth in firm size was due to a combination of new technologies and the resultant process of market expansion. The new technologies which contributed to the emergence of large corporations were of two types: first, there were the new technologies which led to the creation of new sectors, thus providing new productive opportunities; second, other technologies were enabling in the sense that they allowed the transport and communication required for the geographical enlargement of markets. Examples of the former could be found in the chemical and electrical industries. Examples of the latter technologies were the railways, refrigeration and the telegraph. According to Chandler (1977, pp. 287–289), the modern corporation was created by the integration of mass production with mass distribution.

Thus, technology has shaped and accompanied the evolution of the modern firm since the industrial revolution. However, the mechanisms whereby technology affected industry and the firm changed substantially with the institutionalization of R&D.

3.2.2 The institutionalization of R&D

Today R&D is a common function of both modern economic systems and most manufacturing firms, at least in developed countries; even in developing and emerging countries, a growing percentage of firms do some R&D. However, R&D as an independent economic function is little more than a hundred years old. We could say that R&D is the result of an increasing division of labour, influenced partly by the growing utilization of science in industry during the XIXth century, and partly by the considerable enlargement of markets that such utilization of science indirectly contributed to. R&D is a result of an increasing division of labour in the sense that although both learning and knowledge had always been part of human activities, in previous times learning had generally been obtained as a joint product of production activities. Using a modern terminology, before R&D activities existed learning had occurred by 'learning by doing'. The institutionalization of R&D gave rise to a separation of learning activities from production activities. We could say that R&D differed from learning by doing because it was *learning by not doing*. In this sense Freeman and Soete (1997) and Penrose (1959, 1995) are right when they consider that the emergence of R&D was a true revolution fundamentally changing modern industry.

The word 'revolution' implies that R&D was a complete break with respect to past trends. Of course, scientific activities had previously existed, but their volume was extremely low with respect to even that of R&D in the late XIXth century. Furthermore, until the second half of the century, the evolution of technology tended to be separate from that of science. Technologies themselves were called the industrial arts. During the XIXth century, and even before large R&D laboratories were created, science started to exert a growing influence on technology. Historians differ as to the extent of such influence. For example, although most historians would probably agree that innovations in some industries (textiles, steam engine, railways, steel, etc.) fundamentally contributed to the industrial revolution, there is still disagreement about the extent to which such innovations were affected by science (see Landes, 1969; Hobsbawm, 1968; Musson, Robinson 1969; Mokyr, 1990, 2010; Lipsey et al., 2005). While it seems that science started having some effect on industry during the industrial revolution, such effect could not be measured by R&D expenditures or by the citation of scientific work by patents. The institutionalization of R&D had to wait until the end of the XIXth century.

Two very important events marked the beginning of the institutionalization of R&D. First, around the mid-XIX century the German, or von Humboldt, university system for the first time combined systematically higher education and research (Murmann, 2003). Second, during the second half of the XIX century, some firms, mostly in Germany and the USA, started to create their own internal R&D laboratories (Murmann, 2003, Mowery, Rosenberg, 1989, Freeman, Soete, 1997). The German University system was later largely imitated and improved upon. The adoption of R&D by firms proceeded rapidly, but it is only after the Second World War that R&D became a systematic component of both the economic system and firms in developed countries (Mowery, Rosenberg, 1989, Freeman, Soete, 1997; Penrose, 1959, 1995).

Two very important questions can be raised at this point: first, why did the internalization of R&D occur at this particular moment? And second, why was R&D internalized in vertically integrated corporations rather than being produced in specialized research institutions? A tentative answer to the first question could be that only at this moment science had made enough progress to be applied systematically to industry. This answer is subject to many caveats. It is undoubtedly true that the progress of disciplines like chemistry and physics had been particularly fast in the period between the end of the XXth century and the beginning of the XXth century. However, it is clear that the relationship between science and technology had not been then and did not become subsequently one of passive application of science to technology. On the contrary, especially during the early part of the XIXth century, the role of science tended to be mainly concentrated on support activities like chemical analysis, or in general and often ex-post rationalization of processes which had been developed empirically. Important examples are the use of chemical analysis in the selection of iron ores in steel making (Mowery, Rosenberg, 1989) and the development of thermodynamics following the progress of the steam engine. The contribution of academic research to the development of the German chemical industry was probably an exceptional case, and it was largely due not only to the organization of science but to the coevolution of scientific institutions, intellectual property rights and political institutions (Murmann, 2003). Furthermore, Layton (1974) and Vincenti (1990) have shown that technology creates knowledge in a form different from that of science.

The second question was related to the organization of industrial R&D. In principle, three modes of organization could have been expected to occur: first, industrial R&D could have been carried out in academic institutions; second, it could have been located in specialized firms or research organizations; third, it could have been done in large, vertically integrated corporations. Although examples of all three types of organization existed, by far the most common form of internalization of industrial R&D was the internalization in large, vertically integrated corporations. In this sense the institutionalization of industrial R&D proceeded in parallel with the emergence of the large corporation.

The reasons for the dominance of this form of organization of industrial R&D can be found in the particular features of knowledge as a product of human activities. Knowledge is an at least partly public good in the sense that (i) a given piece of knowledge can be reused indefinitely without being consumed and that (ii) it is difficult to prevent agents who have not paid for the creation of a given piece of knowledge from using it. In this sense internalization into large, vertically integrated corporations would have largely reduced the risk that knowledge created by a specialized organization external to the corporation could be equally available to its competitors, thus increasing the appropriability of knowledge. The internalization into large corporations was the dominant form of organization of industrial R&D from the end of the XIXth century until the 1970s.

Starting from the 1970s a process of vertical disintegration, or externalization, of R&D started to be observed (Langlois, 2004). This process occurred in the form of inter-firm technological alliances, sometimes described as innovation networks (see, for example, Freeman (1991), Hagedoorn (1993, 1995), Saxenian (1991), Mowery (1989), Powell et al. (1996), Hakansson (1987), Callon (1991)). This phenomenon seemed to be a reversal of the previous trend, and it was part of the evidence used by Langlois (2004) to argue that Chandler's visible hand was vanishing. This does not seem to be happening (Dosi et al., 2007). However, in a number of knowledge-intensive sectors, high-tech start-ups and innovation networks have become a new form of industrial organization in addition to large, vertically integrated corporations. The precise reasons for this transition are related both to the dynamics of knowledge and to the evolution of industrial organization.

During the period 1950–1990, there has been a change described by Das Gupta and David (1994) as the transition between the old and the new economics of science. The old economics of science (Nelson, 1959; Arrow, 1962) insisted on the public character of science and in particular on its lack of appropriability. Such public good features would have affected the social organization of knowledge production. For example, in most circumstances highly risky fundamental research was likely to be carried out in public research organizations (PRO) while firms and private research organizations would focus on more applied and less risky research. Furthermore, IPRs needed to be designed to protect the interests of the inventor by granting them a temporary monopoly as an inducement to innovate. Also, in these conditions, the internalization of R&D in corporations seemed eminently sensible as a way of limiting the possible leakages of knowledge outside the boundaries of the firm.

The new economics of knowledge differed from the old one by stressing not only the influence of the properties of knowledge but also that of the social organization of knowledge production. Thus, amongst other differences, the new economics of science differed from the old one as to the cost of imitating a given piece of knowledge relative to that of creating it. The basis for the existence of patents is the need to compensate for the relative cheapness of imitation by awarding the inventor a temporary monopoly. However, as Cohen and Levinthal (1989) pointed out, imitation of a given technology requires carrying out R&D in the same technology in order to create the required absorption capacity. To the extent that the cost of creating the required absorption capacity becomes comparable to that of innovating, knowledge turns out to be much less public than it was previously thought, thus substantially undermining the case for IPRs.

The recognition of the importance of spillovers was another important development which took place in the 1980s. Although the involuntary character of spillovers can be rather doubtful, the large amounts of knowledge above the one internally created by a corporation can exert a powerful impact on the economic system at different levels of aggregation. At the macroeconomic level, spillovers are the externalities resulting from increasing returns to knowledge generation that can account for the long-run continuation of growth (Romer, 1990). At the level of the firm, spillovers pass from being an expression of waste in knowledge production to that of being a powerful resource which enhances the collective performance of industries and economies.

Another change which is likely to have an important impact on the firm and industrial organization is the rate of knowledge production and utilization. According to Agarwal and Gort (2001), the average delay between the creation of a new idea and its industrial utilization fell from 39 years at the end of the XIXth century to three years at the end of the XXth century. This increased rate of utilization is likely to have stretched the capabilities of incumbent large firms to learn, thus favouring the emergence of high-tech start-ups and innovation networks.

4 Empirical applications

4.1 The knowledge base of the firm

The general framework previously described can be used to derive empirical applications. This section will be concerned with the way firms and sectors create and use knowledge. The concept of the knowledge base (KB) of firms will be used here to show how that can be done. The logical extension of the previous analysis would be to identify the variables used by firms at given times and the correlations established between these variables. In order to do empirical research, we would need to have access to data sets containing the variables present in the knowledge base of each organization at different times. Such data sets do not exist and their construction is likely to be very costly. As a consequence of this data limitation, the representation of the KB thus obtained is approximate since it does not include all of the possible contributions to it. The KB of a firm, even of the most science based, is not purely scientific, but it contains many components. That this is the case is recognized in the literature, where concepts such as core competencies (Prahalad, Hamel, 1990) and complementary assets (Teece, 1986) describe different parts of the KB. The method that will be described takes into account only the scientific or technological components of the KB and needs to be complemented by other types of information to provide a complete representation of the KB. A complete representation of the KB would include also an 'organizational' network, describing the subsets of the firm creating each piece of knowledge. The reconstruction of such organizational network requires information that is available to firms themselves and which they might not be willing to share. Thus, for the moment, we focus on the types of knowledge that firms use. In the cases where the scientific and technological components of the KB constitute a good approximation for the overall KB, for example, in highly science-based industries, this approach can give us interesting and meaningful results. In these cases, it is possible to derive a graphic representation of the scientific and technological components of the KB by means of lexicographic analysis (Saviotti, de Looze, Maupertuis, Nesta, 2003) and to calculate a number of properties of the KB. These two applications will be briefly described here in Sections 4.2.1 and 4.2.2. The same approach can be extended to higher levels of aggregation, such as industrial sectors, regions or countries (Nesta, Saviotti, 2005, 2006; Krafft et al., 2014).

The study of firms' (and organizations') KBs is a very important component of the creation of an economics of knowledge. In this section two different methods to map the KB and to measure its properties will be described. In both cases we start by identifying some basic units of knowledge. In principle we could attempt to find all the variables corresponding to a given piece of knowledge. This is generally impossible and we use instead more aggregate units of knowledge, such as the technological classes contained in patents or the themes contained in patents or publications. The representation of the KB that we obtain by examining, for example, the patents of a firm is a network in which the nodes are constituted by our units of knowledge and the links by the interactions of the units of knowledge. In the work described here, the interactions are measured by the co-occurrence of the units of knowledge in the patents or in the other sources of information that we are using.

The two methods we used to study firms' KBs are different in that they refer to different levels of aggregation. The first method, *lexicographic analysis (LA)*, detects the units of knowledge in the texts that we use as sources of information. LA can detect in the text of patents short phrases corresponding to technological themes, or alternatively the technological classes contained in the patent. The links of these units are determined by their frequency of co-occurrence in the patents used. This provides us with a graphic representation of the network of knowledge constituting the KB at a given time. Repeating the study at different times, we can map the evolution of the KB and relate it to changes in firm strategy, firm organization, etc. (see Saviotti et al., 2003, 2005). In other words, LA allows us to represent the 'brain' of the firm.

The second method we use starts by constructing a matrix of co-occurrences of technological classes and provides us with a more aggregate representation of the KB. In particular, it allows us to measure some of the properties of the KB, such as its coherence, specialization, differentiation and similarity. On the basis of these measures, it is possible to show that the KB of a firm is a determinant of the firm's performance (Nesta, Saviotti, 2005, 2006). These two methods are complementary. LA provides us with a more disaggregate representation, by means of which we can enter the firm's KB, while the method based on co-occurrence matrices gives us measures of the resultant properties of each KB. The graphic representation we show here (Figures 4.1–4.5) was obtained by means of LA.

4.2 Knowledge properties

A theory of the firm needs to be able to connect changes in the KBs of firms, such as those shown in the previous example, with the overall performance of the firm. The representation of the KB of the firm used here reinforces the idea that knowledge is not a homogeneous entity of which we can measure the quantity as if it were a weight, but a structure having properties depending on the corresponding network. We can expect these properties, rather than the presence of a given 'quantity' of knowledge, to affect firm performance. The most fundamental of these properties are the *coherence* of the KB, its *cognitive distance* and its *variety*. The coherence of the KB describes the capability of the firm to combine different types of knowledge, the cognitive distance measures the dissimilarity between the KB of a firm at a given time and (i) its KB at a different time, or (ii) the KB of another firm at the same time. The variety of the KB of a firm measures the extent of its diversification. These properties can be very useful in understanding the evolution of the firm. For example, if a new technology that could be either a threat or an opportunity for the firm were to emerge, the firm would be forced to change its KB by learning some parts of the new technology. The change in the KB could be expected to reduce the ability of the firm to combine the types of knowledge contained in its KB, thus leading to a temporary fall in its coherence. The extent of such fall can be expected to depend on the cognitive distance between the new technology and the knowledge presently contained within the KB. Thus, learning a new technology which has a large CD with respect to the present KB is likely to be more difficult than learning a very similar one. The larger the CD between the knowledge to be learned and the existing KB, the greater the fall in coherence is likely to be. A large increase in CD can be expected to occur in the presence of discontinuities that give rise to the emergence of new paradigms, to be followed by subsequent phases of incremental innovations. In the initial phases, in which exploration dominates, search occurs in very far away regions of knowledge space, thus giving rise to competence disrupting technological change. This search which entails a high degree of novelty and uncertainty (Saviotti, 1996) is undertaken in the expectation that it can open important avenues of future development. Once a technological trajectory is established by radical innovations, exploitation will tend to dominate exploration, and search will be conducted through a process of organized search mainly within familiar areas of the knowledge space, resulting in lower levels of uncertainty (Krafft et al., 2014, Grebel et al., 2006) (Figure 4.1).

The variety of the KB of a firm is likely to increase to the extent that the firm diversifies. This diversification can occur either at the intra-sector level or at the inter-sector level, corresponding to the two trajectories for diversification described in Chapter 5. As the new knowledge is integrated into the KB, the variety of technological knowledge shifts from unrelated to related, and the search process focuses on a smaller number of profitable combinations. As the new paradigm matures, the bits of knowledge that are combined are likely to be characterized by lower levels of cognitive distance and higher levels of coherence. This representation of knowledge can be used to provide an operational distinction between exploration and exploitation: the transition from the former to the latter occurs as intra-firm cognitive distance falls, coherence rises and variety shifts from unrelated to related. Correspondingly, search changes from random to organized (Krafft et al., 2014; Grebel et al., 2006) (Figure 4.1).

Furthermore, a KB can be defined and mapped for levels of aggregation higher than the firm, such as industrial sectors or national economic systems.

4.2.1 Mapping the knowledge base (KB) of firms

The mapping of the KB of the firm is carried out by means of Lexicographic Analysis (LA), a linguistic engineering technique. The KB of the firm is represented as a network in which the nodes are the technological classes of the patents held by the firm and the links are reconstructed by measuring the frequency of co-occurrence of the technological classes. The frequency of co-occurrence measures the strength of the link. In this sense, the representation of the KB that will be provided here is compatible with the concept of knowledge as a co-relational structure and with its representation as a network.

The problem studied consisted of the change of strategy of two chemical firms, Hoechst and Rhone Poulenc, to become life science firms, followed

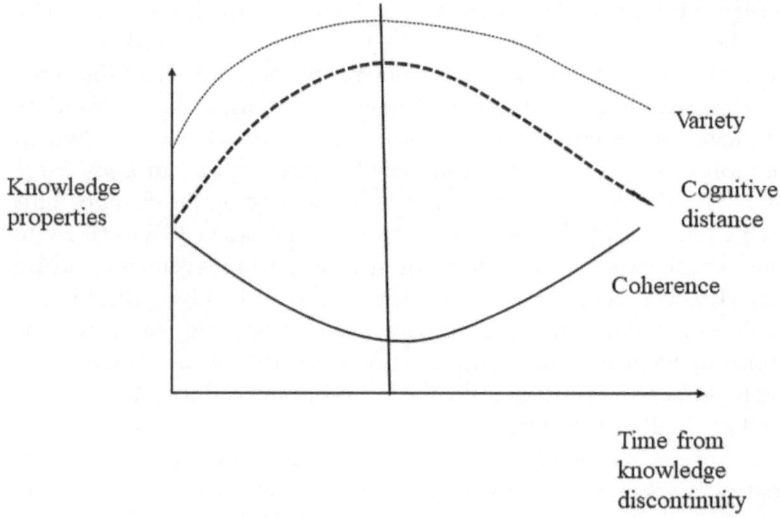

Figure 4.1 Evolution of the properties of knowledge in the presence of a discontinuity.[7]

by the merger of the two firms to form Aventis, a pharmaceutical firm. The KBs of the two firms were mapped before and after their change of strategy and compared to that of Aventis after the merger. The following results were obtained:

i The KBs of both Rhone Poulenc and Hoechst changed as expected from the announced change of strategy by incorporating new biological classes. For reasons of space, only the KB of Rhone is shown. That of Hoechst is shown in Saviotti et al. (2003, 2005).
ii After the change of strategy, the KBs of Rhone Poulenc and Hoechst remained segmented being weakly linked to the residual chemical classes only through a node, corresponding to a mostly commercial class A61K. This weak connection is likely to indicate an incomplete integration of the new and the old components of the KB.
iii After the merger, the KB of Aventis is no longer segmented and shows a well-integrated network with a more even distribution of links over the nodes.

This example highlights one of the possible applications of LA to study knowledge creation in firms: changes in KB following a strategic re-orientation of firms. Other possible applications exist to the study of the following topics: (i) relationship between knowledge dynamics and organizational dynamics, (ii) mergers and acquisitions, (iii) innovation.

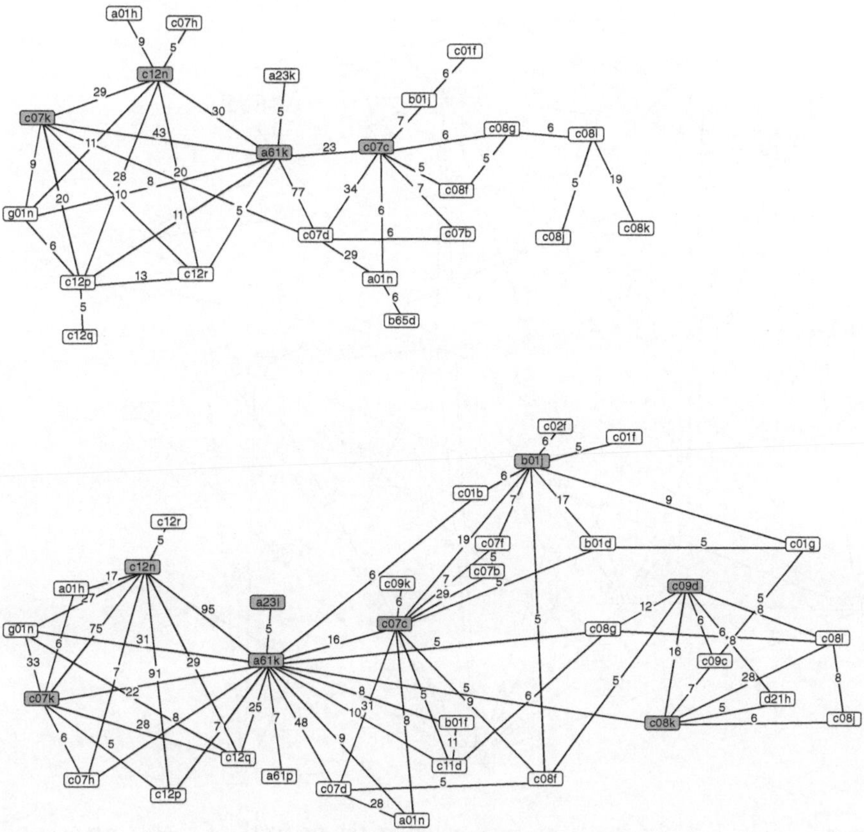

Figure 4.2 Network representation of the changing knowledge base of Rhône Poulenc between the periods (1990–1992) (above) and (1996–1998) (below). Each of the labels that constitute the nodes in the figure corresponds to a technological class. Class A61K, indicated by an arrow, separates biotechnology-related classes, on its left, from chemistry related classes, on its right.

4.2.2 The relationship between the properties of the KB and firm performance

As was pointed out in Section 3.1.6, we can expect the performance of a firm to be affected by the properties of its KB, the most important of which are coherence, cognitive distance and variety. As already pointed out there, cognitive distance and variety measure the dissimilarity and the differentiation of the KB. The concept of coherence deserves some more detailed comments. That a coherent firm can be more competitive or effective than an incoherent

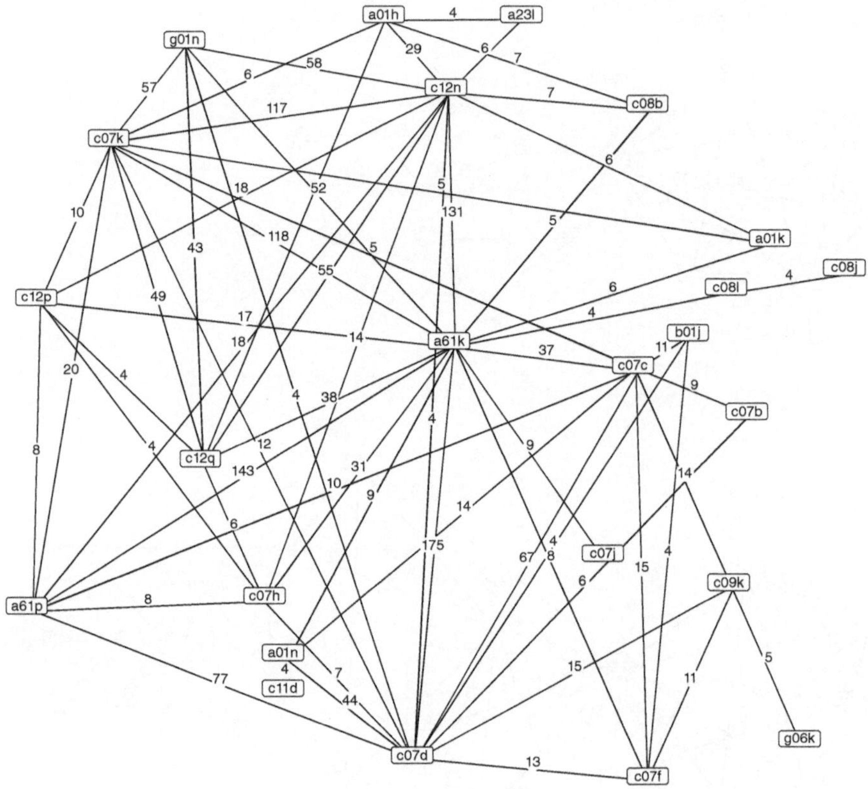

Figure 4.3 The KB of Aventis, as represented by the network of co-occurrences of the technological classes used by the firm in its patents. The technological classes are represented by the symbols in the boxes on the nodes of the network.

firm has for a long time been suspected. This hypothesis could not be properly tested in the absence of a method to measure coherence. Such a method was devised by Teece et al. (1994), based on the products of firms. It could then be ascertained whether or not coherent firms were more or less frequent than incoherent ones (e.g. conglomerates). In a knowledge-based economy, the coherence of the KB of a firm can be expected to be at least as important as the coherence of the outputs of the firm. Furthermore, it is important to understand the meaning of coherence. Teece et al. (1994) were talking about *relatedness*, but relatedness can be both similarity and complementarity. Nesta (2001) calculated the coherence and other properties of the KB of biotechnology firms. In this research, coherence was interpreted as predominantly complementarity.

The measurement of these properties relies on the joint utilization of different types of knowledge represented by technological classes or themes.

In a coherent KB, different classes can be expected to be connected while the entry of completely new classes is likely to give rise to poorly connected network nodes. In the subsequent evolution of the KB, we can expect the new classes to become increasingly connected to the pre-existing ones, thus leading to a recovery of the level of coherence. Furthermore, the cognitive distance of the KB at different times, as well as its variety, is to be affected by the entry of new classes and nodes and by their number and strength of links. The expected evolution of these properties of the KB is shown in Figure 4.1. The first step towards these measurements is the construction of a matrix of technological co-occurrences starting from a database, including all the patents awarded in a given field of technology during a period of time. The construction of this matrix relies implicitly on the representation of knowledge as a network. Starting from the frequencies of co-occurrence found in this matrix, we can calculate the values of a number of relevant properties of the KB. For the procedure used for these calculations, see Nesta and Saviotti (2005, 2006, 2014). It is to be observed that, contrary to the mapping of the KBs of individual firms shown in Figures 4.2 and 4.3, the measurement of these properties is based on a population of firms and other patent holders. The study of these populations was carried out by measuring the above properties or by plotting the networks of technological classes mapping the KB of the population of firms and other patent holders at different times.

The relationship between knowledge dynamics and firm performance can be explored by testing econometrically the existence of correlation between a number of independent variables, including the properties of the KB, and a dependent variable measuring one of the possible dimensions of firm performance. In two separate papers, Nesta and Saviotti (2005, 2006) used either technological performance, defined as the number of patents that a firm can produce during a given period of time, or the value of Tobin's Q, which measures stock market performance. In these two papers, both properties of the KB turned out to be significant and robust determinants of the performance of firms in biotechnology, although their impact on firms in different sectors dependent on biotechnology varied. This application completes the logical chain leading from knowledge generation to its industrial applications.

4.2.3 The dynamics of knowledge-intensive sectors

In this section a brief description of the evolution of the KB of biotechnology will be given. This was part of a study of three knowledge-intensive sectors (KIS), biotechnology, telecommunications, and electronics, in order to test the idea that recent changes in industrial organization, such as the emergence of innovation networks, were at least partly determined by the dynamics of knowledge. Biotechnology, telecommunications, and electronics were chosen for this study[8] because they have a higher-than-average knowledge intensity. They were studied for the period 1981–2003 using the EPO patent database. In the initial phase of the project the knowledge base of the three sectors was studied by measuring related and unrelated variety, coherence and cognitive distance. Furthermore, the networks representing the knowledge base of biotechnology at different times have been plotted.

These three sectors are not only knowledge intensive but have been affected by an important discontinuity in their knowledge base. For example, modern or third-generation biotechnology, which emerged due to advances in molecular biology, changed radically the knowledge base of firms in the pharmaceutical and in the agrochemical industries by replacing organic chemistry as their main source of knowledge. Likewise, telecommunications and electronics were deeply affected by the emergence of the transistor. Here only the results obtained for biotechnology will be discussed as an example.

Figures 4.4–4.6 show that for biotechnology the variety of the knowledge base increased, the coherence increased and the cognitive distance fell during the period 1981–2002. Furthermore, unrelated variety was dominant until 1983 while related variety became dominant in the following period. As previously pointed out, the low initial value of coherence fits very well with the recent emergence of a knowledge discontinuity. The rise in variety, both related and unrelated, means that after its emergence the new knowledge base of the pharmaceutical and agrochemical industries started diversifying by identifying new extensions and applications. The shift away from unrelated to related variety means that the process of diversification of the knowledge base started by exploring large parts of the knowledge space but that, after a number of promising applications were identified, continued by differentiating 'around' these applications. This transition, which in previous papers (Grebel et al., 2006) had been called from *random* to *organized search*, is likely to occur systematically when a knowledge discontinuity emerges. The fall in cognitive distance confirms the previous interpretation. We can expect

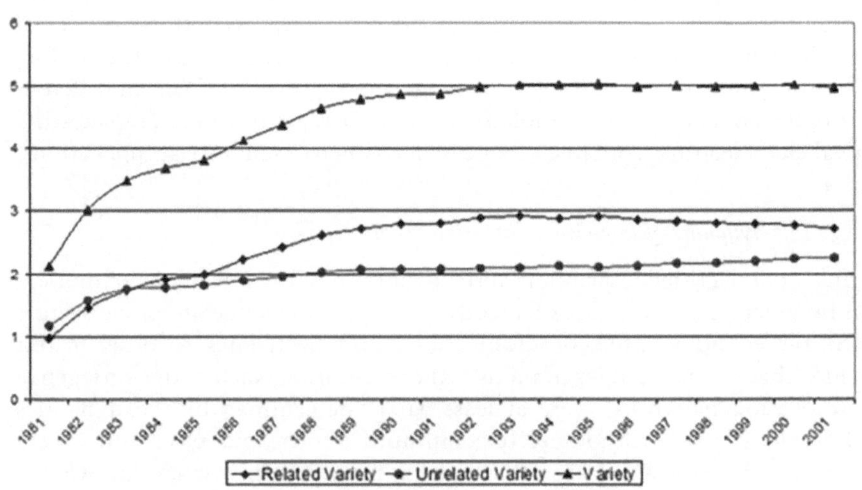

Figure 4.4 Variety of the knowledge base of biotechnology.

that when firms start using a radically new type of knowledge the cognitive distance between their present and past knowledge base is suddenly going to increase. After the principles of the new knowledge have been absorbed, as the new paradigm moves to maturity, we can expect cognitive distance to fall even in the presence of a continued differentiation of the knowledge base. As the search moves away from unrelated to related variety, further progress occurs by means of the same set of concepts.

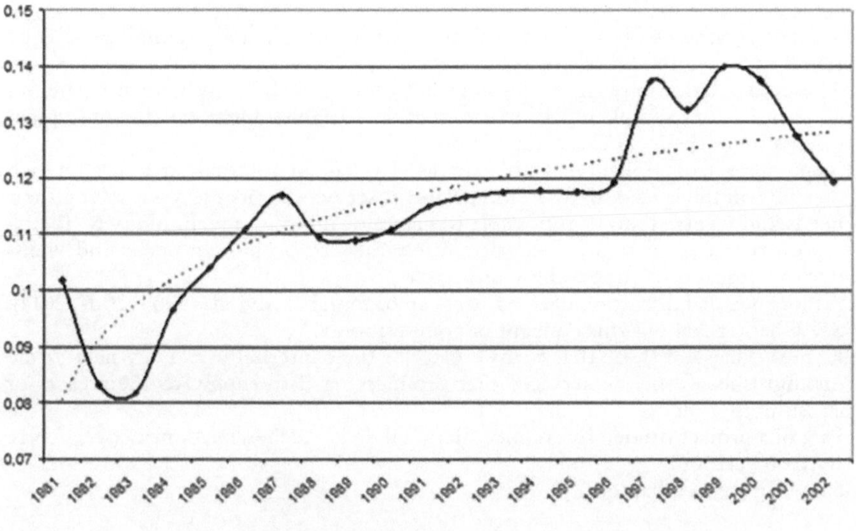

Figure 4.5 Coherence of the knowledge base of biotechnology.

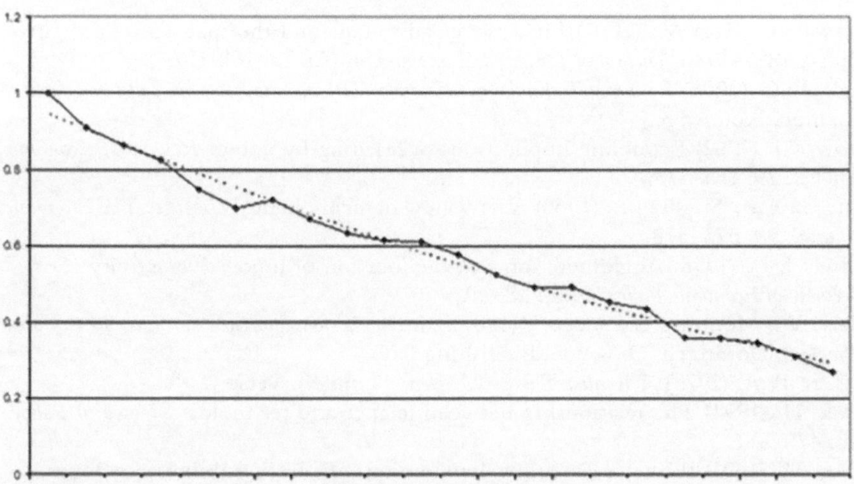

Figure 4.6 Cognitive distance of the knowledge base of biotechnology.

The examples given in this section showed how the properties of the KB can be measured and how they can be related to the economic performance of firms and sectors. Further consequences of these properties are the formation of technological alliances and innovation networks. Further consequences of these properties are explored in Saviotti and Catherine (2008), Saviotti (2014) and Krafft et al. (2014).

Notes

1 Further treatment of the relationship between science and technology can be found in Section 2.2.5 of this chapter.
2 These co-relations are never absolute but they are valid only within particular conditions, for example ranges of values of the variables. Here, see the subsequent discussion of the local character of knowledge.
3 Remember from Chapter 1 that an MMA has an internal structure, which depends on the laws of nature, and performs services for its users, satisfying their needs and wants. Thus, it is possible to create or improve a technology by focusing on the laws of nature (scientific disciplines) or on human needs and wants (technological disciplines, engineering etc.).
4 A more detailed discussion of this aspect can be found in Saviotti (2004, 2007, 2014).
5 See Chapter 2 about this concept of competition.
6 Here services are those that firms create for their internal use. They need to be distinguished from the services that products need to supply to their users or consumers, as defined in Chapter 1.
7 Part of a project funded by Agence National de la Recherche, contract N° ANR ICJC06_141306.
8 Same figure in Chapter 6.

References

Agarwal R., Gort M. (2001) First mover advantage and the speed of competitive entry, 1887–1986. *Journal of Law and Economics*, 44(April): 161–177.

Antonelli C. (2008) *Localised Technological Change: Towards the Economics of Complexity*, London, Routledge.

Arrow K.J. (1962) Economic implications of learning by doing. *Review of Economic Studies*, 29: 155–173.

Atkinson A.B., Stiglitz J.E. (1969) A new view of technological change. *The Economic Journal*, 99: 573–578.

Audretsch D. (1998) Agglomeration and the location of innovative activity. *Oxford Review of Economic Policy*, 14(2): 18–29.

Balzer, W., Moulines U., Sneed J. (1987) *An Architectonic for Science, The Structuralist Program*, Dordretch, D. Reidel Publishing Co.

Bhaskar, R.A. (1975) *A Realist Theory of Science*, London, Verso.

Brooks H. (1994) The relationship between science and technology, *Research Policy*, 23: 477–486.

Callon M. (1991) Réseaux Technico-Économiques Et Irréversibilités, in Boyer R., Chavance B., Godard O. (Eds), *Les Figures De L'irréversibilité En Economie*, Paris, Editions de l'Ecole des Hautes Etudes en Sciences Sociales. ISBN 2-7132-0961-7, pp. 195–230.

Chalmers A.F. (1980) *What Is This Thing Called Science?* Milton Keynes, Open University Press.

Chandler A.D. (1962) *Strategy and Structure*, Cambridge MA, MIT Press.

Chandler A.D. (1977) *The Visible Hand*, Cambridge, MA, Harvard University Press.

Cohen M., Levinthal D. (1989) Innovation and learning: the two faces of R&D, *Economic Journal*, 99: 569–596.

Cohen, M., Levinthal D. (1990) Absorptive capacity: a new perspective on learning and innovation, *Administrative Science Quarterly*, 35: 128–152.

Cowan R., David P., Foray D. (2000) The explicit economics of knowledge codification and tacitness. *Industrial and Corporate Change*, 9: 211–254.

Das Gupta P., David P. (1994) Toward a new economics of science. *Research Policy*, 23(5): 487–521.

Dosi G., Gambardella, A., Grazzi M., Orsenigo L. (2007) Technological revolutions and the evolution of industrial structures. Assessing the impact of new technologies upon size and boundaries of the firms, LEM working paper 2007/12, Scuola Superiore Sant'Anna, Pisa, Italy.

Fleming L. (2001) Recombinant uncertainty in technological search, *Management Science*, 47 (1): 117–132.

Fleming, L., Sorenson, O. (2001) Technology as a complex adaptive system: evidence from patent data. *Research Policy*, 30(7): 1019–1039.

Franck R. (1999) La pluralité des disciplines, l'unité du savoir et les connaissances ordinaires, *Sociologie et Société*, XXXI: 129–142.

Freeman C. (1991) Networks of innovators: a synthesis of research issues, *Research Policy*, 20: 499–514.

Freeman C., Soete L. (1997) *The Economics of Industrial Innovation*, London, Pinter.

Georgescu-Roegen N. (1971) *The Entropy Law and the Economic Process*, Cambridge, MA, Harvard University Press.

Gibbons M., Limoges C., Nowotny H., Schwartzmann S., Scott P., Trow M. (1994) *The New Production of Knowledge-The Dynamics of Science and Research in Contemporary Societies*, London, Sage.

Grebel T., Krafft J., Saviotti P.P. (2006) On the life cycle of knowledge intensive sectors, *Revue de l'ofce*, June, 97 bis (5): 63–85.

Griliches Z. (1979) Issues in assessing the contribution of research and development to productivity growth, *Bell Journal of Economics*, 10(1): 92–116.

Griliches Z. (1988) *R&D and Productivity. The Econometric Evidence*, Chicago, Chicago University Press.

Hagedoorn J. (1993) Understanding the rationale of strategic technology partnering: Interorganizational Modes of Cooperation and Sectoral differences. *Strategic Management Journal*, 14: 371–385.

Hagedoorn J. (1995) Strategic technology partnering during the 1980s: trends, networks and corporate patterns in non-core technologies. *Research Policy*, 24: 207–231.

Hakansson H. (1987) *Industrial Technological Development. A Network Approach*, London, Croom Helm Limited.

Hannah L. (1976, 1983) *The Rise of the Corporate Economy*, London, Methuen.

Hayek N. Ed. (1947) The use of knowledge in society, in *Individualism and Economic Order*, Chicago, The University of Chicago Press, 77–91.

Hayek N. (1978) *New Studies in Philosophy, Politics, Economics the History of Ideas*, London, Routledge, 184.

Hirshleifer J. (1988) *Price Theory and Applications*, Englewood Cliffs, NJ, Prentice Hall.

Hobsbawm E.J. (1968) *Industry and Empire*, Harmondsworth, Penguin Books.

Johnson B., Lorenz E., Lundvall B.A. (2002) Why all this fuss about codified and tacit knowledge? *Industrial and Corporate Change*, 11(2): 245–262.

Joseph G.G. (1991) *The Crest of the Peacock: Non-European Roots of Mathematics*, London, Penguin Books.

Katila R., Ahuja G. (2002) Something old, something new: a longitudinal study of search behaviour and new product introduction. *Academy of Management Journal*, 45(6): 1183–1194.

Knight F. (1921) *Risk, Uncertainty and Profit*, New York, Houghton Mifflin.

Krafft J., Quatraro F. (2011) The dynamics of technological knowledge: from linearity to recombination, in Antonelli C. (Ed), *Handbook on the Economic Complexity of Technological Change*, Cheltenham, Edward Elgar, 181–200.

Krafft J., Quatraro F., Saviotti P.P. (2014) The dynamics of knowledge-intensive sectors' knowledge base: evidence from biotechnology and telecommunications. *Industry and Innovation*, http://dx.doi.org/10.1080/13662716.2014.919762

Kuhn T.S. (1962) *The Structure of Scientific Revolutions*, Chicago: The University of Chicago Press.

Landes D.S. (1969) *The Unbound Prometheus: Technological Change and Industrial Development in Western Europe from 1750 to the Present*, Cambridge, Cambridge University Press.

Langlois R.N. (2004) The vanishing hand: the changing dynamics of industrial capitalism. *Industrial and Corporate Change*, 12(2): 351–385.

Lawson T. (1997) *Economics and Reality*, London, Routledge.

Layton E.T. (1974) Technology as knowledge, *Technology and Culture*, 15: 31–41.

Lipsey R., Carlaw K.J., Bekar C.T. (2005). *Economic Transformations: General Purpose Technologies and Long-Term Economic Growth*, Oxford, Oxford University Press.

Loasby B. (1999) *Knowledge, Institutions and Evolutionary Economics*, London, Routledge.

Machlup F. (1962) The *Production and Distribution of Knowledge in the United States*, Princeton, NJ, Princeton University Press.

Mansfield E. (1980) Basic research and productivity increase in manufacturing. *American Economic Review*, 70: 863–873.

Mokyr J. (1990) *The Lever of Riches: Technological Creativity and Economic Progress*, New York, Oxford University Press.

Mokyr J. (2002) *The Gifts of Athena: Historical Origins of the Knowledge Economy*, Princeton, NJ, Princeton University Press.

Mokyr J. (2010) The contribution of economic history to the study of innovation and technical change: 1750–1914. *Handbooks in Economics*, edition 1, volume 1, Elsevier, 11–50.

Mowery D.C. (1989) Collaborative ventures between us and foreign manufacturing firms. *Research Policy*, 18(1): 19–33.

Mowery D.C., Rosenberg N. (1989) *Technology and the Pursuit of Economic Growth*, Cambridge, Cambridge University Press.

Murmann J.P. (2003) *Knowledge and Competitive Advantage: The Co-evolution of Firms, Technologies and National institutions*, Cambridge, Cambridge University Press.

Musson A.E., Robinson E. (1969) *Science and Technology in the Industrial Revolution*, Manchester, Manchester University Press.

Nelson R.R. (1959) The simple economics of basic scientific research. *Journal of Political Economy*, 67: 297–306.

Nelson R.R. (1994) The co-evolution of technology, industrial structure, and supporting institutions. *Industrial and Corporate Change*, 3(1): 47–63.

Nelson R., Winter S. (1982) *An Evolutionary Theory of Economic Change*, Cambridge, MA, Harvard University Press.

Nelson R.R., Rosenberg N. (1993) Technical innovation and national systems, in Nelson R.R. (Ed), *National Systems of Innovation: A Comparative Study*, Oxford: Oxford University Press, pp. 3–21.

Nesta L. (2001) Cohérence des bases de connaissances et changement technique: une analyse des firmes de biotechnologies de 1981 à 1997 PhD Thesis, GAEL Grenoble Applied Economics Laboratory.

Nesta L., Saviotti P.P. (2005) Coherence of the knowledge base and the firm's innovative performance: evidence from the U.S. pharmaceutical industry. *Journal of Industrial Economics*, 53: 123–142.

Nesta L., Saviotti P.P. (2006) Firm knowledge and market value in biotechnology. *Industrial and Corporate Change*, 15: 625–652.

Nesta L. Saviotti P.P. (2014) Coherence of the knowledge base and the firm's innovative performance: evidence from the U.S. Pharmaceutical Industry, in Link A.N., Antonelli C. (Eds), *Recent Developments in The Economics of Science and Innovation*, Cheltenham, Edward Elgar, 245–267.

Nightingale P. (1998) A cognitive model of innovation. *Research Policy*, 27: 689–709.

Nooteboom B. (1999) *Inter-Firm Alliances: Analysis and Design*, London, Routledge.

Nooteboom B. (2000) *Learning and Innovation in Organizations and Economies*, Oxford: Oxford University Press.

Nooteboom B. (2007) Transaction costs, innovation and learning, in Hanusch H., Pyka A. (Eds), *Elgar Companion to Neo-Schumpeterian Economics*, Cheltenham, Edward Elgar, 1010–1044.

Ormerod P. (2015) *The Economics of Radical Uncertainty*, 9, 2015–41 | November 20, 2015 | http://dx.doi.org/10.5018/economics-ejournal.ja.2015-41

Penrose E. (1959, 1995) *The Theory of the Growth of the Firm*, Oxford, Oxford University Press.

Pinch, T.J., Bijker W.E. (August 1984) The social construction of facts and artefacts: or how the sociology of science and the sociology of technology might benefit each other. *Social Studies of Science* 14: 399–441. http://dx.doi.org/10.1177/030631284014003004

Polanyi M. (1958) *Personal Knowledge: Towards a Post-Critical Philosophy*, London, Routledge.

Popper K.R. (1934) *The Logic of Scientific Discovery*, London, Hutchinson.

Popper K.R. (1972) *Objective Knowledge, An Evolutionary Approach*, Oxford: Oxford University Press.

Powell W., Koput K.W., Smith-Doerr L. (1996) Inter-organisational collaboration and the locus of innovation: networks of learning in biotechnology. *Administrative Science Quarterly*, 41: 116–145.

Prahalad C.K., Hamel G. (1990) The core competences of the corporation. *Harvard Business Review*, 68(3): 79–90.

Romer P. (1990) Endogenous technical progress, *Journal of Political Economy*, 98 (5): S71–S102. Part 2: The Problem of Development: A Conference of the Institute for the Study of Free Enterprise Systems. (Oct., 1990).

Rosenberg N., Birdzell L.E. (1986) *How the West Grew Rich*, New York, Basic Books.

Rosenbloom R.S., Christensen C.M. (1994) Technological discontinuities, organizational capabilities, and strategic commitments, *Industrial and Corporate Change*, 3(3): 655–668.

Saviotti P.P. (1996) *Technological Evolution, Variety and the Economy*, Cheltenham, Edward Elgar.

Saviotti P.P. (2004) Considerations about knowledge production and strategies, *Journal of Institutional and Theoretical Economics*, 160: 100–121.

Saviotti P.P. (2005) On the co-evolution of technologies and Institutions, pp 9–31 in Weber M., Hemmelskamp J. (Eds), *Towards Environmental Innovation Systems*, Berlin, Heidelberg, New York, Springer.

Saviotti P.P. (2007) On the dynamics of generation and utilisation of knowledge: the local character of knowledge, *Structural Change and Economic Dynamics*, 18: 387–408.

Saviotti P.P., Catherine D. (2008) Innovation networks in biotechnology, in Holger Patzelt, Thomas Brenner (Eds), *Handbook of Bioentrepreneurship*, New York, Springer, pp. 53–82.

Saviotti P.P., de Looze M.A., Maupertuis, M.A. (2005) Knowledge dynamics and the mergers of firms in the biotechnology-based sectors, *Economics of Innovation and New Technology*, 14: 103–124.

Saviotti P.P., de Looze M.A., Maupertuis M.A., Nesta L. (2003) Knowledge dynamics and the mergers of firms in the biotechnology-based sectors, *International Journal of Biotechnology*, 5: 371–401.

Saxenian A. (1991) The origins and dynamics of production networks in silicon valley, *Research Policy*, 20(5): 423–437.

Shannon C.E., Weaver W. (1949) *The Mathematical Theory of Communication*, Urbana, University of Illinois Press.

Simon H.A. (1965) *Administrative Behaviour,* 2nd Ed, New York, Free Press.

Smith A. (1776) *The Wealth of Nations*, Penguin English Library, 1972 and following reprints.

Sorenson O., Rivkin J.V., Fleming L. (2006) Complexity, networks and knowledge flow, *Research Policy*, 35(7): 994–1017.

Stichweh R. (1992) The sociology of scientific disciplines: on the genesis and stability of the disciplinary structure of modern science, *Science in Context*, 5(01): 3–15. http://dx.doi.org/10.1017/S0269889700001071, Published online: 26 September 2008.

Teece D.J. (1986) Profiting from technological innovation, *Research Policy*, 15: 285–305.

Teece D.J., Rumelt R., Dosi G., Winter S.G. (1994) Understanding corporate coherence: theory and evidence, *Journal of Economic Behavior and Organisation*, 22: 1–30.

Tushman M.L., Anderson P. (1986) Technological discontinuities and organizational environments, *Administrative Science Quarterly*, 31: 439–465.

Vincenti W.G. (1990) *What Engineers Know and How They Know It*, Baltimore, MD, Johns Hopkins University Press.

Weber M. (1968) *The Protestant Ethic and the Spirit of Capitalism*, London: Unwin University Books, first British edition, 1930.

Weitzmann M.L. (1998) Recombinant growth, *Quarterly Journal of Economics*, 113: 331–360.

5 Structural change, differentiation, and economic development

In the previous chapters we introduced what we consider the fundamental entities of innovation, that we call Man-made Artefacts (MMAs), and we explained that any two MMAs are qualitatively different (Chapter 1). Then, in Chapter 2, we discussed the distinction between qualitative and quantitative change and its implications for many MMAs, such as demand and competition. In Chapter 3 we introduced a general form of socioeconomic behaviour that we call adaptive, which should encompass optimizing rationality as a special case. In Chapter 4 we discussed human knowledge as an activity which is in principle separable from production but which has a growing influence on it. In fact, most of the development that occurred since the industrial revolution is likely to have been growingly affected by changes in human knowledge. In the present chapter we move from entities and behaviour to aggregate and dynamic patterns of change. Here we start with economic growth and development. The analysis of qualitative change introduced in Chapters 1 and 2 will be used to analyse the structure of an SES and to see how this affects economic development.

The concept of growth entails a purely quantitative measure of the change in the 'size' of an SES, or its value. The concept of development is much broader and encompasses many qualitatively different components, such as different sectors, corresponding to different economic activities, but also many types of institutions and organizations. The combination of the various components of the SES and their interactions constitutes the structure of the SES. Growth and development are related in the sense that changes in the structure of the SES affect its growth potential but also that growth tends to induce changes in the structure of the SES. This interaction of different components of the system has already been referred to as the coevolution of different components of the SES (Chapter 1). As was previously pointed out, the use of the term 'SES' derives from the non-complete separability of strictly called economic activities from other activities that, although not strictly economic, affect the economic ones.

It is our conviction, although not one that is shared by all economists, that economic growth in the long run cannot be sustained without changes in the structure of the economic system, or that structural change is a determinant

DOI: 10.4324/9781003294221-5

of growth. We will start by distinguishing approaches to economic growth and development that analyse growth without structural change. Subsequently, we will analyse the relationship between structural change and variety, pointing to the importance in recent research of variety enhancing structural change. Our discussion will be based on a broader concept of structure than the one adopted by the precursors and early exponents of the literature on structural change. Our conception of structure will be systemic, based on the components of a system and on their interactions.

In this chapter we will endeavour to show that neither economic development nor economic growth as we know them could have been taking place without structural change. Furthermore, we will refer to recent developments in the literature pointing towards a type of structural change which is both variety and complexity enhancing. In particular, the type of structural change we are discussing leads to the diversification of the SES and is required to maintain growth in the long run. Thus, in this chapter, we will explain why and by what mechanisms structural change contributes to long-term economic growth and development.

We will start by laying out some stylized facts that will be the source of phenomena and processes to be explained and will be the testing ground for our theories and models. We will be concerned with the long run because we think that some important trends and mechanisms occur over periods of time which are long with respect to the average duration of human life and, even more so, with respect to the typical time horizon of human beings and human organizations. Yet, for their apparent distance from us, some long-run trends affect our everyday activities and SESs need to adapt to them both to take advantage of their opportunities and to limit their inherent damages.

1 From stylized facts to theoretical understanding

1.1 Stylized facts

A stylized fact that will be very important in this book is the gradual differentiation of SESs which occurred in the course of human history. One of the earliest forms of differentiation occurred with transition from hunters and gatherers to settled agriculture. The higher efficiency in food production was accompanied by the emergence of other (non-food production) activities, such as those involving traders, priests and administrators (Diamond, 1997). It would have been impossible to develop without inventing new kinds of work (Jacobs, 1969).

> They (our remote ancestors) expanded their economies by adding new kinds of work. So do we. Innovating economies expand and develop. Economies that do not add new kinds of goods and services, but continue only to repeat old work, do not expand much nor do they, by definition, develop.
> (p. 49)

We could also say that the production of tools was the basis for the differentiation of human activities. However, although this trend has certainly accelerated since the time of the industrial revolution, and even more so since the beginning of the XXth century, Adam Smith was already aware that the more developed SESs were more diversified than the less developed ones:

> Though in a rude society there is a good deal of variety in the occupations of every individual, there is not a great deal in those of the whole society.... In a civilized state, on the contrary, though there is little variety in the occupations of the greater part of individuals, there is an almost infinite variety in those of the whole society.
>
> (Smith, 1776, p. 430)

Two types of division of labour were at the basis of this diversification: the first, which has remained closely associated with the name of Adam Smith, and that we will call Smithian, consists of dividing a process giving rise to a given output (e.g. pins) into a growing number of steps, where each worker would carry out one step and pass the result to the next worker; the second which consists of creating new technologies, which can give rise to new production processes and new types of output. Both of them were present in Adam Smith, although the former was described in much greater detail and remained closely associated with his name. The latter form of division of labour was arising from

> those who are called philosophers or men of speculation, whose trade is not to do anything but to observe everything; and who upon that account are often capable of combining the powers of the most distant and dissimilar objects. In the progress of society philosophy, or speculation, becomes the principal or sole trade and occupation of a particular class of citizens.
>
> (Smith, 1776, p. 115)

This second type of division of labour is the result of innovation and we will call it Schumpeterian because, although it was already present in Adam Smith, it was much more central in Schumpeter's work. In a sense, changes in both forms of division of labour are the result of innovation, the former of organizational innovation and the latter of technological innovation. In this book we will use the term 'innovation' in a general sense, including technological, organizational and institutional innovation. In what follows, we will see that the process of differentiation of SESs is due to the interaction and coevolution of innovations of these three types. The differentiation of SESs led to a change in their structure through the emergence of new components (new sectors, new institutions, new organizational forms) and by their changing interactions.

Three stylized facts which have heavily affected the differentiation of the SES since the industrial revolution, and even more so since the beginning of the XXth century, are the increasing efficiency of productive processes (ST1), the rise in the number of industrial sectors (ST2) and the increasing output quality and internal diversification of existing sectors (ST3).

(ST 1) The efficiency of productive processes increases in the course of time. Productive efficiency will be defined in Section 2.
(ST 2) The net number of distinguishable industrial sectors resulting from the emergence of new sectors and the extinction of pre-existing ones increases in the course of time.[1 2]
(ST3) The output quality and internal diversification of most sectors increase in the course of time.

Each of these trends constitutes a long-term trajectory. Due to these trajectories and their interactions, the output variety of the industrial subsystem increased at both the inter-sectoral and the intra-sectoral levels of aggregation.

These changes in production were accompanied by several institutional changes, such as the emergence of the factory system (Mokyr, 1990), the modern firm (Rosenberg, Birdzell, 1986), different types of corporations (U and M form) (Chandler, 1962, 1977), the R&D function (Freeman, Soete, 1997), and the diffusion of education (Goldin, Katz, 2008). Furthermore, a number of reforms in workers' rights, health care and social assistance gave rise to what we now call a welfare state[3] (Fraser, 1973; Esping-Andersen, 1990). These changes amounted to a profound modification of the structure of the SES by introducing many new components and interactions. Furthermore, the same changes made the boundaries between economic and non-economic activities much fuzzier, correspondingly rendering the concept of 'homo economicus' more problematic. In some cases, the new components existed previously but were of marginal importance in the societies of their time, while now they employ a large share of manpower and are the source of important economic activities. For example, in advanced industrialized countries, the healthcare system generates a large part of the demand for pharmaceutical products and medical equipment.

The considerable increase in the average level of education of the populations of industrialized countries combined with the exponential growth of knowledge production gave rise to what is called a knowledge-based society or a knowledge-based economy, in which knowledge becomes the most important factor in economic growth and development. The emergence of the knowledge-based society was not a sudden phenomenon but a gradual one which began in the second half of the XIXth century and acquired an increasing momentum in the XXth century. The development of a knowledge-based society was discussed in greater detail in Chapter 4, but here we wish to stress that it included the emergence of a new economic function, R&D (Freeman, Soete, 1997), the very considerable increase in importance of education (Goldin, Katz, 2008) and the growing importance of human capital relative to physical capital (Becker, 1964).

The previous stylized facts do not provide a complete description of the economic development which occurred in the XIXth and XXth centuries but highlight two trends: first, the differentiation of the SES was not limited to the productive sectors of the economy but involved other activities and institutions which were not previously considered as economic but which affected heavily the economic system; second, the new activities did not emerge and develop independently but interacted in the course of time, giving rise to considerable changes in the structure of the SES.

1.2 Efficiency and creativity

To start with we need to define some fundamental concepts. First, we will use the definition of efficiency introduced in Chapter 1 as the ratio of the output obtained to the inputs used, when the type of output remains qualitatively constant. Productivity, whether labour or total factor, is usually considered a factor affecting the capacity of country or a region to grow. Productivity is assumed to play this important role due to the expectation that it measures the efficiency of a national or a regional economy. We introduce a different definition of efficiency because we think that both labour and total factor productivity measure not just efficiency but a combination of efficiency and value. Our definition has the advantage that an increase in efficiency coincides with a reduction in the environmental impact of the production process, since the same quantity of outputs can be obtained with lower quantity of inputs.[4] Furthermore, our definition of efficiency provides a better guide to economic policy than productivity: reducing the quantity of inputs required to produce one unit of output reduces both costs and environmental impact, giving rise to a win-win situation. The same thing cannot be said of productivity: in the present economic system it is possible to develop new MMAs which supply better services than existing ones and can find a large market while using larger quantities of inputs which have a harmful impact on the environment. However, our definition of efficiency cannot by itself explain the development occurred since the industrial revolution. To understand this, we need to introduce a second concept in addition to efficiency. We call *creativity* the capability to conceive new products and services qualitatively different from any pre-existing ones. In Chapters 1 and 2 we already discussed the difference between qualitative and quantitative change and the important role that both can play in economic development. Thus, a new sector will be new and will be classified in a new statistical category if it is qualitatively different from any pre-existing one.[5]

In most cases it is not difficult to decide whether two goods or services are qualitatively different or not. Thus, shoes and cars are clearly qualitatively different goods. However, there are a number of cases in which to distinguish between qualitative and quantitative change is not completely straightforward. In spite of these limitations, the difference between qualitative and quantitative change is still extremely useful.[6] A further source of ambiguity stems from the fact that even if a new sector is created by a qualitatively new good or service, during the subsequent evolution of the sector any further modifications of the given good or service can constitute an incremental and mostly quantitative change. Thus, although shoes and cars are qualitatively different goods, two different car models are considered different versions of the same good with different product quality.

Furthermore, product quality is measured by means of the values, or levels, of a number of common product characteristics (Lancaster, 1966). In other words, not only is quality measured, which already seems a contradiction in terms, but it is measured in terms of a common set of product characteristics. Of course, we are here in the presence of two types of creativity which differ for their inherent uncertainty: radical uncertainty for the case in which a completely new product is created and a more moderate uncertainty, almost merging with calculable risk, for the creation of a new model of a given product. However, the two of types of creativity are drastically different. Both types of creativity are different from efficiency but have very different implications for the life cycles of technologies and sectors.

Thus, both efficiency and creativity contributed to the observed process of economic development. However, the two variables did not act independently but interacted continuously. To understand this point, we can ask whether output growth could continue indefinitely in an SES having a constant structure, that is constituted by the same activities and sectors, but in which there was only efficiency growth. In this case the same type of outputs would be produced all the times with a constantly falling amount of labour per unit of output. In particular, the labour intensity of production processes could be expected to fall as production efficiency increased. The unit cost of outputs would then fall and, unless demand for them increased to the same extent, labour displacement could follow. This could be avoided by several mechanisms that we generally call compensation. For example, compensation for the labour displacement due to increasing productive efficiency could occur if the falling cost and price of outputs induced a rise in their demand sufficient to raise employment to produce a higher output. Other compensation mechanisms have been discussed in the literature since Ricardo and the main ones have been reviewed by Vivarelli (1995, 2007a, 2007b, 2014):

1. New machines
2. New investments
3. Decrease in wages
4. Increase in incomes
5. New products

These mechanisms have variable effectiveness in compensating for the labour displacement due to increasing productive efficiency. Vivarelli finds that

'New products'[7] is the most effective in this respect. However, 'New products' can be those which are qualitatively different from any pre-existing ones and which give rise to new sectors, or new variants of pre-existing products. Although we admit that all the compensation mechanisms listed by Vivarelli (1995, 2007a, 2007b, 2014) can play a role, we focus in particular on the creation of new economic activities and new sectors resulting from the emergence of new products and services because we consider it the most important compensation mechanism. We consider this the most important compensation mechanism because (i) there is growing empirical evidence that many new sectors have been created since the industrial revolution and that they have enormously contributed to economic growth (Chandler, 2009) and (ii) the output and employment share of incumbent sectors keeps falling in the course of time (Metcalfe et al., 2005; Fabricant, 1940, 1942).

None of the mechanisms listed by Vivarelli could alone have contributed to lasting economic growth. No price elasticity of demand was likely to provide full compensation whatever the rate of fall of price for outputs of existing sectors. The emergence of new sectors can be explained by the relative rates of growth of income elasticity of demand and of price to elasticity of demand (Saviotti, 2001): when income per capita increases consumers prefer to purchase new goods and services rather than more of the old ones. This stylized fact was first observed by Engel (1857) who noticed that as their income increased households spent a declining share of it on food and necessities. However, even if the total saturation of incumbent sectors assumed by Pasinetti (1981, 1993) does not always occur (Chai, Moneta, 2010), in general the rate of growth of demand for a given output type tends to fall in the course of time (Saviotti, Pyka, 2017), providing an inducement for the emergence of new sectors.

Thus, we have established that the creation of qualitatively new economic sectors could not be due to productive efficiency alone but required the presence of both creativity and efficiency as previously defined. To complete our analysis, we have to explain how creativity originates. To do this, we can use the distinction between routines and search activities introduced by Nelson and Winter (1982) and consider that all economic activities can be classified into one of these two categories. We expect existing routines to contribute to the continuously increasing efficiency of productive processes, thus creating a surplus which can be used to finance search activities. In turn, search activities become the source of a pool of new ideas that can be developed to create new sectors. Thus, in the same way in which an economic system driven only by productive efficiency would find a bottleneck, search activities could not be carried out without the surplus generated by rising productive efficiency. In other words, efficiency and creativity are complementary and search activities are the source of creativity.

Search activities scan the external environment to understand its constituting entities and the laws governing it. As a consequence, search activities enhance our ability to modify our external environment contributing to create future production routines that will substitute or complement existing ones. The necessary consequence of this is the change in the structure of the SES, by the emergence of new activities and by the changing share of all activities, new and old. Thus, structural change occurs and it is a necessary condition for the long-run continuation of economic development. However, not only new sectors emerge and old sectors disappear, but more new sectors have been created than pre-existing ones substituted. There is growing empirical evidence that growth is accompanied by a growing output variety in the production system (Funke, Ruhwedel, 2001a, 2001b; Imbs, Wacziarg, 2003; Frenken et al., 2007; Saviotti, Frenken, 2008; Hidalgo et al., 2007; Hidalgo, Hausmann, 2009; Felipe et al., 2012). This implies that more new sectors have been created than pre-existing ones substituted. Thus, although horse-driven coaches have been substituted by cars, buses and trains, we still produce food, clothing and housing. Furthermore, radio, television and telephones substituted the sending of messages by other means, including mail sent by horses, pigeons and smoke signals. Also, new materials such as plastics did not completely substitute wood and steel but created many new possible uses. Thus, overall, the net number of activities constituting the economic system has been increasing in the course of economic development and this has compensated for the potential labour displacement induced by growing productive efficiency in pre-existing sectors.

In the course of time, both creativity and productive efficiency alter the structure of the SES: the former by adding new sectors and eliminating some pre-existing ones, the latter by changing the output shares of pre-existing sectors. Thus, structural change is not an epiphenomenon of economic development but an essential component of it. Furthermore, the structural change involved here is unidirectional, an arrow of time in which higher levels of development are achieved by increasing the output variety of the SES. This implies that the Schumpeterian concept of creative destruction cannot be interpreted as the substitution of pre-existing goods services and processes by new ones because this would lead to output variety remaining constant in time. However, creative destruction still exists because the output share of incumbent goods, services and processes tends to fall in the course of time (Metcalfe et al., 2005; Fabricant, 1940, 1942). Creative destruction is based on the joint effect of productive efficiency and creativity which needs to squeeze the past in order to create the future.

1.3 Structural change, differentiation and economic development

The previous considerations amount to saying that the output variety of an SES needs to increase for economic development to continue in the long run. Thus, not only the type of economic development that contributes to economic growth involves structural change, but it involves a unidirectional form of structural change, an arrow of time, according to which the output variety of the SES needs to increase in the course of time (Saviotti, 1996). Using a model called TEVECON, Saviotti and Pyka (2004) demonstrated that the development bottleneck identified by Pasinetti (1981), due to the imbalance between continuously growing productivity and saturating demand, could be overcome if the fall of employment in older sectors was compensated by the employment created by new sectors. In subsequent papers (Saviotti, Pyka, 2008a, 2008b), they introduced a demand function containing output quality and output diversification (Eq. 5.1), thus representing the two trajectories ST2 and ST3 two compensation mechanisms, the emergence of new sectors and their internal diversification. These two trajectories are not independent but contribute both to the differentiation of the economic system and to the compensation discussed before.

$$D_i^t = k_{pref,i} D_i^0 D_{Disp,i} \frac{Y_i * \Delta Y_i}{p_i} \tag{5.1}$$

The impact of these two trajectories was then compared (Saviotti, Pyka, 2013) by means of two scenarios called Low Quality (LQ) and High Quality (HQ), where the former consisted only of inter-sector differentiation while the latter included both inter- and intra-sector diversification. Interestingly, the macroeconomic growth path of the two scenarios turned out to be very different. While the rate of growth of employment would have been higher in the LQ scenario (Figure 5.1), this result would have been obtained by holding wages and the quality of human capital constant in the course of economic development (Figures 5.3 and 5.4). Furthermore, the rate of income creation would have been higher in the LQ scenario during the early phases of economic development but would have become higher in the HQ scenario during later phases (Figure 5.2). On the contrary, the HQ scenario would have led to increasing wages and quality of human capital, and to a higher rate of growth of income after an initial period. These results imply that if there had been a choice between favouring full employment and favouring a higher rate of growth of income, the former would he been chosen initially and the latter in subsequent phases. It is worth noticing that the small humps on the curves in Figures 5.1 and 5.2 correspond to the Industry Life Cycles (ICLs) of the sectors generated during economic development. Such ICLs are much shorter in the LQ scenario, when product quality does not change, and much longer in the HQ scenario, when product quality keeps increasing. The reason for this different duration of ICLs is that, in the absence of changes in product quality, market saturation occurs more quickly when every potential buyer has bought one unit of the product. Conversely, when product quality increases and products become increasingly diversified, potential buyers have a wider range of options, for example, to jump from a product model to another one of higher quality and price. This lengthens the ICL and increases its cumulative value along the ICL. The two cases correspond to *volume saturation* (LQ) and *value saturation* (HQ). Thus, volume saturation occurs much more rapidly, requires relatively low values of human capital, and leads to lower wages than value saturation.

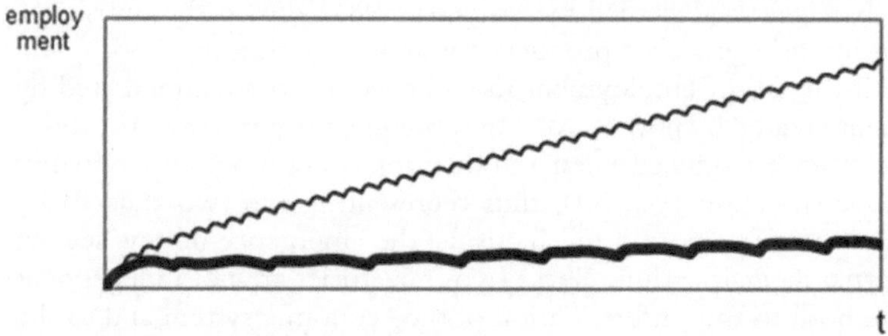

Figure 5.1 Effect of the transition from the LQ to the HQ scenario on aggregate employment. Light curve LQ, thick curve HQ.

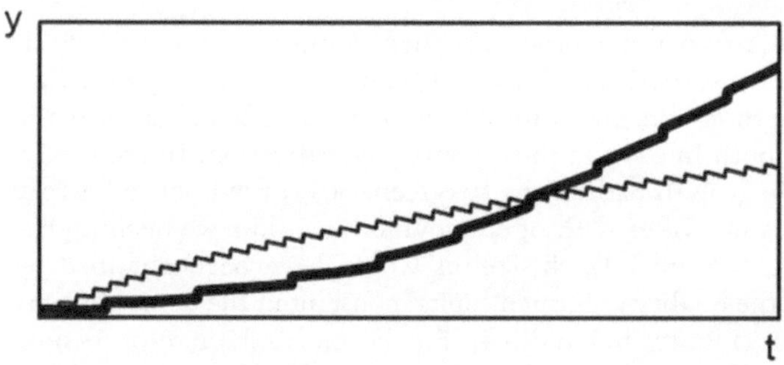

Figure 5.2 The effect of the transition from the LQ to the HQ scenario on patterns of income generation. Light curve LQ, thick curve HQ. Y = income, t = time.

This finding can explain the intra-industry distribution of production locations and the flows of intra-industry trade: multinationals producing multi-characteristic products such as cars, electrical appliances and portable telephones tend to produce the high-quality models in countries having higher levels of competencies and wages and the low-quality models in countries having lower levels of competencies and wages. Furthermore, corresponding to this distribution of production, low-quality product models tend to be exported predominantly from low-wage countries to high-wage countries and high-quality product models from high-wage countries to low-wage countries. An additional difference between the LQ and HQ scenarios is the evolution of demand. As shown in Figure 5.5, demand grows much more rapidly in the HQ scenario than in the LQ scenario. Furthermore, as disposable income, product quality and diversification increase during economic development, the shape of demand curves changes by including an initial upward-sloping part because the bestselling models are not the cheapest ones (Figure 5.5). In other words, while both inter-sector differentiation (ST2) and intra-sector diversification (ST3) contribute to creating new employment, thus compensating for the employment displacing effect of growing

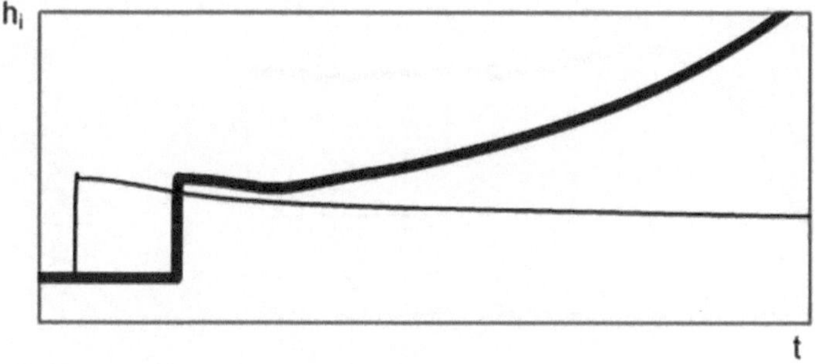

Figure 5.3 The effect of the transition from the LQ to the HQ scenario on the quality of human capital, h_i. Light curve LQ, thick curve HQ.

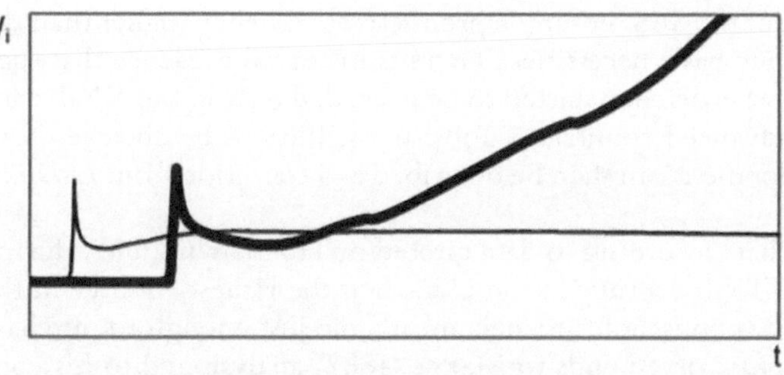

Figure 5.4 Effect of product quality on sectoral wages. Light curve for LQ, thick curve for HQ.

efficiency, the mechanisms by which this occurs are quite different for ST2 and ST3.

A further trend in long-run economic development is due to the combination of an asymmetry between the nature of consumption and the rate of growth of productive efficiency. Although differentiation consists of the emergence of new sectors, these sectors are not all the same. First, some of the sectors correspond to the production of 'basic necessities' of biological origin without which human beings cannot survive. These necessities include food, clothing and housing. Unless these necessities are satisfied, the supply and demand of other types of goods and services corresponding to 'higher' forms of consumption cannot be created. In other words, if all of consumers' income had to be spent on basic necessities, no income would be left for the purchase of other goods and services corresponding to 'higher' forms of consumption.[8] The creation of the disposable income required to purchase 'higher' types of goods and services involved an increase in the productive efficiency of basic necessities which gave rise to a surplus which in turn became the disposable income, enabling the purchase of 'higher' types of goods and services. Thus,

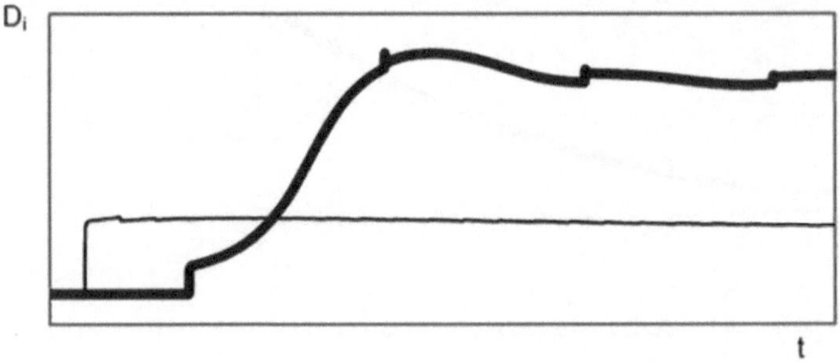

Figure 5.5 Effect of product quality on sectoral demand. Light curve for LQ, thick curve for HQ.

the diversification of the SES requires a productive efficiency higher than the one needed to supply basic necessities. There is historical evidence that such threshold productive efficiency started to be exceeded only in the XXth century in the most advanced countries (Hobsbawm, 1968). The observed path of economic development can then be described as a transition from *necessities to imaginary words*.

Let us observe that, according to data quoted by Hobsbawm (ibid), during the whole of the XIXth century in the UK, then the richest country in the world, working-class households earned an income just enough to purchase basic necessities. This corresponds to Marx's (1887) analysis and to his conclusion that capitalism would only pay workers enough to ensure their physical survival. The question which then arises is: why did this change in the XXth century? Was it simply the automatic result of a natural increase in productive efficiency or was it the rise of the working class and of its capacity to challenge the established capitalist order? Or, was the transition to imaginary worlds a compensation mechanism required to avoid the efficiency-induced bottleneck described in Section 1.2? To separate these mechanisms is likely to be extremely difficult. It is even possible, and we would say likely, that these different mechanisms have operated together in a coevolutionary fashion.

Finally, let us observe that the transition from necessities to imaginary worlds represents a unidirectional path, unlikely to be reversed unless a dramatic fall in productive efficiency occurred. The process of economic development can then be interpreted as a gradual move away from a human life dominated by biological constraints to one in which man-made constraints increasingly dominate human history.

The growth in size of each sector and the overall economic system can induce a form of differentiation by specialization. As the market corresponding to a given sector grows in size it becomes possible to develop separate subsets of the same output into different ones. Examples of this specialization process are the emergence of cars, trucks and buses from what was once a horseless coach, or that of civilian and military airplanes from the first flying machines.

1.4 Services

The above discussion was centred on manufacturing, but most of employment today is in services. In a sense the gradual shift to services can be considered another compensation mechanism contributing to preserving employment in the presence of the effect of labour substitution effect of increasing productive efficiency. Although services are a residual and heterogeneous category, some general features can be found for the sector (Miles, 2005):

1 Many service products are intangible ones.
2 Many service products are often consumed and produced during supplier-client interaction at a given time and place.
3 Many services are highly information-intensive with a preponderance of office-based work or communicative and translational activities.

However, intangible services are less different from manufactured goods than what we could think. From the twin characteristic representation of physical products given in Chapter 1, it follows that today most production is production of services, whether in an embodied or in a disembodied form. Services are supplied in an embodied form by heterogeneous multi-characteristics physical products having a materially based internal structure and supplying services. In this case the knowledge base of producers needs to cover aspects related to the manipulation of matter (e.g., melting and shaping materials, the nature of combustion processes) and to the needs and wants of consumers. However, for disembodied, or direct, services, knowledge related to the manipulation of matter is likely to be relatively less important than knowledge related to the needs and wants of consumers.

Historically, the scientific fields that progressed more rapidly from the early part of the industrial revolution to the second half of the XXth century (chemistry, physics, metallurgy, etc.) improved greatly the capacity of human beings to produce energy and manipulate matter. This gave rise to a very rapid increase in the output of some manufacturing sectors (textiles, steel, chemicals, etc.). During the second half of the XIXth century, the relationship between science and technology became more systematic and intense through the creation of German University system and the institutionalization of industrial R&D (Hounshell, Smith, 1988; Reich, 1985, Murmann, 2003). This led to the creation of new sectors or subsectors, such as fine chemicals, pharmaceuticals and electricity (Freeman, Soete, 1997; Freeman Louca, 2001). The enormous increase in output that the innovations creating these sectors induced gave rise to an increased administrative workload, but there was no corresponding improvement in the technology required to document and process the increased flows in matter, energy and information. Innovations such as the typing machine facilitated the task of representing, classifying, and communicating the information about these increased flows, but could not eliminate the rise in employment in administrative activities. The planning, estimating and layout departments of firms which grew together with the 'Scientific Management' movement in the USA originated the large engineering and record-keeping divisions of modern corporations (Braverman, 1974, p. 126). While the objective of Scientific Management was to deprive at least a part of workers of 'thinking' jobs, it is extremely unlikely that it did not increase the efficiency of administrative work, even if not to the extent required to catch up with the efficiency growth of matter manipulation operations. In other words, the increasing efficiency in matter manipulation had not been matched by a corresponding increase in information storage and processing. In the presence of this mismatch, it became possible to reduce employment per unit of output in matter manipulation faster than in the corresponding activities involved in information storage and processing. Consequently, the share of employment involving information processing, that we can call administrative activities, increased at the expense of the activities involving matter manipulation. This is likely to have happened to an extent superior to that shown by employment statistics since today, even in manufacturing sectors, most employment is in office-based administrative functions. The differential rate of growth of efficiency in manufacturing relative to services is likely to fall in future due to the progress in ITCs. Although ITCs increased the efficiency of both matter manipulation and information processing, they are likely to have affected the latter more than the former (Miles, 2005). Consequently, one of the possible compensation mechanisms that contributed to keep employment high could become less effective (Frey, Osborne, 2017).

Other service activities that are less closely related to manufacturing, such as education, health care and tourism, have enormously increased in advanced industrialized societies. These would not have been considered economic in the past but interact heavily with manufacturing activities. As examples of these interactions, we can think about the impact of education on product quality (eResources Chapter 5), healthcare policies on the pharmaceutical industry or innovations in transport and telecommunications on tourism. The emergence of all these activities redefined the structure of the SES and affected heavily the distribution of employment.

1.5 Structure, order and change

The concepts of order and structure imply that the most elementary components of an economic system cannot be assembled randomly but that they need to be organized according to some order. Such order, or structure, is not invariable in the course of time, but can undergo both qualitative and quantitative changes. Qualitative change gives rise to the emergence of new components, qualitatively different from pre-existing ones. Quantitative changes modify the *size* of the whole system or the *relative sizes* of its components. The structure of a complex economic system is constituted by its components and their interactions. The structure of an economic system can be defined at several levels of aggregation, ranging from micro to meso (Dopfer, Foster,

Potts, 2004; Dopfer, Potts, 2008; Dopfer, 2013) and to macro. In principle, we can expect aggregate outcomes, such as overall output, employment, or growth, to depend on the structure of the economic system considering all the possible levels of aggregation. The calculation of such aggregate outcomes with all the possible levels of aggregation would be extremely costly if not impossible. Thus, approximate representations considering only some levels of aggregation are developed. The simplest such representation is the macro-macro, in which aggregate outcome (e.g., growth) can be calculated starting from other macro variables (e.g., labour or capital). Despite its simplicity, a macro-macro representation is insufficient, because it neglects the potential influence of micro and meso variables on aggregate outcomes. A macro-macro representation eliminates structural change.

In order to understand what growth would resemble if there were no structural change, let us consider the hypothetical case in which the economic system had a constant number of components/sectors but their output could grow in the course of time. Furthermore, if the rate of growth of output were to be the same for all components/sectors, there would be growth without structural change since the output share of all components/sectors would remain constant over time. Such growth pattern does not resemble that of any country over any extended period. In this case, which can be called *proportional growth*, there would be only quantitative growth. On the contrary, typically over the long run, growth occurs with the emergence of new sectors, with their internal diversification and with changing sectoral output and employment shares (Metcalfe et al. 2005; Fabricant, 1940, 1942). According to Pasinetti (1981, 1993), the above type of growth pattern could occur if the rate of growth of efficiency were the same for all sectors and if it were the same as the rate of growth of demand for all sectors. Such conditions are not observed in general and their absence explains why structural change is systematically associated with growth.

Qualitatively new goods and services are usually created by Schumpeterian entrepreneurs in a situation of limited knowledge and without the institutions required for the new technology to develop fully. Furthermore, generally the new technology needs complementary infrastructures and industries supplying inputs or services. The classic example is, of course, the automobile, which needed institutions defining how it had to be used for the benefit of mankind, roads and motorways on which it could travel, industries producing the required fuel and lubricants. In addition to these direct interactions, the new technology induced indirect interactions with the structure of cities and with tourism, enabling both to occur over much larger spaces than it would have been possible before. The process described here for the automobile is an example of the coevolution of technologies, infrastructures, and institutions (Nelson, 1994; Perez, 1983; Murmann, 2003; Saviotti, 2005; Geels, 2002a, 2002b, 2004). We wish to stress that coevolution is by no means a rare process but that it plays a fundamental role in economic development by accelerating the emergence of new technologies and by amplifying their potential markets. In a network representation, we can expect a new node corresponding to a new economic species and a new technology to induce (a) the shrinking or disappearance of older nodes and links, and (b) the formation of new nodes and links, contributing to change dynamically the structure of the economic system. If we represent an economic system as a network, the variety of the economic system is likely to rise since in general the number of new activities and the corresponding nodes can be expected to be greater than that of the disappearing activities. Thus, we expect (i) the variety of the network representing a given economic system to increase during economic development, and (ii) the density or connectivity of the network to rise or fall depending on the ratio of the rates of creation of new nodes and of the formation of new links.

All what has been said so far in this chapter implies that economic development could never have occurred without structural change. Does this statement allow us to say that structural change is a determinant, or even a cause of economic growth? Probably, the term cause should be reserved for factors like labour, capital, raw materials, energy, or even innovation and knowledge. These are primary determinants which modify the structure of the economic system. The extent of structural change depends on the balance between efficiency and creativity. In turn, the resulting growth depends on the rate at which new sectors are created, the shape of their industry life cycles and the market-size corresponding to each sector. Thus, rather than a cause of growth, structural change can be considered a *mechanism* that transforms primary factors into a given quantity and quality of outputs. If such factors were combined in ways that do not lead to structural change, growth would be unlikely to be economically sustainable in the long run. This shows that the determinants of growth cannot be located only at the microeconomic level but also at intermediate (meso) levels of aggregation, where the structure of the system changes. Furthermore, the concept of causality becomes problematic in the presence of coevolution. In this case, if two or more factors interact with positive feedback reinforcing each other, can we then say which one is the cause? For a given set and quantities of primary factors, the resultant growth depends on the strength of interactions in the feedback loops. Consequently, we can still say that structural change is a mechanism leading to growth and that it enables the continuation of growth in the long run.

2 Structural change and differentiation in the literature on economic growth and development

2.1 A typology of models

2.1.1 Level of aggregation

All models of growth establish relationships, or connections, between several variables that are descriptors of the economic system. All existing growth models can be classified according to the level of aggregation at which such variables are measured. All models can then be classified as Macro to Macro (MAMA), Meso to Macro (MEMA) or Micro to Macro (MIMA).

MAMA models cannot be based on structural change since by definition they exclude the structure of the system. However, the papers describing some MAMA models, although formally excluding system structure from their mathematical treatments, could contain important insights about structural change. The advantages of MAMA models are essentially due to their simplicity, in that they considerably reduce the number of variables required to represent the economic system and the computational costs involved. Furthermore, they produce results that are intuitive and quite suitable to be transformed into policies. Their obvious limitations stem from their lack of structure: macro policies are in principle affected by the internal structure of the system but in ways that the MAMA models do not reveal.

MIMA models connect micro and macro variables of the system. They are the 'best' models in the sense that they are the most complete and provide the most exhaustive representation of the economic system. They can produce the same results as MAMA models plus many more. They can predict the effects of changing both micro and macro variables on the fine structure of the system. Clearly, MIMA models are superior to MAMA, but their obvious disadvantages are the extremely high data requirements and computational costs. Even today MIMA models are prohibitively expensive.

MEMA models are an intermediate case between MAMA and MIMA in the sense that they connect meso (Dopfer, Foster, Potts, 2004; Dopfer, Potts, 2008; Dopfer, 2013) and macro variables of the system. In complex systems there are several meaningful intermediate levels of aggregation, as opposed to infinitely many possible intermediate levels of aggregation. Fifty biological cells or 25 individuals are not meaningful levels of aggregation unless they are connected by interactions making them interdependent, as they would be in a biological organ or in a firm. Thus, the meso levels of aggregation are themselves part of the structure of the economic system in the sense that two economic systems with the same micro components but with different meso components are likely to perform differently. MEMA models are less complete than MIMA models but more, or much more, complete than MAMA models. Consequently, both their data requirements and their computational costs are intermediate between those of the other two types.

Clearly, both MIMA and MEMA models are explicitly structuralist, in the sense that they contain a representation of the structure of the economic system. Early growth models were generally MAMA models. This can partly be explained by their much lower data requirements and computational costs. Recently, increasing information about micro and meso aspects of economic systems has been inserted into growth models.

2.2 The emergence of unidirectional structural change

In this section we intend to review the main trends in the literature on economic growth and development to see to what extent they considered structural change and the type of unidirectional structural change that leads to a growing diversification of the economic system. This section is a summary of the paper by Saviotti, Pyka and Jun (2020), to which interested readers are referred for a more extended discussion. This section does not intend to be an exhaustive survey of all the papers ever published on growth and structural change, but it is more narrowly focused on the evolution from the early growth models, typically macro to macro (MAMA), to unidirectional, or variety-increasing, growth models, by the gradual inclusion of some structural features, endogenous technological change, and an endogenously variable number of sectors.

2.2.1 Level of aggregation

All the papers from those by Harrod (1939) and Domar (1946) to those of Solow (1956, 1957) were based on MAMA models, in which connections between different macro variables were established. MAMA models were simple and compact because they did not require any information about the structure of the SES, conceived as the components of the SES and their interactions. However, this advantage was paid for by the impossibility to establish any macroeconomic effects of micro and meso variables. Starting from the late 1980s, endogenous growth models (Romer, 1990; Aghion Howitt, 1992, Grossman, Helpman, 1991, 1994) started incorporating features such blueprints arising from R&D, different types of capital goods or product quality, belonging to intermediate levels of aggregation. The possibility to map empirically the structure of an SES by representing its sectors and the flows between them was established by the development of input output analysis (Leontieff, 1951, 1986). Models incorporating an explicit representation of different sectors were developed in different research traditions, for example, by Pasinetti (1981, 1993) at the Cambridge School, Saviotti and Pyka (2004, 2008a, 2008b, 2013) and Ciarli et al. (2019) in an evolutionary approach. Recently, empirical analysis based on networks allowed us to distinguish between related and unrelated variety (Frenken et al., 2007) and to construct a map of the product space of the world (Hidalgo et al., 2007; Hidalgo, Hausmann, 2009).

2.2.2 Stability vs change

While Harrod (1939) was worried about the stability of growth, considering both self-amplifying and self-reducing deviations from equilibrium, the subsequent neoclassical literature on growth, from Solow's papers (1956, 1957) and until endogenous growth ones, did not explicitly focus on the problem, but replaced it with the concept of balanced growth. According to Solow's model (1988), the economy converges to a balanced growth path, a situation where each variable of the model is growing at a constant rate. Balanced growth is opposed to the boom-and-bust nature of economic cycles. The concept of balanced growth is derived from Kaldor's (1957) stylized facts about (1) real output per man, (2) stock of real capital, (3) ratio of 1 and 2, (4) rate of profit on capital, (5) rate of growth of output per man in different countries and (6) high share of profits in income tends to have a high ratio of investment to output. An economy growing according to the first three or four rules is said to be in a balanced growth path (Solow, 1988, pp. 3–4). Recent literature (Whelan, 2004; Grossman et al., 2017) provided partial confirmation for the existence of balanced growth paths. We can observe that a balanced growth path is not necessarily the same thing as general equilibrium.

An explicit rejection of the concept of general equilibrium appeared in Kaldor's work (1972) following his attempt (Kaldor, 1956, 1957) to construct a coherent economic theory by combining Keynesian macroeconomics with the theory of imperfect competition. In this work Kaldor used a technical progress function rather than a production function; and adopted the concept of cumulative causation, first introduced by Myrdal, in which variables are linked in the determination of major processes. Hicks inherited the non-equilibrium nature of economic transformations from Kaldor (1972) and Joan Robinson (1956, 1973) (Lavoie, 1998). In his late work Hicks (1965) thought that an economy could not be all the time in a state of equilibrium but that it would spend at least part of the time in transition, or in a *traverse*, between different equilibrium states. In this way the work of Hicks and his followers (Amendola and Gaffard, 1998) opened the way for the analysis of a system out of equilibrium.

The rejection of general equilibrium was present beginning in evolutionary models of growth in which, following Schumpeter, innovation is expected to destroy any existing equilibrium (Schumpeter, 1911, 1934); Nelson Winter, 1982; Dosi, Nelson, 1994; Nelson, 1995; Arthur, 1989; Arthur et al., 1997; Saviotti, Metcalfe, 1991). In Schumpeter's work equilibrium can at best exist in periods in which the circular flow is not disrupted by innovations. As was pointed out in Chapter 3, in an innovative SES a general equilibrium cannot exist as a real state but only as an attractor determining the direction of change of the SES. General equilibrium can then be conceived as a special type of stability that can very rarely be attained. The most general problem is then the relationship between stability and change in SESs during economic development.

2.2.3 Qualitative vs quantitative change, heterogeneity

The role of qualitative change in economic development is very difficult to study and has in the past been avoided by concentrating on quantitative change. Sraffa (1963) questioned the possibility to measure capital at a macroeconomic level and pointed out that capital is a highly heterogeneous entity that could contain electric motors, steam engines, tractors, or lasers, that were qualitatively different and that could not simply be added up. The fact that capital components are qualitatively different could be held to imply that even if it were possible to additively aggregate different types of capital at a given time, the subsequent development of the economic system would depend on the differential rates of growth of its meso and micro components. Furthermore, Sraffa stressed that while capital depended on the rate of profit the rate of profit depended on capital. This potential circularity in reasoning is not just a mistake or a rare occurrence, but an example of the coevolution of two interdependent variables. While that seemed an anomaly in the 1930s it could be perceived as quite a normal mechanism of economic development today. This awareness of the role of qualitative change in economic development had to wait for the creation of input output analysis (Leontieff, 1951, 1986) in order to provide empirical applications and for Pasinetti's work (1981, 1993) to develop a model incorporating structural change.

2.2.4 Variety

This work established that the structure of the economic system could be mapped and that changes in that structure allowed the long-term continuation of economic development. However, input output analysis had to assume a constant number of sectors and it could not predict the direction of change of variety. In Pasinetti's work the imbalance between increasing efficiency and saturating demand can be overcome by the creation of new sectors. Thus, whether variety of the SES increases or decreases depends on the balance between the creation of new sectors and the extinction of older ones. In Saviotti and Pyka (2004, 2008, 2013), older sectors do not disappear, but their share of output and employment keeps falling in the course of economic development. Thus, not only there is structural change, but structural change is unidirectional, leading to a progressive diversification of the SES, an arrow of time accompanying economic development.

Amongst evolutionary growth models, the early ones (Nelson, Winter, 1982; Silverberg et al., 1988, Chiaromonte, Dosi, 1993; Silverberg, Verspagen, 1994; Verspagen, 1993) did not explicitly address the changing variety and diversification of economic systems. The first evolutionary growth model to explicitly focus on variety and diversification was that by Saviotti and Pyka (2004, 2008, 2013; Pyka et al., 2018). One of the main features of this model is the link between the 'saturation' of pre-existing sectors and the induced emergence of new sectors. Saturation is here intended to represent not only market saturation but also the effect of the intensity of competition due to the imitation of the innovation initially introduced by Schumpeterian entrepreneurs. Such saturation transforms an initially innovative sector into a part of the Schumpeterian circular flow and induces entrepreneurs to explore new ideas to achieve a temporary monopoly. The second important feature is the fact that diversification occurs both at the inter-sectoral level and at the intra-sectoral level. Thus, when a new sector is created (inter-sector diversification), its output does not remain constant, but keeps changing due to an increasing output quality and intra-sector diversification. Thus, the Saviotti-Pyka model[9] is not just an endogenous growth model, but one in which the number of sectors is endogenously variable. It shows that the long-term continuation of economic growth and development is only possible if the output variety of the economic system keeps increasing.

2.3 Empirical studies of unidirectional structural change

The previous modelling work was accompanied by many empirical papers which introduced the important distinction between related and unrelated variety (Frenken et al., 2007, Boschma, 2017; Kogler et al., 2013 refs) and showed that development was accompanied by a growing diversification and complexification of products (Hidalgo et al., 2007; Hidalgo, Hausmann, 2009). The distinction between related and unrelated variety depends on the similarity of the knowledge inherent in different technologies, or on its inverse, cognitive distance (Nooteboom et al., 2007). In this sense an increase in related variety would occur when a firm diversifies its technology towards one which is very similar to it, or which has a small cognitive distance with respect to it. Conversely, unrelated variety increases when a firm diversifies towards a technology very different with respect to its present one. We could expect related variety to be easier to achieve, to entail less risk and to have a faster payoff than unrelated variety. However, the latter could have a greater scope. In the study that introduced the distinction (Frenken et al., 2007), as well as in most of the very large number of papers that followed,[10] related variety was found to be far more effective in creating employment and growth than unrelated variety. As the empirical evidence accumulates it becomes clear that, although the important role of related variety is confirmed, economic development cannot occur simply by related variety (Saviotti, Frenken, 2008; Pinheiro et al., 2021). Thus, although the relative role of related and unrelated variety has not been definitively clarified, these studies provide a powerful confirmation that regional economic systems need to diversify in order to grow.

While the papers on related variety were generally focused on the national or regional level, other papers carried out studies at an international level. Due to the absence of production data, the first empirical studies of diversification at the international level had to use trade data. Funke and Ruhwedel (2001a, 2001b) showed that export variety was a factor leading to economic development. Imbs and Wacziarg (2003) showed that in general countries at low level of economic development diversified until they reached an intermediate level of economic development but then re-specialized again. In two very important papers, Haussman, Klinger (2007) and Hidalgo et al. (2007) derived from trade data the product space of different countries, in which products are distributed according to their proximity. Based on the product space, Hidalgo and Hausmann (2009) calculate for each product indexes of diversification and complexity. Typically, countries at high levels of economic development export non-ubiquitous, highly diversified, and complex products, while countries at low levels of economic development export ubiquitous, less diversified and less complex products.[11] Hidalgo et al. (2007) predict that countries at a given level of economic development are most likely to diversify towards products which have a high proximity with respect to those they are presently producing. To the extent that proximity is similar to relatedness, the common conclusion is that at both the national and the regional levels the most likely type of diversification is towards products that are related, or have a high proximity to the ones presently produced. In other words, economic development is more likely to proceed by small steps than by big jumps. These papers confirmed that structural change is an important determinant of a variety increasing economic development that we can consider an arrow of time.

2.3.1 Endogenous vs exogenous change

Although innovation was considered an important factor contributing to economic development at least since the industrial revolution, its importance was taken for granted, as if did not need to be demonstrated or analysed. This was true even in the work of Marx (1867, 1954), probably the most comprehensive analysis of the capitalist economy of the XIXth century. This apparent oversight was in fact justified by the then infrequent nature of innovation. At the time most innovations were introduced by individual inventors who used minimal levels of resources with respect to the ones invested in capital goods. That ceased to be the case as the resources invested in R&D increased massively during the XXth century (Freeman, Soete, 1997). This increase in the level of resources allocated to R&D amounted to a redefinition of the boundaries of the SES, making innovation endogenous. The changing role of R&D was formally accepted in endogenous growth models (Romer, 1990; Aghion Howitt, 1992) and in evolutionary models (Kwasnicki, 1996, 2007).

2.3.2 Decreasing vs increasing returns

The presence of increasing returns is a subject that for a very long-time worried economists for its incompatibility with perfect competition and general equilibrium. The paper by Allyn Young (1928), one of the earliest papers to discuss it, had initially a limited impact but was recently rescued, as interest in increasing returns was revived by evolutionary economists. Arthur (1989, 1996) pointed out that learning by doing and network externalities could give rise to lock-in and potential inefficiency, while David (1985) showed how a particular technology, the qwerty keyboard, could for a long time dominate typing machines even if it was not the most efficient arrangement of keys. These papers accepted that existing technologies could, at least for some time, develop with increasing returns, but tended to emphasize some of their negative effects. Thus, an SES which had some technologies developing with increasing returns would end up with those technologies being relatively inefficient, or non-optimal, over extended periods. Now, no SES could have all its technologies developing with increasing returns all the time. At best we could expect real SESs to contain a mixture of technologies with increasing and deceasing returns, and even that a given technology could alternate between periods of increasing and decreasing returns in different phases of its life cycle. Increasing returns could then operate as an autocatalytic reaction proceeding at growing speed until a constraint, such as the exhaustion of an ingredient involved in the process, arose. Furthermore, an SES that contained some processes occurring with increasing returns would inevitably end up showing path dependence as the choices made amongst competing technologies in their early stages could lead to different development paths.

In this section we discussed how the concept of unidirectional, variety increasing structural change emerged within economics and how it contributed to interpret economic development. Other concepts that are now being borrowed from other disciplines or research traditions, such as order, structure, chaos, irreversibility, coevolution, complexity, variation selection and concepts which are rare in the economics literature, will be discussed in Chapter 6 about the nature of evolutionary theories.

3 Present state and future developments

So far, in this chapter, we have briefly surveyed the evolution of growth models, leading in the end to models of unidirectional structural change endogenously generating growing output variety. We do not expect existing growth models of this type to be the final point of an intellectual trajectory, but an intermediate point towards greater realism and exhaustiveness in the representation of economic systems and of their internal mechanisms of interaction. We explored the models evolving from MAMA to MEMA and to MIMA and to multisectoral; from an exogenous to an endogenous representation of innovation and technological change; from an implicit to an explicit representation of sectors. The models we selectively surveyed come from different research traditions. Neoclassical economists stressed coherence at the expense of relevance, realism and accuracy. Neoclassical growth models were conceived as if they could be deductively derived from a series of basic axioms and be compatible with the assumptions of general equilibrium and perfect knowledge. The neoclassical theories of production and innovation were constructed as extensions of the earlier theory of demand, making assumptions that enabled production and innovation to be represented by equations formally similar to demand. For example, a Cobb-Douglas production function corresponded to a demand function (Pasinetti, 1981). Cambridge structuralists, and in particular Pasinetti, claimed to have constructed a theory of production not vitiated by the need for formal similarity with that of demand and thus endowed with greater realism and relevance. Such theory was more closely linked to the work of classical economists such as Ricardo, which led it to be called neo-Ricardian, and it was combined with input-output analysis. This made Pasinetti's work the first explicit representation of an economic system that was multisectoral, dynamic, and that could potentially predict the need for an increasing output variety. Evolutionary economists placed an even greater emphasis on relevance and realism and shifted the focus of research from production to innovation. Methodologically, evolutionary economics moved further away from a deductive approach and became far more inductive, with a growing emphasis on long-term trends. All these developments were accompanied by an increasing computational capability which contributed to simulated as opposed to analytically solvable models. The recent rise of agent-based models (see Pyka, Fagiolo, 2007) is an example of this trend. We do not pretend to compare the different models in terms of their explanatory power or predictive ability: most of the models have different objectives and the empirical evidence required for their testing is often absent. This is particularly true for models aiming to study long-term trends, the predictions of which can only be compared to historical observations and stylized facts. In this context we can still perceive a trend towards models incorporating more detailed features of modern economic systems, even if at the expense of reduced coherence and formal elegance.

So far, we explored the diversification of the economic system by considering the increasing number of sectors and their internal diversification. However, even when sectors are explicitly represented, their interactions with other sectors or activities that had not been traditionally considered were not often analysed carefully. There is growing evidence that industrial sectors coevolve with various types of institutions (Nelson, 1994; Perez, 1983, 2002; Freeman, Perez, 1988). A recent example is the coevolution of education and innovation and their influence on economic development (Saviotti et al., 2016). The idea that different components of the economic system could interact giving rise to feedback loops was present in the concept of cumulative causation, first put forward by Myrdal (1957, pp. 12–13) and adopted by Kaldor (1966). However, the presence of this type of interactions was not incorporated into models (but see Goodwin, 1967) or placed on a more general foundation until much later. Recent work stressed the connections between evolutionary economics, including the increasing diversification of the economic system, with complexity theory (Silverberg and Verspagen, 1995; Dosi, Virgillito, 2017; Hidalgo et al., 2007; Hidalgo, Hausmann, 2009). In this more general context, coevolution can be considered a very important component of economic development capable of contributing to the emergence of new sectors and activities and to the formation of increasingly ordered structures.

The scope of this chapter has been narrowed to the path leading to the emergence of growth models representing explicitly a multisectoral economic system, leading endogenously to a growing number of sectors and a growing output variety. While this gives the paper a much more precise focus than a general survey of growth models involving a type of structural change, one might wonder if the focus is not too narrow, or, in other words, if the phenomenon studied is of sufficient importance to deserve such attention.

Both biological and social systems are characterized by an overall irreversibility. While some local equilibria can exist and a limited local reversibility of some phenomena can occur, neither the life of biological organisms nor that of human communities can be lived backwards. In fact, the irreversibility of the universe is predicted by the second law of thermodynamics. However, the second law predicts that this irreversibility is associated with a growing entropy, and thus with growing disorder. At first the increasing order and complexity that we can observe in the evolution of biological and social systems seems to contradict the second law. This is not the case since recent developments in the thermodynamics of irreversible processes (Prigogine and Stengers, 1984; Nicolis and Prigogine, 1989; Haken, 1983; Allen, 2007; Arthur, 2007a, 2007b) show that for some types of systems, which are called open systems and are far enough from equilibrium, both the diversification and the order of the systems can increase. This is compatible with the second principle of thermodynamics because this local increase in order is more than compensated by an increase in disorder somewhere else in the universe. Thus, the predicted and observed increasing diversification of economic systems confirms the possibility that transitions in social systems can lead to greater order and diversification.

The previous conclusion about the possibility of increasing order and diversification in social systems applied only to open systems, which is far from equilibrium. Systems are open when mass, energy and information can flow through their boundaries. According to this definition, social systems are open, and increasingly so in a globalized world. However, given the importance of general equilibrium in economics, the fact that increasing order and diversification are observed only far from equilibrium seems to require some thought. On the one hand, for neoclassical economists, general equilibrium is the proof that the economic system can provide an ideal coordination and is, in a sense, the best possible state; on the other hand, phenomena and trends similar to those observed are predicted to occur only far from equilibrium. These two concepts probably reflect the different and possibly contrasting objectives of the two approaches: to explain why economic systems are stable for neoclassical economics, to explain why and how economic systems change for evolutionary economics and complexity science. Of course, both stability and change are required to provide a complete explanation of the evolution of economic systems. No doubt, further research will be required about this problem.

Notes

1 There is no database that allows us to measure accurately the output variety of the economic system at the level of goods and services. However, it is increasingly difficult to find homogeneous output types. Most consumer goods and durables are increasingly diversified. Broad technological classes, such as transport or telecommunications, have become increasingly diversified (Saviotti, 1996). At the level of trade or technological classes, strong evidence of diversification can be found in Section 2.2.

2 In this chapter we will call differentiation the emergence of new sectors due to new products (ST2) and internal diversification the intra-sectoral increase in the quality range of existing products.

3 The term 'welfare state' is perhaps the most common to describe several institutional approaches in which the state provided citizens with education, health care, pensions, paid for holidays and other forms of social assistance. Other terms used for similar institutional arrangements are the social state, or l'état-providence. The different terms correspond to different institutional arrangements, typically varying on a national scale. There is a general recognition that the first example of a welfare state occurred in Bismarck's Germany in the second half of the XIXth century. In the subsequent period, and in particular since the Second World War, a welfare state in some form was adopted in most industrialized countries. The national differences in the implementation of the welfare state have been discussed by Esping-Andersen (1990). We are not denying the existence of such differences, but rather focusing on the common trend leading to the formation of welfare states and following from the industrialization which began with the industrial revolution (Fraser, 1973). This point will be further discussed in Chapters 7 and 8.

4 Here we are assuming that the changes in process technology required to reduce the numbers of inputs required to produce one unit of output are not outweighed by the extra costs and environmental impact of the modified process technology computed over the life cycle of the technology itself.

5 The distinction between efficiency and creativity corresponds closely to that between cost competitiveness and technological competitiveness introduced by Bogliacino and Pianta (2009). The main effect of an increase in efficiency is a reduction in costs. The main effects of creativity can be (i) new products or (ii) new production processes using new types of capital goods. (i) is likely to create more new markets and new employment than (ii).

6 A more extended discussion of this difference can be found in Chapter 1 and Saviotti (2007).

7 The second and third of the three trajectories cited before show that new products can be both the ones that create new sectors and the new, high-quality models of pre-existing products. However, Saviotti and Pyka (2013) showed that the macroeconomic implications of the two for employment, income generation, wages and human capital are quite different. Thus, the statement that 'new products' is the most effective mechanism to compensate for employment destruction is an oversimplification.

8 Here see Chapter 1 on wants and needs, Chapter 8 on extended basic needs.

9 The model developed by Saviotti and Pyka, with recent collaboration by Jun, is called TEVECON. A more complete description of it can be found at: https://www.researchgate.net/publication/292130135 TEVECON Description of Model, DOI: 10.13140/RG.2.1.1626.9841.

10 For a more extended bibliography, see Saviotti, Pyka and Jun (2020).

11 For other studies following a similar approach, see Felipe et al. (2012), Freire (2017), Saracco et al. (2015) and Tacchella et al. (2012).

References

Aghion P., Howitt P. (1992) A model of growth through creative destruction. *Econometrica*, 60: 323–351.

Allen P. (2007) Self-organization in economic systems, in Hanusch H., Pyka A. (Eds), *Elgar Companion to Neo-Schumpeterian Economics*, Cheltenham, Edward Elgar, 1111–1148.

Amendola M., Gaffard J.L. (1998) *Out of Equilibrium*, Oxford, Oxford University Press.

Arthur W.B. (1996) Increasing returns and the new world of business. *Harvard Business Review*, Jul–Aug 74(4): 100–109.

Arthur W.B. (1989) Competing technologies, increasing returns, and lockin by historical events. *The Economic Journal*, 99: 116–131.

Arthur W.B. (2007a) Complexity and the economy, in Hanusch H., Pyka A. (Eds), *Elgar Companion to Neo-Schumpeterian Economics*, Cheltenham, Edward Elgar, 1102–1110.

Arthur W.B. (2007b) *Complexity and the Economy*, Oxford, Oxford University Press.

Arthur W.B., Durlauf S.N., Lane D.A. (1997) *The Economy as an Evolving Complex System II*, Boston, MA, Addison–Wesley.

Becker G.S. (1964) *Human Capital: A Theoretical and Empirical Analysis with Special Reference to Education*, Chicago, University of Chicago Press.

Bogliacino F., Pianta M. (2009) The impact of innovation on labour productivity growth in European industries: Does it depend on firms' competitiveness strategies? IPTS working paper on corporate R&D and innovation no. 13/2009.

Boschma R. (2017). Relatedness as driver of regional diversification: a research agenda. *Regional Studies*, 51(3): 351–364.

Braverman H. (1974) *Labor and Monopoly Capital: The Degradation of Work in the XXth Century*, New York, Monthly Review Press.

Chai A., Moneta A. (2010). Retrospectives: Engel curves. *Journal of Economic Perspectives*, American Economic Association, 24(1): 225–240.

Chandler A.D. (1962) *Strategy and Structure*, Cambridge, MA, MIT Press.

Chandler A.D. (1977) *The Visible Hand*, Cambridge, MA, Harvard University Press.

Chandler A.D. (2009) *Scale and Scope: The Dynamics of Industrial Capitalism*, Cambridge, MA, Harvard University Press.

Chiaromonte F., Dosi G. (1993) Heterogeneity, competition and macroeconomic dynamics. *Structural Change and Economic Dynamics*, 4: 39–63.

Ciarli T., Lorentz A., Valente M., Savona M. (2019) Structural changes and growth regimes, *Journal of Evolutionary Economics*, 29: 119–176. https://doi.org/10.1007/s00191-018-0574-4

David P. (1985) Clio and the Economics of QWERTY, *The American Economic Review*, 75(2), Papers and Proceedings of the Ninety-Seventh Annual Meeting of the American Economic Association (May, 1985): 332–337.

Diamond J. (1997) *Guns, Germs, and Steel, The Fates of Human Societies*, New York, Norton.

Domar E.D. (1946) Capital expansion, rate of growth, and employment, *Econometrica*, 14(2): 137–147.

Dopfer K. (2004) The economic agent as rule maker and rule user: Homo Sapiens Oeconomicus. *Journal of Evolutionary Economics*, 14: 177–195.

Dopfer K. (2013) Evolutionary economics, chapter 14, in Faccarello G., Kurz H.D. (Eds), *Handbook of the History of Economic Analysis*, Volume II, *Schools of Thought in Economics*, Cheltenham, Edward Elgar, 175–193.

Dopfer K., Foster J., Potts J. (2004) Micro–meso–macro, *Journal of Evolutionary Economics*, 14: 263–279. https://doi.org/10.1007/s00191-004-0193-0

Dopfer K., Potts, J. (2008) *The General Theory of Economic Evolution*, London and New York, Routledge.

Dopfer K., Potts J. (2009) On the theory of economic evolution. *Evolutionary and Institutional Economics Review*, 6(1): 23–44.

Dosi G., Nelson R.R. (1994) An introduction to evolutionary theories in economics. *Journal of Evolutionary Economics*, 4: 153–172.

Dosi G., Virgillito M.E. (2017) In order to stand up you must keep cycling: change and coordination in complex evolving economies. *Structural Change and Economic Dynamics*, 56(2): https://doi.org/10.1016/j.strueco.2017.06.003

Engel E. (1857) Die Productions –und consumtions –Verhältnisse des Königreichs Sachsen, *Bulletin de l'Institut International de Statistique 9.*

Esping-Andersen, G. (1990) *The Three Worlds of Welfare Capitalism*, Princeton, NJ, Princeton University Press. ISBN 9780069028573

Fabricant, S. (1940) *The Output of Manufacturing Industries, 1899–1937*, New York, National Bureau of Economic Research, Inc., xxiv, 685.

Fabricant, S. (1942) *Employment in Manufacturing: 1899–1937*, New York, NBER.

Felipe J., Kumar U., Abdon A., Bacate M. (2012) Product complexity and economic development, *Structural Change and Economic Dynamics*, 23: 36–68.

Fraser D. (1973) *The Evolution of the British Welfare State: A History of Social Policy since the Industrial Revolution*, London, Palgrave Macmillan.

Freeman C., Perez C. (1988) Structural crises of adjustment, business cycles and investment behaviour, in Dosi G., Freeman C., Nelson R., Soete L., Silverberg G. (Eds), *Technical Change and Economic Theory*, London, Pinter, 38–66.

Freeman C., Louça F. (2001) *As Time Goes By, from the Industrial Revolution to the Information Revolution*, Oxford, Oxford University Press.

Freeman C., Soete L. (1997) *The Economics of Industrial Innovation*, London, Pinter.

Freire C. (2017) Economic diversification: explaining the pattern of diversification in the global economy and its implications for fostering diversification in poorer countries, UNU MERIT Working paper, #2017-033, ISSN 1871-9872.

Frenken K., van Oort F.G., Verburg T. (2007) Related variety, unrelated variety and regional economic growth. *Regional Studies*, 41(5): 685–697.

Frey C.B., Osborne M.A. (2017) The future of employment: how susceptible are jobs to computerisation? *Technological Forecasting and Social Change*, 114(C): 254–280.

Funke M., Ruhwedel R. (2001a) Product variety and economic growth: empirical evidence for the OECD countries, *IMF Staff Papers*, 48(05): 1–1.

Funke M., Ruhwedel R. (2001b) Export variety and export performance: empirical evidence from East Asia, *Journal of Asian Economics*, 12: 493–505.

Geels F.W. (2002a) Technological transitions as evolutionary reconfiguration processes: a multi-level perspective and a case-study, *Research Policy*, 31: 8–9, 1257–1274, 17 p.

Geels F.W. (2002b) *Understanding the Dynamics of Technological Transitions: A Co-Evolutionary and Socio-Technical Analysis*, Twente, Twente University Press.

Geels, F.W. (2004) From sectoral systems of innovation to socio-technical systems: insights about dynamics and change from sociology and institutional theory. *Research Policy*, 33(6–7): 897–920.

Goldin C., Katz L. (2008) *The Race between Education and Technology*, Cambridge, MA, Harvard University Press.

Goodwin B.R. (1967) A growth cycle, in Feinstein, C.H. (Ed), *Socialism, Capitalism and Economic Growth*, Cambridge, Cambridge University Press, 54–58.

Grossman G.M., Helpman E., Oberfield E., Sampson T. (2017) Balanced growth despite Uzawa. *American Economic Review*, 107(4): 1293–1312. https://doi.org/10.1257/aer.20151739

Haken H. (1983) *Synergetics*, Berlin, Springer Verlag.

Harrod R.F. (1939) An essay in dynamic theory, *The Economic Journal*, 49(193): 14–33.

Haussman R., Klinger B. (2007) The structure of the product space and the evolution of comparative advantage, CID working paper series 2007.146 Harvard University, Cambridge MA, April 2007.

Grossman G.M., Helpman E. (May, 1991) Quality ladders and product cycles, *The Quarterly Journal of Economics*, 106(2): 557–586.

Grossman G.M., Helpman E. (1994) Endogenous innovation in the theory of growth. *Journal of Economic Perspectives*, 8(1): 23–44.

Hicks J.R. (1965) *Capital and Growth*, Oxford, Clarendon Press.

Hidalgo C.A., Hausmann R. (2009) The building blocks of economic complexity, *PNAS*, 106(26): 10575.

Hidalgo C.A., Klinger B., Barabasi A.-L., Hausmann R. (2007) The product space conditions the development of nations. *Science*, 317: 482–487.

Hobsbawm E.J. (1968) *Industry and Empire*, Harmondsworth, Penguin Books.

Hounshell D.A., Smith J.K. (1988) *Science and Corporate Strategy: Du Pont R and D, 1902–1980*, Cambridge, Cambridge University Press.

Imbs J., Wacziarg R. (2003) Stages of diversification, *The American Economic Review*, 93(1): 63–86.

Jacobs J. (1969) *The Economy of Cities*, New York, Vintage Books.

Kaldor N. (1956), Alternative Theories of Distribution, Nicholas Kaldor, *The Review of Economic Studies*, Vol. 23, No. 2. (1955–1956), pp. 83-100.

Kaldor N. (1957) A model of economic growth, *The Economic Journal*, 67(268): 591–624.

Kaldor N. (1966) Causes of the *slow rate* of *economic growth* of the *United Kingdom*, Cambridge, Cambridge University Press.

Kaldor N. (1972) The irrelevance of equilibrium economics, *The Economic Journal*, 82(328): 1237–1255.

Kogler D.F., Rigby D.L., Tucker I. (2013) Mapping knowledge space and technological relatedness in US cities. *European Planning Studies*, 21(9): 1374–1391. https://doi.org/10.1080/09654313.-2012.755832

Kwasnicki W. (1996) *Knowledge, Innovation and Economy*, Cheltenham, Edward Elgar.

Kwasnicki W. (2007). Schumpeterian modelling, in Horst Hanusch & Andreas Pyka (Eds), *Elgar Companion to Neo-Schumpeterian Economics*, chapter 25, Cheltenham, Edward Elgar Publishing, 389–404.

Lancaster K.J., (1966) A new approach to consumer theory, *Journal of Political Economy*, 14: 133–156

Lavoie M. (1998) Au-delà de la traverse sectorielle de Hicks : croissance insoutenable et flexibilité du système productif. *Cahiers d'économie Politique* 2004/1 (n46) : 131–146.

Leontieff W. (1951) *The Structure of the American Economy*, 1919–1939, 2nd ed., White Plains, NY: International Arts and Sciences Press.

Leontieff W. (1986) *Input-Output Economics*, Oxford, Oxford University Press.

Marx K. (1867, 1954) *Capital*, London, Lawrence and Wishart.

Metcalfe J.S., Foster J., Ramlogan R. (2005) Adaptive economic growth, *Cambridge Journal of Economics*, 30: 7–32.

Miles I. (2005) Knowledge intensive business services: Prospects and policies, *Foresight*, 7: 39–63.

Mokyr J. (1990) *The Lever of Riches: Technological Creativity and Economic Progress*, New York, Oxford University Press.

Murmann J.P. (2003) *Knowledge and Competitive Advantage: The Co-evolution of Firms, Technologies and National Institutions*, Cambridge, Cambridge University Press.

Myrdal, G. (1957) *Economic Theory and Underdeveloped Regions*, London: University Paperbacks, Methuen.

Nelson R.R. (1994) The co-evolution of technology, industrial structure, and supporting institutions, *Industrial and Corporate Change*, 3(1): 47–63.

Nelson R.R. (1995) Recent evolutionary theorizing about economic change, *Journal of Economic Literature*, 33(1): 48–90.

Nelson R., Winter S. (1982) *An Evolutionary Theory of Economic Change*, Cambridge, MA, Harvard University Press.

Nicolis G., Prigogine I. (1989) *Exploring Complexity*, New York, Freeman.

Nooteboom B., Van Haverbeke W., Duysters G., Gilsing V., Van den Oord, A. (2007) Optimal cognitive distance and absorptive capacity. *Research Policy*, 36(7): 1016–1034.

Pasinetti L.L. (1981) *Structural Change and Economic Growth: A Theoretical Essay on the Dynamics of the Wealth of Nations*, Cambridge, Cambridge University Press.

Pasinetti L.L. (1993) *Structural Economic Dynamics*, Cambridge, Cambridge University Press.

Perez C. (1983) Structural change and the assimilation of new technologies in the economic system, *Futures*, 15: 357–375.

Perez C. (2002) *Technological Revolutions and Financial Capital: The Dynamics of Bubbles and Golden Ages*, Cheltenham, Edward Elgar, 198 pages, ISBN 1 84064 922 4.

Pinheiro F.L., Hartmann D., Boschma R., Hidalgo C.A. (2022) The time and frequency of unrelated diversification, *Research Policy*, 51(8): 1–24.

Prigogine I., Stengers I., (1984) *Order Out of Chaos*, London, Fontana.

Pyka A., Fagiolo G. (2007) Agent-based modelling: a methodology for neo-Schumpeterian economics, in Hanusch H. Pyka A. (Eds), *Elgar Companion to neo-Schumpeterian Economics*, Cheltenham, Edward Elgar, 467–492.

Pyka A., Saviotti P.P., Nelson R.R. (2018) Evolutionary perspectives on long run economic development, in Nelson R.R., Dosi G., Helfat C., Pyka A., Saviotti P.P., Lee K., Dopfer K., Malerba F., Winter S. (Eds), *Modern Evolutionary Economics, An Overview*, Cambridge, Cambridge University Press, 143–167.

Reich L.S. (1985) *The Making of American Industrial Research*, Cambridge, MA, MIT Press.

Robinson J. (1956) *Accumulation of Capital*, London, Palgrave MacMillan.

Robinson J. (1973) *An Introduction to Modern Economics*, Maidenhead, Mc Graw Hill.

Romer, P. (1990) Endogenous technical progress, *Journal of Political Economy*, 98 pp. S71–S102.

Rosenberg N., Birdzell L.E. (1986) *How the West Grew Rich*, New York, Basic Books.

Saracco F., Di Clemente R., Gabrielli A., Pietronero, L. (2015) From innovation to diversification: a simple competitive model, PLOS ONE. https://doi.org/10.1371:journal.pone.0140420.

Saviotti P.P. (1996) *Technological Evolution, Variety and the Economy*, Cheltenham, Edward Elgar.

Saviotti P.P. (2001) Variety, growth and demand, *Journal of Evolutionary Economics*, 11: 119–142.

Saviotti P.P. (2005) On the co-evolution of technologies and institutions,in Weber M., Hemmelskamp J. (Eds), *Towards Environmental Innovation Systems*, Berlin, Heidelberg, New York, Springer, 9–32.

Saviotti P.P. (2007) Qualitative change and economic development, in Hanusch H., Pyka A. (Eds), *Elgar Companion to Neo-Schumpeterian Economics*, Cheltenham, Edward Elgar, 820–838.

Saviotti P.P., Frenken K. (2008) Export variety and the economic performance of countries, *Journal of Evolutionary Economics*, 18: 201–218.

Saviotti P.P., Metcalfe J.S. (1991) *Evolutionary Theories of Economic and Technological Change: Present Status and Future Prospects*, Chur, Reading, Harwood Academic Publishers. Reprinted by Routledge (2020).

Saviotti P.P., Pyka A. (2004) Economic development by the creation of new sectors, *Journal of Evolutionary Economics*, 14(1): 1–35.

Saviotti P.P., Pyka A. (2008a) Micro and macro dynamics: industry life cycles, inter-sector coordination and aggregate growth, *Journal of Evolutionary Economics*, 18: 167–182.

Saviotti P.P., Pyka A. (2008b) Product variety, competition and economic growth, *Journal of Evolutionary Economics*, 18: 323–347.

Saviotti P.P., Pyka A. (2013) From necessities to imaginary worlds: Structural change, product quality and economic development, *Technological Forecasting & Social Change*, 80: 1499–1512.

Saviotti P.P., Pyka A., Jun B. (2016) Education, structural change and economic development; *Structural Change and Economic Development*, special issue on Complexity and Economic Development, 38: 55–68. http://dx.doi.org/10.1016/j.strueco.2016.04.002

Saviotti P.P., Pyka A., (2017) Innovation, structural change, and demand evolution: does demand saturate? *Journal of Evolutionary Economics*, 27:337 – 358 DOI 10.1007/s00191-015-0428-2

Saviotti P.P., Pyka A., Jun B. (2020) Diversification, structural change, and economic development. *Journal of Evolutionary Economics*, 30(5): 1301–1335, https://doi.org/10.1007/s00191-020-00672-w

Schumpeter J. (1911) *The Theory of Economic Development*, Cambridge, MA, Harvard University Press (1934, original edition 1911).

Silverberg G., Dosi G., Orsenigo L. (1988) Innovation, diversity and diffusion: a self-organisation model. *The Economic Journal*, 98(393): 1032–1054.

Silverberg G., Verspagen B. (1994) Learning, innovation and economic growth: a long run model of industrial dynamics, *Industrial and Corporate Change*, 3: 199–223.

Silverberg G., Verspagen B. (1995) *Evolutionary Theorizing on Economic Growth*, IIASA Working paper WP-95-78.

Smith A. (1776) *The Wealth of Nations*, Penguin English Library, 1972 and following reprints.

Solow R.M. (1956) A contribution to the theory of economic growth, *Quarterly Journal of Economics*, 70: 65–94.

Solow R.M. (1957) Technical change and the aggregate production function, *Review of Economics and Statistics*, 39: 312–320.

Solow R.M. (1988) *Growth Theory: An Exposition*, Oxford, Oxford University Press.

Sraffa P. (1963) *Production of Commodities by Means of Commodities*, Bombay, Vora &Co. Publishers.

Tacchella A., Cristelli M., Caldarelli G., Gabrielli A., Pietronero L. (2012) A new metrics for countries' fitness and products' complexity. *Science Reports*, 2: 723.

Verspagen B. (1993) *Uneven Growth between Interdependent Economies*, Avebury, Aldershot.

Vivarelli M. (1995) *The Economics of Technology and Employment*, Cheltenham, Edward Elgar.

Vivarelli M. (2007a) Innovation and employment technological unemployment is not inevitable—some innovation creates jobs, and some job destruction can be avoided, IZA Vol. 2015,154.

Vivarelli M. (2007b) Innovation and employment, in Hanusch H., Pyka A. (Eds), *Elgar Companion to Neo- Schumpeterian Economics*, Cheltenham, Edward Elgar, 719–732.

Vivarelli M. (2014) Innovation, employment, and skills in advanced and developing countries: a survey of the economic literature, *Journal of Economic Issues*, 48(1): 123–154.

Whelan K. (2004) New evidence on balanced growth, stochastic trends, and economic fluctuations, Research Technical Paper 7/RT/04 Central Bank and Financial Services Authority of Ireland.

Young A.A. (1928) Increasing returns and economic progress. *The Economic Journal*, 38(152): 527–542.

6 Complexity and evolutionary theories

Evolutionary theories have been extensively used in biology and growingly in several other disciplines. In economics a revival of interest in these theories began with the 1982 book by Nelson and Winter *An Evolutionary Theory of Economic Change*. Although we can trace the beginning of an evolutionary style of theorizing in the social sciences to the end of the XVIIIth century (Hayek, 1982, pp. 22–23), this modern revival of evolutionary theorizing in economics owes its origin to the growing importance of innovation in modern societies. After the Second World War, the resources allocated to R&D and innovation increased enormously with respect to the past. Although at the beginning R&D was concentrated in a very small number of countries, by the end of the XXth century it had become a normal component of the economic activities of most countries. As Freeman and Soete (1997) have observed, the emergence of R&D was a true revolution in the sense of introducing a completely new activity into the world economic system. It consisted of separating learning from doing, or of inventing learning *without* doing. While the outcomes of this revolution were undoubtedly positive, they required new tools to understand and evaluate their efficacy. A growing number of scholars did not find in the economic theories of the 1960s the tools which could have helped them to understand the emergence and dynamics of innovation. The then dominant research tradition, neoclassical economics, seemed to hide the nature of innovation. The assumption of perfect knowledge on the part of economic agents, the possibility of optimization and the existence of general equilibrium seemed to be incompatible with the perceived nature of innovation. The presence of qualitative change and the consequent possibility of discontinuities and radical uncertainty (see Chapter 1) implied that at least in a number of situations human knowledge could be very limited.

Agents' decision-making procedures could then not be expected to rely always on optimization. Furthermore, the concept of general equilibrium seemed to be less and less adapted to describe the world which innovation helped to create. To more and more people, innovation seemed the ingredient that could disrupt existing equilibria rather than lead to them.

DOI: 10.4324/9781003294221-6

It needs to be stressed that the modern revival was not the first foundation of evolutionary theories. In fact, a style of evolutionary theorizing had been present in the social sciences since the end of the XVIIIth century (Hayek, 1982) and it had achieved its most explicit application in biology. As will be seen later, the new wave of evolutionary theories, which we will henceforth call modern evolutionary theory, was very early on affected by the success of the evolutionary approach in biology and borrowed from it some concepts.

In the rest of this chapter, it will be shown that modern evolutionary theories have been developed as an attempt to remedy the perceived limitations of neoclassical economics for what concerns the analysis of innovation. A crucial question which has been hanging over evolutionary theories and to which this book will try to give an answer is whether evolutionary theories can be a specialized subset of economics dealing only with innovation or whether it can be a general substitute of neoclassical economics useful to analyse all possible types of economic phenomena. Whatever the answer which can be given to this question, the construction of an evolutionary theory of economic behaviour is a very ambitious project which could hardly be expected to succeed in 30 years. The time scale for the construction of neoclassical economics has been considerably longer than that (Mirowski, 1989).

A more explicit and detailed attempt to compare adaptive and optimizing behaviour has been made in Chapter 3. In this chapter we are going to follow the evolution of evolutionary theories since the 1970s, from the initial phase of empirical studies to the construction of a more elaborate theoretical framework for the study of innovation to the extension of evolutionary theories to phenomena other than innovation. Furthermore, we will situate the recent development of evolutionary theory in its historical antecedents and we will maintain that the construction of a more complete and coherent evolutionary economic theory needs to consider the recent developments of complexity theory. This path will entail building bridges and connections with different research traditions both in economics and in other disciplines. Although such a development path seems to go in the required direction to construct a general economic theory, so far evolutionary theories seem to have become more fragmented (Robert, Yoguel, 2016; Tavares Silva, Teixeira, 2006). The simultaneous presence of a trend towards an extension of the range of phenomena studied by a theory and of a greater specialization seems to be perfectly natural. In this sense evolutionary theory would behave as an innovation which was created in a niche but that in its subsequent diffusion to other parts of the economic system needs to be adapted to each new niche. In the end such an evolutionary path can be successful and give rise to a theoretical structure which can have a wider scope and encompass neoclassical economics as a more limited subset only if a degree of coherence for the whole structure can be obtained. In what follows, we try to establish the main research traditions that contributed to the development of evolutionary economics and the main differences with respect to neoclassical economics.

1 Antecedents and recent developments

1.1 Evolutionary and constructivist rationalisms as alternative modes of knowledge

The recent revival of evolutionary economics is not completely new, although its emphasis on innovation is. According to Hayek (1982), the beginning of an evolutionary approach to different fields of human knowledge can be detected in the work of empiricist philosophers of the late XVIIIth century, and in particular in that of Hume. These philosophers reacted to a form of rationalism that had accompanied the scientific revolution in the XVIIth century and that aimed at replacing the traditional forms of knowledge which were not based on reason. According to Hayek (1982), the main exponent of this orientation, which he called *constructivist rationalism*, was Descartes, who maintained that statements which could not be derived as logical deductions from explicit premises had to be rejected. Here, following Hayek, we will call this type of rationalism *constructivist*. This type of rationalism justified and accompanied the progress of the physical sciences during the XVIIth and XVIIIth centuries, giving rise to the belief in the existence of a new and superior form of knowledge. Furthermore, the same approach to knowledge was expected to be in principle applicable to the social sciences, an attitude that is often referred to as scientism.

This sense of certainty about human knowledge was heavily criticized by British empiricist philosophers, the most important of whom can be considered Hume. Having started with the project to 'apply the method of natural science to human nature and to create a science of man', he ended up with an extremely sceptical view of human reason, denying even the validity of the relationship of cause and effect (Losee, 1977, pp. 104–105). Hayek considers that a form of rationalism different from the constructivist one, and that he calls evolutionary, has started to be developed on this basis. He maintains that knowledge and information are highly dispersed amongst individuals in a group and that no one has the knowledge and information required to design the rules and institutions that can create and preserve the extended order which makes the group or community superior to a set of isolated individuals.

Hayek is very critical of constructivist rationalism, especially in the social sciences which do not have the same type of simple systems that allowed the physical sciences to prosper in their initial phases. Although Descartes did not stress the application of constructivist rationalism to the social sciences, Hayek (1982, p. 10) places Rousseau in the same research tradition and credits him with the idea that existing institutions could be redesigned to make human beings free, thus supplying the intellectual basis for the French Revolution. On the contrary, Hayek thinks that existing institutions and rules emerged through a process that we could call blind search, in which groups and communities adopted rules which gave them a different capacity to survive in each EE. The 'best' rules were those found in the communities that had the greatest capacity to survive and became dominant without any member of the communities having a clear knowledge about the effect of such rules.

These comments are not intended to provide a complete discussion of the philosophical debate between rationalism and empiricism but only to distinguish two types of rationalism, called by Hayek constructivist and evolutionary, which in our view correspond to the main differences between neoclassical and evolutionary economics. In the social sciences, these types of rationality give rise to the expectation that (i) rules and institutions inherited from tradition can be redesigned according to reason and give rise to better, or perfect, forms of society (constructivist rationalism), or that (ii) existing rules and institutions were not designed with a specific objective, but emerged through a process of search and group selection in which groups having 'superior' rules prevailed (evolutionary rationalism). Thus, neoclassical economics assumes perfect knowledge and optimizing rationality while evolutionary economics assumes a more limited, although constantly improvable, knowledge. The methodologies of the two research traditions follow from these epistemological differences. Neoclassical economics privileges the deduction of results from certain premises while evolutionary economics favours a more inductive approach in which the detection of patterns and trends is accompanied by the search for mechanisms.

By far the most successful application of an evolutionary approach to a field of human knowledge was given by the work of Darwin (1859). Several attempts to apply ideas derived from Darwinian biology to the social sciences were subsequently made at different stages. However, according to Hayek (1982, pp. 18–19), Darwin was not the creator of an evolutionary approach but learned it from social scientists. Whether Hayek is right or not about the origin of an evolutionary approach, it is quite clear that Darwin established a mode of knowledge that could be an alternative to a mechanical analogy and that could act as a template to be applied to other fields of human knowledge.

Early attempts to apply Darwinism to the social sciences could be found in the work of Herbert Spencer (1892) and Veblen (1898) (see also Hodgson, 1993; Saviotti, 1996). The work of Spencer was one of the examples of social Darwinism. Social Darwinists held that the life of man in society was a struggle for existence ruled by the 'survival of the fittest'. As we saw in Chapter 3, unfit organs inherited from a previous external environment (EE) survive in biological evolution. In biology, where it was originally studied, the statement should be modified to 'the survival of the relatively better'. In the social sciences the external environment seems to have been moving away from the one that would have led to the 'survival of the fittest', for example, by increasing industrial concentration or by the policies protecting existing firms or organizations. Thus, rather than being a correct interpretation of biological or social evolution, the 'survival of the fittest' became the basis for highly conservative and racist conclusions, justifying the existence of natural inequalities amongst individuals and undermining attempts to reform society since, as social Darwinists maintained, they interfered with a 'natural' process. Social Darwinism acquired a considerable importance in the late XIXth century but subsequently declined and created a bad reputation for attempts to apply biological theories to human societies.

Veblen made explicit use of Darwin's ideas applying them to the study of institutions. According to him, they owe their origin to habits of thought, which in turn come from instincts. Variation, selection, and inheritance were present in Veblen's work. Institutions were both the units of selection and the replicator. Furthermore, institutions were relatively stable and could transmit variety from one period to the next, ensuring that selection had relatively stable units on which to operate. Veblen's work was not marred by any conservative or racist connotations. On the contrary, he was perceived as a radical critic of existing society, and especially of the wealthy leisured class. However, his fundamental pessimism and his lack of a complete system of thought contributed to the relative neglect of his work by the economics profession (Saviotti, 1996).

After Veblen the only contribution to the use of biological explanations in economics is the well-known statement by Marshall (1949) that 'the Mecca of economics lies in economic biology rather than in economic dynamics. Although Marshall realized that the subject matter of economics was more similar to that of biology than to that of physics, he never followed this intuition in his work. He realized the value of a biological metaphor more than he used it (Hart, 2013).

These early attempts to use a biological approach to economics did not find any follower until Alchian (1950, 1953), who explicitly adopted a population perspective, suggesting that only firms which realized positive profits can survive. Thus, Alchian placed at the centre of his analysis a selection mechanism based on realized profits and a population approach, focusing on a population of firms rather than on a representative one. He suggested that the economic counterparts of genetic heredity, mutation and natural selection are imitation, innovation, and positive profits (1950, 1973, p. 74) (Andersen, 1994, p. 12).

Although pioneering, Alchian's work was incomplete and could not give rise to a proper evolutionary approach. Winter (1964) criticized Alchian's approach by pointing out that the selection mechanism was not adequately specified and that it was not clear whether the process of variety creation was strong enough to exclude suboptimal modes of behaviour (Andersen, 1994, p. 13). In the work of Winter, we start seeing the beginning of a synthesis between Alchian's work on the selection mechanism, Simon's work on behavioural routines (Lazaric, 2000) and Schumpeter's ideas on innovative behaviour.

The biological concepts that survived in modern evolutionary theories are (Andersen, 1994).

variation
selection
inheritance
population approach

Variation consists of all the types of innovation that can be generated within SESs. Of course, the meaning of variation can be different with respect to a biological system due to the greater intentionality it can have in an SES. Such intentionality must neither be overestimated nor be neglected. When trying to develop an innovation, firms, R&D laboratories, or research institutions have objectives, but such objectives are usually defined in a broad way, the more so, the more fundamental the type of research involved. By definition no innovation can be the outcome of a carefully planned process in which the result is exactly predictable. Important contributions to knowledge occur only when the outcome involves a considerable extent of surprise. Radical innovations involve qualitative change and radical uncertainty, while the most incremental ones are characterized by quantitative change, limited uncertainty, and calculable risk. During a technological life cycle or during a technological paradigm, the type of change varies from qualitative to quantitative and radical uncertainty becomes calculable risk (see Chapters 1 and 2). Thus, the extent of the intentionality of an innovation can vary between the uncertainty of very basic research and the high predictability of very applied research or of an incremental innovation. Thus, innovations can vary for their degree of intentionality, which is never zero. This is enough to differentiate social systems from biological systems.

In the form described so far, the basic concepts of an evolutionary approach are particularly suited to the analysis of biological organisms and species. The greater intentionality of human decision-making, as opposed to that of biological organisms, seemed to be an important potential difference with respect to that of biological species. A debate arose about the supposed Lamarckian character of human decision-making, as compared to the purely Darwinian one of biological species (Nelson, 2006, 2007a, 2007b). Such debate has recently been summarized and criticized by Hodgson and Knudsen (2006, 2007, 2008, 2010), who maintain that it is possible to develop a Universal Darwinism, which is in principle capable of encompassing both biological species and human communities. Here we can only briefly summarize their highly articulate treatment of the subject. An appropriate starting point can be the irreducibility of culture and institutions to biological factors. Consequently, selection can be multilevel, occurring at different levels, both genetic and social. Furthermore, selection can occur at a group level, a possibility that has been gradually accepted in biology but that acquires an even greater importance in the social sphere. Hodgson and Knudsen introduced the concepts of *interactors* and *replicators* as general analogues of genotype and phenotype. In a general sense, interactors are entities that can interact with their EE. As a result of this interaction, their population can survive and grow or shrink. Interactors contain replicators which carry the information required to make copies of themselves. Generative replicators are a special class of replicators that are capable of augmenting complexity in evolving systems. Habits and routines are examples of replicators and sometimes of generative replicators. Thus, replication contributes to inheritance and generative replication can contribute to variation. Hodgson and Knudsen reject Lamarckism as an alternative to Darwinism. They observe that intentionality exists but that rarely if ever innovators can foresee the consequences of their innovations. Thus, intentionality exists but is typically accompanied by a variable amount of unpredictability. Furthermore, intentionality should not be simply accepted but explained by an evolutionary theory.

1.2 From innovation studies to Nelson and Winter

Another strand of the literature that contributed to the formation of a modern evolutionary economics consisted of a field loosely called innovation studies. Although innovation had been present for a very long time in human societies, up to the XIXth century it had been introduced very infrequently by individual inventors. With the industrial revolution, the size of innovations and their impact on the development of human societies increased enormously. In the second half of the XIXth century, the production of innovations acquired a more systematic basis by means of the institutionalization of R&D in new style universities and industrial firms. After the Second World War these early developments were followed by a very rapid diffusion of R&D at the international level, thus requiring large investments and effectively endogenizing innovation. The considerably increased scale of innovation and its impact on both defence and economic activities created the need for an evaluation of the effectiveness of the corresponding investments. This led to the emergence of a new stream of innovation studies. Innovation was previously considered a phenomenon which, while potentially having an important economic impact, was not intrinsically economic in its origin and nature. Since to understand innovation was very difficult based on the then existing economic theories, initially most innovation studies were very empirical and constituted what could be considered a natural history of innovation (Freeman, 1982; Coombs et al., 1987). Yet out of this empirical approach arose a series of general concepts about innovation patterns, such as dominant designs, technological regimes, paradigms, and trajectories, that have already been described in Chapter 2. These concepts were combined with the work of Schumpeter and that of Simon, Cyert and March in Nelson and Winter's (1982) book, which then became the formal beginning of a modern evolutionary economics.

From Schumpeter N&W borrowed the emphasis on innovation as the fundamental driver of economic development and from that of Simon, Cyert and March (1963) the concept of a limited human knowledge. Thus, N&W replaced optimizing with satisficing behaviour and maintained that firms followed routines. Routines were also the economic counterpart of genetic heritage. They were the memory of the firm, provided continuity by being passed on from one generation of personnel to the next and saved on information costs. In N&W variation was caused by innovation, which they defined as a change of routines, a change that was induced by the failure to achieve the firm's objectives. Furthermore, for N&W knowledge was 'local' in the sense that firms tended to operate in the vicinity of the same combination of factors of production that they had been previously using moving only incrementally from there. Although they described the concept of local knowledge in a capital and labour space, the concept is easily generalizable to other dimensions of the environment in which firms operate. For example, we can expect the knowledge base (KB) of firms to remain for relatively long periods within the same dimensions of knowledge space by constantly using the same patent classes. Changes in which the KB of the firm incorporates new patent classes are likely to be infrequent and to constitute knowledge discontinuities. Such a discontinuity can occur when there is a change of technological paradigm in a field that the firm needs to learn. In a sense the location of the firm in a particular position of knowledge space can be considered a higher-level routine that will be changed infrequently.

N&W incorporated some biological concepts in their evolutionary theory but made a limited use of biological analogies. Their approach owes much more to Schumpeter, Simon, Cyert and March than to biology. Although the work of Simon (1965, 1969), and Cyert and March (1963) does not seem to show any direct link to Hayek and his purported origin of an evolutionary approach, N&W contribution could be interpreted as the continuation of a trend to consider human knowledge limited, although enormously improvable. It may seem a contradiction that a book stressing the central role of innovation in economic development simultaneously places such a great emphasis on the limits of human knowledge. However, the possibility of unlimited learning is quite compatible with the idea that no theory can ever be definitively proved right (Popper, 1934) or that the evolution of human knowledge can go through periods of revolutionary as well as more incremental change (Kuhn, 1962). An evolutionary approach is by no means irrational, but it is opposed to a constructivist rationality, a different type of evolutionary rationality.

If the example of biology exerted a considerable influence on evolutionary economics, there were non-negligible differences in the ways in which evolutionary economists used it. Some predecessors to evolutionary economics, such as Schumpeter (1911, 1934) and Penrose (1952), even objected to the use of biological ideas in economics. Obvious differences between the two are the existence and role of knowledge and of institutions in SESs, as compared to their virtual absence in animal species. Of relevance, given the emphasis of modern evolutionary economics on innovation, is the presence of search activities. These are activities by means of which individuals or organizations scan the external environment (EE) to understand it and to prepare suitable alternatives to present routines. That search activities have one or more objectives suggested to some evolutionary economists that variation in sciences is not completely random as in biology but has an at least partly intentional character. As pointed out in Section 2.1, this gave rise to the idea that economic evolution is more Lamarckian than Darwinian (Hodgson, Knudsen, 2006, 2007; Nelson, 2006, 2007a, 2007b). Not everyone agrees and the possibility to develop a generalized Darwinian approach to SESs has been proposed by Hodgson and Knudsen (HK) (2010).

Perhaps unsurprisingly, no consensus exists on the matter. The limits of human knowledge and the frequent occurrences of unexpected results in search activities tell us that economic evolution is not fully Lamarckian although the wide differences in uncertainty corresponding to different types of innovation, radical or incremental, tell us that it may not be fully Darwinian. We recognize that this debate has produced some very useful and interesting results but prefer to analyse socioeconomic phenomena in terms of adaptive behaviour, as discussed in Chapter 3. Thus, adaptation of a firm or a region to a change in the EE can involve more or less profound changes in routines, knowledge bases (KBs) and institutions. For example, the creation of completely new outputs, qualitatively different from pre-existing ones, is likely to entail a profound change not just of its routines but also of its KB and of its competencies, requiring massive and discontinuous changes of personnel and organizational forms. However, the very incremental changes that occur during the more mature phases of technology, industry or product life cycle can be introduced almost without changes in existing routines, KB and organizational structure. The former conditions (more drastic, almost qualitative changes) are encountered at the emergence of completely new sectors or knowledge types, such as automobiles, aircraft, television, antibiotics, electricity, and railways.

We can conclude this section by saying that constructivist and evolutionary rationalisms are two different approaches to knowledge that have existed and competed for an explanation of phenomena in the social sciences.[1] As far as the differences between biology and economics are concerned, our point of view is that they both are complex systems and that an adequate theoretical approach to both needs to be based on theories of complexity. We will come back to this point later in the chapter. We could summarize our analysis so far by saying that evolutionary and constructivist rationalisms correspond to different types of theoretical approaches to the study of biology and economics, and that we consider an evolutionary approach superior for long-run patterns of economic development.

1.3 Structure, order and change

We have so far characterized modern evolutionary economics as the outcome of a long process of development of an evolutionary mode of theorizing, as an alternative to constructivist rationalism. We now pass to a different aspect of evolutionary theories exemplified by the concepts of order or structure.

These two concepts are almost synonyms and have been used in different parts the literature. Hayek (1982) referred to the extended order which exists in socioeconomic systems due to the rules that govern such systems. The structure of a complex system can be defined by 'the properties of the parts and the laws of their interactions' and the system is complex when inferring the properties of the whole from the parts and the interactions is not a trivial matter (Simon, 1969, p. 195). Biological and social systems have a structure. The emergence and extinction of animal species or social classes give rise to profound changes in their structure that can be considered qualitative. From a different point of view, biological and social systems are not random assemblies of their more micro components but ordered systems in which individual identities, group structures and patterns of interactions are far from random and enjoy considerable stability. Major qualitative changes in these structures can occur, but they tend to be infrequent with respect to more incremental changes which occur all the time. In this sense we can see that there is a potential conflict between the study of long-term evolution and that of short-term changes. In fact, a complete science should be able to deal with both, but the intellectual tools used for each of these tasks may well be different. Here we just wanted to point out that in evolutionary economics the concept of order, or structure, is the counterpart of equilibrium in neoclassical economics. The need that all economic theories need to face is the relationship between order and change.

Another not often recognized precursor of evolutionary economics was Marx, although neither he nor his followers ever acknowledged the similarity. We consider that Marx's work was evolutionary not because we share his conclusion that capitalism will inevitably be replaced by communism, but because of his mode of analysis. The central assumption of Marx's work was that patterns of human evolution are determined by class struggle. While the classes that he identified (proletariat and bourgeoisie) are not necessarily the same in different historical periods, the generalizable principle is that in each society there is enough heterogeneity in capabilities, income, and power to determine the formation of different groups having conflicting interests and opinions about the allocation of resources, outcomes and rewards. The dynamics of these conflicts is likely to interact with the dynamics of technology and that of nation states, giving rise to complex patterns of development. Thus, Marx's theory is essentially dynamic, not just in the sense that changes necessarily occur in the course of time, but that such changes can give rise over relatively long periods to profound transformations in the structure of SESs, such as the one between feudalism and capitalism. There is no reason why such dynamics should end at a given time in history, as Marx himself assumed with the transition to communism, thus being unfaithful to his own methodology. The presence of group conflicts as a driving force for the development of SESs will be discussed again in Chapter 7. Here our purpose is to show that Marx was a very important precursor of evolutionary theories in the social sciences. He was not directly influenced by biology, but his style of explanation resembles more that of biology than one based on constructivist rationalism.

Although Schumpeter was by no means a Marxist in his conclusions, he was deeply influenced by Marx. Part 1 of CSD[2] begins with a long chapter on Marx, examined as a prophet, a sociologist, an economist, and a teacher. However, just the fact that Schumpeter quotes Marx is not a complete explanation of the influence that Marx had on him. CSD is an analysis of the reasons for which even a creative and dynamical system like capitalism is destined to be replaced by socialism. Although such prediction may sound very similar to that of Marx, the mechanism whereby the transition to socialism was expected to occur was very different from the one that Marx had proposed. The working class did not play an important role in Schumpeter's work. In fact, in his early work, Schumpeter stressed the heroic character of the entrepreneur who introduced radical innovations into the economic system, overcoming the resistance of those who opposed change. In this phase Schumpeter borrowed ideas from theories of the elite. He maintained that the disruptive effects of innovation could not be introduced by the masses alone but that it required the presence of the entrepreneur (Andersen, 2009). However, he differs radically from Marx in rejecting the latter's theory of the immiseration of the working class. Also, he does not consider the bourgeoisie and the masses to be necessarily enemies but sees the possibility of collaboration between the two (CSD, p. 19).

According to Schumpeter, the crisis of capitalism and its eventual replacement by socialism are not due to the efforts of the working class but to the rationalist attitude that the industrial bourgeoisie created that did not stop at 'the credentials of kings and popes, and could go on to attack private property and the whole scheme of bourgeois values' (CSD, p. 143). Furthermore, such rationalist attitude created a 'vested interest in social unrest' (CSD, p. 146). Thus, the internal contradictions of the industrial bourgeoisie were expected by Schumpeter to be responsible for the transition to socialism. Contrary to Marx, Schumpeter did not look forward to this transition. He just expected it to be inevitable. Schumpeter was a great admirer of capitalism but expected its eventual replacement by socialism to be inevitable.

It is interesting to consider the role of innovation both in the creation and in the expected final demise of capitalism. In his early work in TED,[3] Schumpeter (1934) stressed the role of the entrepreneur as the hero of capitalist evolution, introducing innovations into the economic system in the expectation of a temporary monopoly and facing greater resistances and uncertainty as opposed to managers who just administered the existing activities of the economic system, that he called the *circular flow*. In CSD he shifted to a different position by saying that the formation of monopolies and oligopolies was not as disruptive of capitalist creativity and of social welfare as many economists expected, but could contribute to innovation. The large corporations that were becoming common in mature industrialized countries were capable of innovating. Their large R&D labs would eventually replace the individual entrepreneur. Using a modern evolutionary terminology, innovation could be completely routinized.

These two different mechanisms of introduction of innovation have given rise to the distinction between Schumpeter Mark 1 and Schumpeter Mark 2, corresponding to two different technological regimes (Winter (1984), Malerba and Orsenigo (1993, 1997), Breschi et al. (2000), Malerba (2007)). Each technological regime is defined by opportunities, appropriability, cumulativeness, generic knowledge, and specific knowledge, while innovation patterns are described by technological entry and exit, concentration of innovative activities and stability in the ranking of innovators (Table 6.1). High technological opportunity tends to favour the entry of new innovators while low technological opportunity is likely to favour incumbent innovators. High cumulativeness favours incumbent innovators and low cumulativeness leaves more chances to enter to new innovators. Stability in the ranking of innovators is high if appropriability and cumulativeness are high. The type of existing knowledge base can have a considerable influence on observed patterns of innovation. According to Breschi et al (2000) and Malerba (2007), a generic knowledge base tends to favour incumbent firms with large R&D laboratories, which can have a high absorptive capacity (Cohen, Levinthal, 1989) while specialized knowledge in the applied sciences is equally available to new and incumbent innovators (Table 6.1).

We agree with this analysis except for the nature of the knowledge base. We think that the presence of discontinuities arising from qualitative change in knowledge is at least as important as the distinction between generic and specialized knowledge. The R&D laboratories of large diversified firms (LDFs) are likely to have a high absorptive capacity for the types of knowledge that they have already been using but a very low one for qualitatively new types of knowledge. Thus, during the phases after the emergence of a new technological paradigm (Dosi, 1982), we can expect new innovators coming from universities or basic research to have a better absorptive capacity for the new technology than any of the incumbent firms or R&D laboratories. However,

Table 6.1 The relationship between patterns of innovation and technological regimes, from Malerba (2007)

Pattern of innovation → *Technological regime ↓*	*Concentration (CONC)*	*Stability (STAB)*	*Entry and exit (ENTRY)*
Opportunities (OPP)	+/−	+/−	+
Appropriability (APP)	+	+	−
Cumulativeness (CUM)	+	+	−
Generic Knowledge (KBA)	+		−
Specific Knowledge (KAP)	−		+

the relative advantage of Schumpeterian entrepreneurs and Large Diversified Firms (LDFs) can shift from the former to the latter during the life cycle of a technology, as the new technology matures and the relevant competencies become more easily available. The evolution can be analysed in terms of the properties of knowledge described in Chapter 4 (Krafft et al., 2014). At the emergence of a discontinuity, the cognitive distance (CD) between the knowledge base of incumbent Large Diversified Firms (LDFs) and that of the technology constituting the new paradigm is very high and only researchers from universities or basic research institutions can create innovative start-ups (SUs) that have a high absorption capacity for it. In these conditions, the coherence of the new technology, defined as the possibility to combine the new technology with other types of knowledge, new or old, is very low and hampers the possibility to develop industrial applications of the new technology. When the new technology matures, CD falls as LDFs acquire the relevant competencies, absorption capacity and coherence increase back to normal levels, thus facilitating industrial applications (Figure 6.1).

Then the advantage shifts from SUs to LDFs, as shown by their relative changes in centrality (Saviotti, Catherine, 2008). High CD corresponds to low barriers to entry for SUs and to high barriers to entry for LDFs. High coherence (COH) corresponds to high cumulativeness and tends to favour the concentration of innovation, shifting the advantage to LDFs.

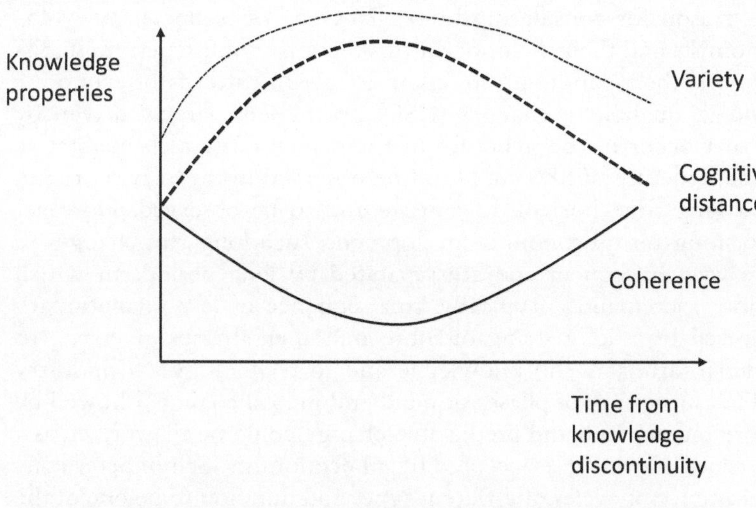

Figure 6.1 Evolution of the properties of knowledge in the presence of a discontinuity. This figure represents the KB of a sector with a constant technology. The diagram representing the knowledge base of a sector undergoing transitions between qualitatively different technologies would be given by the combination of different diagrams similar to that of Figure 6.1, one for each technology.

The previous analysis shows that there has not been a definitive transition from Schumpeter Mark 1 to Schumpeter Mark 2. On the contrary, Schumpeterian entrepreneurs, giving rise to high-tech SUs, and Schumpeter Mark 2 LDFs coexist, being more complements than substitutes. Of course, the assumption that innovation could be completely routinized was highly debatable. Both pieces of evidence from non-capitalist systems and recent capitalist development indicate that large corporations are certainly capable of innovating, but that they cannot create all the innovations required to explain observed patterns of economic development. The high-tech Start-Ups (SUs) that were fundamental for the emergence of electronics, ITC and biotechnology are almost pure examples of entrepreneurial innovation (Saviotti, Catherine, 2008), corresponding to Schumpeter Mark 1. However, large, diversified firms (LDFs) are highly capable of transforming radical innovations into products. SUs are more characteristically playing the role of disruptive innovators (ibid), but they are very rarely capable of transforming themselves into LDFs (ibid). Thus, a given sector can shift from a Schumpeter Mark 1 mechanism to a Schumpeter Mark 2 mechanism during its industry life cycle (ILC). Furthermore, a sector that has attained a Schumpeter Mark 2 state can be rejuvenated by the emergence of a new technology which challenges the one the sector is using. The impact of biotechnology on the pharmaceutical and agrochemical industries and that of semiconductors on computers are relevant examples. Thus, both industries and technologies can have a cyclical behaviour, but the two do not necessarily coincide. A new technology can either create a new sector or transform an existing one.[4]

The main reason for considering both Marx and Schumpeter as evolutionary economists and their inclusion in this section about structure, stability and change is their common interest in long-run patterns of economic evolution and in qualitative changes (CSD, pp. 82–86), largely driven by innovation, that occur in the structure of SESs. Naturally, such qualitative changes in the structure of SES could not be observed in the very short run but needed a long time-horizon to emerge and to be observed. However important for long-term economic development, such long-run changes in structure are very infrequent and are separated by long periods in which change is more incremental. Typically, this sequence of few revolutionary changes followed by a long string of more incremental ones gives rise to discontinuities in artefacts and knowledge and to technology and industry life cycles. This succession of phases of rapid and radical change followed by others of more incremental and predictable change could be interpreted as a cycle. Some types of cycles are accepted by all economists. Schumpeter considered the existence of cycles of different types and duration to be one of the most important aspects of economic development. Recently, Schumpeterian, and evolutionary economists have become interested in long waves and in the role played by technological innovation in them (Freeman, Perez, 1988; Freeman, Louça, 2001; Perez, 2002).

Both Marx and Schumpeter were more interested in change than in stability. In fact, Schumpeter was much more aware than Marx of the dichotomy and was interested in it all throughout his career (Andersen, 2009). He included the circular flow in his representation of the economic system and was a great admirer of Walras, although he clearly stated that economic development did not arise from the circular flow but could only be caused by innovation. In both cases the concept of a general equilibrium did not fit easily in their work. The emphasis on long-term patterns of economic development cannot suffice to understand fully the day-to-day functioning of economic systems. It follows that the relationship between stability and change is still at the heart of the social sciences.

In this context, it is important to list Pasinetti (1981, 1993) as an important structuralist. Once more, the changes in the economic system which occurred between Schumpeter and Marx affected his work. By the 1970s, the economic system had become much more highly differentiated and structural change much easier to observe. Furthermore, the computational capability available to economists had enormously increased and enabled empirical and modelling work that would have been inconceivable in previous generations. The development of input-output analysis which became a powerful tool for empirical and modelling work on structural change could not have been developed without the use of computers. Pasinetti was neither an evolutionary nor a neoclassical economist, but developed his work in the intellectual environment of the Cambridge capital controversy (see Chapter 5). Although he was never an evolutionary economist, to the extent that structure and order is a relevant component of evolutionary economics, he deserves to be mentioned as an important influence on the development of evolutionary economics. With respect to Marx and Schumpeter, Pasinetti developed a much more analytical approach and placed at its centre the instability potentially arising from the tension between the growth of productive efficiency and that of demand. He suggested that the creation of new sectors, which in Chapter 5 we called creativity, could avoid this instability, and allow economic development to continue in the long run. Thus, productive efficiency and creativity are complementary components of economic development. Recent research, both empirical (Hidalgo et al., 2007; Hidalgo, Hausmann, 2009; Funke, Ruhwedel, 2001a, 2001b; Saracco et al., 2015) and modelling (Saviotti, Pyka, 2004, 2008, 2013), substantially confirmed Pasinetti's ideas and showed that not only continued growth and economic development require structural change, but a particular type of unidirectional structural change in which output variety keeps growing and becomes an arrow of time.

1.4 Rules and institutions

The importance of structure and order cannot be fully understood without taking into account the role of institutions other than the firm and the market. Neoclassical economics focused on an extremely narrow range of institutions. Thus, while an approach aimed at studying an economic system at constant institutional structure can have some advantages, such as, for example, achieving a more precise and analytical representation of the system, it achieves this by excluding from its observation space some phenomena that cannot be analysed by the same approach. Given that changes in institutions tend to be slower than other economic phenomena (North, 1990, Chapter 13; Perez, 1983), it is quite likely that a relatively parsimonious intellectual approach neglecting some institutions and their changes will perform poorly in the study of long-run phenomena. This is noticeable in the study of modern SESs, let us say of the XXth and XXIst centuries, in which non-market institutions have grown at least as much as those directly related to markets. Furthermore, these non-market institutions are not independent of markets but coevolve with them.

Institutions are required for the collective adaptation of a group or community to its EE to be superior to individual adaption à la Robinson Crusoe (Chapter 3). Institutions suppress some types of behaviour and prescribe others to ensure that the collective outcomes the group can potentially achieve, be they economic, political, or military, are not wasted due to antisocial, egoistic individual behaviour. In this sense institutions provide the alignment of individual behaviours required for collective adaptation to be superior to individual adaptation. To achieve this objective, institutions need to have an ethical and legal foundation. Virtually all human societies had some form of myth to explain the origin of morality. For example, in Plato's *Protagoras* Zeus took pity of hapless humans and, to make up for their weaknesses relative to other animals, he gave them a moral sense and the capacity for law and justice, so that they could live in larger communities and cooperate with one another (Encyclopaedia Britannica, Knowledge in Depth, Vol. 18, 627, 1988; about this point see also Hodgson, 1988, pp. 23–24).

Furthermore, given that collective adaptation is based on division of labour and on coordination, institutions are required to define both. The different types of human activities and their interactions are defined by formal or informal institutions. As previously pointed out, division of labour and trade would not provide any advantage unless they were coupled with the coordination of different steps or elementary activities. In some cases, the invisible hand (Smith, 1776) provides the required coordination. However, in a wide range of circumstances, rules and institutions are required to provide coordination. The fundamental importance of language and writing can be understood in this sense. Furthermore, an advanced division of labour in pin making would not result in any enhanced output unless coordination between individual steps were present. The productive advantages of an assembly line could not be achieved unless each worker were able to carry out the required operations when the previous workers complete their tasks. Thus, by defining the belonging of individuals to subgroups and their interactions, institutions contribute to create the order or structure of a particular SES.

In addition to ruling out undesirable behaviour and providing coordination, institutions reduce the uncertainty present in the EE, both the one deriving from the actions of other individuals or organizations and the one arising from the evolving knowledge of the physical world or of socioeconomic systems. Economic activities would be severely restricted if we were not secure walking in the streets of cities or moving between the places where we practise our activities. The uncertainty-reducing role of institutions is particularly important in economic activities. Furthermore, and increasingly so, uncertainty arises about the knowledge firms and organizations need to use, both for what concerns the physical and the social world. The EE of firms is extremely complex. To acquire and interpret all the information needed to map this EE and to predict its future evolution is far beyond the capabilities of any firm. Although it may seem paradoxical, innovation, by increasing the variety of the economic system, keeps increasing the range of uncertainty present in an SES. However, the lack of information[5] is not the only barrier to the coordination of individual activities. According to North (1990, p. 20), the uncertainty of our EE is due essentially to two reasons: (i) human motivation and (ii) deciphering the environment. (i) Human behaviour is not just wealth-maximizing but also includes altruism and self-imposed constraints; (ii) we decipher the EE by processing information by means of pre-existing mental constructs through which we understand our EE and solve problems. Our subjectively derived mental constructs diverge amongst individuals and show no tendency to converge. Furthermore, they tend to be longer lived than short-term changes in the EE, such as product types and fashions. Thus, both human behaviour and our EE are far more complex than assumed by rational choice and orthodox economics. Institutions and rules exist to reduce the uncertainty and keep it within manageable boundaries. The overall complexity and knowledge required to coordinate human and organizational behaviour is likely to have increased with economic development: according to North (Chapter 4, p. 28) transaction costs rose from 25% to more than 45% of national income during the XXth century.

Another feature of institutions that contributes to their importance in socioeconomic evolution is their character of habitual behaviour. Veblen (1899) was the first to propose that institutions could be considered habits of thought. This definition has recently been rescued and elaborated by Hodgson (1988). Habits of thought exist because 'fully conscious rational deliberation about all aspects of behaviour is impossible because of the amount of information and computational competence involved' (ibid., p. 124). Habits can greatly reduce the complexity of everyday life by using a fixed pattern of behaviour instead of getting involved in global rational calculations involving very large amounts of information and requiring knowledge that is often beyond the competencies of most or all individuals. The routines used by firms and other organizations are an example of habitual behaviour.

In turn, institutions are composed of rules. Social rules can be defined as statements prescribing or forbidding some types of behaviour. Here, differently from Dopfer, Potts (2008), we distinguish social rules from cognitive statements, which define connections between observables and variables in the natural environment (see Chapter 4). Although in principle both can be considered as relationships between different concepts, the former refers to relationships between inputs and outputs, or between actions and outcomes, while the latter describe relationships which are invariant with respect to human actions. Examples of both are:

1 Thou shalt not kill
2 $e = mc^2$ where e = energy, m = mass and c = speed of light

Technological statements can be considered an intermediate case since they describe actions required to obtain some types of social outcomes. Technological statements are in principle relationships, or connections, between (a) the natural world, physical and biological, related to the internal structure of artefacts, and (b) the services supplied to users and consumers[6] (see Chapter 1, mapping) which are more closely related to the social world. Creation of a new man-made artefact (MMA) involves combining raw materials extracted from the physical and biological world in order to supply services to the users of the given artefact. In a general sense, this means establishing connections between (a) the physical and biological world and (b) the services that manipulating it could produce for human users and consumers. Both (a) and (b) come from different networks of knowledge, with the connections in (a) being invariant with respect to human actions while the connections between (a) and (b) and those within (b) are statements aimed at improving human welfare.

All these rules contribute to create order or structure. Institutions are sets of rules hierarchically organized and connected to an overarching objective. Institutions contribute to order by limiting the types of behaviour allowed in a community to generate the collective adaptation that makes the community superior to a set of independent individuals. For that to happen, certain types of behaviour must be excluded or encouraged. For example, neither murder nor taking justice into one's own hands is allowed.

The previous considerations lead to two sets of questions, one related to stability and one to change. First, why do institutions exist and how did they come about? We have already seen that, according to Hayek (1982, pp. 18–19), institutions were not designed to achieve specific objectives or based on a sound knowledge that allowed people to predict their outcomes but that they came about by blind variation and group selection. Thus, some institutions turned out to be 'better' by increasing the frequency of occurrence of the respective communities without any individual having precise knowledge of how those institutions were likely to work. We think Hayek was somewhat excessive, since constructivist rationalism inspired the creation of institutions which, although themselves incomplete, contributed in important ways to socioeconomic evolution. In other words, the creation of institutions was not based on completely blind variation but included a component of intentional design. This was true even long before the scientific revolution, as the many myths about morality demonstrate.

Even when institutions contribute to give a high adaptability to the respective community, they cannot be said to be fair or efficient. Institutions are hardly ever impartial with respect to the needs and rewards of the different members of a community. The more powerful members and groups within a community are likely to affect the formation of institutions more than the less powerful ones (North, 1990). Furthermore, the efficiency of institutions can only be defined with respect to some objectives. A community which is very fit in each EE and with a given objective is not necessarily going to retain its high fitness if the EE or the objective changes while preserving the same institutions. An example of the effect of changing objective and EE in each community is given by the changing rates of reproduction as SESs increase their level of economic development. In most societies in human history, families tried to produce as many offspring as they could, thus behaving very similarly to most other animal species. Since the XXth century, and at times differing for each country, rates of reproduction and family sizes fell very rapidly. It is possible to interpret this transition as arising from the combination of (i) increasing levels of education involving longer periods in life spent learning and rising costs per child, and (ii) the creation of forms of social security that could replace the care supplied by children to ageing parents. Today, in a highly developed SES, many children would be both impractical and not necessary. Consequently, countries experience falling fertility as they move towards higher levels of economic development. This transition will be discussed in greater detail in Chapter 7. Here this example was used to show that the concept of the efficiency of institutions is problematic and that it could at best be used for a constant objective and in a constant EE.

Institutions that were initially developed to carry out some fundamental functions, such as language, the law and religion, still operate, although in a different form, in every society. As the lives of communities evolve, existing institutions need to adapt by incorporating rules defining behaviour in new fields. For example, the development of settled agriculture required new competences needed to measure or document inputs or outputs (see Box 6.1). Technology can play a very important role in this respect. In addition to the example of settled agriculture, other examples like trade or the construction of buildings and roads needed the creation of new rules to define acceptable behaviour in these activities. In general, all new activities require new rules and institutions. However, it would not be correct to say that technologies and innovations cause the formation or the change of institutions. The appropriate institutions created after the emergence of a new technology substantially modify the subsequent development of the same technology. For example, the development of standards in the industries producing and using new materials substantially reduced the uncertainty involved in the exchange and application of these materials, contributing to expand the corresponding markets (Freiman, Quinn, 1970; Royce Institute, 2021) Organizational innovations can be as important as technological innovations in inducing the formation or change of institutions. The increase in firm size and industrial concentration that occurred at the end of the XIXth century induced the establishment of antitrust regulations and laws (Rosenberg, Birdzell, 1986). Thus, innovations, technologies and institutions coevolve and give rise to the creation of positive feedback loops which greatly accelerate the emergence and growth of new activities and markets. Of course, institutional changes occur also for political reasons, related to the distribution of resources and power amongst different social groups. Examples of institutions arising for political reasons are labour unions and political parties. We will discuss further political changes in institutions in Chapter 7.

Box 6.1 Mathematics in Egypt

Measurements were of fundamental importance in Egypt. There the parcels of land allocated to individuals by the Pharaoh, and from which the Pharaoh extracted an annual tax, were subject to periodic flooding. Both to allocate the parcels and to estimate the loss incurred by farmers due to the flooding, the services of surveyors known as harpedonaptai (literally rope stretchers) were required. The system of measurement together with other pursuits requiring practical arithmetic and mensuration contributed to the development of Egyptian mathematics and civilization. Thus, institutions (parcel allocation, taxation) coevolved with division of labour in society (profession of rope stretchers) and with the creation of knowledge (mathematics).

Source: Joseph, G.G. (1991) *The Crest of the Peacock*, London, Penguin pp. 58–59.

The relationship of institutions to economic evolution is based on the related concepts of order and structure discussed in the previous section. Order was considered by Hayek (1982, Chapter 2) a more appropriate concept than equilibrium for economics. Structure is a property of a complex system. There is order when the entities constituting the system are not all equal and are not arranged randomly. The existence of both order and structure requires the presence of differentiation in its constituting elements, the organization of these elements in distinguishable subsets and the presence of interactions between these subsets. In other words, the existence of order and structure requires a sufficient diversity, or variety, in its constituting elements and a reduction in the number of degrees of freedom in their interactions. The reduction of the degrees of freedom is obtained by limiting the possible interactions of the elementary components, which has the effect of combining different elements into subsets separated by distinguishable interfaces. Each subset contains an artificial combination of component elements of particular types. An example of such a system is a firm, which employs only some types of individuals organized in different subsets (divisions, departments, etc.) with specific patterns of interactions. In a firm, as in every other type of organization, not everyone talks to everyone else. On the contrary, only some types of interaction and communication are allowed.

The structure of an SES changes during economic development, and such changes tend to be relatively slow with respect to generational changes, sometimes occurring over several centuries. The expansion of any technology would be severely limited unless institutions defining the rules for its utilization existed. Technologies can have positive or negative effects for human communities and the function of institutions is to encourage the generation of positive effects while excluding the negative ones. By so doing appropriate institutions do not just limit the utilization of technologies by reducing their potential impact or market size. On the contrary, institutions allow an expansion of the market size or of the field of application of a technology far beyond what it could have achieved in a pre-institutional situation. For example, aviation could never have achieved the size it has today without the complex set of rules that govern it now. Typically, new technologies are created by Schumpeterian entrepreneurs in an a-institutional environment. While in the early phases of their life cycle very simple institutional arrangements can suffice, the technology can only grow beyond a given size if very complex institutional arrangements are developed. For example, when there were very few airplanes, they were all small, had a limited range and could land and take off from simply prepared fields; very simple rules could suffice to ensure that the positive effects of aviation predominated over the negative ones. Today, when hundreds of thousands of flights cross the skies every year, the set of rules required to ensure that this huge flow of air traffic occurs without serious accidents and provides substantial benefits to users and consumers has grown correspondingly. Such a coevolutionary path is by no means unique to aviation. A similar story of increasingly complex institutional arrangements accompanying the growth of technologies and their respective markets can be written for railways, cars, electrification, and telecommunications amongst others. Thus, we can expect technologies to emerge in an a-institutional environment and to require increasingly complex institutions to grow to their maximum possible size. In other words, we expect technologies and institutions necessarily to coevolve in order to generate the patterns of economic development that have been historically observed.

It this sense it is worth observing that infrastructures play a role similar to that of institutions, in that their presence is required for given technologies to be able to supply services to users and consumers at a large scale. An infrastructure is a physical device of such a large size as to require an investment greater or much greater than the one needed to set up a production plant of the given technology. In turn, once set up the infrastructure is available to all producers, users, and consumers of the given technology. Infrastructures can enormously enlarge the potential market for the outputs of a given technology. To appreciate this effect, it suffices to think how the number of today's cars could fit and could produce their transport services on the roads of the year 1910. Furthermore, today's cars are very different from those of 1910 and the changes in motor car technology introduced up to the present are partly due to the nature of existing infrastructures: modern cars could not go very far on unpaved roads full of huge potholes. Roads, bridges, airports, electricity, and telecommunications networks are examples of infrastructures.

Thus, to reach its maximum potential development, the technology giving rise to a particular industry needs complementary institutions and infrastructures that coevolve with it. Together with technologies, institutions and infrastructures create positive feedback loops that can amplify and speed up the development of a new technology. Not only they can enlarge the market corresponding to a given technology, but they can create additional employment in complementary institutions, infrastructures, and sectors. An example of the last type of complementarity is given by the petroleum refining industry. When the industry was founded in about 1859 (Waddams, Solomon, 2018; Nguyen et al., 2005), its most important applications were heating and lighting. Starting from the beginning of the XXth century the industry had to change its pattern of refining to supply the different fractions that can be used by cars and airplanes. These forms of complementarity act as *multipliers* (Llerena, Lorentz, 2022) and external increasing returns that had been identified by Allyn Young (1928).

2 Complexity and evolutionary theories

We consider that the reason for the use of biology in evolutionary economics stems from the intrinsic similarity of their subject matters. Although this intrinsic similarity is somehow related to the fact that human beings are a biological species, this cannot fully account for their similarity. This similarity consists of the complex nature of social and biological systems. Several scholars maintain that there can be a general level of explanation at which both biology and the social sciences can be studied by means of the theory of complexity (Allen, 2007, 2001, 1976; Allen et al. 2006, 2007; Foster, 2005; Dopfer, 2013; Hodgson, Knudsen, 2010; Arthur, 2015, 1989; Arthur et al 1997; Lane, 2011; Haken, 1983, Beinhocker, 2006; Kirman, 2011). The name 'theory of complexity' is somewhat deceptive in the sense that a full theory of complexity does not exist. In fact, even on the definition of complexity, there is no absolute agreement. However, several important developments in complexity science[7] have received widespread attention in the scientific community and have been awarded important scientific prizes. Such developments originated from several scientific fields. Complex systems and complex behaviours started to be studied in the 1950s in physics, chemistry, and biology (Nicolis, Prigogine, 1989; Prigogine, Stengers, 1983; Simon, 1962, 1969; Frenken, 2006) Allen et al (2007). Here we will focus on a small number of aspects of complexity which are generally judged to be important, such as interactivity, dynamics, open and closed systems, order and structure, positive feedback and increasing returns. It must be pointed out that complexity can provide a common interpretative framework for different types of systems, at quite a general level of analysis, but that each system has its specificity.

2.1 Interactivity

One of the most important features of complex systems is the interactivity of their components. For a long time, this made it impossible to calculate the dynamics of such systems. A complex system is composed of elements, or components, which are interacting in a non-simple way and of a boundary with its external environment (Simon, 1962, 1969). However, in many situations, the interactions between the elements of the system are difficult and costly to compute. Thus, until recently, systems of this type could not be studied because they were beyond the computational capabilities of the time. The aggregate properties of these systems were not intuitively derivable. Systems of this type exist within chemistry, physics, biology, and the social sciences. However, what existed only in some of these fields were what we could call *Simplifiable systems.* Some properties of these systems were determined by a small number of their elements that were interacting in a simple way. Simple here means interactions that were described by functions that could easily be calculated with the mathematics of the time and allowed to predict some aggregate properties of the given systems. Examples of such systems are those studied by Ptolemaic astronomy (Kuhn, 1957, 1962) and classical mechanics (Lipsey et al., 2005). Of course, such systems were not intrinsically simple. It is just that some of their aggregate properties were affected by very few properties of their constituting elements. The earth, the sun, planets and stars are far from simple, but their orbits are mostly determined by their mass and their gravitational attraction. It is not by chance that Simplifiable systems were the first to be understood and represented in a mathematical way.

Simplifiable systems hardly exist in biology and the social sciences.[8] Thus, for a long time, it was considered that the subject matter of these disciplines could not be understood by the same laws and theories used to study the behaviour of mechanical systems (Vico, 1725; Hume, 1740; Hayek, 1989). The success obtained in studying mechanical systems contributed to the scientific revolution and to the growing belief that human beings could modify their external environment by means of scientific knowledge (Mokyr, 2016; Mirowski; 1989). The schism between these two types of rationality does not seem equally large today given the progress made by the thermodynamics of irreversible processes and by our computational capabilities (Nicolis, Prigogine, 1989; Haken, 1983). That is one of the reasons for which we did not completely follow Hayek when he stated that constructivist rationalism was not appropriate to the study of the social sciences. Although he would have been right in asserting that the scientific knowledge that existed in the XIXth century was not suitable to study the social sciences, at a high level of generality modern complexity theory can be used to study different types of systems, including biological and social ones (Leydessdorff, 2001).

2.2 Stability and change

If calculating the structure of a complex system had been impossible up to a given time, calculating its dynamics would have been even more difficult. Yet, some of the intuitive properties of those systems that evolutionary economists and complexity theorists focus on are examples of dynamical systems that are strikingly different from the properties of those systems that neoclassical economists have been studying. The dichotomy between equilibrium economics and complexity economics (Arthur, 2007, 2015; Beinhocker, 2006; Kirman, 2011) exists not because equilibrium economics does not have a dynamic. Rather, the dynamics present in equilibrium economics allows only for temporary deviations from equilibrium. The equilibrium position in such a system can be shifted only by external, or exogenous, forces. Once the perturbation is over, the system reverts to its equilibrium position. In this sense one needs to make the implicit assumption that the period during which the perturbation acts and the system is out of equilibrium is short, as we have seen in Chapter 3 on adaptive behaviour. Thus, what matters in equilibrium economics is that general equilibrium is intrinsically stable.

On the contrary, complexity economics studies social systems that are intrinsically unstable. However, the instability in complexity economics is largely endogenously generated (Arthur, 2007; Kirman, 2011; Antonelli, 2011), or at least has significant endogenous components. Furthermore, complex SESs are not in a permanent chaos but change is occurring within an ordered SES, destroying parts of the existing SES, creating new components, and moving the SES towards a more differentiated and more complex state (Saviotti, Pyka, 2004, 2013; Hidalgo et al., 2007; Hidalgo, Hausmann, 2009). Thus, this instability is not to be understood as a negative feature of complex economic systems but rather as the source of their creativity. It is not clear why an SES that is in general equilibrium and in which no one should be induced to change could change and grow.

A complex SES will never be in equilibrium and there will always be some members of the population who are particularly innovative and try to introduce innovations into the SES. In other words, there will be micro diversity (Allen et al., 2006). Typically, such innovators are Schumpeterian entrepreneurs. They have a broad but not very detailed idea of the innovation they wish to implement. Thus, even when an entrepreneur is successful, the new technology or organizational form is not generated by a precisely designed plan but is the result of the interactions of the constituting elements, some of which modify endogenously the SES and in turn are affected by its new state. In the course of time, the innovation does not remain in the state in which it was created by an entrepreneur, but is gradually modified to adapt to the environment in which it is adopted. In turn, the social environment itself needs to change in order to allow a growing diffusion of the innovation, for example, by the creation of infrastructures, appropriate institutions, and complementary industries. In other words, the new technology or organizational form created by an innovation needs to coevolve with other components of an SES to amplify the process of diffusion and the size of the corresponding markets. In this sense an SES is different from a complex physical or chemical system, and even from a biological system. The components of a physical or chemical system can be affected by the aggregate state of the system but cannot purposely modify the system. In other words, they can at most adapt to the state of the system (ADTO), but not adapt the system to their requirements (ADOF).[9] Agents in an SES have some form of knowledge that allows them to react to changes in their environment (ADTO) and even to change purposefully their environment (ADOF). Such knowledge is never perfect and it does not allow economic agents to predict accurately the result of their actions. This is particularly true for entrepreneurs introducing into an SES radical innovation qualitatively different from anything that existed before. In the early stages of this process, characterized by high and radical uncertainty, a new technology becomes better known, more efficient and more differentiated while in subsequent and more mature stages incremental and more predictable improvements become increasingly important (Dosi, 1982; Nelson, Winter, 1977; Abernathy, Utterback, 1975). Thus, during the early stages of the life cycle of industries or technologies, qualitative change dominates while in the later stages quantitative change becomes dominant. Thus, although even equilibrium economics has some form of dynamics, for example, in terms of growth equations, it does not have the dynamics of *qualitative change.* Such dynamics is much more difficult to study and only recent developments in complexity science and irreversible thermodynamics allowed significant progress to be made. The conditions leading to the emergence of new types of phases, life forms, activities, sectors, and institutions are discussed in the following subsection.

2.3 Order and disorder

In Section 2.3 the concepts of structure and order have been considered very important in the development of an evolutionary approach. However, the existence of order itself was observed rather than explained. It is not clear why economic changes should lead to ordered states rather than to disordered ones. The structure of an SES depends on the patterns of division of labour and coordination that exist within it. Although the price system can provide coordination in a wide range of situations, it cannot explain the changing structures of SESs. The Roman Empire, the medieval society and the XXIst century SES had quite different structures. They differed in their methods of production, in their activities (economic and non-economic), in their institutions and organizational forms. However, are the methods of production, institutions, organizational forms, and development paths that we can observe the only possible ones? Or could there have been different structures and development paths? Is there any reason for expecting processes of change to lead systematically to gradually more ordered, differentiated, and complex states than those that preceded them? In general, due to the second law of thermodynamics, the transformations of physical and chemical systems and of their surroundings, which form a *closed system*, are expected to give rise to more disordered states, corresponding to an increasing entropy. Since entropy is a property that measures disorder, this law means that all the natural processes lead to final states that are more disordered than the initial ones from which the process started.

If economic transformations must satisfy the same requirement, then the final state of any process of economic development should be more disordered than initial state. This conclusion seems to be in stark contrast with various observed aspects of economic development. Man-made artefacts, such as machines, buildings, and electrical devices, seem to be much more ordered than the raw materials from which they were produced (see Chapter 1). In fact, the processes of production of man-made artefacts consist of taking high-entropy raw materials and transforming them into low-entropy products (Chapter 1). Furthermore, modern industrial and post-industrial societies are both more diversified and more ordered than primeval societies or communities. Of course, the same observation of growing order and complexity can be made for biological systems, and it was in the past a reason for thinking that such systems could not develop according to the same laws as physical or chemical systems (Von Bertalanffy, 1950). However, recent developments in irreversible thermodynamics have shown that a particular type of systems, called open systems, can undergo transitions leading to final states that are more ordered and more diversified than the initial ones (Haken, 1978; Prigogine, Stengers,1984; Nicolis, Prigogine,1989; Hidalgo, 2015; Allen, 2006, 2007; Beinhocker, 2006).

Systems are open when they have flows of matter, energy and information going through their boundaries. By definition they exist only away from equilibrium since equilibrium is the state in which no flows go through the boundaries of the system. Consequently, the rate of flow through the system boundaries of matter, energy and information measures the distance from equilibrium. The possibility for change processes to lead to final states more ordered and more differentiated than the initial ones occurs only when a threshold distance from equilibrium, consisting of a minimum flow rate of matter, energy, and information through their boundaries, is attained (Prigogine, Stengers, 1984; Nicolis, Prigogine, 1989). For flow rates higher than the minimum, open systems can undergo transitions to final states more ordered than the initial ones. On the contrary, closed systems, through the boundaries of which there are no flows, can achieve states of equilibrium, corresponding to the maximum disorder and entropy.

Although these findings come from the thermodynamics of irreversible processes, they are applicable to all systems, including biological and social ones. As in Chapter 1, an increasing disorder corresponds to a higher entropy. According to the second law of thermodynamics, a closed system can be expected to evolve spontaneously towards a state of growing entropy and to attain the maximum entropy at equilibrium. Since the whole universe is a closed system, its entropy can be expected to increase for any transition occurring within it. Consequently, the combined entropy of a process occurring in an open system and that of the rest of the universe needs to be greater than zero. Open systems can undergo transitions to final states of lower entropy because their fall in entropy is more than compensated by an increase in entropy somewhere else in the system, but they can do that only away from equilibrium.

The possibility to create more ordered structures in an open subsystem requires the creation of more disorder somewhere else. As seen in Chapter 1 (p. xx; Georgescu Roegen, 1971; Hidalgo, 2015), the creation of ordered structures constituted by technological artefacts requires the creation of greater disorder in the form of wastes and pollution. Thus, all processes using energy and raw materials lead in the end to an increase in entropy. This creates an immediate link to the relationship between technology and the environment. A general statement of our environmental problem can be formulated as follows: we need to reduce the total entropy produced by all human processes below a level that our environment can absorb (Deutscher, 2008; Ayres, 1998), corresponding to what Georgescu-Roegen (1971) called a viable technology. Of course, the broad principle that reducing the energy used below a given limit will necessarily reduce the entropy produced below the 'viable' threshold does not give us a complete recipe to create a sustainable SES.

2.4 Irreversibility and path dependence

Irreversibility is an easily observed phenomenon. Most people would not expect the life of biological organisms to be reversible or the pieces of a milk bottle fallen onto the floor to automatically recombine. Yet the idea that the material world was in principle reversible dominated classical physics between the scientific revolution and the XIXth century. Even then physicists did not dispute that some observed processes seemed to be irreversible, but thought that irreversibility was due to our ignorance rather than being a fundamental of property of the physical world (Prigogine, Stengers, 1984, p. 208). This started conflicting with the development of the steam engine and the birth of thermodynamics in the XIXth century. It then started being accepted that not only there were irreversible processes by which mechanical energy could be degraded, but that this degradation could constitute a fundamental law of the universe. The introduction of entropy, a function designed to measure the degradation of mechanical energy, led to the formulation of the second law of thermodynamics, stating that all natural processes led to a rise in entropy and were irreversible. The statistical interpretation of entropy by Boltzmann revealed that entropy measured disorder and that the second law of thermodynamics meant that the universe was likely to become gradually more disordered. This link between irreversibility and disorder seemed to conflict with the observation of ordered structures in biological organisms, manufactured objects, and forms of social organization. Georgescu-Roegen (1971) pointed out that these ordered structures did not violate the second law of thermodynamics because their order was more than compensated for by the various wastes involved in their production. In fact, according to Beinhocker (2006), it is the transformation of high-entropy materials into low-entropy products that creates value. Thus, the production of man-made artefacts (MMAs) creates ordered structures to supply valuable services to users and consumers (Chapter 1).

Equilibrium economics assumes negative feedbacks, or diminishing returns, in order to ensure a unique, predictable equilibrium (Arthur, 2007, 2015). For this reason, the presence of positive feedbacks, or increasing returns, has always troubled economists. We have seen in Chapter 5 how the pioneering intuition of Allyn Young (1928) about increasing returns was for a long time neglected. Quite likely, what delayed the acceptance of increasing returns was not the absence of phenomena indicating their presence but the need felt by economists to preserve the existence of equilibrium. When positive feedbacks, or increasing returns, exist, a different set of phenomena can occur. In general, in these phenomena, deviations from equilibrium are not systematically damped but can be amplified, leading the system to a different structure, or affecting its dynamics in unexpected ways. Thus, in chemistry, autocatalytic reactions can lead a system to the formation of chronologically or spatially ordered patterns (Nicolis, Prigogine, 1989) while in economics the competition of technologies can lead to multiple equilibria, lock-in and potential inefficiency. Such inefficiency can arise, for example, from the presence of learning effects which improve the performance of a technology and make it better than another technology which was potentially superior (Arthur, 1989; David, 1985). In SESs path dependence is generated by the existence of institutions, some of which persist even in the presence of important societal changes which seem incompatible with the given institutions.

2.5 Coevolution

Reference has already been made several times to coevolution as a very important mechanism in economic development. Relevant examples were those of the coevolution of innovation and demand, or that of technologies and institutions. As was pointed out, coevolution involved positive feedback between the interacting components of an SES in which each component reinforced the other, thus potentially accelerating processes of change and leading to the emergence of a new structure. In this sense coevolution is equivalent to an autocatalytic reaction. Perhaps the most important and neglected form of coevolution is that of human communities and their natural environment.

The implicit assumption that was made since the time of the industrial revolution amounted to considering the natural environment as a bottomless pit from which infinite amounts of resources could be extracted and into which infinite amounts of wastes could be dumped. To start adapting to our natural environment, coevolving with it is perhaps our greatest challenge today.

Here it may be useful to remind ourselves of the differences between the two related concepts of self-organization and coevolution. Self-organization is a process in which some form of overall order arises from local interactions between parts of an initially disordered system. However, coevolution is a more dynamical concept in which the components of a system interact, leading to an outcome different from that which would be obtained by the same but not interacting components. Thus, while in both cases the interactions between components are essential, self-organization focuses more on the order that can be achieved by means of these interactions and coevolution stresses the development path(s) to which the same interacting components can give rise.

3 Ontology

Several scholars stressed ontology as one of the most important dimensions to define the nature of evolutionary economics (Hodgson, 2010; Witt, 2008). The work of different economists could be considered evolutionary to the extent that it shared the same ontology or that it was based on the same entities. Witt (2008) lists the ontological level (what basic assumptions are made about the structure of reality), the heuristic level (how the problems are framed to induce hypotheses) and the methodological level (what methods are used to express and verify theories). This distinction seems particularly important concerning the use of biological analogies in evolutionary economics: some authors used it just as a heuristic device while others, such as Veblen (1898), Georgescu-Roegen (1971), Hayek (1988) and North (2005), adhered to a naturalistic, Darwinian world view. This view considers that human beings are just one more biological species living in an environment and subject to its constraints. The approach called Universal Darwinism advocates a combination of a heuristic based on an abstract analogy to Darwinian concepts and a naturalistic ontological position (Hodgson, 2002; Hodgson, Knudsen, 2006, 2012). Of course, this does not imply that the same laws and patterns of change can apply unchanged to both biological species and human communities.

However, the distinction between ontology and heuristics as factors defining evolutionary economics is not absolute. Ontology cannot be such an exclusive determinant of the nature of theories even if it can certainly contribute to the way a theory is conceived. The ontology underlying a theory can change, depending on the development of the same or other theories. For example, the fundamental entities of biology or cosmology changed in the course of time, depending on the progress of physics and chemistry. In fact, after the mid-to-late XIXth century, all disciplines, at least in the physical sciences, could have shared the same atomistic ontology and physics could hold out the promise of the unification of all science. In fact, it is the conception of physics that became dominant at the time that had a very important impact on the development of neoclassical economics (Mirowski, 1989, p. 201). Of course, while the methodology of neoclassical economics mimicked the development of physics, it could not immediately adopt its same ontology. At the time neoclassical economics was created, biological organisms and social organizations could not be explained based on physics. It took more than half a century for that hurdle to be overcome and for biology itself to acquire the same ontology as physics and chemistry. This distinction was only overcome in the XXth century with the progress of molecular biology and the thermodynamics of irreversible processes. In other words, what is an ontological difference at a given time can become an ontological similarity at subsequent time. However, while this in principle implied that social systems could be governed by the same laws as physics or as biology, this did not immediately transform the social sciences into a passive application of physics or biology. Even in this case disciplines like biology and physics remain separate although sharing a common ontology.[10] Even when they share the same ontology, different disciplines and theories do not have internal structures that map easily onto one another. Thus, although ontology is an important potential determinant of the formation of theories and disciplines, it does interact with methodology and heuristics (see Chapter 5). This means that the distinction between ontology and methodology is more fluid and less discrete than hypothesized by Witt (2008).

In spite of ontology not being such exclusive determinant of the formation of theories, the exclusion of the biological nature of human beings can have very important implications for the development of a theory. A change in ontology seems to have occurred in economics after the industrial revolution: land has been abandoned in favour of a man-made world in which only production remained. Paradoxically, this started with classical economics but continued with neoclassical economics, where the production function only contained capital and labour but no land, although such production function was logically derived as an extension of the consumption function. If the biological nature of human beings had not been excluded by economics, we might have realized sooner the problems we were creating for ourselves by considering our EE as a bottomless pit into which we could dump all what we wanted.

As for methodology, although it is unlikely to be the primary variable in the definition of evolutionary economics, it has a non-negligible importance. For example, there is a correspondence between the worldview of neoclassical economics and that of XIXth century physics, and with the emergence and use of the concept of energy (Mirowski, 1989). The mimicking of physics by neoclassical economics was not limited to the adoption of a worldview but included the adoption of the mathematical techniques used in it (ibid).

However, more modern mathematical techniques and discoveries in physics and chemistry, such as system dynamics, agent-based modelling (see Pyka et Fagiolo, 2007; Dosi, Roventini, 2019) or network theories, enable the treatment of more complex types of change than those studied by neoclassical economics. It is perhaps not by chance that despite his efforts to learn and apply mathematics to economics, Schumpeter never managed to do it. The mathematics of his time was simply unsuitable for this purpose.

The question raised by the conclusion of the previous paragraph is whether continuity and differences are due to ontology or some other reason. Without wanting to exclude ontology, we propose another source of continuity and differences. This arises from the division of labour in knowledge production that gives rise to different disciplines, research traditions, specialties, etc. (Chapter 4). Each discipline chooses a subset of social or natural reality and tries to identify the entities, observables, structures, and mechanisms within it in order to understand how it is likely to evolve in the course of time. Different disciplines can compete by trying to suggest different explanations for the same phenomena or be complementary by supplying explanations for related but not identical phenomena. In this context, it is clearly possible for evolutionary economics to consider human beings as biological species but to focus on their 'artificial' man-made activities while biology would consider human beings another biological species but focus on their biological properties and mechanisms, without any of the two denying the biological nature of human beings. Admittedly, the boundary between the two disciplines would be somewhat fuzzy as phenomena such as health and nutrition would be studied by both but in different ways. In this sense it would be possible for biology and evolutionary economics to share the same ontology. Furthermore, to the extent that the origin of life can be explained by natural processes arising from non-living matter, such as simple organic compounds (Luisi et al., 1999; Kitadary, Maruyama, 2018), both biology and evolutionary economics would share the same ontology based on a common origin.

4 A comparison of evolutionary and neoclassical economics

In this chapter we discussed evolutionary and neoclassical economics as consisting of two broadly different world views rather than of discrete research traditions separated by well-defined boundaries. In this section we attempt to provide a comparison of these worldviews by means of three dichotomies: knowledge vs uncertainty, stability vs change, interactivity vs independence (Table 6.2). In the presence of total and radical uncertainty, only choices by trial and error are possible. However, only very limited amounts of knowledge are enough to drastically reduce uncertainty and to limit choices to a finite although sometimes still wide range. This situation has been described in Chapters 2 and 4 as characterized by entrepreneurial knowledge, the type of knowledge available to entrepreneurs when they create a radical

Table 6.2 Aspects of the different worldviews corresponding to evolutionary economics and neoclassical economics

	Knowledge vs uncertainty		*Stability vs change*		*Independence vs interactivity*	
	Knowledge	*Uncertainty*	*Type of change*	*Dynamics*	*Coordination*	*Coevolution*
Neoclassical	Perfect	Calculable risk	Exogenous + quantitative	Equilibrium + instantaneous adjustment to exogenous shocks	Automatic: individuals + coordination by invisible hand	Irrelevant
Evolutionary	Always progressing but incomplete	From radical uncertainty to calculable risk	Long and short range Endogenous +exogenous, qualitative + quantitative	Permanent change alternating between qualitative and quantitative	Transactions, complex and costly, Institutions, Intertemporal coordination	Structure, multi-stability path dependence irreversibility

innovation and they have only a broad understanding of all the implications of their innovation for the SES in which it is adopted and improved. During technology or industry life cycles, uncertainty changes from very high and radical to very limited and approximately calculable risk. In this low uncertainty limit, evolutionary economics approaches neoclassical economics, although general equilibrium can never be attained. However, there is no clear-cut limit defining the boundary between radical uncertainty and calculable risk.

Another very important difference between evolutionary economics and neoclassical economics is given by their relative time horizons. Qualitative and structural changes are much more visible in the long run. They generally occur according to time scales different and longer than those of some short-run phenomena, such as the duration of daily work, fashion cycles or average life expectancy. Such changes are very difficult or impossible to predict and this has very strong implications for the reliability and durability of human policies. This aspect will be discussed further in Chapter 7.

Notes

1 About the competition between theories see Chapter 4.
2 CSD: Capitalism, Socialism and Democracy
3 TED: Theory of Economic Development
4 Here see the trajectories leading to output variety and to intra-sectoral product diversification in Chapter 5.
5 See information overload.
6 See Chapter 1, about twin characteristics.
7 Complexity science is not a discipline but a different approach to knowledge.
8 See Allen et al. (2006) for an analysis of types of knowledge related to different levels of complexity.
9 See Chapter 3 for adaptive behaviour.
10 On the division of labour in the formation of different disciplines see Chapter 5.

References

Abernathy W.J., Utterback J.M. (1975) A dynamic model of process and product innovation. *Omega*, 3(6): 639656.

Alchian A.A. (1950) Uncertainty, evolution and economic theory. *Journal of Political Economy*, 58(2): 211–222.

Alchian A.A. (1953) Biological analogies in the theory of the firm: comment. *American Economic Review*, 43: 600–603.

Allen P. (1976) Evolution, population dynamics and stability. *Proceedings of the National Academy of Sciences, USA*, 73(3): 665–668.

Allen P. (2001) Knowledge, ignorance and the evolution of complex systems, in Foster J., Metcalfe J.S. (Eds), *Frontiers of Evolutionary Economics*, Cheltenham, Edward Elgar, 313–350.

Allen P. (2007) Self-organization in economic systems, in Hanusch H., Pyka A. (Eds), *Elgar Companion to Neo-Schumpeterian Economics*, Cheltenham, Edward Elgar, 1111–1148.

Allen P., Strathern M., Baldwin J. (2006) Evolution, diversity and organization, in Garnsey E., McGlade J. (Eds), *Complexity and Co-evolution*, Cheltenham, Edward Elgar, 22–60.

Allen P.M., Strathern M., Baldwin, J.S. (2007) Complexity and the limits to learning. *Journal of Evolutionary Economics*, 17: 401–431. https://doi.org/10.1007/s00191-006-0051-3

Andersen, E. S. (2009) *Schumpeter's Evolutionary Economics: A Theoretical, Historical and Statistical Analysis of the Engine of Capitalism*. Anthem Press, London, New York, Deli.

Andersen E.S. (1994) *Evolutionary Economics: Post Schumpeterian Contributions*, London, Pinter.

Antonelli C. (Ed) (2011) *Handbook on the Economic Complexity of Technological Change*, Cheltenham, Edward Elgar.

Arthur W.B. (2015) *Complexity and the Economy*, Oxford, Oxford University Press

Arthur W.B. (1989) Competing technologies, increasing returns, and lockin by historical events. *The Economic Journal*, 99: 116–131.

Arthur W.B. (2007b, 2015) Complexity and the economy, pp 1102–1110 in Hanusch H., Pyka A. (Eds), *Elgar Companion to Neo-Schumpeterian Economics*, Cheltenham, Edward Elgar.

Arthur W.B., Durlauf S.N., Lane D.A. (1997) *The Economy as an Evolving Complex System II*, Boston, MA, Addison–Wesley.

Ayres R.U. (1998) The second law, the fourth law, recycling and limits to grow INSEAD Working Paper, 98/38/eps/cmer.

Beinhocker E.D. (2006) *The Origin of Wealth, The Radical Remaking of Economics and What It Means for Business and Society*, Boston, MA, Harvard Business School Press.

Breschi S., Malerba F., Orsenigo L. (2000) Technological regimes and Schumpeterian patterns of innovation. *Economic Journal*, 110(463): 388–410.

Cohen M., Levinthal D. (1989) Innovation and learning: the two faces of R&D, *Economic Journal*, 99: 569–596.

Coombs R., Saviotti P.P., Walsh V. (1987) *Economics and Technological Change*, London, MacMillan.

Darwin C. (1859) *On the Origin of Species* (1st ed.), London, John Murray.

David P. (1985) Clio and the economics of QWERTY. *The American Economic Review*, 75(2), Papers and Proceedings of the Ninety-Seventh Annual Meeting of the American Economic Association (May, 1985): 332–337.

Deutscher G. (2008) *The Entropy Crisis*, Singapore, London, World Scientific.

Dopfer K. (2013) Evolutionary economics, chapter 14, in Faccarello G., Kurz H.D.(Eds), *Handbook of the History of Economic Analysis*, Volume II, *Schools of Thought in Economics*, Cheltenham, Edward Elgar, 175–193.

Dopfer K., Potts, J. (2008) *The General Theory of Economic Evolution*, London and New York, Routledge.

Dosi G. (1982) Technological paradigms and technological trajectories: a suggested interpretation of the determinants and directions of technical change. *Research Policy*, 11: 147–162.

Dosi G., Roventini A. (2019) More is different… and complex! the case for agent-based macroeconomics. *Journal of Evolutionary Economics*, 29(1): 1–37.

Encyclopaedia Britannica, Knowledge in Depth, Vol. 18, 627, 1988.

Foster J. (2005). From simplistic to complex systems in economics. *Cambridge Journal of Economics*, 29: 873–892.

Freeman C. (1982) *The Economics of Industrial Innovation* (2nd ed.), London, Pinter.
Freeman C., Louça F. (2001) *As Time Goes By, from the Industrial Revolution to the Information Revolution*, Oxford, Oxford University Press.
Freeman C., Perez C. (1988) Structural crises of adjustment, business cycles and investment behaviour, in Dosi G., Freeman C., Nelson R., Soete L., Silverberg G. (Eds), *Technical Change and Economic Theory*, London, Pinter, 38–66.
Freeman C., Soete L. (1997) *The Economics of Industrial Innovation*, London, Pinter.
Freiman, S. Quinn, G. (1970) How standards help bring new materials to the market, *Astm Standardization News* (Accessed April 27, 2022) https://www.nist.gov/publications/how-standards-help-bring-new-materials-market
Frenken K. (2006) *Innovation, Evolution and Complexity Theory*, Cheltenham, Edward Elgar.
Funke M., Ruhwedel R. (2001a) Product variety and economic growth: empirical evidence for the OECD countries. *IMF Staff Papers*, 48(2): 225–242.
Funke M., Ruhwedel R. (2001b) Export variety and export performance: empirical evidence from East Asia. *Journal of Asian Economics*, 12: 493–505.
Georgescu-Roegen N. (1971) *The Entropy Law and the Economic Process*, Cambridge, MA, Harvard University Press.
Haken H. (1983) *Synergetics*, Berlin, Springer Verlag.
Hart N. (2013) *Alfred Marshall and Modern Economics*, Basingstoke, Palgrave MacMillan.
Hayek F. (1982) *Law, Legislation, and Liberty*, London, Routledge.
Hayek F. (1988) *The Fatal Conceit: The Errors of Socialism*, London, Routledge.
Hidalgo C. (2015) *Why Information Grows, The Evolution of Order, from Atoms to Economies*, Penguin Random House.
Hidalgo C.A., Hausmann R. (2009) The building blocks of economic complexity. *PNAS* 106(26): 10575.
Hidalgo C.A., Klinger B., Barabasi A.-L., Hausmann R. (2007) The product space conditions the development of nations. *Science*, 317: 482–487.
Hodgson G.M. (2002) Darwinism in economics: from analogy to ontology, "*https://econpapers.repec.org/article/sprjoevec/" Journal of Evolutionary Economics*, 2002, vol. 12, issue 3, 259-281.
Hodgson G.M. (1988) *Economics and Institutions*, Cambridge, Polity Press.
Hodgson G.M. (1993) Institutional economics: surveying the 'old' and the 'new'. *Metroeconomica*, 44: 1–28.
Hodgson G.M. (2010) A philosophical perspective on contemporary evolutionary economics, *Papers on Economics and Evolution*, Max Planck Institute of Economics, Evolutionary Economics Group.
Hodgson G.M., Knudsen T., The nature and units of social selection, J Evol Econ (2006) 16:477–489 DOI 10.1007/s00191-006-0024-6
Hodgson G.M., Knudsen T. (2007) Dismantling Lamarckism: why descriptions of socio-economic evolution as Lamarckian are misleading. *Journal of Evolutionary Economics*, 17(3): 349–352.
Hodgson G.M., Knudsen T. (2008) In search of general evolutionary principles: Why Darwinism is too important to be left to the biologists. *Journal of Bioeconomy*, 10: 51–69. https://doi.org/10.1007/s10818-008-9030-0
Hodgson G.M., Knudsen T. (2010) *Darwin's Conjecture: The Search for General Principles of Social and Economic Evolution*, Chicago, Chicago University Press.
Hume D. (1740) *A Treatise of Human Nature: Being an Attempt to introduce the Experimental Method of Reasoning into Moral Subjects*. London, John Noon, 1739.

Kirman A. (2011) *Complex Economics: Individual and Collective Rationality*, London, Rutledge.

Kitadary N., Maruyama S. (2018) Origins of building blocks of life: a review. *Geoscience Frontiers*, 9(4): 1117–1153.

Krafft J., Quatraro F., Saviotti P.P. (2014) The dynamics of knowledge-intensive sectors' knowledge base: evidence from biotechnology and telecommunications. *Industry and Innovation*, https://doi.org/10.1080/13662716.2014.919762

Kuhn T.S. (1957) *The Copernican Revolution*, Cambridge, MA, Harvard University Press.

Kuhn T.S. (1962) *The Structure of Scientific Revolutions*, Chicago: The University of Chicago Press.

Lane A.D. (2011) Complexity and innovation dynamics, in Antonelli C. (Ed), *Handbook of the Economic Complexity of Technological Change*, Cheltenham, Edward Elgar.

Lazaric N. (2000) The role of routines, rules and habits in collective learning: some epistemological and ontological considerations. *European Journal of Economic and Social Systems*, 14(2): 157–171.

Leydessdorff L. (2001) *A Sociological Theory of Communication: The Self-organization of the Knowledge-based Society*, uPUBLISH.COM: Universal Publishers.

Lipsey R., Carlaw K.J., Bekhar C.T. (2005) *Economic Transformations: General Purpose Technologies and Long-Term Economic Growth*. Oxford, Oxford University Press.

Llerena P., Andre Lorentz A. (2022) Alternative theories on economic growth and the co-evolution of macro-dynamics and technological change: a survey. hal-00279328

Losee J. (1977) *A Historical Introduction to the Philosophy of Science*, Oxford, Oxford University Press, 104–105.

Luisi P.L., Walde P., Oberholzer T. (1999) Lipid vesicles as possible intermediates in the origin of life. *Current Opinion in Colloid & Interface Science*, 4: 33–39.

Malerba F. (2007) Patterns of innovation and technological regimes, pp 344–359 in Hanusch H., Pyka A. (Eds) *Elgar Companion to Neo-Schumpeterian Economics*, Cheltenham, Edward Elgar, 344–359.

Malerba F., Orsenigo L. (1993) Technological regimes and firm behavior. *Industrial and Corporate Change*, 2(1): 45–71.

Malerba F., Orsenigo L. (1997) Technological regimes and sectoral patterns of innovative activities. *Industrial and Corporate Change* 6(1): 83–116.

Marshall A. (1890) *Principles of Economics*, London, MacMillan, 8th edition (1949).

Mirowski P. (1989) *More Heat than Light: Economics as Social Physics, Physics as Nature's Economics*, Cambridge, Cambridge University Press.

Mokyr J. (2016) *A Culture of Growth: The Origins of the Modern Economy*, Princeton, NJ, Princeton University Press.

Nelson R.R. (2006) Evolutionary social science and universal Darwinism. *Journal of Evolutionary Economics*, 16(5): 491–510.

Nelson R.R. (2007a) Comment on 'Dismantling Lamarckism: why descriptions of Socio-Economic evolution as Lamarckian are misleading', by Hodgson and Knudsen. *Journal of Evolutionary Economics*, 17(3): 349–352.

Nelson R.R. (2007b) Universal Darwinism and evolutionary social science. *Biology and Philosophy*, 22(1): 73–94.

Nelson R., Winter S. (1977) In search of useful theory of innovation. *Research Policy*, 6: 36–76.

Nelson, R. Winter, S. (1982) *An Evolutionary Theory of Economic Change*, Cambridge, MA, Harvard University Press.

Nguyen P., Saviotti P.P., Trommetter M., Bourgeois B. (2005) Variety and the evolution of refinery processing. *Industrial and Corporate Change*, 14: 469–500.

Nicolis G., Prigogine I. (1989) *Exploring Complexity*, New York, Freeman.

North Douglass C. *(2005), Understanding the Process of Economic Change*, Princeton, Princeton University Press.

North D.C. (1990) *Institutions, Institutional Change and Economic Performance*, Cambridge, Cambridge University Press.

Pasinetti, L.L. (1981) *Structural Change and Economic Growth*, Cambridge University Press.

Pasinetti L.L. (1993) *Structural Economic Dynamics*, Cambridge, Cambridge University Press.

Penrose E.T. (1952) Biological analogies in the theory of the firm, *American Economic Review*, 42: 804–819.

Perez C. (1983) Structural change and the assimilation of new technologies in the economic system. *Futures*, 15: 357–375.

Perez C. (2002) *Technological Revolutions and Financial Capital: The Dynamics of Bubbles and Golden Ages*, Cheltenham, Edward Elgar, 198 pages, ISBN 1 84064 922 4.

Popper K. (1934) *The Logic of Scientific Discovery*, London, Hutchinson.

Prigogine I., Stengers I. (1984) *Order Out of Chaos*, London, Fontana.

Pyka A., Fagiolo G. (2007) Agent-based modelling: a methodology for neo-Schumpeterian economics, pp 467–487 in Hanusch H., Pyka A. (Eds), *Elgar Companion to Neo-Schumpeterian Economics*, Cheltenham, Edward Elgar, 467–492.

Robert V., Yoguel G. (2016) Complexity paths in neo-Schumpeterian evolutionary economics, structural change and development policies. *Structural Change and Economic Dynamics*, 38: 3–14.

Rosenberg N., Birdzell L.E. (1986) *How the West Grew Rich*, New York, Basic Books.

Royce Institute (2021) Materials-4.0-A-Role-for-Standards.pdf https://www.royce.ac.uk/content/uploads/2021/06/

Saracco F., Di Clemente R., Gabrielli A., Pietronero L. (2015) From innovation to diversification: a simple competitive model, *PLOS ONE*. https://doi.org/10.1371:journal.pone.0140420

Saviotti P.P. (1996) *Technological Evolution, Variety and the Economy*, Cheltenham, Edward Elgar.

Saviotti P.P., Catherine D. (2008) Innovation networks in biotechnology, pp 53–82 in Holger Patzelt, Thomas Brenner (Eds), *Handbook of Bioentrepreneurship*, New York, Springer, 53–78.

Saviotti P.P., Pyka A. (2004) Economic development by the creation of new sectors. *Journal of Evolutionary Economics*, 14(1): 1–35.

Saviotti P.P., Pyka A. (2008) Micro and macro dynamics: industry life cycles, inter-sector coordination and aggregate growth. *Journal of Evolutionary Economics*, 18: 167–182.

Saviotti P.P., Pyka A. (2013) From necessities to imaginary worlds: structural change, product quality and economic development. *Technological Forecasting & Social Change*, 80: 1499–1512.

Schumpeter J. (1911) *The Theory of Economic Development*, Cambridge, MA, Harvard University Press (1934, original edition 1911).

Simon H.A. (1965) *Administrative Behaviour*, 2nd Ed, New York, Free Press.

Simon H.A. (1962) The architecture of complexity. *Proceedings of the American Philosophical Society*, 106: 467482, reprinted in: Simon H.A. (1981) *The Sciences of the Artificial*, Cambridge, MA, MIT Press.

Simon H.A. (1969, 1981) *The Sciences of the Artificial*, Cambridge, MA, MIT Press.

Smith A. (1776) *The Wealth of Nations*, Penguin English Library, 1972 and following reprints.

Spencer H. (1892) *Essays Scientific, Political and Speculative*, New York, Appleton.

Tavares Silva S., Teixeira A.C. (2006) On the divergence of evolutionary research paths in the past fifty years: a comprehensive bibliometric account, FEP working Papers, N° 229 (2006) CEMPRE, Oporto University.

Veblen T.B. (1899) *The Theory of the Leisure Class: An Economic Study in the Evolution of Institutions*, New York, Macmillan.

Veblen T. (1898) Why is economics not an evolutionary science?, *Quarterly Journal of Economics*, 12: 374–397.

Vico G. (1725) *Principi di una Scienza Nuova*, Naples, Felice Mosca.

Von Bertalanffy L. (1950) The theory of open systems in physics and biology. *Science*, 111: 23–29.

Waddams A.L., Solomon L.H., et al. (2018) Petroleum refining, Encyclopædia Britannica, Encyclopædia Britannica, Inc., November 09, URL: https://www.britannica.com/technology/petroleum-refining

Winter S.G. (1964) Economic natural selection and the theory of the firm. *Yale Economic Essays*, 4: 225–272.

Winter S.G. (1984) Schumpeterian competition in alternative technological regimes. *Journal of Economic Behavior & Organization*, 5(3–4): 287–320.

Witt U. (2008) What is specific about evolutionary economics? *Journal of Evolutionary Economics*, 18: 547–575. https://doi.org/10.1007/s00191-008-0107-7

Young A.A. (1928) Increasing returns and economic progress. *The Economic Journal*, 38(152): 527–542.

7 Evolutionary political economics

1 Introduction

In the introduction to this book, we said that if evolutionary economics wants to become a general interpretative framework for economic behaviour and change, it cannot focus only on innovation in a narrow sense. In this chapter we will go back to say that innovation has changed the world and that it remains one of the most powerful forces contributing to its continued development. This is not in contradiction with our initial objective since, as we have already seen before, innovation does not act alone and independently, but by necessity it coevolves with institutions, organizational forms, and infrastructures. This happened because existing institutions can create conditions that are favourable both to the emergence of innovation and to the utilization of innovation and technology in society. These considerations were developed at a very general level in the previous chapters of this book. In this chapter we will start to explore the possible links of evolutionary economics with the political sphere, in terms of the coevolutionary paths linking the two. In one chapter we can hardly hope to do more than to scratch the surface of such a virtually boundless subject that could easily fill not one but many books. We will focus on a limited number of examples and concentrate on the basic links connecting economic activities, innovation, and political institutions.

2 Innovation and political institutions

Since the beginning of history all human communities needed to acquire and use the resources required to achieve their overarching objectives. In primeval communities the objectives could be simplified to survival and procreation or, in other words, to individual and collective survival over different periods of time. From these overarching objectives followed some more detailed ones, involving, for example, the acquisition of food and shelter, these being the most basic resources. Different human communities had their own endowments, for example of physical strength and mental capabilities, which were unevenly distributed both within each community and

DOI: 10.4324/9781003294221-7

between different communities. Furthermore, all human communities lived in an external environment (EE) in which the resources required for survival and procreation were distributed unevenly. For example, some subsets of EE could be very rich in food and shelter and others very poor. Also, human communities could migrate and fight for resources. Even if in some subsets of the EE food and shelter were initially plentiful, scarcity was likely to be created by population growth. Even in such simple communities there could be a type of dynamics. For example, a human community finding itself in a resource- 'poor' EE could migrate in search of a better one and find it, but occupied by another community. The invading and the incumbent communities would then fight to compete for the local resources.

Although the previous considerations were specific to very simple types of human communities, all the subsequent and much more complex types of communities needed resources to pursue their objectives. However, what changed radically in the course of human history are the types of resources used and the objectives pursued. Whereas in very simple communities' food and shelter would suffice as resources, in a modern society the range of resources used would be far wider, including things like bicycles, computers and portable telephones or services like health care, cinema or holidays. Furthermore, the objectives pursued in modern societies are far more varied than just survival and reproduction. For example, education, employment, and professional development became as important as or more important than survival and reproduction. How these changes took place and how they were affected by innovation and technological change are crucial questions in the understanding of human history.

As far as political institutions are concerned, the crucial question is whether political choices can affect investment decisions, research programmes and production strategies leading to wealth creation, to reasonable income distribution and altogether to an improvement in the living conditions of the populations of SESs. The answer to this question would be positive if it were possible to demonstrate that there is only one type of political system that is superior to all others in creating a combination of material and social welfare and of freedom. A partial answer to this question exists: not all types of political system are equally capable of providing material wealth, social welfare and freedom. Perhaps the best example of this during the XXth century was the Soviet Union, the collapse of which was due to its inability to stimulate the innovation and creativity that could lead to growing output, welfare, and freedom.[1] As a consequence, it became increasingly difficult to compete in armaments with the USA without unduly increasing the share of GDP allocated to military expenditures (Wolf, Popper, 1992). Furthermore, the same type of political system can be declined in many versions with widely varying outcomes in terms of wealth creation, distribution, and quality of life. Hall and Soskice (2001) distinguished between liberal market economies (LMEs), in which firms tend to rely more on market mechanisms, and coordinated market economies (CMEs), in which firms depend more heavily on non-market relationships to coordinate their actions with other actors and to construct their core competencies. While Hall and Soskice conclude that there is no substantial difference between the long-term economic performance of LMEs and of CMEs, they maintain that the former have a greater propensity for radical innovation and the latter for incremental innovation. These expected differences amongst varieties of capitalism could in fact be compatible with similar economic performances: for example, a CME country could compensate its lower propensity to create radical innovations with a greater capability to develop these innovations once they have been created elsewhere. They compare the USA and Germany as examples of LME and CME countries.

The attractive simplicity of Hall and Soskice's distinction of capitalist economies into LMEs and CMEs and the corresponding intuition that the former tend to specialize in radical innovation while the latter tend to specialize in incremental innovation are likely to be responsible for their large impact on several disciplines and research traditions, ranging from economics to political science to business studies to innovation studies. The large number of studies that quoted or criticized Hall and Soskice (H&S) pointed out some of their weaknesses. Such weaknesses are of three types: (i) the potential difficulties inherent in identifying radical and incremental innovations (Akkermans et al., 2009); (ii) the neglect of other disciplinary contributions (Almond, Gonzalez Menendez, 2006; Feldman and Kogler, 2010; Rodríguez-Pose and Di Cataldo, 2015; Hancké et al., 2007); (iii) the assumption that there can be only one optimal development path.

Akkermans et al. (ACL) point out that H&S compare LMEs and CMEs focusing just on the USA and Germany, showing that each country produces relatively more patents in technology classes that are likely to contain radical innovations: semiconductors and biotechnology for the USA, incremental innovations (transport, etc.) for Germany. Furthermore, the two countries are compared in the 1983–1984 and 1993–1994 periods, neglecting that the share of radical innovations in each class tends fluctuate in the course of time since technologies generally follow life cycles, typically initiated by a radical innovation and followed by a long stream of incremental innovations[2, 3] (Abernathy, Utterback, 1975; Dosi, 1982). The share of radical innovations in each class tends to fluctuate in the course of time since technologies generally follow life cycles, typically initiated by a radical innovation and followed by a long stream of incremental innovations[4] (Abernathy, Utterback, 1975; Dosi, 1982). Furthermore, there is considerable evidence that innovations within a technology class, irrespective of their radical or incremental nature, tend to cluster in specific geographical locations (Feldman, Kogler, 2010), thus raising further doubts about H&S interpretation. ACL adopt a more sophisticated approach to the detection of radical innovations based on the work of Trajtenberg (1990), Trajtenberg et al. (1997) and Shane (2001) which assumed that a radical innovation would be more cited, used in a wider range of applications, and based on more diverse types of knowledge than an incremental one. Furthermore, ACL made the comparison of LMEs and CMEs more relevant by extending it to 23 countries, even placing some of them in a third group of Mediterranean Market Economics (MMEs). Finally, ACL pointed out that some of H&S's results run counter to earlier work based on patent statistics for a much broader set of countries that focused on other aspects than LME vs CME differences, such as differences in country size (Archibugi, Pianta, 1992). In addition to the above difficulties, H&S neglect other disciplinary contributions by focusing exclusively on firm coordination without taking into account that other institutions could affect the choice and the performance of technologies. Within economic geography, the coevolution of institutions and technologies is only just beginning to receive the attention it deserves (Hall, Soskice, 2001; Feldman, Kogler, 2010; Rodríguez-Pose, Di Cataldo, 2015). Rather than a discrete dichotomy of the two types LME and CME, the state of MEs can be described as a distribution of socioeconomic systems (SESs) contained between the above two extremes, in which each SES combines different degrees of the same set of activities and institutions. For example, Sweden, a CME country in ACL classification, combines a high degree of employment protection with a large stock market, given the size of the country (Almond, Gonzalez Menendez, 2006).

In terms of our previous analysis, H&S can be summarized as (i) being based on the assumption that there is one optimal development path and (ii) being based on the hypothesis that the structure of an SES is likely to affect its observed development path. Additionally, H&S do not specify the time horizon on which the comparison of LME-CME should be carried out. As H&S admit, if we use the macroeconomic growth rate to compare the performance of different MEs, LMEs and CMEs cannot be separated. Consequently, either no ME of the two types follows an optimal development path or there is no optimal development path and different MEs follow similar development paths based on similar[5] structures of their SESs. In fact, the range of system structures compatible with a 'good' economic performance can be quite narrow, so that differences in the type, size and interactions of SES components are limited. In this case very large deviations from the structures observed for the 'good' SESs would condemn other SESs to an inferior economic performance. Then, the communist system of the Soviet Union would have been an example of large deviations from capitalist SESs which made it impossible for the Soviet Union to compete with them.

The economic development that followed the collapse of the Soviet Union can be interpreted as a limited convergence on accepting some capitalist institutions and mechanisms, combined with other institutions and mechanisms aiming to (i) compensate for the unequal distribution of wealth and power that capitalist economic development would spontaneously produce and (ii) compete economically or militarily with other similar SESs. Whereas immediately after the collapse of the Soviet Union future economic development seemed to be destined to be led by MEs, the subsequent rise of China to world power changed the situation to a confrontation between two different styles of capitalist development: a Western democratic one and a Chinese, state-led, authoritarian one. Contrary to the Soviet Union, China is rapidly catching up with the West by constructing a very successful NIS (Lundvall, Rikap, 2022). This raises again the question of the superiority of a given political system in stimulating innovation and creating economic development in a different form. Could a socioeconomic system combining capitalist mechanisms of economic development with a strict political control of society outperform an innovative Western democratic system? The Chinese government seems to believe so and is presenting the Chinese model of economic development as a superior alternative to the Western democratic one. However, recent attempts by the Chinese government to drastically increase its control of the economy could considerably affect China's economic performance. This is unlikely to stop China's economic development and to reduce it to a secondary power, but it could affect the competition between the Chinese and the Western model. Whatever the success of China's development strategy, we can expect a new geopolitical order dominated by the USA and China to emerge in the world system. Amongst the factors likely to affect the structure of the future world system technological capabilities are likely to play a very important role, although they will need to be accompanied by political institutions that can limit the inequalities that are spontaneously generated by a highly innovative system, a topic that will be discussed in the next chapter.

In the following section of this chapter, we will explore how the coevolution of innovation, technologies and political institutions since the industrial revolution contributed to the observed patterns of socioeconomic development at different levels of aggregation.

3 On the interactions between innovations, technologies and institutions in recent history

From the creation of tools to the construction of water mills, roads and bridges, innovation always played a role in human history (Mokyr, 1990). However, it is only since the industrial revolution that innovation started to contribute systematically to self-sustaining economic development. By contributing systematically, we mean that innovations started to become relatively frequent, that they were widely adopted within SESs and that their impact on economic development was clearly established. When we say that innovation contributed to self-sustaining economic development, we mean that the growth which then started could continue cumulatively in the course of time, without being limited to short bursts followed by a return to an almost zero growth path. That this was a novelty after the industrial revolution can be seen in Figure 1.1. This kind of economically self-sustaining growth needs to be distinguished from the sustainability that is being discussed now, that is based on the reduction of the environmental impact of human activities on the external environment (EE). In fact, the economically self-sustaining growth that began with the industrial revolution has been at least partly due to the implicit assumption that the impact of human activities on our EE was likely to be negligible. This aspect of the problem will be discussed later. Now we start by exploring how the coevolution of innovation, technologies and institutions transformed the previous no growth pattern into one of economically self-sustaining growth.

We are now going to explore the interactions between innovations and technologies on the one hand, and the political evolution on the other hand. We are not trying to establish the causes of either technological or political events, but to explore the coevolution of technologies and institutions. In coevolution the growth of one factor can lead to the growth of one or more other factors, which in turn affect positively the growth of the initial factor(s) in a positive feedback loop. Once these factors are in place, they can collectively determine the rate of growth of some macroeconomic variables, such as output and population. They could still be considered determining factors, but their overall effect on macroeconomic variables would depend both on their amount *and* on their interactions. Typically, such a situation gives rise to non-linear dynamics, in which at least some of the terms in any dynamical equation are joint functions of more than one factor. This feature of coevolution makes it a relatively simple example of complexity and a potential mechanism enhancing the emergence of a new system configuration qualitatively different from any pre-existing ones. When there is coevolution what is important to establish is the set of factors contributing to a given process and their interactions. Once the set of factors is in place, the mechanism can operate, leading to self-sustaining growth until some limit is attained. Such a limit could be a finite supply of one or more of the relevant factors. In general, no such self-sustaining growth path can be expected to last indefinitely. However, the beginning of the coevolution requires a minimum amount of all the basic factors. This minimum amount could be considered a necessary condition for the *emergence* of a new *configuration* of an SES qualitatively different from any pre-existing ones. However, once these emergence conditions were in place, the mechanism that kept the system going could lead to a faster growth than it would have been if the different contributing factors were acting independently.

3.1 The rise of manufacturing

The first fundamental characteristic of industrial capitalism was the presence of *capital*, which combined with labour led to a considerable rise in productive efficiency. The new machines used in the factory system replaced the putting-out system in which artisans worked at home using their tools and then sold the product of their labour to merchants (Mokyr, 1990; Landes, 1969). The much larger size and cost of the new machines used in the factory system limited their property to a few individuals who could access the financial resources required. Clearly, financial institutions were an important further component of coevolution (Hodgson, 2021). These machines were owned by industrial capitalists, who employed workers. In turn, workers sold their labour to the capitalists in exchange for wages. It is to be observed here that at the beginning of the industrial revolution the terms 'capital' and 'capitalists' were new and started to be used only in the mid-XIXth century (Hobsbawm, 1975). These innovations were the basis for the creation of two new social classes: the industrial capitalists and the proletariat. The interests of these two classes were opposite because the capitalists tried to pay wages as low as possible to make a profit while workers tried to raise wage levels in order to achieve reasonable working conditions and a fairer distribution of resources and power in society.

We do not need here to agree with the Marxian hypothesis of the gradual impoverishment of the working class, but simply to observe that the interests of the two classes were antithetical and would lead to the class struggle that marked heavily the political evolution of the XIXth and XXth centuries. In this class struggle workers were not alone. Starting from the second half of the XIXth century, new political parties and movements were created to defend the interests of the working class. It is in this period that Marxism emerged and that socialist and communist parties started to be organized (Hobsbawm, 1975). We are certainly not able to discuss in detail the above class struggle except by observing that it was at the centre of the political evolution of both industrialized and pre-industrial countries at least until the collapse of the Soviet Union.

The class struggle took the form of demands by the working class and its representatives for better working conditions and a fairer society. Such demands which were typically resisted by industrial capitalists. The tensions thus originated at the international level gave rise to two very different solutions: (i) private property was identified as the fundamental cause of the injustices created by industrial capitalism and an alternative political system was created to eliminate it; (ii) a more reformist development path was chosen in which private property and the capitalist mode of production were retained, but in which the state took the responsibility to compensate for the unfair distribution of resources and power that this mode of production inevitably generated. The former led to communist regimes and the latter to what we will call capitalist democratic regimes. This bifurcation did not arise immediately after the industrial revolution, but it took a long time for it to be created: the Russian Soviet Republic, created in 1917, and the Soviet Union, created in 1922, were the first communist societies while capitalist democratic countries only emerged after the Second World War. A common feature of the developed countries that after the Second World War they did not become communist was the creation of a welfare state (Esping-Andersen, 1990)[6] in which governments took responsibility for helping the most disadvantaged members of society. During the 1950–1980 period, some features of the welfare state were shared by most governments of capitalist countries, but the differences in its implementation were such that Esping Andersen divided welfare states into liberal, conservative, and social democratic. Although forms of government assistance for poor people were not historically new, the scale and institutional complexity they acquired in modern welfare states were incomparably greater than in any previous society. It is quite likely that there was a threshold of economic development below which a welfare state would not have been sustainable, but above which it became both economically sustainable and socially advantageous. The welfare state played an important role in the competition between the revolutionary communist and the reformist democratic regimes to be the dominant form of political organization of industrialized countries during most of the XXth century.

At this point we can already observe that a large part of the political evolution of the XXth century was due to events and forces set in motion by the industrial revolution more than 100 years before. The political events that we analysed in the previous paragraph were limited to intra-country politics, although they happened in parallel in many countries. Two other types of political phenomena related to the industrial revolution occurred at the international level. From the beginning of the industrial revolution until the 1850s, the UK was the unchallenged industrial leader of the world. In the second half of the XIXth century, a small number of European countries started to imitate the industrial revolution, thus competing for power with the UK. The main challengers of the UK were first Germany and later the USA (Landes, 1969, 1999), their competition being largely dependent on the success they had in imitating the industrial revolution. Here the term 'imitating' does not mean that the revolution had created a set of routines that remained unchanged and that could be simply copied.[7] On the contrary, it is quite clear that the industrial revolution did not remain unchanged after having been created. Already during the XIXth century it underwent several substantial changes which were responsible for the continuation of the self-sustaining growth initiated by the IR and which gave rise to changes in the group of countries that could be considered industrialized. Thus, the industrial revolution changed by adding to the initial technologies (textiles, steam engine, etc.) some new ones (organic chemicals, electricity) that were more science dependent. In these technologies, Germany acquired a decisive leadership (Freeman, Louça, 2001; Murmann, 2003) that later passed to the USA. Such an attempt by Germany to acquire its place in the world has contributed to the emergence of two world wars and has been considered an example of the so-called Thucydides trap, in which a war occurs between one or a series of incumbent powers and an emergent power. Such changes in technology, which have been considered by some scholars as new industrial revolutions (Freeman, Louça, 2001), were very important in determining the emergence of new economic powers, but their effects were not as spectacular as the emergence of the class struggle between capitalists and workers. However, in the second half of the XXth century, economic progress provided the citizens of advanced capitalist countries with a variety of goods and services[8] that, together with the welfare state, led these countries to outperform communist ones.

The industrial revolution not only enormously increased the average income and wealth of industrializing countries, but had a powerful effect on economic inequality both at the country and the world level. The above-described processes were not independent, but interacting, although proceeding at different speeds. The intra-country class struggle between workers and industrial capitalists was due to an extremely and increasingly uneven distribution of income and power generated by the industrial revolution. That a capitalist system spontaneously generated great amounts of wealth and high levels of inequality is not an accident, but follows from the naturally uneven distribution of rewards earned by the entrepreneurs or capitalists and by other members of society. This uneven distribution of economic rewards occurred both at the country and at the world level. Thus, the industrial revolution gave rise to an increasing wealth and power gap both at the country and at the world level (Milanovic, 2016). The inter-country inequality kept increasing until after the Second World War while the intra-country one went through periods of increasing and decreasing income inequality. In the early XIX century where you were born (location-based inequality)[9] was a far more important determinant of your economic condition than the position you occupied in your society (class-based inequality). The situation has been reversed since the 1980s due to the emergence of newly industrializing countries and globalization (Milanovic, 2016).

By the end of the XIXth century, a small number of European countries, the UK and its early imitators, had accumulated an economic and military superiority that allowed them to conquer or dominate the rest of the world. This happened in the form of the total political subjection of some non-European countries, which were directly administered by European powers and became colonies, or in the combination of formal independence and a growing industrial and military weakness in other non-European countries. The processes of (a) intra-country class struggle between workers and industrial capitalists, (b) inter-country competition for industrial, technological and military superiority amongst early industrializing ones and (c) the colonization of large parts of Africa and Asia by European industrial powers happened in parallel over some periods of time, but at quite different speeds. Thus, the British Empire reached its maximum extension long after the UK had been leapfrogged by Germany as the industrial and technological leader of the world. Now we will explore these three processes in order to see how they developed and interacted amongst themselves and with other trends that were already in place.

The competition between communist regimes, represented mostly by the Soviet system, and the capitalist democratic societies, the leader of which were the USA, gave rise to the world order which prevailed from the Second World War to the collapse of the Soviet Union in 1989. By world order we mean a particular configuration of the world economic and political system which is relatively stable over extended periods of time. Typically, such stability is obtained by the dominance of one or a small number of countries. Thus,

Britain dominated the world order of the XIXth century with a secondary role for France, while the USA and the Soviet Union dominated that of the XXth century. The transition from the British-dominated world order to the one dominated by the USA and the Soviet Union resulted from a gradual improvement in the economic performance of the USA relative to that of Britain, with the two world wars and the economic crisis that began in 1929 playing important roles. A similar transition in the world order is occurring now, leading probably to the emergence of a new political oligopoly dominated by the USA and China, with secondary roles possibly played by Russia, the EU and India.

The three long-term trends – (i) intra-country struggle between industrial capitalists and the proletariat, (ii) the inter-country competition amongst the countries that were already industrialized and those that were in the process of becoming so, (iii) the inter-country struggle between industrialized colonial powers – even at a very aggregate level, did not explain all the world evolution during the XIXth and XXth centuries. We focused on them because, on the one hand, they were very important trends, and, on the other hand, they were all dependent on the existence of the industrial revolution (IR) and on the coevolution of technologies and institutions that started with the IR. It would be excessive to state that the above trends provided a complete description of world development in the XIXth and XXth centuries. Older trends and power structures were still in place and affected world development. For example, the Spanish, Portuguese, and Dutch colonial empires had been established long before the British one and Britain needed to compete with them. However, these early colonial empires started to collapse in the XIXth century, when the British Empire was still expanding. Although the much earlier decline of the Spanish and Portuguese colonial empires is unlikely to be fully explained by the absence of an industrial revolution in those colonial powers, it seems quite clear that from the XIXth century onwards innovation and technology became factors increasingly contributing to world leadership.

Technological change and the capability to innovate have become fundamental ingredients in the ability of a country to develop economically and to attain a reasonable level of political autonomy. In order to do this, different countries must construct a national innovation system (NIS) (Lundvall, 1992; Nelson, 1993; Edquist, 1997, 2005; Fagerberg, Shrolec, 2008). In particular, full catching up by an LDC occurs when a follower country manages to reach the economic frontier, defined as the level of GDP per capita of the most advanced countries; the technological frontier, defined as a level of technological capabilities similar to that of the most advanced countries; and a level of institutional development comparable to that of the most advanced countries.[10] The concept of the NIS is not based simply on a particularly high allocation of resources to science, technology and innovation but also includes the presence of institutions that define the ways in which the creation and distribution of income and wealth occur. For example, the economic performance induced by the construction of a national innovation system was a very important factor contributing to the shift of world leadership from the UK to the USA. In the end, the collapse of the Soviet Union was at least partly due to its inability to innovate while the recent rise of China has been accompanied by the construction of a very effective NIS (Lundvall, Rikap, 2022).

After discussing the interactions between science, technology, and the political sphere after the industrial revolution, we can now start exploring what we can expect to happen in future. First, the competition between communist regimes and those that we called capitalist democratic came to an end with the collapse of the Soviet Union. For a while some commentators believed mankind had reached the end of history (Fukuyama, 1992) which would have been constituted by the world dominance of liberal capitalism.[11] Not only such a prediction turned out to be wrong, but the seeds of instability and change could have been detected before the collapse of the Soviet Union. What from the 1950s onwards had seemed to be the prevailing form of social organization, that we called capitalist democratic, started to be attacked by both capitalists and communists. Such form of social organization could be heroically simplified as grafting onto early capitalism some of the institutions that socialist movements had been demanding for the population and for workers. By the 1960s such an attempt seemed to have succeeded in stabilizing capitalist societies and in allowing them to resist more revolutionary changes, thus contributing to destabilize the Soviet Union. The creativity of capitalism, combined with some injections of socialism, defeated the Soviet attempt to create a communist society. Some communist regimes survived, but to do that they had to change radically their economic policies, by admitting some forms of work organization that were typically capitalist. The foremost example of this strategy is China. However, the apparent victory of the capitalist democratic order was more fragile than it seemed. Such liberal democratic order had been designed for a society constituted mainly by a small fraction of capitalists and by a large fraction of workers. In a slow and difficult-to-perceive way, the composition of society started to change, thus undermining the social democratic order. The change was due to the coevolution of several factors, one of which was the transition from a manufacturing to a service society. In the latter form of social organization, the class structure changed dramatically, reducing the population share of manufacturing workers and increasing that of other workers, mostly employed in services and often having short-term and insecure contracts.

Second, the adoption of the industrial revolution by follower countries continued apace, although in an updated version. The technological frontier towards which catching-up countries needed to move kept advancing in the course of time. After the end of the Second World War, Japan, South Korea, Taiwan, Singapore, and China rapidly industrialized, sometimes leapfrogging in some fields the early industrial powers. Yet, if we consider the industrial revolution a revolution that once initiated in a country could potentially diffuse to all other countries, it took a very long time to reach the present diffusion and even now this diffusion is far from complete. India is clearly on a path towards industrialization and some other countries could follow. This trend started to reduce income inequality amongst countries, which had been rising since the early XIXth century (Milanovic, 2016, p. xx).

We could interpret all these changes in terms of the concept of *asymmetry*, the asymmetrical distribution of institutions, wealth, economic and military power in the world system (Pisani-Ferry, 2020). The asymmetry of the world system increased considerably from the industrial revolution to the Second World War, then it seemed to start decreasing in the 1970s with the rapid catching up of some Asian countries (Japan, South Korea, Singapore, Taiwan) and even more so with the catching up of China from the 1990s. Although such trend could be interpreted as pointing towards the end of world asymmetry, it is very unlikely to go that far. There are still many countries, if not continents, which are stuck in poverty or in middle-income traps. The most likely outcome in the XXIst century is a new world order constituted by a political oligopoly different from the one that dominated the XXth century. In fact, the likelihood of a homogeneous world is not very high for at least two reasons: first, according to Kindleberger (1973, p. 28), an asymmetry, constituted by one or few dominating countries, is required to maintain the stability of the world system; second, the distribution of innovations in the world system is extremely unlikely to ever be symmetrical. The origin of innovation has always been distributed asymmetrically amongst countries and regions. Furthermore, while innovations diffuse away from where they were created, they keep being improved upon by their early creators. This stream of improvements raises the barriers to the further diffusion of the innovations, contributing to maintain a skewed distribution of technological and learning capabilities in the world economic system.[12] Furthermore, new innovations can crop up somewhere else and give rise to new waves of diffusion. Thus, once more, no final state of the world system can be imagined, since even when existing technologies have completed their life cycles, new innovations can emerge somewhere else and give rise to new diffusion processes.[13]

3.2 From manufacturing to services

The intra-country struggle between industrial capitalists and the proletariat was initiated by the industrial revolution and based mostly on manufacturing. This struggle heavily affected the political evolution of the XIXth and XXth centuries and seemed to find its ultimate stage in the welfare states created in the second half of the XX century. In these societies, workers were represented politically by parties and unions, enjoyed high levels of employment and security, and achieved standards of living far beyond the basic necessities of life (Matsuyama, 2002; Saviotti, Pyka 2013). Almost free education and health care, paid for holidays and generous pensions became increasingly available to large shares of the population of industrialized countries. The period between the end of the Second World War and the 1970s was called the Golden Years of capitalism (Kindleberger, 1967, Marglin, Schor, 1991, United Nations, 2017) and seemed to represent the best combination of economic creativity and of social justice that had ever been achieved. The idea that an important threshold in social development had been achieved started to be shaken by the first oil crisis of the 1970s and has by now eroded expectations of future welfare. Several phenomena, including globalization, the emergence of new technologies and the impact of human activities on the natural environment, have increased uncertainty about the possibility of future social progress.

To understand the coevolution of globalization, the emergence of new technologies and the impact of human activities on the natural environment is one of our present challenges. However, the welfare states from the 1950s to the 1970s had an intrinsic tendency to instability that would have manifested itself even without globalization, new technologies and the environment. Welfare states were created at a time in which manufacturing represented a very large share of total employment designed to provide good working conditions and quality of life for large groups of workers who shared a common social identity. The growing productive efficiency of the economy always constituted a potential threat to manufacturing employment. The problem had been identified by Ricardo (1817) and analysed in greater detail by Marx (1867). However, until the recent past, the potential reduction in employment due to increasing productive efficiency never manifested itself at a macroeconomic level as a consequence of two compensating trends: first, simultaneously with a reduction in employment per unit of output in more mature sectors, new sectors created by innovations generated new forms of employment (Saviotti, Pyka, 2004, 2008, 2013, Pyka et al., 2018), examples of which were cars, computers, televisions, telephones, etc.; second, as already pointed out, even when employment in the new manufacturing sectors started to decline, employment grew rapidly in services, which by the 1980s had become the main source of it in mature industrialized countries.

There are multiple reasons for this transition to service societies, largely dependent on the fact that services are a residual and highly heterogeneous category. Thus, the factors contributing to the growth of employment in health care, education or tourism are likely to be very different. Several scholars have attempted to point out that some services are much more dynamic and innovative than others, for example, by singling out sectors with high knowledge intensity (Peneder et al., 2001). Many studies focused on Knowledge-Intensive Business Services (KIBS) (see, for example, Hertog, 2001; Muller, Doloreux, 2007). At a more general level, many studies challenged the idea that service sectors were not innovative or that innovation in services would proceed by the same mechanisms as in manufacturing activities (Gallouj, Windrum, 2008; Windrum, 2007; Gallouj, 2002; Metcalfe, Miles, 2000; Gallouj, Weinstein, 1997).

Despite the heterogeneity of services, there is one underlying factor that can be expected to contribute to all types of services as well as to manufacturing activities. From the beginning of the industrial revolution until the first half of the XXth century, most new knowledge and innovations were concentrated in scientific fields and industrial sectors which involved the manipulation of matter. Examples of these fields were physics, chemistry, electricity, electronics, and engineering disciplines. Most manufacturing sectors benefited from progress in these fields. The enormous increase in the output and throughput of manufacturing industry since the industrial revolution created huge information requirements. These were due not only to the increasing volume of output and throughput but also to the growing differentiation of the economic system. Information is required to account for all the stocks and flows of matter and energy in the economic system. The number of these stocks and flows can be expected to increase with the variety of the economic system and with the diversification of foreign trade amongst others, because the number of interfaces between sectors and activities increases faster than their number. It is then quite likely for information requirements to have grown more rapidly than the corresponding stocks and flows.[14] No scientific or technological development comparable to that relative to matter manipulation occurred in the storage and processing of information until the second half of the XXth century.

During the XIXth century, the demand for information processing required to manage the rising amount of manufacturing output, the emergence of large corporations and the increasing geographical dispersion of their activities (Chandler, 1977) grew rapidly. Throughout most of the XIXth century, this demand was satisfied by an equally rapid increase in the employment of clerical workers. Until about the 1880s the office work was predominantly based on labour using very simple tools, such as pencils paper (Braverman, 1974; de Witt et al, 2002). The mechanization of office work started in the 1880s with the introduction of typing and calculating machines. Furthermore, at about the same time, there were attempts to design office work along the same lines as shop floor work in manufacturing firms (Braverman, 1974). These technologies and management methods raised the efficiency of office work but the most important advances in information processing had to wait until after the Second World War with the advent of the digital computers.

The technology that in the end had a decisive effect on efficiency in the storage and processing of information was the digital computer (Copeland, 2017; Mahoney, 1988). Although some technologies to store and process information had been devised from the antiquity, they were only adapted to deal with quantities of data that by today's standards seem extremely small. Thus, the developments of language and mathematics were initially used to document the amounts of cereals stored or the size of cultivated fields (Joseph, 1991). Early computers, such as Pascal's 'Pascaline', created in the XVIIth century, were based on mechanical technology and had a very limited computing capability (Copeland, 2017; Southern Illinois University, 2016). Important progress in computing speed only occurred with the advent of electromechanical computers in the 1940s and even more so in the 1960s when vacuum tubes were replaced by semiconductors. At this point the relative efficiency of computing started growing much faster than that of mechanical, chemical, or electrical technologies, because of the famous Moore's law[15] (see also Petropoulos et al., 2019).

It is then quite likely that from the beginning of the industrial revolution until the Second World War the efficiency in the manipulation of matter increased more rapidly than efficiency in the storage and processing of information. These trends in the evolution of matter manipulation and in the storage and processing of information can partly explain the evolution of manufacturing and services. To the extent that the efficiency in matter manipulation increased faster than that in the storage and processing of information, we can expect employment per unit of output to fall faster in the former than in the latter. The obvious consequence of this would have been an increasing employment share of service activities as compared to shop floor activities, even in manufacturing firms.

One of the first analyses of this problem was carried out by Baumol (1967). He did not specifically refer to the difference between manufacturing and services, and he did not even mention the distinction between mater manipulation and information processing, but he called 'technologically progressive' the economic activities that experience high rates of productivity growth and 'technologically stagnant' those that experience persistently low rates of productivity growth. In the course of time, the latter were likely to show rising costs relative to the former and to suffer from declining demand and employment, contrary to the observed rise in employment share for services. It may seem contradictory for employment to increase faster in the less efficient activities, such as information processing technology, than in the more efficient matter manipulation technologies. However, such contradiction would have been real only if manufacturing and service activities were *substitutes*. In some cases, they are *complementary* activities. For example, this happens in supermarkets, where the purchase price of goods and services sold is likely to include the production cost of physical goods combined with services such as packaging, shipping, and distribution costs. This complementarity could have continued until the disposable income of consumers rose faster than the purchase price of goods and services, even if this purchase price included a growing share of cost due to low productivity[16] services.

Of course, in addition to the relative rates of growth of efficiency in matter manipulation and in the storage and processing of information, other factors can explain the transition towards a society in which the largest share of employment is in services, a trend also called tertiarization. Like in the storage and processing of information, some factors are supply-based while in other cases demand-based factors affect employment in services. For example, after the Second World War, education, measured by the average number of years of schooling of the population, has more than doubled in most industrialized countries (Roser, Ortiz-Ospina, 2016). This not only increased the cultural level and the quality of human capital of the population in industrialized countries, but required a massive increase in education employment, thus contributing to the growth of output and disposable income. Thus, the growth of education was affected by both demand and supply. The increasing knowledge intensity of production required human capital of increasing quality, which had to be supplied by the education system. In turn, the growing wages paid to workers of higher quality human capital raised the demand for higher quality goods and services (Saviotti, Pyka, 2013) and the demand for education in the population.[17] Incidentally, this was a good example of the coevolution of innovation, education, demand, and employment (eResources, Chapter 5).

In addition to education, other sectors that had a very high rate of growth of employment share are health care and tourism. The considerable growth of both can be explained by the construction of the welfare state, including rights such as a shorter working week, affordable health care, generalized pensions and security of employment (Boulin et al., 2006). We could then say that these rights were obtained by the working class as a result of political struggle (Esping-Andersen, 1990). Although this is certainly true, it needs to be complemented by other factors. In Chapter 5 it was stressed that full employment in the presence of increasing productive efficiency could be achieved by (i) the emergence of new sectors and their increasing internal diversification, be they manufacturing or services, and by (ii) the shortening of working times. Thus, those rights that were obtained by political action benefitted also from the existence and complementarity of growing productive efficiency and creativity.[18] Furthermore, the existence of the same rights created a growing demand for various types of services, including travel and holidays.

The trend towards a growing employment share of services lasted until quite recently but it is not clear whether it can continue forever. The inversion in the relative growth of efficiency in matter manipulation and in the storage and processing of information seems to work against that, thus raising doubts about the possibility that employment in services can continue to provide a form of compensation for the falling employment-creating capacity of manufacturing (Chapter 5). However, trends like the growth in health care or education are likely to be favoured by population ageing or by the growing knowledge required to work or simply to participate meaningfully in social life. For example, knowledge of ITC is increasingly required to purchase goods and services (e.g. plane and train tickets, book cinemas and theatres), obtain health care, interact with government (ask for documents, pay taxes), etc. However, any prediction about future employment in services is made more problematic by the loose definition of the sector and by the changing boundaries between manufacturing and services. First, as already pointed out, services are a residual category, what is left when primary industries and manufacturing are accounted for. Even the distinction between material and immaterial output is insufficient. A type of convergence between manufacturing and services that did not rely so much on the progress of ITC and that had been observed by economists consists of the increasingly heterogeneous nature of material goods. Such goods are not purchased for their material nature but for the services they supply (see Chapter 1). There still are homogeneous goods sold in very large quantities, which correspond to the concept of commodity. Since commodities are homogeneous, the demand for them depends uniquely on their price. On the contrary, heterogeneous products can span a very wide range of services, qualities and prices. Most consumer goods and durables are increasingly of this type. Cars, computers, portable telephones, electrical appliances, etc. are just some examples. This heterogeneity is not specific to material goods but also applies to services. Holiday packages or financial products are examples of heterogeneous services. Thus, physical goods supply services in an embodied form whereas 'pure' service activities supply services in a disembodied form. In both cases, the final services are increasingly supplied with a growing capital intensity. The corresponding type of capital equipment is often, but not only, related to ITC. Thus, consumers can purchase transport services either in an embodied form, purchasing cars, or in a disembodied form, by purchasing them from railway companies or airlines. Different types of transport services, embodied or disembodied, can compete.[19] Furthermore, recent technological or industrial developments are difficult to classify as manufacturing or services.

Based on the previous considerations, a generalized representation of production,[20] including the production of both material and immaterial outputs, could be expressed as follows:

> Production can be defined as the transformation of inputs into outputs, where inputs can be human capital of variable quality, materials and energy, capital goods used either for matter manipulation or for information storage and processing. The outputs of this production can be services supplied either in an embodied form, as physical goods, or in a disembodied form, as pure services. Some embodied services, which are then called self- services, can be partial or total substitutes for disembodied services.
>
> (Chapter 1)

The convergence towards a generalized supply of services due to increasing heterogeneity of physical products has been amplified by the progress of ITC. The most important trend contributing to the convergence of manufacturing and services has been the common use of ITC in firms and organizations that produce both physical goods and immaterial services. This contrasts with a stereotype of service organization in which services were supplied by people with a minimal use of technologies. Education would be a classical example, in which the knowledge of teachers was supplied to pupils with the use of pencil, papers, writing boards and printed documents. Today most service organizations have become intensive users of ITC. ITC has become the unifying feature, increasingly used by both services and manufacturing firms. ITC itself is highly capital- and energy-intensive: hardware and software are jointly used in computers and portable telephones; huge computing centres supply the needs of firms and organizations. Even at the level of firms the production of products and services cannot be so easily separated and the situation can be described as the production of a product-service continuum (Kowalkowski et al., 2017) in which most firms produce a mixture of both.

Some examples can show that new firms combine features typical of both manufacturing and services. Firms gathering very large quantities of data (big data) can enter fields of manufacturing that require such data. A clear example of this is Google, which by collecting geographical information was able to start developing autonomous vehicles, thus potentially becoming a competitor for established car manufacturers. In turn, such manufacturers need to develop capabilities in big data and autonomous vehicles. A further example is given by Amazon. Is it a service or manufacturing firm? Its first objective was to sell books, but having access to a huge collection and relying on advanced delivery system. However, rather than a book seller, it acted mostly as a bridge between suppliers of books scattered all over the world and consumers. As compared to a typical supermarket, it acted as a supermarket of supermarkets. In this sense it could become a worldwide seller of everything. To achieve this objective, Amazon needed to combine advances in ITC and in firm organization, in both of which the firm made substantial progress becoming a leading cloud computing supplier. Furthermore, it is developing innovations in unrelated fields such as space travel.

3.3 Recent trends: globalization, neoliberalism, AI, knowledge-based economy and society

Although the transition from manufacturing to services has contributed to creating employment, it has in the meantime undermined the welfare state that was constructed after the Second World War to improve the condition of the working class in advanced post-industrial societies. Because of that transition and of the continuous increase in productive efficiency of manufacturing industry, the employment share of manufacturing has rapidly declined falling to values of about 10% in several countries (Pilat et al., 2006; Rose, 2018). If we bear in mind that even within manufacturing firms most employment is of administrative type, we can easily understand why traditional working-class employment has been fast disappearing. The gradual reduction in employment in manufacturing has sometimes been referred to, often with a negative connotation, as a case of deindustrialization. In fact, this trend is the natural consequence of the higher rate of productivity growth in manufacturing with respect to services. However, the different pace with which the shift from manufacturing to services occurred in various countries has sometimes been associated with difficulties in economic development. According to Rowthorn and Ramaswamy (1997), the observed differences in rates of deindustrialization depended on the trade patterns of the countries considered. Whereas from a macroeconomic point of view employment in manufacturing and services could be considered equivalent, from the social point of view the two types of employment differ. For example, both the social identity of service workers and their propensity to unionize are considerably different (Dolvik, Waddington, 2002; Vissen, 2019). These differences were compounded by the growth of neoliberalism which followed the oil crises of the 1970s. These crises interrupted the long period of growth subsequent to the Second World War that had been called the golden years of capitalism (Marglin, Schor, 1991). Starting from the 1970s not only growth slowed down but the Keynesian policies that had previously been effective began to fail. While before Keynesian policies had enabled to control the trade-off between growth and inflation, from the 1970s onwards the phenomenon called stagflation began to be observed: inflation was no longer accompanied by growth but coexisted with a stagnant economy. The proponents of neoliberalism maintained that the slowdown of the economy was due to excessive state intervention, excessive regulation, and an excessively generous welfare state (ZBW, 2012; Lindbeck, 2006, Hartman, 2005; Palley, 2018). Although the term 'neoliberalism' was not very rigorously defined, it nevertheless represents well the broad direction of change away from the welfare state and the Keynesian consensus that dominated the political systems of developed countries from 1945 to the 1970s.

3.3.1 Globalization

Although recently most commentators discussing globalization focused on the period after the Second World War, globalization in its modern form[21] started in the XIXth century when the Corn Law in the UK led to the end of mercantilism (Rodrik, 2011). The first wave of globalization lasted until 1914 and was followed by a return of protectionism between the two world wars. A new wave that started after the Second World War can be divided into two periods differing for some important institutional changes. The first period was defined by the Bretton Woods agreements which largely eliminated the protectionist barriers established between the two wars but tried to find a reasonable balance between rules favouring globalization and rules safeguarding the capacity of nation states to create specific policies in their interest. The beginning of the second period was induced by the growing difficulties experienced by the Bretton Woods regime, which became evident during the 1970s. The second period proceeded to dismantle the remaining exceptions protecting national interests in order to achieve a more complete form of globalization. This second period is now encountering growing difficulties due to the dissatisfaction it generates in many countries.

Quite apart from their specific features, all forms of globalization require technologies and institutions that enable the exchange of goods, services, and financial resources all over the world system. Thus, railways, steamships, the telegraph, and military technology enabled the first phase of globalization while airplanes and ITC played a very important role in the two subsequent periods. Together with technologies, institutions defining trade and capital movements or underpinning financial stability and property rights were required. For example, the gold standard provided financial stability in the XIXth century and the US dollar played the equivalent role in the Bretton Woods agreements (Rodrik, 2011). Thus, globalization in all its forms required the coevolution of technologies and institutions.

An important influence on the development of globalization was played also by neoliberalism, an intellectual orientation that emerged in the 1970s and had important implications in foreign policy and international relations by removing some barriers to globalization. According to the so-called Washington consensus, all barriers to trade, as well as all forms of protection of industry and industrial policy, were inefficient and to be avoided. However, although trade is generally beneficial in most situations, there are conditions in which a limited degree of protection could improve the performance of some countries or social groups. For example, according to Rodrik (2007), all the most impressive developing countries of the second half of the XXth century, including Japan, South Korea, Taiwan, Singapore and more recently China, used Import Substitution Industrialization (ISI). Previously ISI had acquired a bad reputation by being associated with the relatively poor economic performance of Latin American countries after the 1970s (Sachs, Warner, 1995, 2001; Coatsworth, Williamson, 2002). In fact, this relatively poor economic performance was not necessarily due to the intrinsic nature of ISI but due to the way in which it was applied. Japan, South Korea, Taiwan, and Singapore combined ISI with policies emphasizing learning and exports. In this way barriers to the import of some technologies needed to be only temporary and could be lifted when the infant industry had reached the level of competitiveness required to participate in international trade (Chang, 2002). In other words, ISI can be beneficial if it is limited in time, coupled with learning, and followed by a switch to Export-Oriented Industrialization (EOI). This switch never occurred effectively in Latin American countries (Irwin, 2021).

A further problem created by globalization was given by the damages inflicted upon some old industrialized countries and regions. There is an intrinsic tendency for the efficiency of given technologies and industries to increase in the course of time during their life cycle, leading to a fall in the amount of labour required to produce one unit of output. This tendency is intrinsic to technologies, but can be accelerated by the entry of new industrializing countries (NICs) into technologies previously used by Old Industrialized Countries (OICs). This happened since the Second World War with the entry of Japan, South Korea, Taiwan and, lately, China. European countries and the USA became incapable to compete in some technologies and industries which were at the basis of their economic model. Thus, the inducement to structural change that would have emerged more slowly in a closed market was accelerated by globalization. The adaptation of OICs to this threat could have been based on two strategies: (i) reduce their own unit costs to the level of NICs, or (ii) try to create new products and services in which they (OICs) had a temporary monopoly. Although an increase in productive efficiency would have been required in all cases, strategy (i) alone was likely to lead to great social tensions because it would inevitably have required a reduction in labour costs and social expenditures to levels comparable to those of NICs. Strategy (ii) was superior, but required to increase the knowledge intensity of the OICs. Not all the OICs could undergo this transition. Those countries that failed to implement strategy (ii) are now facing severe difficulties, including a faster shrinking of the working class than it would have been the case in a closed SES.

The above-mentioned strategies to adapt to globalization in OICs and LDCs were rarely completely successful. In principle, globalization can introduce a tension in international relations by denying some nation states the right to protect and assist communities or activities from international competition (Rodrik, 2011). ISI is an example of protection based on the infant industry argument, stating that an industry new to a less developed country (LDC) cannot from its very foundation compete with the most advanced industry of highly developed countries (DCs) and needs to be protected until it is able to compete internationally. In other words, the protection needs to be temporary, until the protected industry has had the time to learn. ISI is just an example of the protection that national governments can supply to their citizens and organizations. The possibility for nation states to compensate for the disadvantages of globalization was allowed in the Bretton Woods-GATT agreements, which regulated the first wave of globalization after the Second World War and lasted until the 1970s, but was subsequently forbidden in the agreements leading to the formation of the World Trade Organization (WTO) (Rodrik, 2011). The growing opposition to the present form of globalization is likely to require that nation states recover the power to compensate the effects of uncontrolled globalization. However, it seems quite unlikely that globalization can be completely reversed. An alternative to a regain of national power would consist of creating forms of international governance capable of finding the right balance of the advantages and disadvantages of international trade for each country.

3.3.2 Neoliberalism

This combination of increasing productive efficiency of manufacturing, of the shift to services, of globalization was reinforced by the advent neoliberalism. This change of political philosophy did not amount to a complete uprooting of the welfare state but initiated a trend towards a gradual reduction in state intervention, in the power of labour unions and in the frequency and strength of regulations. It gave rise to a trend towards shorter and more insecure work contracts, including a growing reliance on employment agencies, that transformed into short-term contracts even those that had previously been long-term and highly secure forms of employment contracts. Combined with the transition to a service society, globalization and the advance of neoliberalism contributed to creating an increasingly fragmented society in which distinct groups did not feel adequately integrated and represented. Such groups are much more heterogeneous than the working class of industrial memory. They share only a disaffection and a lack of trust in the society in which they are living but they may have different preferences, corresponding to the different complaints they have about the society of which they are part. Standing (2011) called the collection of these groups the 'precariat', where the term indicates individuals who are insecure and incomplete citizens, in the sense of being denied some of the rights that a proper citizen would have. According to Standing, the precariat is growing and absorbing people from different social groups, such as the remnants of the working class; the people having short-term, insecure and poorly paid work contracts; the old who accept poorly paid jobs to compensate their low pensions; and the immigrants. Quite apart from the details of this situation, the fragmentation of society described above constitutes the destruction of the social base for which the welfare state had been designed. The present situation is likely to be a state of transition that will need a redesign of the welfare state in order to accommodate the diverging requirements of the relevant social groups.

Although the shift towards neoliberalism was not heavily influenced by technology, its effect is now being reinforced by the advances of artificial intelligence (AI). If neoliberalism has been responsible for the destruction of the social base of the welfare state, its effect is being reinforced by the capacity of AI to replace not only relatively unskilled jobs but also jobs of increasing creativity. This employment displacing capability of AI has induced several scholars to predict a future in which it will be impossible to create full employment for the whole of society (Frey, Osborne, 2013, 2017; Brynjolfsson, McAfee, 2011). While it is undoubted that AI can substitute more creative human activities than previous forms of automation, it is not clear that the impact of AI on employment can be substantially different from that of previous forms of automation. In fact, in the past, large-scale technological unemployment has been avoided by means of compensating forces, the most important of which in our opinion are the creation of new activities which compensate for the employment displacement of pre-existing activities (Vermeulen et al., 2018; Saviotti, Pyka, 2004, 2008, 2013, see Chapter 5) and the shift to services. However, the effect of AI is likely to reduce some types of service employment, thus potentially decreasing the effectiveness of the shift to services as a compensating force. This problem is discussed in a more detailed way in the following section. Before passing to the discussion of policies that could adapt the welfare state to the new social base, we need to discuss human decision-making, and how it is affected by human knowledge.

3.3.3 Knowledge-based economy and society

A very important ongoing trend in economic development is represented by the transition towards a knowledge-based economy and society. By definition this is a society in which the average knowledge level of the population is very high with respect to recent history. For example, the average number of years of education passed from about 5 to about 13 in the second half of the XIXth century in industrialized countries (Roser, Ortiz-Espina, 2016; Barro, Lee, 2010, 2001, 1996, 1993). Such a rising share of education in average lifetimes is considered a factor that contributed and is increasingly contributing to economic development (; Barro, 1991; Barro, Lee, 2001; Cohen, Soto, 2007). In general, an increase in the duration and quality of education raises the salary and the human capital of educated individuals (Karasiotou, 2012; Mincer, 1981). In turn, human capital contributes positively to economic development (Lindahl and Krueger, 2001; Cohen, Soto, 2007).

Such a positive relationship cannot be interpreted as implying that more education is always better in whatever form it comes. Levels of education can vary in a population for their duration, quality, and specialization, and for the effects they have on the economic performance of educated individuals. Not all types of education necessarily make an equally meaningful contribution to the development of a country (Pritchett, 2001). Thus, we need to distinguish between the quantity and quality of education. For example, in the case of highly developed countries, the duration of schooling seems not to contribute significantly to economic development unless it is corrected for the quality education, as measured by PISA tests (Lindahl, Krueger, 2001). Whereas an increase in the level of education of the population of a country is in many senses a benefit, it can also give rise to social tensions. It is not just the average level of education but also its distribution that matters. A potential problem inherent in the growing amount of knowledge that we produce and use in highly developed SESs is constituted by its increasing dispersion in a growing number of individuals. Consequently, the number of interfaces between different pieces of knowledge increases more rapidly than their number. This leads to growing coordination problems when different pieces of knowledge need to be used together. And, it is not clear how the price system can help us to overcome this coordination problem.

In a highly knowledge-intensive SES, we could expect a policy involving the allocation of educational resources based on capabilities and merit to be most effective in creating high quality human capital. Such a policy would constitute a meritocracy. Although meritocracy undoubtedly has some advantages, as compared to the allocation of educational resources based on social relations or wealth, it is not necessarily easily compatible with democracy. If the ratio of the most valuable competencies and human capital to the least valuable ones was very high and growing in the course of time, it could lead to a similarly skewed ratio of salaries. To the extent that salaries are based on competencies and human capital, this could lead to a growing income inequality.[22] If we consider that (i) the lowest competencies and salaries may not be enough to purchase the basic needs of life and that (ii) the differential ability of very high-income people to influence political decisions, we can realize that a 'pure' meritocracy could be incompatible with democracy. Meritocracy could deny some members of an SES the access to basic needs and lead them to feel estranged from the society in which they live. A similar trend, involving a growing income inequality and a growing difficulty in the access to top quality education, seems to be occurring in several old industrialized countries (OICs) (Milanovic, 2016). The possibility that education can contribute to the increasing income inequality experienced in most old industrialized countries (OICs) after the 1980s (Piketty, 2014) implies that meritocracy and democracy are not necessarily easily compatible. In fact, the distribution of education can severely distort democracy by endowing individuals and groups much more effective means to influence political decision-making than those available to the general population.

3.3.4 Long-term trends

As we previously pointed out, within the development of SES, we can identify processes occurring simultaneously at very different speeds. Some of these processes can be very long range, some cyclical and others secular. Some very slow processes may not be identified until they reach a critical threshold, above which they can no longer be neglected. The beginning of such processes is typically determined by discontinuities, such as the emergence of a new technological paradigm. We have already mentioned cyclical phenomena such as technology or industry life cycles. The reason for discussing these processes here is that they are much more difficult to detect them than short-range ones.

Two types of these processes will be discussed here due to their close relationship with innovation and technological change. The first of these processes is long waves. Cyclical phenomena in economics have been known for a very long time. Schumpeter (1939) described three types of cycles, which he called Kitchin (3–5 years), Juglar (7–11 years) and Kondratieff (45–60 years) based on their duration. All of them can be affected by innovation. Here we will focus on long waves. They are periodic fluctuations in the capitalist system which have duration of between 45 and 60 years. The names of these waves are associated with the Russian economist Kondratieff. He was not the discoverer of long waves, but amongst the early proponents of these fluctuations he made the most concerted effort to study them statistically. Here we do not intend to provide a comprehensive review of the literature in a field that has been very intensely studied. Rather, we will rely on interpretations of long waves proposed in the Neo-Schumpeterian and evolutionary literature because they stress the relationship between innovation and long waves. The most recent studies of long waves (Freeman, Louça, 2001; Perez, 2002; Tylecote, 1992, Silverberg, 2007) place technology and innovation at the centre of their interpretation. We do not privilege these interpretations because they constitute a form of technological determinism. On the contrary, their authors consider long waves originated by the coevolution of new technologies and other aspects of the SES. They do not adopt a form of technological determinism but consider that technology and innovation coevolve with other components of an SES, such as culture, political and economic institutions, respect, and creation of conditions favourable to science and technology (Freeman, Louça, 2001). For example, the first industrial revolution was not the result of some innovations irrupting in the UK and by themselves giving rise to a new way of producing things and a greatly increased production capacity. The fact that the industrial revolution occurred in the UK has been widely attributed to a combination of a few factors, including a culture favourable to personal initiative, a great respect for science and technology, a relatively open and tolerant political system (Landes, 1969, 1999; Mokyr, 1990).

To show that all these factors reinforced one another, Freeman and Louça (2001) cite the publication of Adam Smith's *The Wealth of Nations* in 1776 as the book that provided an almost perfect rationalization of the profit-seeking activities on the new industrialists and merchants (p. 177). At that time, they were an emerging group in a society the elite of which still consisted of landlords. The interests of these two groups differed. Smith's *The Wealth of Nations* convinced industrialists and merchants that they were serving the community by pursuing their self-interest. While landlords favoured the protection of agriculture, industrialists and merchants were more favourable to free trade (ibid., p. 179). Policies aimed at protecting the interests of the latter were gradually introduced, but it was not until the repel of the Corn Laws in the 1840s that conditions favourable to free trade were established.

Thus, within a coevolutionary approach, technology and innovation contribute powerfully to socioeconomic development. Not all technologies are equal. Some are more important than others and function as the centre of clusters or networks driving economic development. These are called *carrier branches* and resemble what other scholars not committed to long waves called general-purpose technologies (GPTs) (Bresnahan, Trajtenberg, 1995; Lipsey et al., 2005). Even without considering other factors, different technologies interact amongst themselves, each reinforcing the others. Thus, advances in the use of coal allowed the production of steel of increasing quality which in turn was the basis for the development of railways and mechanical engineering (Freeman, Louça, 2001). Different groups of technologies, clustered around some dominant ones, are used to explain the emergence and decline of different long waves. For example, water-powered mechanization in the first long wave, steam power and railways in the second wave, electricity in the third wave, oil, and transport technologies in the fourth wave, computerization of the whole economy in the fifth wave (see table II,1 in Freeman, Louça, 2001 and table 2.3 in Perez, 2002). Again, this is not technological determinism but the coevolution of technologies and institutions. While Freeman and Louça stress the role of culture and political institutions, Perez (2002) focuses predominantly on the interaction of technologies and financial institutions. The innovations leading to new technologies become interesting for investors as the old technologies belonging to a previous paradigm mature, leading to declining returns on investment. After the emergence of new technologies (the big bang) occurring within technological organizations, financial organizations start being interested in them and tend to dominate the further development of these technologies. This leads to the coevolution of technologies and financial organizations, which accelerates the further growth of both knowledge about the new technologies and investment in them. The expectation that the very high returns initially obtained by investment in the new technologies can continue forever leads to a period of *frenzy* ending with the formation of financial bubbles, giving rise to a *turning point*. In the ensuing recession, there is a rebalancing of the roles of financial (FK) and productive capital (PK), leading to a period of *synergy*, followed by a gradual increase in the markets for the new technologies, a growing industrial concentration of their producers, the *maturity* of the same technologies and a fall in the rate of return on their investment. The door is then open for the emergence of a new techno-economic paradigm and for the corresponding *surge* of new technologies.

The fact that we cite long waves does not imply that we believe they are cycles in the strict sense of the term. Rather, we think that they are very strong evidence of the out-of-equilibrium nature of capitalist economic development, which proceeds through struggle, discontinuities and alternative phases of prosperity and depression. Although the introduction of financial capital and organizations represents an advance with respect to a model focusing exclusively on technologies, there are other phenomena potentially affecting the cyclical nature of long-term cycles, for example, by affecting differentially the length of their cycles for different paradigms. Examples of these phenomena are geopolitical changes in world order, or the impact of human activities on the natural environment. The transition from British to American leadership at the head of the world order at the end of the Second World War came on the tail of the economic crisis that began in 1929, a crisis to which the technologies which were then new are likely to have contributed. While these changes in world order could have a quasi-cyclical behaviour interacting strongly with that of technologies and financial institutions, the impact of human activities on the natural environment seems to have a long-term *secular* character. This impact, initially almost unperceived, started accumulating gradually in the EE without being generally noticed and only much later reached a critical mass. How this secular trend interacts with long-term cycles is a point deserving some serious thoughts. The main point made here is that such long-term trends are more difficult to detect and interpret than short-term ones. The question that then arises is: 'can or should we try to make policies about such long-term trends?' We could at this point recall the famous sentence by Keynes that 'in the long run we are all dead' and disagree slightly with it by saying that 'we might all be dead long before the long run if we do not think about it'. Although we are incapable of predicting the future development of the world SES, we are likely to be better prepared to adapt to important changes in it if we explore possible future scenarios than if we wait for changes to happen and try to adapt afterwards. This question will be further analysed in Chapter 8.

3.4 Environmental impact

The impact of human activities on the EE started to be noticed only after the Second World War, although its beginning coincided with the beginning of the industrial revolution. In principle, such impact had always existed but it had been perceived as important mostly at the 'local' level (Wilde, 2019; Enright, 2018; Encyclopaedia Britannica, 1988). In fact, as the industrial revolution unfolded, the idea of a 'law of progress' predicting the inexorable, irreversible, advance of humankind towards a golden age on Earth took shape in the writing of scholars such as Comte, Spencer, and Marx (Pisani, 2006). Previous preoccupations with this impact only existed in the writings of Malthus (1798) regarding the limited amount of land usable for agriculture or about the working conditions within industrial plants or about the health in areas surrounding them. Even after the earliest studies documenting the growing impact of human activities on the EE were published, a consensus about the need to limit it was quite late to emerge. Early pioneers of environmental studies tried to show that human activities were moving towards a scale at which severe and possibly irreversible damages would occur (Meadows et al., 1972; Commoner, 1971, Georgescu Roegen, 1971; Boulding, 1966; Daly, 1977, 1991). Here we are not trying to provide an exhaustive survey of environmental studies but to analyse the impact of human activities on the EE as a very long-term process, stretching our capabilities to predict, analyse and adapt to such processes. The questions which then arise are: why did it take so long for the awareness of such a problem to emerge? And, if we started now to change human activities to make them compatible with our EE, how long would it take for our EE to go back to the state it had before the beginning of the industrial revolution? Concerning the first question, if one had extrapolated the rates of growth of output starting from the beginning of the XIX century, one could at least have suspected that at some future time the amounts of man-made wastes would have exceeded the carrying capacity of the planet earth. The reasons for such a lack of concern about the EE are multiple, but they are all examples of the barriers to adaptation of human communities to their EE.

The first barrier to be considered is a cognitive barrier. While at the beginning of the XIXth century a simple extrapolation of output would have been in principle possible, it would have encountered a few cognitive barriers: (1) an extrapolation of the overall output of human activities would have required a choice of the countries to be included. At the beginning of the XIXth century, when the UK was the only industrialized country but when India and China were still responsible for relatively large shares of world output, the extrapolation was likely to give results quite different from the historically recorded ones. Even today, although we have much more sophisticated models of world output, such prediction would be impossible to obtain. That at some point we would have been approaching a 'dangerous concentration' of human wastes would have been equally difficult. Today some areas of concern have emerged, such as climate change, the loss of biodiversity, the pollution by plastics of oceans and water streams. However, even in such areas, our ability to analyse the phenomena and to suggest solutions for the relevant problems is still insufficient despite the considerable progress made in human knowledge after the XIX century. The capability to analyse the highly complex phenomena affecting the EE was completely lacking until the emergence of ITC started providing adequate computational capabilities. Although even today the capability to analyse such complex phenomena is still limited at the conceptual level, it is rapidly improving as recent IPCC reports (IPCC, 2021) show.

The above limitations of human knowledge open the door to the discussion of the political barriers hindering the adaptation of human beings to climate change. Many studies have pointed out that the impact of the technologies that emerged since the industrial revolution varies a lot. Early critics of their effect on the EE pointed out that an essential difference between the periods before and after the industrial revolution is the enormously increased reliance in the latter on stocks of energy and raw materials accumulated during geological evolution, as opposed to flows coming from nature, which dominated in the former. Whereas such distinction was pointed out early by Georgescu Roegen (1971), one of the earliest examples to forecast the likely shortages of raw materials that could follow from the continuation of present trends was the MIT study (Meadows et al., 1972). Such a study seemed to many people too alarmist (Cole et al., 1973) and eventually exploration activities and innovation substantially increased the known and usable stocks of raw materials.

Leaving aside the fact that the limits predicted by the MIT study were only slightly displaced and not eliminated, the debate illustrates the nature of the political barriers opposing the human adaptation to the environmental problem. Many existing technologies have been conceived and developed to produce artefacts and services by means of fossil fuels and raw materials present in finite concentrations. Such technologies represent a large share of existing investment and employment across many interconnected industrial activities. The owners of these activities are likely to oppose any changes that substantially reduce their share of existing output and employment. The huge investment embodied in existing industrial structures represents a huge political and economic barrier to our adaptation to environmental impact. At the international level, a similar division exists between countries rich in raw materials and countries rich in knowledge. In this sense the environmental problem has an eminently political nature, pitting exponents of old and dirty industries against those of newer and cleaner ones. In fact, a solution to our EE problem consists of designing a development path that can make human activities compatible with a sustainable SES, avoiding the default solution that would involve simply stopping all the environmentally dangerous technologies. The design of such transition path is still outside our capabilities. It is in any case a task of very tall order, consisting not of substituting existing technologies with cleaner ones, but of designing a considerably different system in which different activities will be connected in different networks, and in which the concepts of growth and development will be substantially redefined.

The conclusion of this section is that we have created a problem for which we have no complete solution. In any case a solution would need to consider both the cognitive and political barriers delaying the achievement of a solution that is environmentally and politically sustainable.

4 Human decision-making

In the previous section, we discussed how the emergence of the welfare state represented a very late adaptation of capitalist societies to the class struggle between workers and industrial capitalists which had started with the industrial revolution. We saw how such adaptation occurred very late when increasing productive efficiency was drastically reducing employment in manufacturing, thus eating away the social basis for which the welfare state was designed. Services, which has become the main sector of employment, does not have the same characteristics as industrial employment. Employment in services is more heterogeneous, including jobs ranging from work in a MacDonald restaurant to working in the media or financial organizations. This heterogeneity leads to very different political preferences of the groups constituting service employment (Standing, 2011). Thus, the social basis of the welfare state which had dominated old industrialized countries after the Second World War has largely disappeared and is being replaced by a collection of groups that have different political preferences deriving from the extent to which they feel happy and integrated in the society in which they live. The form of welfare state we still have is no longer adapted to the changing social basis and will need to be redesigned.

Before discussing the nature of the changes required, we need to reflect here on the nature of human decision-making. The previous discussion showed that human beings' capacity to predict all the effects of their decisions, and in particular long run ones, is quite poor. This is not to deny the enormous progress that has been made in human knowledge. On the contrary, our knowledge of the physical and biological world has allowed us to understand phenomena ranging from elementary particles to the intimate nature of biological organisms to the structure and dynamics of the universe. However, when a technological or organizational innovation emerges, our knowledge of it is very incomplete. Typically, an innovation is first adopted based on some of its properties which are perceived as contributing positively to human welfare or organizational performance. During its subsequent diffusion, other properties, which we can consider secondary, can start acquiring a growing importance. The impact of these secondary properties can start to affect negatively human welfare, the more so the more they move towards a *saturation* of the subset of the environment in which they are used. Examples of this *saturation* due to secondary properties are the traffic congestion and pollution originated by cars, or the security problems and the stockage of nuclear wastes for nuclear power.

There are several reasons for which our knowledge is incomplete. As we discover new observables and new phenomena, we discover new problems that we had not necessarily anticipated. Furthermore, all our knowledge is constituted by connections between variables, and our total knowledge is poorly connected, in the sense that it is impossible to derive most variables from some other variables. Furthermore, scientific knowledge establishes general statements, which are obtained by abstracting away the specific details of each system within a large class. Consequently, general statements are applicable to large classes of systems, but they do not constitute a complete description of any specific system within the class. Such complete description can be obtained by combining a set of general statements with a much more detailed description of the specific aspects of the system considered. This explains why the discovery of new general statements can help us imagine the creation of new technological artefacts (MMAs). However, to create working prototypes of such artefacts we need to acquire a lot of extra knowledge about specific aspects of the relevant systems.

Second, the physical and social worlds in which we live are highly complex, and the latter possibly increasingly so. This implies that the most important components and variables of these worlds are (i) difficult to identify and (ii) interacting amongst themselves. In the past progress has been achieved first in the disciplines that were studying *simplifiable systems*. These are systems that, while being intrinsically complex, possess some components and properties that can be understood in isolation from all the other variables of the same system. Mechanics and astronomy are relevant examples. The laws of both were derived by focusing on a small set of properties and interactions, namely the mass and position of the relevant bodies and a law of interaction, gravity. Both terrestrial and celestial bodies possess many more properties, but such properties are not interacting directly with those which were used in mechanics and astronomy. Not all systems are simplifiable. For example, for a long time, biological organisms were considered impossible to study using the laws of mechanics. Biological organisms do not possess components and properties which are independent of other properties and are non-simplifiable.[23] As a consequence, fields in which progress was made during the early part of the industrial revolution were those in which the findings of chemistry and physics could be applied more easily.[24]

Third, the evolution of social systems contains processes that can occur simultaneously but at quite different speeds. For example, the industrial revolution started more than 200 years ago, but the establishment of forms of social organization aimed at reducing the tensions generated within society took a long time to emerge. Likewise, the impact of the industrial revolution on the physical and biological environment began simultaneously with the revolution itself but it took an even longer time for it to be observed and to become part of policy makers' preoccupations. The simultaneous occurrence of trends with different time scales is accompanied by different intensities of interaction of such trends. For example, while the class struggle between workers and capitalists developed continuously over 200 years, the impact of human activities on our environment accumulated without being perceived until it reached a critical mass.

We neglected here the limitations of human knowledge described by Kahneman et al. (2021), either for what concerns *noise* or for *cognitive biases*. We think that noise could have slowed down the progress of knowledge but not prevented the eventual attainment of correct theories, because, at least in some fields, there is a criterion to test the value of theories by the correspondence of their predictions with empirical results. However, cognitive biases have been part of the history of science and technology, for example, scientific and technological paradigms (see Chapter 1).

The reasons for this inherent inability to predict the final outcomes of present decisions can be classified into three groups: (1) the tension between abstract general knowledge and specific knowledge; (2) the intrinsic and possibly increasing complexity of the physical and social environment in which we live; (3) the very different time horizons of simultaneous processes occurring in our system and environment.

Due to the previous limitations, new technologies and new organizational forms are generally introduced without a full understanding of their implications. This is particularly true of Schumpeterian entrepreneurs, who introduce radical innovations, which are accompanied by radical uncertainty. For example, the enhanced mobility that cars could provide dominated initially their life cycle, if security could be assured for both passengers and the general public. Problems like pollution and traffic congestion were much slower to come and only became relevant when car density attained very high values. Similarly, the environmental impact of industrialization was neglected for a very long time after the industrial revolution. However, even politicians introduce institutions and policies without a full understanding of their implications and future effects. In the presence of a very complex environment, our approach generally is to focus on those that appear to be the main phenomena and variables affecting the system.

Logically, variables that are changing very slowly tend not to be observed or to be judged irrelevant for the phenomena we are studying. This problem is compounded by the limited duration of human life. Phenomena that are very long with respect to human life do not receive as much of our attention as those that are urgent and short term. In addition to the previous considerations, systems that are intrinsically complex and do not possess simplifiable sub-systems are more difficult to study and progress there has been historically much slower.

Consequently, both for new technologies and for new organizational forms, the balance between advantages and disadvantages can vary quite considerably during their life cycle. Unexpected problems crop up and gradually slow down or reverse their progress. The example of pensions will help to clarify the situation.

Example 1. Pensions

Pensions available to people at the end of their working life are one of the main components of the welfare state. Although nobody challenges the concept of a pension, its funding is becoming increasingly problematic. This is not the result of the impoverishment of advanced capitalist societies, but of the way in which pensions have been funded, which is itself the consequence of the coevolution of a few factors. The main funding mechanism, which is now becoming difficult to sustain, was based on contributions to the pensions of retired people made by people at work. Such a mechanism worked well in the societies with relatively high rates of growth of output and population in which the welfare state was initially introduced. However, as the rates of growth of output and of population slowed down, this funding mechanism became unsustainable. A falling rate of growth of population entails a decreasing ratio of people at work to people who are retired, inevitably requiring a growing fiscal pressure on people who are working. Furthermore, improving health care, supplied as part of the welfare state, increased life expectancy, thus contributing to population ageing and reducing the ratio of working people to retired people. Falling rates of growth of output compounded the problem.

Why did these changes in the funding mechanism of pensions occur? Could they not have been foreseen by the planners of the welfare state? The answer we can give now to the previous question is relatively simple. Rates of growth of population tend to fall as the level of education in a society increases and as the availability of social services reduces the need for children to assist old parents. Although both increasing levels of education and improved social services were themselves highly positive, they destabilized the main pension funding mechanism. Fertility rates, education, health care and pensions interact in ways that have not been anticipated by any welfare state. The main interactions of fertility rates, education, health care and pensions are represented in Figure 7.1 and Table 7.1.

Remedies to fund pensions started to be developed only after rates of population growth had fallen and pension funding began to weigh too heavily on

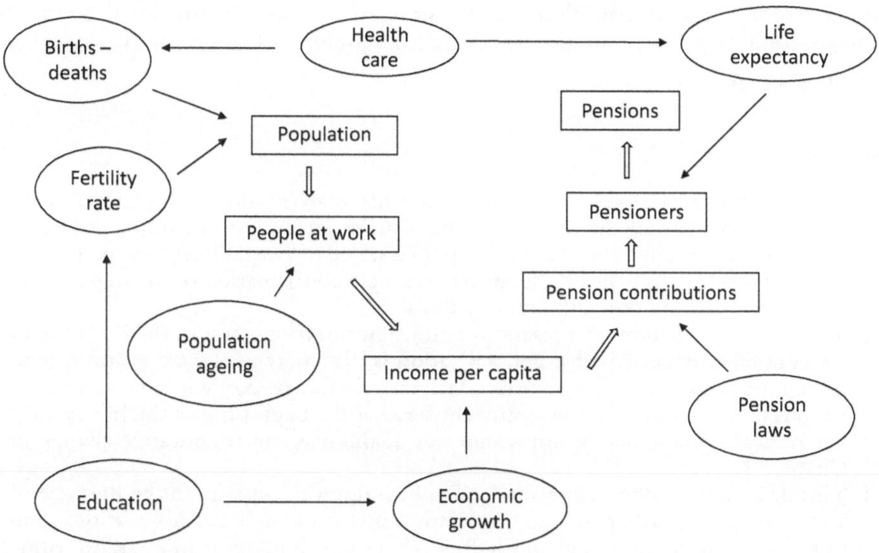

Figure 7.1 Main coevolutionary interactions affecting pensions.

Table 7.1 Dynamics of pension interactions with pay-as-you-go model (Figure 7.1)

Table 7.1
Dynamics of pension interactions with pay-as-you-go model (fig 7.1.)
↓Fertility rate ➡ ↓ Average population age ➡↑pensioners share in population + ↓population share of workers ➡ falling pension contributions
↑Education diffusion ➡ ↓ fertility rate ➡↓ Average population age
↑ Health care ➡ ↑ Life expectancy ➡ ↓ Average population age ➡↑pensioners share in population + ↓population share of workers
↑Pension laws ➡ ↑ or ↓ pension contributions

➡ = leads to; ↓ decreasing; ↑ increasing pension contributions.

public budgets. Alternative ways of funding pensions which are not affected by rates of population growth consist of calculating pensions based on the contributions made by individuals during their working life (contributive), rather than on payments made by people who are working (pay-as-you-go or redistributive model), or of providing pensions with *defined contributions* rather than *defined benefits* (Kuné, 2001; Siebert, 1997; Castanheira, Galasso, 2011).

Additional methods could be to raise retirement age reflecting increased life expectancy, and complement pensions with various forms of savings (Dunnewjik, 2002). To what extent such changes will solve the problem of funding pensions is not clear.

Notes

1 This is certainly an oversimplification, but the strategy adopted by China to try and avoid the fate of the Soviet Union, which consisted of including a dose of capitalism at the core of its economic policies, and of a capitalism in which innovation would play a central role, provides ample confirmation of the importance of innovation in all contemporary systems.

2 This does not exclude the presence of radical innovations later in the life cycle of a technology. An acceptable generalization is that incremental innovations tend to be much more numerous in the life cycle of a technology while radical innovations less numerous and typically clustered at the beginning of the life cycle.

3 See radical vs incremental innovations vs qualitative and quantitative change in Chapter 2.

4 This does not exclude the presence of radical innovations later in the lifecycle of a technology. An acceptable generalization is that incremental innovations tend to be much more numerous in the lifecycle of a technology while radical innovations less numerous and typically clustered at the beginning of the lifecycle.

5 By similar structures here we mean structures having the same components with similar values of their 'sizes and their interactions.

6 The beginning of the welfare state is often considered the establishment of a pension system by Bismarck in 1889.

7 The period since the beginning of the industrial revolution has been divided into several sub-periods by economic historians. Here we do not wish to dispute the appropriateness of these divisions and we will come back to them later. We think the trends discussed in this section operate over periods longer than those of each of these sub-periods of the industrial revolution.

8 Here see how increasing output variety and diversification contributed to rising wages, human capital and demand in Chapter 5.

9 The expressions location-based inequality and class-based inequality have been introduced by Milanovic (2016).

10 The concept of catching up is obviously an oversimplification that would make sense only if there was only one possible development path, driven by one variable. This is clearly not the case since multiple structures and multiple development paths can exist for different capitalist countries, as evidenced by the discussion in the introduction to this chapter. The concept of catching up can only be used as a broad multidimensional change of SESs towards states that are similar but never identical.

11 What some authors called liberal capitalism we would call here capitalist democratic capitalism. Here we leave aside the different varieties of existing capitalisms (Hall, Soskice, 2001) not because we consider them irrelevant, but because as compared to the Soviet system, they were generally more creative. Of course, after the collapse of the Soviet Union, the differences between various types of capitalism became more relevant. The present competition between different political systems is now between the Western democratic system and the Chinese authoritarian state capitalism. Once more innovation and technology will play a fundamental role in determining the outcome of this competitive process.

12 See Chapter 6 on a general interpretation of the diffusion of innovations based on forces and flows.
13 In a related vein see Dosi and Yu (2018).
14 Here see North (1990, Chapter 4) about the growth of transaction costs during the XXth century.
15 Moore's law is the observation that the number of transistors in a dense integrated circuit doubles about every two years.
16 Productivity in services is difficult to measure. Thus, the actual productivity of some services could have been higher than the one officially reported. However, this complementarity would have existed even if the real productivity of services had been lower than that of manufacturing.
17 See also Chapter 5.
18 About the definitions of productive efficiency and creativity see Chapter 5.
19 Different types of transport services are not complete substitutes and can compete only over a subset of their relative ranges.
20 See Chapter 1.
21 Some scholars set the beginning of globalization much earlier, but for our purposes in this book we prefer to focus on the globalization that began with the industrial revolution.
22 Here see the discussion in Chapter 8.
23 See definition of simplifiable in Chapter 6.
24 This does not imply that the innovations of the early part of the industrial revolution were directly derived from the previous progress of science. About this point see Chapter 5.

References

Abernathy W.J., Utterback, J.M. (1975) A dynamic model of process and product innovation. *Omega*, 3(6): 639656.

Akkermans D., Castaldi C., Los B. (2009) Do 'liberal market economies' really innovate more radically than 'coordinated market economies? Hall and Soskice reconsidered. *Research Policy*, 38(1): 181–191.

Almond P., Gonzalez Menendez M. (2006) Varieties of capitalism: the importance of political and social choices. *Transfer: European Review of Labour and Research*, 12: 407. https://doi.org/10.1177/102425890601200309

Archibugi D., Pianta M. (1992) Specialization and size of technological activities in industrial countries: the analysis of patent data. *Research Policy*, 21: 79–93.

Arthur, W.B., Durlauf, S.N., Lane, D.A., (1997) *The Economy as an Evolving Complex System II*. Addison–Wesley, Boston, MA.

Barro R.J. (1991) Economic growth in a cross section of countries. *The Quarterly Journal of Economics*, 106(2): 407–443.

Barro R.J., Lee J.W. (1993) International comparisons of educational attainment. *Journal of Monetary Economics*, 32: 363–394.

Barro R.J., Lee J.W. (1996) International measures of schooling years and schooling quality. *American Economic Review*, 86: 218–223.

Barro R.J., Lee J.W. (2001) International data on educational attainment: updates and implications. *Oxford Economic Papers*, 53(3): 541–563.

Barro R.J., Lee J.W. (2010) A new data set of educational attainment in the world, 1950–2010, *NBER Working Paper* No. 15902.

Baumol W.J. (1967) Macroeconomics of unbalanced growth: the anatomy of urban crisis. *The American Economic Review*, 57(3): 415–426.

Boulding K. (1966) The economics of the coming spaceship earth, in H. Jarrett (Ed.), *Environmental Quality in a Growing Economy*, Resources for the Future, Baltimore, MD, Johns Hopkins University Press, 3–14.

Boulin J.Y., Michel Lallement M., Messenger J.C., Michon F. (Eds) (2006) *Decent Working Time: New Trends, New Issues*, Geneva, International Labour Office.

Braverman H. (1974) *Labor and Monopoly Capital: The Degradation of Work in the XXth Century*, New York, Monthly Review Press.

Bresnahan T., Trajtenberg M. (1995) General purpose technologies 'Engines of growth'? *Journal of Econometrics*, 65(1): 83–108. https://doi.org/10.1016/0304-4076(94)01598-T

Brynjolfsson E., McAfee A. (2011) *Race against the Machine*, Lexington, MA, Digital Frontier Press.

Castanheira M., Galasso V. (2011) Which reforms for a fair and sustainable pension system? *Reflets et perspectives de la vie économique* 2011/2013 (Tome L), pages 187 à 202.

Chandler A.D. (1977) *The Visible Hand*, Cambridge, MA, Harvard University Press.

Chang H.J. (2002) *Kicking Away the Ladder–Development Strategy in Historical Perspective*, London, Anthem Press, 2002.

Coatsworth J.H., Williamson J.G. (2002) The roots of Latin American protectionism: looking before the great depression. NBER WorkingPaper8999http://www.nber.org/papers/w8999

Cohen D., Soto M. (2007) Growth and human capital: good data, good results, *Journal of Economic Growth*, 12: 51–76. https://doi.org/10.1007/s10887-007-9011-5

Cole H.S.D., Freeman C., Jahoda M., Pavitt K.L.R. (Eds.) (1 April 1973). *Models of Doom: A Critique of the Limits to Growth*, New York, Universe Publishing. ISBN 0876631847.

Commoner B. (1971) *The Closing Circle: Nature, Man, and Technology*, New York, Knopf.

Copeland B.J. (2017) The modern history of computing. *The Stanford Encyclopaedia of Philosophy* (Winter 2017 Edition), Zalta E.N. (Ed.), https://plato.stanford.edu/archives/win2017/entries/computing-history/.

Daly H.E. (1977, 1991) *Steady-State Economics: Second Edition with New Essays*, Washington DC, Island Press.

de Witt et al., (2002) Innovation junctions: office technologies in the Netherlands, 1880–1980. *Technology and Culture*, 43: 50–72

Dolvik J.E., Waddington J. (2002) Private sector services: challenges to European trade unions. *Transfer*, 8(3): 356–376.

Dosi G. (1982) Technological paradigms and technological trajectories: a suggested interpretation of the determinants and directions of technical change. *Research Policy*, 11: 147–162.

Dosi G., Yu X. (2018) Capabilities accumulation and development: what history tells the theory, LEM Working Paper Series, No. 2018/27, Scuola Superiore Sant'Anna, Laboratory of Economics and Management (LEM), Pisa.

Dunnewjik B. (2002) Four pillars, four solutions: pension reform and insurance opportunities. *Geneva Papers on Risk and Insurance*, 27(4): 540–554.

Edquist C. (Ed.) (1997) *Systems of Innovation: Technologies, Institutions and Organizations*, London and Washington, Pinter.

Edquist C. (2005) Systems of innovation: perspectives and challenges, in Fagerberg J., Mowery D., Nelson R.R. (Eds.), *The Oxford Handbook of Innovation*, Oxford, Oxford University Press, 181–208.

Encyclopaedia Britannica, Legislation for working conditions, Knowledge in Depth, vol. 18 (1988) 7: 81:3b, Chicago, 15th edition.

Enright G. (2018) A history of workplace health and safety – Part 2 April 26, 2018 in https://blog.intelex.com/2018/04/26/history-workplace-health-safety-part-2/

Esping-Andersen G. (1990) *The Three Worlds of Welfare Capitalism*, Princeton, NJ, Princeton University Press. ISBN 9780069028573

Fagerberg J., Shrolec M. (2008) National innovation systems, capabilities, and economic development. *Research Policy*, 37(9): 1417–1435.

Feldman M., Kogler D. (2010) Stylized facts in the geography of innovation, Chapter 8 in *Handbook of the Economics of Innovation*, 1: 381–410.

Freeman C., Louça F. (2001) *As Time Goes By, from the Industrial Revolution to the Information Revolution*, Oxford, Oxford University Press.

Frey C. B., Osborne M. A. (2013) The future of employment: how susceptible are jobs to computerisation? Working paper, Oxford Martin School, Oxford University, September 17.

Frey C.B., Osborne M.A. (2017) The future of employment: how susceptible are jobs to computerisation? *Technological Forecasting and Social Change*, 114(C): 254–280.

Fukuyama F. (1992) *The End of History and the Last Man*, New York, The Free Press.

Gallouj F. (2002) *Innovation in the Service Economy: The New Wealth of Nations*, Cheltenham, Edward Elgar Publishing.

Gallouj F., Weinstein O. (1997) Innovation in services. *Research Policy*, 26(4–5): 537–556.

Gallouj F., Windrum P. (2008) Services and services innovation April 2008. *Journal of Evolutionary Economics* 19(2): 141–148. https://doi.org/10.1007/s00191-008-0123-7

Georgescu Roegen N. (1971) *The Entropy Law and the Economic Process*, Cambridge, MA, Harvard University Press.

Hall P.A., Soskice, D. (Eds.) (2001) *Varieties of Capitalism. The Institutional Foundations of Comparative Advantage*, Oxford, Oxford University Press.

Hancké B., Martin Rhodes M., Thatcher M. (2007) *Beyond Varieties of Capitalism: Conflict, Contradictions, and Complementarities in the European Economy*, Oxford, Oxford University Press.

Hartman Y. (2005) In bed with the enemy: some ideas on the connections between neoliberalism and the welfare state. *Current Sociology*, 53(1): 57–73.

Hertog P.D. (2001) Knowledge-intensive business services as co-producers of innovation January 2001. *International Journal of Innovation Management*, 4(04): 491–528. https://doi.org/10.1016/S1363-9196(00)00024-X

Hobsbawm E. (1975) *The Age of Capital*, London, Widenfeld and Nicholson.

Hodgson G.M. (2021) Financial institutions and the British industrial revolution: did financial underdevelopment hold back growth? *Journal of Institutional Economics*, 17: 429–448.

IPCC (2021) Summary for policymakers. In: Climate Change 2021: The Physical Science Basis. Contribution of Working Group I to the Sixth Assessment

Report of the Intergovernmental Panel on Climate Change [Masson-Delmotte, V., P. Zhai, A. Pirani, S. L. Connors, C. Péan, S. Berger, N. Caud, Y. Chen, L. Goldfarb, M. I. Gomis, M. Huang, K. Leitzell, E. Lonnoy, J. B. R. Matthews, T. K. Maycock, T. Waterfield, O. Yelekçi, R. Yu and B. Zhou (Eds.)]. Cambridge, Cambridge University Press.

Irwin D.A. (2021) The rise and fall of import substitution. *World Development*, 139: 105306. https://doi.org/10.1016/j.worlddev.2020.105306

Joseph G.G. (1991) *The Crest of the Peacock: Non-European Roots of Mathematics*, London, Penguin Books.

Kahneman, Daniel; Sibony, Olivier; Sunstein, Cass R. (2021) Noise: The new book from the authors of 'Thinking, Fast and Slow' and 'Nudge' London, Harper Collins Publishers.

Karasiotou P. (2012) Education and the labor market, *Reflets et perspectives de la vie économique*, Tome LI: 51–72.

Kindleberger C.P. (1967) *Europe's Post-war Growth: The Role of Labor Supply*, Cambridge MA, Harvard University Press.

Kindleberger C.P. (1973) *The World in Depression, 1929–1939*, Berkeley & Los Angeles, University of California Press.

Kowalkowski C., Gebauer H., Oliva R. (2017) Service growth in product firms: past, present, and future. *Industrial Marketing Management*, 60: 82–88.

Kuné J.B. (2001) The controversy of funding versus pay-as-you-go: what remains of the debate? *The Geneva Papers on Risk and Insurance*, 26(3): 418–434.

Landes D.S. (1969) *The Unbound Prometheus: Technological Change and Industrial Development in Western Europe from 1750 to the Present*, Cambridge, Cambridge University Press.

Landes D.S. (1999) *The Wealth and Poverty of Nations*, New York, WW Norton & Company.

Lindahl M., Krueger A.B. (2001) Education for growth: why and for whom? *Journal of Economic Literature*, 39(4): 1101–1136.

Lindbeck A. (2006) The Welfare State – Background, Achievements, Problems IFN Working Paper No. 662, Research Institute of Industrial Economics P.O. Box 55665 SE-102 15 Stockholm, Sweden.

Lipsey R., Carlaw K.J., Bekhar C.T. (2005) *Economic Transformations: General Purpose Technologies and Long-Term Economic Growth*, Oxford, Oxford University Press.

Lundvall B.A. (1992) *National Systems of Innovation*, London, Pinter.

Lundvall B.A., Rikap C. (2022) China's catching-up in artificial intelligence seen as a co-evolution of corporate and national innovation systems, *Research Policy*, 51: 104395.

Mahoney M.S. (1988) The history of computing in the history of technology. *Annals of the History of Computing*, 10: 113–125.

Malthus T. R. (1798) *An Essay on the Principle of Population*. Oxfordshire: Oxford World's Classics, 13. ISBN 978-1450535540.

Marglin S.A., Schor J.B. (Eds) (1991) *The Golden Age of Capitalism: Reinterpreting the Postwar Experience*, Oxford, Clarendon Press.

Marx K. (1867, 1954) *Capital*, London, Lawrence and Wishart.

Matsuyama K. (2002) The rise of mass consumption societies. *Journal of Political Economy*, 110: 1035–1070.

Meadows D.H., Meadows G., Jorgen Randers J., Behrens W.W.III. (1972) *The Limits to Growth*, New York, Universe Books.

Metcalfe S., Miles I. (2000) *Innovation Systems in the Service Economy*, Boston, MA, Kluwer.

Milanovic B. (2016) *Global Inequality a New Approach for the Age of Globalization*, Cambridge MA, London, Harvard University Press.

Mincer J. (1981) Human Capital and Economic Growth NBER Working Paper 1/803.

Mokyr J. (1990) *The Lever of Riches: Technological Creativity and Economic Progress*, New York, Oxford University Press.

Muller E., Doloreux D. (2007) The key dimensions of knowledge-intensive business services (KIBS) analysis: a decade of evolution, Fraunhofer systems and Innovation Research, Working Papers Firms and Region No. U1/2007.

Murmann J.P. (2003) *Knowledge and Competitive Advantage: The Co-evolution of Firms, Technologies and National Institutions*, Cambridge, Cambridge University Press.

Nelson R.R. (1993) *National Innovation Systems: A Comparative Analysis*, Oxford, Oxford University Press.

North D.C. (1990) *Institutions, Institutional Change and Economic Performance*, Cambridge, Cambridge University Press

Palley T. (2018) Re-theorizing the welfare state and the political economy of neoliberalism's war against it, *FMM Working Paper* No. 16 February, Hans-Böckler-Stiftung.

Peneder M., Kaniovski S., Dachs B. (2001) What follows tertiarization? Structural change and the role of knowledge-based services, WIFO Working Papers N° 146 April 2001.

Perez C. (2002) *Technological Revolutions and Financial Capital: The Dynamics of Bubbles and Golden Ages*, Cheltenham, Edward Elgar, 198 pages, ISBN 1 84064 922 4.

Petropoulos G., Marcus J.S., Moës N., Bergamini E. (2019) *Digitalisation and European Welfare States*, Brussels, Bruegel Blueprint Series, Volume 30.

Piketty T. (2014) *Capital in the Twenty-First Century*, Cambridge, MA, Harvard University Press.

Pilat D., Cimper A., Karsten O., Webb C. (2006) The changing nature of manufacturing in OECD economies, OECD_STI working paper 2006/2009.

Pisani J.A. (2006) Sustainable development – historical roots of the concept. *Environmental Sciences*, 3(2) : 83–96. https://doi.org/10.1080/15693430600688831

Pisani-Ferry J. (2020) Le retour des asymétries mondiales. *Le Grand Continent*, October 20. https://legrandcontinent.eu/fr/2020/10/20/pisani-ferry-asymetries/

Pritchett L. (2001) Where has all the education gone? *The World Bank Economic Review*, 15(3): 367–391.

Pyka A., Saviotti P.P., Nelson R.R. (2018) Evolutionary perspectives on long run economic development, in Nelson R.R., Dosi G., Helfat C., Pyka A., Saviotti P.P., Lee K., Dopfer K., Malerba F., Winter S. (Eds), *Modern Evolutionary Economics, An Overview*, Cambridge, Cambridge University Press, 143–171.

Ricardo, D. (1817) *On the Principles of Political Economy and Taxation* (1st ed.), London, John Murray.

Rodríguez-Pose A., Di Cataldo M. (2015) Quality of government and innovative performance in the regions of Europe. *Journal of Economic Geography*, 15(4): 673–706. https://doi.org/10.1093/jeg/lbu023

Rodrik D. (2007) *One Economics, Many Recipes: Globalization, Institutions and Economic Growth*, Princeton, NJ, Princeton University Press.

Rodrik D. (2011) *The Globalization Paradox: Why Global Markets, States and Democracy Can't Coexist*, Oxford, Oxford University Press.

Rose S.J. (2018) Manufacturing employment: fact and fiction. Urban Institute, https://www.urban.org › default › files › publication

Roser M., Ortiz-Ospina E. (2016) Global education. Published online at OurWorldInData.org. Retrieved from https://ourworldindata.org/global-education

Rowthorn R., Ramana Ramaswamy R. (1997) Deindustrialization–its causes and implications, IMF Working Paper 97/42, "Deindustrialization: Causes and Implications," September 1997.

Sachs J.D., Warner A.M. (1995) Economic Reform and the Process of Global Integration, Brookings Papers on Economic Activity, 1.

Sachs J.D., Warner A.M. (2001) Natural resources and economic development, the curse of natural resources. *European Economic Review*, 45(4–6): 827–838.

Saviotti P.P., Pyka A. (2004) Economic development by the creation of new sectors. *Journal of Evolutionary Economics*, 14(1): 1–35.

Saviotti P.P., Pyka A. (2008) Micro and macro dynamics: industry life cycles, inter-sector coordination and aggregate growth. *Journal of Evolutionary Economics*, 18: 167–182.

Saviotti P.P., Pyka A. (2013) From necessities to imaginary worlds: structural change, product quality and economic development. *Technological Forecasting & Social Change*, 80: 1499–1512.

Schumpeter J. (1939) *Business Cycles: A Theoretical, Historical and Statistical Analysis of the Capitalist Process*, New York, McGraw Hill.

Shane S. (2001) Technological opportunity and new firm creation. *Management Science*, 47: 205–220.

Siebert H. (1997) Pay-as-you-go versus capital funded pension systems. The issue, Kiel working paper no. 816, The Kiel Institute of World Economics.

Silverberg G. (2007) Long waves: conceptual, empirical and modelling issues, in Hanusch H., Pyka A. (Eds) *The Edward Elgar Companion to Neo-Schumpeterian Economics*, Cheltenham: Edward Elgar, 800–819.

Southern Illinois University, A Brief History of IT, Technical support newsletter (March 23, 2016) Vol 2, N° 29.

Standing G. (2011) *The Precariat: The New Dangerous Class*, London, Bloomsbury.

Trajtenberg M. (1990) A penny for your quotes: patent citations and the value of innovations. *RAND Journal of Economics*, 20: 172–187.

Trajtenberg M., Henderson R., Jaffe A.B. (1997) University vs. corporate patents: a window on the basicness of innovation. *Economics of Innovation and New Technology*, 5: 19–50.

Tylecote A. (1992) *The Long Wave in the World Economy*, The Current Crisis in Historical Perspective, London, Routledge.

United Nations (2017) Post-war reconstruction and development in the Golden Age of Capitalism Ch 2 in *World Economic and Social Survey*, Department of Economic and Social Affairs.

Vermeulen B., Kesselhut J., Pyka A., Saviotti P.P. (2018) The impact of automation on employment: just the usual structural change? *Sustainability*, 10: 1661.

Vissen J. (2019) *Trade Unions in the Balance*. ILO ACTRAV Working Paper, ILO.

Wilde R. (2019) Public health during the industrial revolution. *ThoughtCo*, Aug. 31, 2019, thoughtco.com/public-health-in-the-industrial-revolution-1221641.

Windrum P. (2007) Innovation in services, in Hanusch H., Pyka A. (Eds.), *The Edward Elgar Companion to Neo-Schumpeterian Economics*, Cheltenham, Edward Elgar, 405–439.

Wolf C., Popper S.W. (Eds) (1992) Defence and the Soviet Economy: Military muscle and economic weakness, Rand Note N-3474-USDP.

ZBW – Leibniz Information Centre for Economics (2012) The welfare state after the great recession. *Intereconomics*, 47(4): 200–229. https://doi.org/10.1007/s10272-012-0422-y

8 Policy implications of evolutionary economics

1 Future trends and policy implications

One of the main objectives of this book was described as showing that the policy implications of evolutionary economics are at least as interesting and meaningful as those of neoclassical economics. To pursue that objective, we can begin our exploration by establishing some general criteria that should guide the policies inspired by evolutionary economics. Such criteria cannot be objectively derived from observed events, although very often they emerge from tensions experienced by citizens of different countries, but their formulation and adoption are affected by value judgements. In the present state of the world system, there are some trends that will occupy analysts and policy makers for the foreseeable future. Some of these trends, which can be called 'world challenges', will be discussed in the light of an evolutionary theory of socioeconomic development. The main objective here is not to have an exhaustive discussion of these challenges, but to show with some examples that meaningful policy implications can be derived from an evolutionary theory of socioeconomic development. These challenges are in fact changes which could be discontinuities and have the potential to challenge existing institutions at the national and international levels, to the point of threatening the future of human civilization. They are:

Geopolitical order
Employment and social security
Welfare state
Environment
Technology and innovation

The focus here will be on employment and social security and on environment. The discussion of employment and social security will address one of the most important themes in the redesign of the welfare state. The discussion of technology and innovation will be underlying all the chapter. Our starting point will be a theme which is not specific to evolutionary economics but that should be central for any theory of socioeconomic systems (SESs), the

DOI: 10.4324/9781003294221-8

distribution of resources. In doing that I will compare the recipe of neoclassical economics with that of evolutionary economics, the latter being based on the Schumpeterian concept of creative destruction, the consequent need for compensation and the ways such compensation could be provided. This will form the basis for the subsequent discussion which will end with environment as the fundamental theme determining the future of human societies.

1.1 Main points of evolutionary economics

1.1.1 Qualitative vs quantitative change, discontinuities

Economic development consists of both qualitative and quantitative changes. The emergence of qualitatively different entities gives rise to discontinuities and leads to life cycles of industries, technologies, etc. However, quantitative changes give rise to continuous changes. These life cycles are started by one or more radical innovations and proceed by incremental innovations leading to a time path similar to punctuated equilibrium. Qualitative changes give rise to radical uncertainty and their effects cannot be predicted in any accurate way. However, quantitative changes give rise to more predictable outcomes, and they entail calculable risk. The emergence of qualitatively new technologies underpins the differentiation of SESs, contributes to economic development (see point 3) and determines the relative wealth and power of different countries.

1.1.2 Adaptive behaviour

Adaptive behaviour is the most common type of economic behaviour and it contains rational optimization as a limited subset. Adaptation can be subdivided into (i) adaptation to changes in the external environment (EE) of human beings (ADTO) and (ii) adaptation of the EE in order to improve the welfare of human beings in it (ADOF). The events that give rise to ADTO can be either completely exogenous to all human beings or created by some human beings for which other human beings must adapt. ADOF is created by some groups of human beings and can then diffuse to other human beings during a time-bound process in which the total changes constituting ADOF are gradually introduced and both the creators and the adopters need to adapt to them. Failure to adapt can occur due to cognitive or political barriers. Such barriers result from the heterogeneity in the structure of SESs and from the different preferences for adaptation of their different components.

1.1.3 General equilibrium

There cannot be any general equilibrium in the context of long-run economic development, including qualitative change. Any time a radical innovation gives rise to a qualitatively different entity, the composition, and the structure of an SES change in an unpredictable way, including the addition of the new entity and all its subsequent developments. Such developments can be described as dynamic sequences of ADOF and ADTO. Consequently, once a life cycle initiated by a radical innovation and by the corresponding qualitative change begins, the SES is continuously changing. A situation of rest that could be described as a general equilibrium could only exist (i) if no new innovations began and if the life cycles of all the previous innovations came to their end, or (ii) if the rate of adaptation of an SES to any innovation was much higher than the rate of introduction of new innovations. No such situation is likely to occur in a restless (Metcalfe, 1994, 1998; Ramlogan, Metcalfe, 2006) capitalist socioeconomic system which is permanently dynamic.

1.1.4 Structural change and differentiation

The lack of any general equilibrium in the SES is shown in a concrete way by the growing output variety accompanying economic development. Output variety grows inevitably by the joint action of growing productive efficiency and creativity. Efficiency increases when a qualitatively constant output can be produced by a falling quantity of inputs. Creativity gives rise to qualitatively new and wholly unpredictable entities. The development observed in the last 200 years could not have occurred by means of efficiency or creativity alone. Growing efficiency would have led to an economic bottleneck in which a falling share of the available labour can produce all demanded output. Creativity can overcome the previous bottleneck by generating new entities, giving rise to new economic activities, but can only do so by the surplus generated by growing efficiency.

1.1.5 Human knowledge is incomplete

Innovations and new technologies are created in a situation of incomplete knowledge. Entrepreneurs create novelty in a situation of radical uncertainty in which it is impossible to predict accurately the future effects of present decisions. Human knowledge has been growing exponentially in the last century but it is still incomplete. However paradoxical it may seem, as we acquire new knowledge, we become aware of problems that before we did not perceive. In other words, the frontier of knowledge is advancing when we move towards it. This implies that uncertainty is more likely to increase than to decrease. When we explore new fields of science and we gradually articulate our local knowledge within these fields, we reduce uncertainty locally within them but we create new uncertainty elsewhere by opening new fields of knowledge. To the extent that economic development has been increasingly knowledge intensive, we are likely to have increased the overall uncertainty surrounding our decision-making. This implies that we are incapable of predicting accurately the effects of our decisions, especially in the long run, and that our decision-making is likely to create new sources of uncertainty.

1.1.6 Long-term processes

Socioeconomic development involves the occurrence of simultaneous processes occurring at different speeds. Long-term processes are more difficult to detect and interpret than short-term ones and are sometimes detected only after they have reached a given threshold. It is important to think about long-term processes even if we know that we cannot predict accurately their development. The countries or regions that will do research about long-term processes will be better able to adapt to their emergence and evolution. Although Keynes was right in saying that 'in the long run I will all be dead', we might be dead long before that unless we think about it. Examples of failure to think about the long run are the present-world crisis and the environmental impact of human activities.

1.1.7 Coevolution of technologies and institutions

New technologies do not emerge and develop in isolation but coevolve with institutions, infrastructures, and organizational forms. Coevolution can accelerate the emergence of new system structures and multiple possible development paths. No technological innovation could have had the impact we observe on the real world unless it had been accompanied by important institutional and organizational innovations. Technology and innovation need to coevolve in order to allow the potential impact of technology to be realized. Consequently, there is no unique path to economic development, but the actual path followed by a country or a region depends jointly on the inventive activity, on the institutional and organizational changes introduced. This implies that the development path followed by a country or a region depends on the institutions and the political priorities of the country. Thus, evolutionary economics needs to consider the interactions of the different components of an SES and become evolutionary political economics.

2 Policy implications

In the introduction to this book, the derivation of policy implications from evolutionary economics was described as one of its main objectives. A recent survey of economic policies conceived in an evolutionary approach (Roberts, Yoguel, 2022) found that most of those policies were created by pragmatic considerations rather than derived from principles of evolutionary theory. In what follows, I will try to focus on a selected number of principles and examples. However, the work presented in this chapter could be an introduction to a re-examination of those previous policies.

The balance between the creation and distribution of income and wealth has been the main economic problem since the beginning of political economy in the debates about the distribution of rents, profits, and wages in the work of classical economists. Every new economic theory needed and needs to come to terms with it. This will be discussed as the first problem to see how evolutionary economics can approach it. The discussion of the first objective will naturally lead to the nature of our SESs, focusing on employment and social security, which underlies the need for a redesign of the welfare state. The second broad policy objective, the impact of human activities on the natural environment, the urgency of which is continuously increasing, will be discussed after. Finally, some expected trends in innovation and technology will be discussed. As was previously pointed out, I do not believe in any form of technological determinism but I think that development proceeds by means of the coevolution of technologies and institutions, where the term 'institutions' needs to be interpreted broadly to include institutions of all types, organizational forms and infrastructures.

2.1 Policy implications of creative destruction

Points 3 and 4 above show that SESs can be expected to keep changing and transforming themselves, although at variable speeds, alternating discontinuities, and periods of gradual change. The questions that could then arise is: why do these changes occur? Who benefits from them? Innovation is one of the main drivers of these changes, although it never acts alone but always in connection with institutions, infrastructures, and organizational forms. There are always, in any type of society, individuals or groups that are either unhappy with the present condition or can imagine a better one and would like to introduce some changes. Innovations are introduced by entrepreneurs whose frequency varies, depending on the type of society or organization. Schumpeterian entrepreneurs expect to achieve a temporary monopoly as a result of their innovations. The advantages of innovation are enjoyed by some entrepreneurs and the organizations in which they work. But, are there any advantages flowing from innovation to members of society? In other words, how are the results of innovation distributed? Although there is some evidence that some innovations created benefits for most members of society, there is general evidence that the benefits of innovation are very unevenly distributed.

The logical starting point for a discussion of the distribution of the benefits of innovation in a capitalist society is the work of Marx. As pointed out in Chapters 6 and 7, such benefits were largely appropriated by capitalists, leaving workers with only the minimum required to ensure their physical survival. According to Marx, this situation that he called 'exploitation' was not only unjust but also potentially unstable and likely to lead to a revolution. We have already seen that Marx's predictions were only partly right and that, by means of the transformation to what was called a liberal democratic society, the capitalist system managed to outcompete the communist system.

Not long after Marx, neoclassical economists supporting the capitalist system tried to demonstrate that no injustice was involved in the capitalist system. Neoclassical economics provided a potential answer to the above question in the marginal productivity theory of income distribution, which was developed a little over a century ago by John Bates Clark in 'The Distribution of wealth', although such answer was related to production rather than to innovation. Essentially, Clark claimed that, contrary to what Marx had maintained, workers did not get less than what they produced, but that both capitalists and workers got what they deserved. The reward that they both received was based on their marginal product. Thus, no injustice was involved in the income distribution prevailing in capitalist society and workers had no reason to complain about it. Clark's preoccupation about the social stability of capitalist society is clearly demonstrated by the following quotation:

> The welfare of the labouring classes depends on whether they get much or little; but their attitude toward other classes—and, therefore, the stability of the social state—depends chiefly on the question, whether the amount that they get, be it large or small, is what they produce. If they create a small amount of wealth and get the whole of it, they may not seek to revolutionize society; but if it were to appear that they produce an ample amount and get only a part of it, many of them would become revolutionists, and all would have the right to do so.
>
> (Bates Clark, 1899)

So, the neoclassical theory of income distribution was born as an ideological response to Marxism. The subsequent development of neoclassical theory reinforced Clark's idea and gave it a more solid analytical content. In particular, the birth of human capital theory in the 1960s extended and reinforced the ideas about wealth distribution proposed in the marginal revolution. All income differences, economists claimed, could be explained by productivity differences.

The concept of Pareto efficiency, or Pareto optimality (Milgrom, Roberts, 1992), currently used in neoclassical economics, does not assume that the outcomes of the capitalist system are necessarily fair or acceptable. Any change to a different allocation that makes at least one individual better off without making any other individual worse off is a Pareto improvement. An allocation is defined as 'Pareto efficient' or 'Pareto optimal' when no further Pareto improvements can be made, in which case it is assumed to have reached Pareto optimality. This leaves open the possibility to compensate the losers in cases that are not Pareto improvements. Thus, an innovation that benefits some members of society while harming others can still be acceptable if the losers can be compensated.

The implications of innovation for income and wealth distribution ought to have been a very fundamental question for evolutionary economists. Whereas they seem to generally accept that innovation creates wealth, its contribution to wealth distribution is much less discussed. Evolutionary economists go as far as accepting that innovation does not create just wealth but that such wealth can be very unevenly distributed, thus creating both winners and losers, as implied by the Schumpeterian concept of creative destruction.

Furthermore, not all members of organizations that largely benefit from innovation are equally rewarded. Thus, existing evidence seems to indicate that the benefits of innovations are unequally distributed within society. Of course, such a concept seems to be at odds with the approach of neoclassical economists to the distribution of wealth.

Schumpeter's concept of creative destruction is the opposite of Pareto efficiency. In all changes in which there is creative destruction there are both winners and losers and Schumpeter does not say anything about the need to compensate losers. Neither Schumpeter nor Pareto is concerned about justice, equality, or fairness. However, examples of processes that occur without any compensation provided abound. Then not all processes that occur, and perhaps not many, are Pareto improvements. Thus, a suitable generalization that describes more accurately what happens in real life is the following:

> Most processes proceed if the gains of the winners are greater than the losses of the losers.

The previous generalization seems to imply that innovations can be accepted if they benefit some members of society, even if at the expense of other members. A more complete conclusion about the usefulness of innovation needs to consider that there is a form of group selection occurring at the level of large communities, which in the present context means nation states and important regions. This selection favours SESs that combine a series of factors, such as above average economic and military performance, which requires a high-quality NIS (Fagerberg, Shrolec, 2008). Thus, the changes occurring in different SESs are likely to depend on several factors: some internal and depending on the interactions of the different components of the SES, some external and related to the economic and military competition at the international level. Changes in particular SESs could then happen even if they make a large part of the relevant population unhappy, to the extent that they affect positively the international competitiveness of a given SES. Thus, although the transition from hunters-gatherers to settled agriculture is now considered to have worsened the 'quality of life' of most members of the relevant communities, it proceeded due to the faster rate of population growth of agricultural communities, which could then outcompete those of hunters-gatherers. Thus, the transition to settled agriculture gave rise to a collective advantage (faster population growth) at the expense of individual disadvantages (worsening quality of life) (Gowdy, 1994; Harari, 2011). This is not an exception but the general situation: most economic transitions, whether they involve qualitative or quantitative change, create advantages for innovators, immediate users of innovation and, possibly but not necessarily, for the whole population. This does not exclude that at least some innovations can benefit people, but confirms the importance of group selection in the evolution of SESs: important innovations create competitive advantages for the country or region where they are created or very largely adopted even when they do not benefit all the country or region inhabitants. That such mixture of individual and collective advantages and disadvantages is likely to occur in the development of all SESs raises some doubts about the nature of progress.

The position taken in this book is that in a just society all members should have the right to an income level that enables them to satisfy those that could be considered *basic needs*. An income distribution determined by wages corresponding to marginal productivities would be in principle unfair because it could not eliminate the possibility that some members' income fell under the basic needs level, a level that corresponds to poverty. However, in Schumpeter's work, no account is taken of the welfare implications of innovation for winners and losers. Thus, neither marginal productivity theory (MPT) nor Schumpeter's work contains an ethical component that protects individual members of society from falling into poverty, even if their role in the economic system or their low marginal product are not due to their 'incorrect' behaviour. For example, the marginal product of people working in firms using a process, the economic viability of which is threatened by another process competing directly with it, could fall drastically or even become zero. Such a situation would occur if the new process produced an output similar to that of the existing process, but with (i) higher quality or (ii) lower price or a combination of the two. This could be the result of an innovation or the entry of a new competitor into the international market. In this case the market share of the firms using the pre-existing process would fall drastically or disappear, leading to an extremely low or zero marginal product of the firms' workers. This would be an example of creative destruction.

The lack of an ethical content and the neglect of the determinants of marginal product external to workers' behaviour do not deny the possibility to use marginal productivity as a device to monitor the state of an economic system, but deny the possibility to consider that income distribution is due solely to marginal productivity. This conclusion becomes particularly important if we accept that (i) innovation is the main determinant of economic progress, and that (ii) it inevitably entails the presence of creative destruction leading to winners and losers. If we expect innovation to have the potential to improve the welfare of all members of society, then it is both just and logical to compensate the losers.

2.1.1 Compensation

The discussion so far showed that even when marginal productivity can be measured accurately, it cannot be the basis to design a prosperous, just and stable society. A society in which the distribution of income is such that many people live in poverty even when they are working cannot be a prosperous, just, and stable society. As we saw previously, Clark's theory of productivity aimed to demonstrate that everyone in a capitalist society receives a reward for their work comparable to their marginal product. However, neither he nor any neoclassical economist ever considered that there is an income threshold below which any income leads to poverty. This threshold consists of what was called basic needs. Basic needs include biological necessities such as food, housing, and clothing, but such needs only allow physical survival. Members of a modern society capable of satisfying the previous biological needs can still be unable to enjoy full human rights and to be proper citizens. Lack of access to education and ITC are two examples of needs which, if left unsatisfied, could socially handicap many members of society. Thus, basic needs evolve with socioeconomic development but in ways that are not always easy to identify.

Even in this case, Schumpeter's concept of creative destruction can lead to important policy implications. One extreme implication would be a form of social Darwinism similar to the one that had acquired some prominence in the second half of the XIXth century, and that was epitomized by the expression 'the survival of the fittest', first used by Spencer (Weinstein, 2019). A much more balanced interpretation, which was not discussed by Schumpeter, would be that it is both just and wise to compensate the losers by giving them enough of the resources generated by creative destruction to enable them to reach the basic needs threshold. Such rationale is not only morally grounded but can have an important economic justification in the need to support the demand coming from the poorest layers of society, for example, in Keynesian demand policies. In fact, such extension of Schumpeter's creative destruction can be considered a combination of Schumpeter and Keynes.[1] The welfare states that emerged in Europe after the Second World War correspond to this interpretation. However, although they could in principle combine the creativity of capitalism with a 'reasonable' distribution of income and wealth, such welfare states are now undergoing a crisis and they may need to be redesigned. The form of compensation required is likely to depend on the underlying social structure, which in turn is likely to change in the course of time due to technology and the international economic system. Thus, the creative destruction prevailing in a highly knowledge intensive society is unlikely to be the same as in a manufacturing society. In this transition, the concept of the state needs to evolve from a bureaucratic one, mostly based on the repetition of a set of routines, to an entrepreneurial one (Mazzucato, 2013), capable of contributing to explore the most important avenues of change and articulating scenarios to adapt to such changes. In particular, the redesign of welfare states to accommodate the different and possibly contrasting interests of different groups in modern SESs is one of the great challenges of our time.

2.1.2 From basic to higher needs

The conclusion reached so far is that although innovation generates both winners and losers, using the income created by innovations, it is possible to compensate the losers. While this seems clear in principle and it has sometimes been done, it leads to the difficult question of how we can provide adequate compensation. A possible approach would be to establish a level of compensation sufficient to enable losers to satisfy their *basic needs*, which define the absolute minimum resources necessary for long-term physical well-being. The amount of income required to satisfy those needs coincides with the poverty line. The 'basic needs' approach was introduced by the International Labour Organization's World Employment Conference in 1976 and was designed to measure absolute poverty in developing countries (ILO, 1976; Streeten et al., 1981).

The minimum definition of basic needs includes what could be considered biological necessities required for physical survival, such as food, shelter, and clothing. Although these biological needs continue to be vital for the survival, being able to satisfy only these needs a citizen of modern developed countries would not be able to have a 'normal' life. The absence of health care or sanitation could seriously endanger the possibility of survival both at the individual level and at the collective level: whereas non-transmissible illnesses can only endanger individual life, contagious ones can risk the life of many individuals and compromise important social functions. The lack of education substantially reduces the career possibility of individuals up to the point of condemning them to a marginal existence. Lack of access to ITC and internet is a serious social handicap, increasingly limiting the capacity of citizens to carry out basic social functions (paying taxes, purchasing train and airline tickets, finding out about social and cultural events etc.).

In Chapter 1 I distinguished between needs, corresponding to biological necessities, and wants, which can be created by innovation and economic development. Thus, in a modern developed SES, the concept of basic needs must be extended to include both biological needs and man-made wants, the list of the latter being likely to become longer as new technologies and new social functions emerge. Furthermore, even the products satisfying basic needs have become much more diversified and of much higher quality (Saviotti, Pyka, 2013). Food and clothing are now available to a large part of the population of many countries at affordable prices and in wide ranges of quality levels (Saviotti, 2018). Also, innovations based on the most advanced fields of science are continuously redefining the production of food, clothing, and housing.

The extension of basic needs discussed in the previous paragraph has been derived from models of innovation and economic development, and mainly from the observed differentiation of the SES discussed in Chapter 5. During the industrial revolution, most people working earned just enough to purchase the minimum required to achieve biological subsistence (Marx, 1867, 1954; Hobsbawm, 1968). This changed during the XXth century, as the share of necessities required for biological survival (food, clothing, and housing) decreased, gradually creating the disposable income that allowed working people to purchase a wider range of goods and services that Saviotti and Pyka (2013) called 'imaginary worlds', but that correspond to man-made wants. Such new consumption is not necessarily of physical objects, but can include a high component of services. The changed structure of consumption in developed countries can be described by a hierarchy of needs (Maslow, 1943), in which higher needs can be demanded when lower needs are potentially satisfied.

A similar evolution of the concept of basic needs was proposed by Sen (1985) (Nussbaum, 2011), although for completely different reasons. He introduced the twin concepts of *functionings* and *capabilities* and focused on capabilities rather than on consumption. Functionings are *beings* and *doings*, which are states of human beings (beings) and various activities (doings) that a person can undertake. Examples of person's states can relate to nourishment (well-nourished, undernourished), temperature (warm or cold house), education (well or poorly educated), social relations (good citizen, criminal). Examples of activities are travelling, caring for a child, being a member of a political party or of a charitable organization. Functionings are in principle available to everyone but not necessarily every human being has access to them. Capabilities are a person's real opportunities to achieve functionings and so to achieve real freedom. Sen's work on capabilities has been very important in establishing the Human Development Index (HDI) (Stanton, 2007; Ranis et al., 2005).

The concepts of functionings and capabilities can be connected to the previous discussion since the new man-made wants created by innovation and economic development define new functionings and require new capabilities. Thus, the increasing variety of outputs and man-made wants accompanying economic development is likely to lead to an increasing diversification of basic needs, a growing variety of man-made wants and a growing list of functionings. However, individuals cannot be expected to acquire automatically the capabilities to achieve new functionings as soon as they are created. For each functioning resulting from innovations that create new wants the required disposable income needs to be created. That depends on the state of the economy and the political system in the SES. Thus, the list of the functionings can be expected to become longer, but the acquisition of the corresponding capabilities is unlikely to occur spontaneously without the presence of public policies supporting the creation of demand. Once more, it is the coevolution of innovation and demand that can lead to growth. In other words, I can formulate the definition of compensation in terms of capabilities. However, it is not just the absolute level of capabilities that matters, but the distribution of resources enabling the formation of capabilities and their accessibility by the different members of the SES that matters. Thus, although the concept of compensation seems straightforward, a precise definition of it involves a great uncertainty and important value judgements.

Although innovation does not necessarily create well-distributed income and wealth, during some periods people at work often achieved an income above poverty level. For that reason, the right to work was included in some national constitutions as a satisfactory way to provide a reasonable income level. However, that employment can lead to a reasonable income level can no longer be taken for granted. A growing number of people have recently become the so-called 'working poor' (Newman, 1999), that is, people who while working and being paid a salary cannot reach the level of income required to purchase the level of goods and services deemed necessary to be full members of a community or a country. Both neoclassical theory and Schumpeter did not consider that (i) the marginal productivity of some individuals might correspond to wages below the poverty line, which corresponds to basic needs or augmented basic needs, and that (ii) losers might not even be able to achieve a revenue below the poverty line.

The consideration that all citizens have the right to an income above the poverty level was added based on considerations that are both normative and positive. On the one hand, the right to an income above the poverty level can be introduced for moral reasons. On the other hand, the same right can be introduced for very pragmatic reasons because citizens below the poverty level have a very limited demand and contribute very little to economic development. The potential of a society in which many people are unemployed or 'working poor' is not attained.

2.2 Employment and social security

The relationship between innovation and distribution is one of the main problems underlying economic development. As was pointed out, 'spontaneous'[2] capitalist economic development creates wealth, but not evenly distributed. I assumed that such a state of affairs is not acceptable and cannot lead to a stable and harmonious society. Consequently, Schumpeterian creative destruction must be corrected by some forms of compensation that protect the weakest members of society by guaranteeing at least the minimum required to purchase what were called the extended basic needs that correspond broadly to Sen's capabilities.[3] In this section employment will be discussed as a means to the creation and distribution of income and wealth. After that the welfare state and the institutional devices used to compensate for the inequalities that spontaneous economic development creates will be briefly analysed.

The problem of unemployment has recently come back to the forefront of attention in connection with the development of ITCs and of artificial intelligence (AI). The main point in the discussion of employment creation and destruction presented in Chapter 5 was that, although technology and innovation have the potential to substitute human labour, such labour displacements can be compensated by the creation of new and more differentiated forms of employment. This follows from the complementary relationship between efficiency and creativity, where the former reduces unit production costs of existing goods and services while the latter gives rise to qualitatively new goods and services leading to new sectors. A similar imbalance between the growing efficiency in matter manipulation and the less rapidly increasing one in information processing was an important influence in determining the shift from manufacturing to services that became the main source of employment in the second half of the XXth century. Furthermore, the shortening of working times contributed to limit the loss of employment all throughout the XXth century. The increasing level of education which occurred in many developed countries during the XXth century contributed by means of a coevolutionary mechanism to raise the quality of human capital and to create the corresponding purchasing power. While the previous ones were supply-based compensating forces, other forms of employment linked to the welfare state were mostly based on the enhanced demand by the populations of developed countries. Examples of these new types of employment can be found in health care, tourism, entertainment, and media. In the past all these forms of compensation contributed to maintain full or quasi-full employment.[4]

The following list summarizes the main compensating mechanisms which I stressed:

- The emergence of new activities producing qualitatively new types of outputs and increasing the output variety of the economic system (creativity)
- The shift to services, due to the higher rate of growth in matter manipulation relative to information processing during the XIXth century and part of the XXth century
- The reduction in working time during the XXth century
- The increasing level of education during the XXth century
- The growth of activities linked to the welfare state

The question which then arises is whether the same mechanisms which were very effective during the XXth century with the creation of industries based on mechanical, chemical and electrical technologies can be equally effective in the XXIst century in the presence of ICTs and globalization. The crucial question that we face now is: can our economic system create new jobs fast enough to compensate for job destruction by (i) the progress of artificial intelligence (AI) which is capable of substituting jobs of increasingly high skills, and (ii) the increasing competition by emerging countries? The reasons for which the answer to these questions could this time be different depend on (i) the relative speeds of the destruction of pre-existing jobs and of the creation of new ones and (ii) the types of jobs that technology is now capable of substituting.

Although continuously growing productive efficiency is a central feature of the capitalist system and it can be expected to reduce employment per unit of output in existing activities, such a tendency has been greatly accelerated by the extremely rapid catch-up of East Asian countries, and of China. Even more recently this trend has been exacerbated by the progress of AI, which can now be expected both to accelerate job destruction and to widen the range of skills and competencies that can be substituted. The rate of efficiency growth in ITC-based activities is an order of magnitude higher than in mechanical, chemical, or electrical technologies. Furthermore, AI can enable the substitution of jobs of increasingly high skills and competencies which are outside the bounds of previous technologies (Frey, Osborne, 2013, 2017; Brynjolfsson, McAfee, 2011). Admittedly, none of this proves that it will be impossible to create enough new jobs or that all new jobs will provide wages above poverty level. However, it seems to be better to be ready to adapt by designing adequate policy and institutional responses.

Furthermore, the answer to this question depends greatly on the geopolitical environment. With respect to the present, in the 1950s nation states were 'relatively' insulated from the international environment. Since the 1990s globalization led to enhanced international interaction, leading for example to global supply chains (GSC)[5] (Gereffi, 1999; UNCTAD, 2013; Lee et al., 2017). While such chains raised productive efficiency and prosperity for those people who could profit from them in different countries, the greater openness reduced barriers to trade and limited the ability of different nation states to create buffers to limit the sufferings of their citizens (Rodrik, 2011). Thus, the enhanced international division of labour represented by GSC is likely to have contributed, together with changes in technology and trends in political ideas, to the growing income inequality experienced in old developed countries since the 1980s and to the crisis of their welfare states.

2.2.1 Emerging policy and institutional trends

It was previously pointed out that for economic development to continue in the long run, a type of structural change in which an output variety increases in the course of time is required (Saviotti, Pyka, 2004, 2008, 2013; Frenken et al., 2007, Hidalgo et al., 2007; Hidalgo, Hausmann, 2009). This is the first compensation mechanism in the previous list. It implies that the composition of employment needs to change in the course of time to adapt to the evolving requirements of the labour market, which makes it impossible to guarantee constant employment in existing activities. While that may happen spontaneously during some periods, there is no certainty that it will happen at all the times. In fact, the periods during which employment seemed to be stable in existing sectors coincided with the presence of many sectors in the early part of their life cycle and/or with high rates of income growth. However, even during these periods, net employment was always due to the balance between job creation and job destruction. Here I can discuss the policies and institutional approaches that could be used when job creation is too slow.

Typically, in a sector subject to high rates of growth in productive efficiency and to intense international competition, excess employment could be found in some sectors. In these conditions to try and keep employment constant without changing technology and work organization would be futile. Given the complementarity between efficiency and creativity, the resources so used would slow down the growth in productive efficiency of the subsidized firms and deny resources to firms in expanding sectors. A much better alternative consists of trying to anticipate the previous changes and to

(A) displace employment from declining sectors subject to international competition to more promising ones, or (B) modify the same sectors by (b1) making them more efficient or by (b2) increasing their output quality. Each of these choices has advantages and disadvantages. Creating completely new sectors (A) has the greatest potential for employment creation because it corresponds to empty markets but faces the greatest uncertainty. Making existing sectors more efficient (b1) can increase their price competitiveness but at the expense of reducing employment. Modify the same sectors by increasing their output quality (b2) faces less uncertainty than (A) but has a lower potential of employment growth.

2.2.2 Structural change and Flexicurity

All these policy options require retraining, sometimes extensive, of workers. A policy called Flexicurity (European Commission, 2013), which intended to combine competitiveness with high levels of social security, was introduced in Denmark and the Netherlands in the 1990s. Flexicurity is a policy intended to combine labour market flexibility in a dynamic economy and security for workers. It is a welfare state model with a pro-active labour market policy. In other words, it is the opposite of a typical liberal market policy in which the government expects the market to get rid of old unwanted competencies and to produce the new demanded ones. The term was first coined by the social democratic Prime Minister of Denmark Poul Nyrup Rasmussen in the 1990s. Flexicurity had both rights and obligations for the unemployed. Thus, while workers had generous unemployment benefits, they had to be prepared to participate in training programmes aimed at improving their competencies to make them better adapted to the present situation of the labour market. The Flexicurity policy has been created to adapt Denmark for a global future (Eurofound, 2009) and to prepare the labour force to a knowledge-based economy in which lifelong learning is required (Lundvall, 2002).

In Denmark Flexicurity was very successful in reducing unemployment to 4% of the labour force. The success of this policy was a demonstration of the incompatibility of job security and employment security: to obtain employment security we must abandon job security. Flexicurity required large levels of resources to be allocated to retraining activities but these additional resources are compensated by greatly reduced unemployment benefits. Although the introduction of Flexicurity was dictated by empirical reasons and was not based on the then dominating neoclassical economic theory, it follows logically from the evolutionary models of economic development described in Chapter 5, which are based on the creation of new activities and sectors and on the growing diversification and increasing quality in existing sectors.[6]

In Denmark Flexicurity has been highly successful: it has reduced unemployment and youth unemployment to very low levels and it has contributed to create a very high labour mobility (Lundvall, 2002). At about the same time, a similar policy aiming to improve the rapid adaptation of the labour force to the changing conditions of the labour market has been adopted in the Netherlands (Bekker, Mailand, 2018).

Flexicurity as a general concept cannot be implemented in the same way in every country. The specific rules and institutions describing it need to be integrated within the institutions of the country considered. The previous existence of some institutions can greatly facilitate its adoption. For example, it is important to recognize that the Flexicurity concept has been developed in countries with high wages and with clear progressive taxation, as in, for example, Denmark. In countries where these conditions are not already present, the adoption of Flexicurity would face a greater barrier. The European Commission (EC) recognized the importance of Flexicurity in the early 2000s, and promoted it to a flagship policy in the mid-2000s. It was included in the Lisbon Agenda, re-confirmed in the EU2020 strategy, and is advocated by guideline 21 of the European Employment Strategy 2007 as being able 'to promote flexibility combined with employment security' (European Commission, 2013).

Both the initial introduction of Flexicurity and its recognition by the EC happened before the crisis that began in 2007. The crisis had a severe effect on employment forcing EU governments to extend social expenditures to support unemployed and economically fragile people. This crisis accentuated the cost reducing aspects of Flexicurity and weakened the most socially progressive and forward-looking ones. Furthermore, it delayed the adoption of Flexicurity by those countries that had low wages and less progressive taxation, which faced a higher barrier (European Commission, 2013; Bekker, Mailand, 2018). Nevertheless, in countries where flexicurity policies Ire/are in place (Nordic and Continental), the effects of the crisis (in terms of unemployment and GDP growth) have been less severe than in other countries characterized by high labour market rigidities.

When it was introduced, Flexicurity was a considerable novelty in that it was in between the two extremes in labour market policies previously existing; that is, the market-oriented policy described above as the freedom to hire and various forms of employment protection which raised different types of barriers to laying off workers. Both had been tried and both of them had shortcomings. Those shortcomings are magnified by some changes in the international economic environment starting from the 1980s onwards. The most important of these changes are (i) globalization and (ii) technological change. Within a very short period, the extent of globalization increased markedly due to the combination of (a) the emergence of newly industrializing countries and (b) that of global supply chains. These two changes are not unrelated since the progress of ITC greatly facilitated the coordination of different steps of production over long distances (Baldwin, 2016, 2018), allowing the delocalization of some production steps to newly industrializing countries and giving rise to global supply chains. Thus, the second wave of globalization was highly dependent on technological change since it was facilitated by falling transport and even more by ITC. In turn, by means of a coevolutionary mechanism, the enhanced production efficiency due to this new international division labour accelerated the production and diffusion of technologies such as the internet and portable telephones.

For old industrialized countries (OICs), globalization and technological change represented both a threat and an opportunity. The opportunity came from the possibility to delocalize the less knowledge-intensive parts of production to countries having lower costs and the availability of finished products at lower prices than it would have been the case otherwise. The threat came from the emigration of the delocalized parts of production and of the corresponding employment (Baldwin, 2016; Sapir, 2006; Acemoglu et al., 2016). Thus, sectors and production processes that had been the monopoly of OICs are suddenly subject to intensified international competition. The natural fall in employment per unit of output due to the increasing efficiency and the improved coordination over long distances following from technological change was then accelerated by the low-cost competition from emerging countries. The joint effect of globalization and technological change provided benefits for the workers having competencies that could still be used in OICs but are a threat for employment and wage levels in the activities that are delocalized (Slaughter, Swagel, 1997; OECD, 2007; Helpman, 2016; Baldwin, 2016). In this sense the second wave of globalization is likely to have contributed to the growing income inequality experienced in OICs.

Flexicurity emerged from the observation of this increased international competitiveness but its conception and introduction are essentially dictated by pragmatic considerations. An interesting question is then if economic theory could have helped policy makers to conceive it. The changes in the world economic environment that occurred since the 1980s can be represented as external, or exogenous, with respect to the nation states of the OICs but affecting them very heavily. If the SESs of OICs had previously been in an equilibrium state, this perturbation would have destabilized the SESs and obliged them to move towards a different equilibrium. According to neoclassical economics, the market would have done it. However, a question that neoclassical theory never asks is: how long would the changes required to achieve the new equilibrium position take? This is the situation for which the statement by Keynes that 'In the long run I are all dead' was pronounced. If the transition time between the two equilibrium positions were to last for a whole generation, the sufferings of the population would be immense. In these conditions the government would be required to intervene. In Chapter 3, I took the position that a general equilibrium of an SES could only exist if after the destabilizing effect of an innovation, which included the emergence of the innovation and all the technological and institutional changes linked to its diffusion, no other innovation would occur. Furthermore, I stated that all changes in an SES occur at a finite speed. Thus, since in modern SESs innovations occur all the time, a general equilibrium could only exist if the changes following the introduction of an innovation were to occur at an infinite speed, in zero time. Such possibility is not only illogical, but it is contradicted by empirical evidence: industry or product life cycles, as well as important institutional changes, can last tens or hundreds of years. Thus, general equilibrium cannot exist in SESs driven by innovation. Such SESs are part of 'restless capitalism' (Metcalfe, 1998; Ramlogan, Metcalfe, 2006) and are undergoing permanent change. If a distinction can be made it is not between equilibrium and disequilibrium but between periods in which qualitative change and radical innovations predominate and periods in which the SES grows quantitatively without important qualitative changes. In the former period, new technologies, new institutions and new organizational forms are introduced, leading to a profound change of structure. In the latter period, the SES grows quantitatively with limited changes in its structure. The former period is characterized by a higher and more radical uncertainty, while in the latter period uncertainty changes towards calculable risk.

Moreover, not only the structure of the SESs keeps changing but it changes in a particular direction, that of an increasing differentiation and an increasing variety (Saviotti, Pyka, 2004, 2008, 2013). All these changes imply a change in the distribution of the competencies used in the SES. As a consequence, it is a mistake to try and delay the displacement of competencies from older sectors in which less labour is required to produce one unit of output to newer sectors where the demand for labour is growing more rapidly. Policies aimed to stabilize employment in mature or declining sectors use resources to subsidize jobs that should disappear and deny resources to newer sectors that would employ logically the existing labour force. A policy attempting to unnecessarily stabilize employment in mature sectors would slow down the growth in efficiency and delay the progress of creativity.[7] Recent empirical research (Frenken et al., 2007, Hidalgo et al., 2007; Hidalgo, Hausmann, 2009) confirms this point of view. These implications of evolutionary growth models correspond exactly, although in a general sense, to the Flexicurity policy. At least in this situation, the policy implications of evolutionary economics are more relevant than those of neoclassical economics. Finally, it is not just structural change that leads to these policy implications but also the speed at which it occurs. In the recent past, the emergence of newly industrializing countries, and of China, has greatly accelerated structural change requiring changes in competencies more than once during working lives.

2.2.3 AI and robotics

Flexicurity was introduced in a period in which the main threat to employment was the joint effect of technological change and increasing international competition in the activities and sectors that had been the preserve of old industrialized countries (OICs). As I have previously seen (Chapters 5 and 7), since the industrial revolution, full or quasi-full employment had been maintained by a combination of increasing productive efficiency and of a series of compensating factors, including the emergence of new activities and sectors, the differential rate of growth of efficiency in matter manipulation and information processing, the shortening of working times, and a series of mostly demand-based factors, such as the development of health care and tourism.

The question which now arises is whether the same factors can be expected to keep full employment in future. In the early 2000s, a change in technology that some scholars consider exceptional and likely to give rise to a different relationship between technology and employment took place. This change consists of an acceleration in the progress of artificial intelligence (AI) (Accenture, 2017; Copeland, 2020). Previously, AI had been considered an academically interesting and promising field, but with very far away technological payoff. In the early 2000s, a technique called 'deep learning'[8] suddenly seemed to shorten the time required to develop practical applications. Not only did AI seem to be capable of substituting human labour, but it did so at an increasing speed and for types of activities that were previously considered too creative to be automated. Some scholars thought this would prevent the creation of full employment and lead to the 'end of work' (Brynjolfsson, McAfee, 2011; Frey, Osborne, 2013, 2017). More recent work (Vermeulen et al., 2018) reaches a more optimistic conclusion, pointing out that although as usual technology can substitute labour, its net employment effect consists of this substitution and a few compensating mechanisms, such as those described in the previous paragraph. These studies use databases on occupations and activities and attempt to predict which ones of these will gain and which one will lose employment. According to this study, some occupations and activities can gain employment while others can lose it. The possible macroeconomic development paths vary between the end of work and the continuation of full employment, but include intermediate stages with a partial loss of employment followed by a full recovery. Although none of these studies can accurately predict future macroeconomic development paths, taken together they exclude that the end of work is the only possible future.

2.2.4 Routines and search activities

Although Flexicurity is based on some specificities of the Danish system, it contains the seeds of a generalized response to labour displacement induced by the joint action of technological change and international competition. The application of the same principles to other countries will require adaptation to their national circumstances. This assumes that the policy measures constituting Flexicurity can keep generating enough new employment to compensate for the one that is being destroyed. A question that is not answered by Flexicurity is how to design training programmes. While it is not exceptionally difficult to redirect workers towards activities in which skill shortages have already been identified, no one can accurately predict the future evolution of an economic system and the new activities that will be created. A useful guide to the creation of new activities can be derived from the distinction between routines and search activities (Nelson, Winter, 1982). Routines are repeated unchanged or with minimal variations for long periods until threats or failures persuade firms that they need to be replaced. Search activities explore the external environment trying to understand it, thus providing the basis for new alternative routines. All economic activities can then be classified in a range going from unchanging routines to the most fundamental search activities. In fact, these would be only the extremes of a range of activities including some intermediary cases. For example, some forms of incremental R&D could already use some routinized components and be somewhere in between routines and completely unstructured search activities. A criterion to distinguish the two could be based on the distinction between radical uncertainty and calculable risk. Activities involving radical uncertainty are pure searches while those involving calculable risk are more incremental searches. Search activities go beyond R&D and are by no means reserved to the physical sciences. Routinized behaviour exists in all forms of human activity, including government health care and the media. Start-ups (SUs) are already an example of firms predominantly carrying out search activities.

The workers displaced from declining sectors could be redirected partly to learning activities that give them the competencies required where there are skill shortages and partly to organizations involved in search activities. These organizations, which could be Start-Ups (SUs), cooperatives or NGOs, can experiment with new activities of potential economic or social usefulness. A sector in which search activities could be highly beneficial is the protection of the environment. As will be pointed out later, the solution of our environmental problem cannot consist of the substitution of more environmentally damaging activities with less damaging ones, everything else being kept constant. The construction of sustainable SES involves a complete change of its structure, including new components, the disappearance of older ones and the reorganization of their interactions. Both the scope for experimentation and the need for it in this field are immense.

Most of these search organizations will have a temporary life and disappear within a short period, but some of them will create new patterns of work, leading to more stable and large-scale employment. In this proposed reorganization, the labour market would be redefined as consisting of people who work, people who learn and people who search, with most people moving between these compartments once or more during their working lives. This type of work organization is appropriate to a knowledge-based society in which (i) production routines are becoming increasingly automated and employing few people, and (ii) the economic system is becoming increasingly differentiated and requiring rapid changes in competencies. I can even imagine a future in which all production based on matter manipulation will be largely or completely automated, with only a limited level of complementary employment surviving. In this case search or social activities would become the predominant form of employment.

2.3 The welfare or social state

The previous considerations were focused predominantly on employment. In the past the right to work was often interpreted as the right to have a fixed job all or most of the time. Such a right seems to have become incompatible with the maintenance of reasonable levels of prosperity and growth in the present circumstances. As previously pointed out, in the SESs of several nation states, there is the problem of the so-called working poor, that is, people that while being employed and earning a wage are below the poverty line. This might be due to technological progress, or to the competition by newly industrializing countries (NICs) having lower labour and social costs. In this case the compensation mechanisms that since the industrial revolution have contributed to maintaining high levels of employment might not be enough in the future. Although I cannot and do not wish to rule out the possibility that spontaneous adjustments in the economic system will automatically lead to full employment, I think it wise to reflect on policy and institutional changes that could avoid unemployment crises. After all, the employment levels observed during the XXth century were obtained by a reduction in weakly working hours from ~60 to ~40 (Huberman, Minns, 2007) and by a considerable increase in the education level of the labour force (Morrison, Murtin, 2007, 2009; Wils, Goujon, 1998). The change stressed here consists of (i) if some types of jobs can have a short duration relative to working lives and that workers may need to be retrained once or more during their working lives, and (ii) assuming that, since the economic activities of the future cannot be accurately predicted, workers made redundant from declining sectors should be redirected to learning or search activities that can give them required competencies or explore potential future economic activities.

I previously pointed out that the welfare states created after the Second World War were probably the best[9] solution to the class struggle that began with the industrial revolution, but that the particular form of the welfare state that was then created became well adapted to the politics, the technology and the international economic environment that occurred since the 1980s. The combined effect of neoliberalism, trends in technology and globalization attacked the legitimacy of the welfare state, reduced the resources at its disposal and widened the gap in income and wealth between the poorest and the richest parts of the population of OICs. Several factors contributed to determine this outcome. The gradual reduction of the tax rate for the richest members of society contributed to magnify the growing income and wealth inequality occurring in OICs (Saez, Zucman, 2019) while simultaneously globalization was threatening the stability of employment for the workers subject to increasing international competition and enriching the people who by virtue of their human capital or their inherited wealth could benefit from it. Globalization was greatly facilitated by falling transport costs and vastly improved communications. The coevolution of these institutional and technological changes destabilized the SESs of OICs by increasing their income and wealth inequality and reducing the resources that could fund the welfare state. In the same period the shift to a service economy reduced the population share of the working class and led to a more fragmented society. In these conditions the welfare state needs a considerable redesign. I am not going here to provide a complete discussion of the desirable institutional design of the welfare state but I will focus on those aspects that depend on the coevolution of technologies and institutions. I start by formulating few basic principles that future institutional design of the welfare state should consider:

1 Every individual, citizen has the right to a reasonable income level, where reasonable means above the poverty level of the time.
2 Every individual, citizen has the right to a meaningful and safe occupation which, while contributing to the collective adaptation of the society in which they live, helps to sustain, and enhance individual identity.
3 To avoid power imbalances, income distribution should not become too unequal.
4 The activities of our global SESs must be transformed to make them sustainable in harmony with our physical and biological environment.

2.3.1 Social salary

In this section I will discuss points (1), (2) and (3). Point (4) will be discussed in the next section. To obtain a continuous and reasonable flow of income, a social salary[10] (SOSA) should in principle be available to everyone. The expression in principle means that the social salary should be used by the smallest possible number of people. Such social salary would replace unemployment benefits and income support but it would be awarded subject to some conditions. Since a large part of unemployment is due to poorly adapted competencies of the labour force, people receiving SOSA should in exchange be prepared to undertake some type of retraining, set up new firms or organizations of the types described in the previous section or participate in them. If the retraining programmes are effective then workers should be able to find new jobs. When the new firms or organizations are successful and grow, the founders and the people participating in them can become employees and replace the SOSA with a normal salary. Given that such new firms or organizations can be expected to have a high rate of failure, people working for them are likely to alternate between work and SOSA. As pointed out in the previous section, this would amount to redefine the labour market as constituted by people who work, people who learn and people who search. The aggregate outcome of having a SOSA would be to continuously improve the human capital of the population.

The level of SOSA should always be above the poverty level to provide a reasonable income, but not too high to discourage the acceptance of employment opportunities. After being awarded to an unemployed worker, SOSA should not be terminated when the worker receives a job offer with a salary just above SOSA. For example, the job offer could involve costs (e.g., transport costs), after which the new real salary would be below SOSA. In this case it would be advisable to leave a residual part of SOSA, called RSOSA, in order to make the new real salary clearly above SOSA. Depending on the nature of the new employment, RSOSA should be reduced or kept constant in the course of time.

Case 1: the new job offer is in a sector that is subject to intense international competition or that is barely economically viable. In this case SOSA could act as a form of income support but would be reduced in the course of time until the real salary becomes equal to SOSA (see Figure 8.1). After that the person would go back to retraining to achieve a better, more stable job. This approach could be used as a transition device in a community highly dependent on a narrow range of activities and competencies that is threatened by extended employment. However, in this case, SOSA should be conceived only as transition device and should not acquire a permanent character.

Case 2: founding of, or participation in, a Start-Up (SU), ONGs or socially useful organizations. To satisfy principle (4), some of these firms and organizations should contribute to reduce the environmental impact of human activities. In this case SOSA could only cover labour costs and should be complemented, when necessary, by forms of help, such as complementary skills and competencies that are normally provided by incubators. To facilitate the transition to a viable firm, SOSA should be cumulable[11] up to a point with income from the SU's activities (Figure 8.2). The members of these organizations should be allowed to keep a RSOSA even after the organization has survived the initial period and become viable, up to maximum value of their salary. In the case of ONGs or socially useful organizations the cost of any services supplied should be based on the customers' income.

Work and employment have always been very important components of the welfare state. Situations such as that envisaged in the prediction of the 'end of work' would make the institutional design of the welfare state very difficult. The previous considerations can provide ways to sustain employment even during periods in which an imbalance occurs between the demand and the supply of jobs. The combination of work and SOSA could keep income per capita at a reasonable level (Point 1). Employment in Start-Up (SU), ONGs or socially useful organizations could contribute to enhance the quality of work and support individual identity (Point 2). However, Point 3 depends largely on fiscal policy. I have already seen that innovation creates wealth but unevenly distributed. Such trend seems to be well represented or even exaggerated by firms like the GAFAS which become real-world powers. Although a discussion of fiscal policy clearly exceeds the scope of this book, in a general sense it can be an important policy instrument used to compensate for the unequal distribution of income and wealth spontaneously generated by innovation. As a consequence, I can expect fiscal policy to become more progressive as it was in the 1950s and 1960s in the USA (Saez, Zucman, 2019).

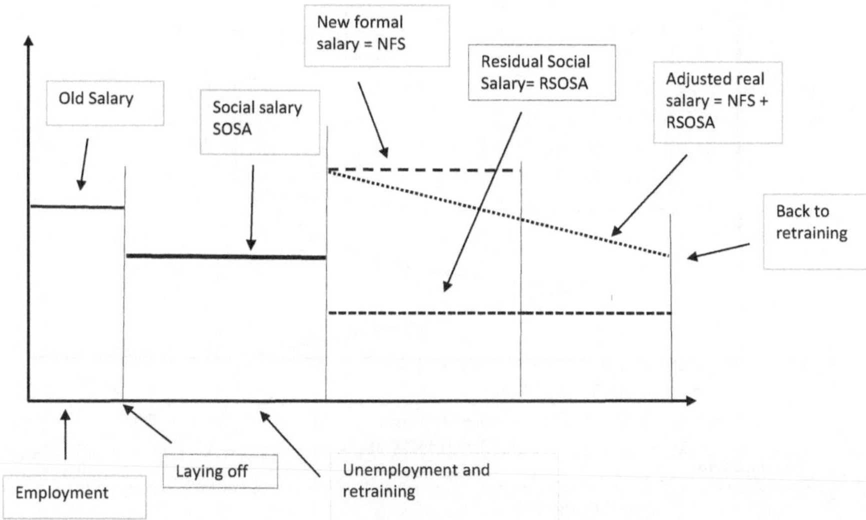

Figure 8.1 Evolution of social salary (SOSA) from (i) employment to (ii) unemployment and retraining, to (iii) new employment with low real salary + residual social salary (RSOSA), to (iv) unemployment and retraining. The period (iii) can be used transition device to allow a gradual transition from older and no longer economically viable activities to new economically viable activities.

As pointed out in Chapter 7, the design of the welfare state implemented in the period between the Second World War and the 1970s was based on the existence of the two social classes of capitalists and workers. Such social structure has by now largely disappeared, and it has been replaced by a more fluid structure with various groups having different political preferences which are not easily represented by traditional political parties. The relative stability of work which was still possible from the 1950s to the 1970s is gradually being replaced by a faster rate of structural change, due to the combination of technological progress and globalization. In these circumstances, even full employment could for many people be a succession of short-term jobs separated by periods of retraining. Whether this is a short-term adjustment or a permanent shift is not yet clear. It seems better to include in the redesign of the welfare state the possibility for people to work and learn during their whole life without undue suffering by means of institutional arrangements adapted to a learning society. The example of the social salary is oriented in this direction.

As was pointed out in Chapter 3, in all modern societies, there is a tension between stability and change. Some countries that are more innovative will force other countries to adapt, either by imitating them or by remaining behind. However, even within the same country, large inequalities or

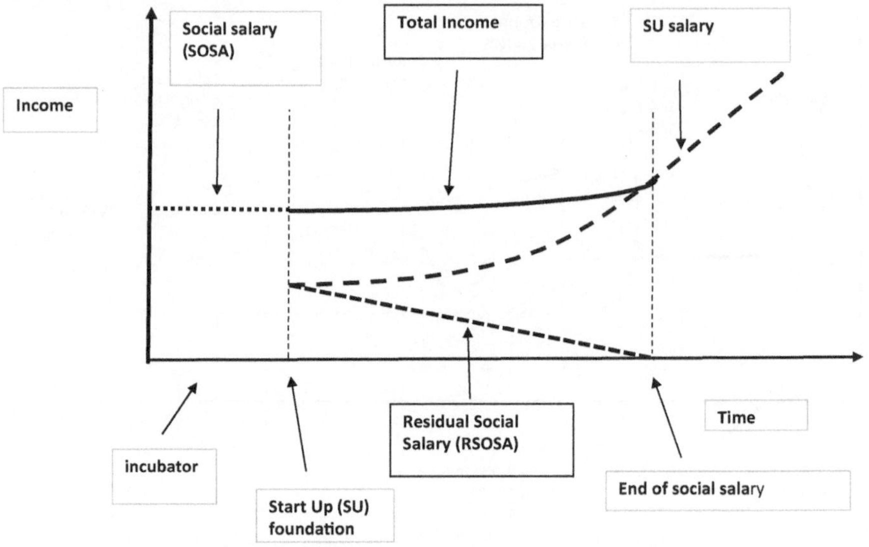

Figure 8.2 Transition from (i) an incubator to (ii) the foundation of a Start-Up (SU) to the economic viability of the SU. The path represented here in not unique. For example, the economic viability of the SU can worsen before recovering and attaining economic viability. The general principle stressed here is that it is better to help entrepreneurs cross the period before the SU attains economic viability (valley of death).

lack of social mobility can make a part of the population feel as if they were not treated as proper citizens. Thus, in any redesign of the welfare state, an appropriate balance between creating and producing on the one hand and solidarity, or cohesion, on the other hand will be needed. In the organization of work described above, social solidarity will be preserved and possibly enhanced by having all of the labour force continuously engaged in working, learning or searching.

2.4 Environment

The impact of human activities on the physical environment is undoubtedly one of our greatest challenges, a challenge that could destroy human civilization as we know it. The role of the environment in this book is not to present a survey of the studies done in this field and the present state of the debate, but rather to outline the directions in which evolutionary economics needs to change in order to be able to provide analyses and policy implications which makes it a general analytical framework to rival neoclassical economics at both the theoretical and policy levels. In order to achieve that evolutionary economics can expand its own field of investigation or form mergers and alliances with other, non-typically neoclassical, fields of knowledge. As a consequence, here I will not discuss specific paths towards a sustainable SES but only establish some general criteria that could distinguish different types of paths and their expected outcomes. For example, the definition of physical goods and services introduced in Chapter 1 is compatible with the second law of thermodynamics and the definition of efficiency adopted here takes into account the physical nature of the inputs used to produce man-made artefacts (MMAs). Furthermore, the possibility that MMAs can be more ordered, and thus to have a lower entropy, than the natural inputs from which they are produced can occur in the open systems studied by non-equilibrium thermodynamics when they are far from equilibrium. Such possibility is not a violation of the second law of thermodynamics because the high entropy of the wastes produced in the process will necessarily more than compensate the loss in entropy of the MMAs. Thus, even if in the production of the ordered structures created by human activities there is a fall in entropy, the overall outcome of the corresponding processes will always lead to an increase in entropy. Furthermore, the coevolution of technologies and institutions, a concept that has been quite central in this book, applies equally well to the relationship between the relationship between human activities and the natural environment. In fact, this relationship after the industrial revolution could be described as a failed coevolution of two interacting components, mankind and the natural environment, in which the former behaved as if the latter did not exist or as if it did not matter. The same phenomenon can be represented as a failed adaptation of human beings to their natural environment in which ADOF was pushed far beyond its legitimate limits.

In Chapter 1, it was pointed out that all material artefacts (MMAs) have two dimensions: their internal structure, constituted by a number of physical, interconnected components and described by a set of technical characteristics; and a set of services supplied to users or consumers intended to satisfy human needs and wants. Such material artefacts are the union of human knowledge about the physical environment and of human needs and wants. The production of all physical technologies requires materials, energy and knowledge. The extraction of materials and the production of energy have an impact on our environment, an impact that has now become too high and that we need to reduce to make our SES sustainable.

From the previous analysis of MMAs, we know that their main impact on the environment is mainly caused by the production of the internal structure (IS). Thus, rather than eliminating all the environmentally damaging product technologies, we need to reduce the environmental impact required to supply a constant flow of services. To do this we need to reduce the environmental impact of the extraction and utilization of all the materials and the energy used in the production of ISs and indirectly in that of the corresponding services. Furthermore, we need to take care of wastes given that all physical technologies have a finite lifetime and create environmentally damaging wastes. The best way to do this consists of creating an 'ecosystem' in which the extraction of materials from the environment is minimized and all the wastes are recycled. This is what is called the circular economy, a concept pioneered by Boulding (1966), although not using the same term. The circular economy has been the object of a very large number of publications (see, for example, Pearce, Turner, 1989), is giving rise to many applied research programmes and is now at the basis of 'A new circular economy action plan: for a cleaner and more competitive Europe' of the European Commission.

In pursuing the above objective, we need to remember that we are running against the second law of thermodynamics, according to which all physical transformations tend to increase entropy. When we create and produce a new physical technology, we take high entropy materials from the environment and by applying energy and knowledge transform them into low-entropy products (Daly, 2007, Georgescu Roegen, 1971; Beinhocker, 2007; Gowdy, 1994; Hidalgo, 2015). Even if we reduce the local entropy of the artefacts we produce, we simultaneously increase total entropy by producing high-entropy wastes. Then, since the overall entropy of the process has to increase, we inevitably export high entropy to other parts of our environment. We need to limit such excess entropy in order to create a sustainable SES. In fact, our earth has a finite but not unlimited capacity to metabolize entropy. While we produce entropy and disorder, the earth uses sunlight and human wastes (CO_2) to create ordered structures (plants) by means of photosynthesis. Thus, we need to reduce the amount of energy we use below the limit corresponding to the maximum entropy that can be absorbed by our environment (Deutscher, 2008, Ayres, 1998; Carsten, 2011; van der Bergh, Gowdy, 2000). In fact, according to Deutscher, we do not have an energy crisis but an entropy crisis.

The case of direct, or disembodied, supply of services can in principle imply a lower production of entropy since the final delivery of services is carried out by human beings or organizations without embodying them in a physical product. However, physical technologies giving rise to entropy and wastes are used in the processes involved in the supply of such disembodied services. Thus, although in principle the disembodied supply of services can lead to a lower environmental impact than its embodied analogue, the two need to be compared case by case with calculations of their environmental impact. A particularly interesting case occurs in the sharing of product technologies which are privately purchased (see the case of car sharing in eResources) but the analysis could be generalized to other situations. Furthermore, a solution of our environmental problem needs to save or replace the services supplied by the environment to recreate natural capital (Pearce, 1992; Lovins et al., 2000).

Whereas the existence of the second law of thermodynamics implies that we cannot keep using a productive system that creates increasing pollution leading to an unsustainable development path, it cannot provide detailed answers to questions such as: (1) is there a finite limit to how much I can pollute, or is such a limit zero? And (2) admitting that there is a sustainable steady state towards which we need to converge, how quickly do we need to get there? In fact, to design development paths leading to such a sustainable steady state is likely to be at least as difficult as to design the steady state itself. Given the previously discussed limitations of human knowledge, at this stage nobody is capable of predicting accurately the potential outcomes of any of the policy decisions we can make. The uncertainty surrounding the potential impact of human activities on the natural environment is so great and so radical that we can only gradually construct scenarios, enrich them as our knowledge and computational capabilities improve, and adjust them to an expanding body of observations and data.

Although many potential development paths that could reduce the impact of human activities on the natural environment are discussed in the literature, two of them, called Degrowth (DG) (DeMaria et al., 2013; Martínez-Alier et al., 2010) and Sustainable Development (SD) (Daly, 1990, 1991, 2002), are the two most important references around which the debate is articulated. These two are conceptual models, or thought experiments, rather than detailed and well worked out development paths. Within this pattern of progress, general theoretical frameworks such as DG and SD help to organize the debate. They differ for their attitude towards the present model of economic development. While DG considers it completely faulty and in need to be replaced by a completely different one, SD implicitly assumes that it is possible to achieve a sustainable SES by reducing the environmental impact of all the technologies used. In other words, DG and SD differ mostly in the design of development paths leading to a sustainable state. Degrowth advocates the downscaling of production and consumption, or the contraction of economies, arguing that overconsumption lies at the root of long-term environmental issues and social inequalities. Degrowth theorists do not expect this contraction to impoverish human societies but to contribute to the enhancement of their well-being by substituting wasteful consumption activities with more meaningful and less polluting ones, such as devoting more time to art, music, family, nature, culture and community. I find this approach extreme and unlikely to be generally acceptable and to lead to a realistic development path.

However, policies corresponding to SD generally assume that reducing the environmental impact to a sustainable level can be achieved by a continuing reliance on the same model by suitably modifying it.[12] For example, the Brutland report (WCED, 1987), one of the earliest public documents to deal with SD, defined it as not only compatible with growth but requiring it (Daly, 1990). When comparing DG and SD, we need to distinguish the absence of growth from its content. We certainly need to drastically reduce all polluting activities, but do we need to eliminate them completely or is there a maximum level of development of human activities that is compatible with the capacity of the natural environment to absorb it? Then, the relevant question becomes: is there a threshold of entropy below which human activities not too dissimilar from the present ones can be physically sustainable? Such a threshold can be provided by the maximum entropy level that the EE can sustain. In its normal functioning, the Earth has the capacity to create order and reduce entropy, for example, by transforming the energy contained in the solar radiation reaching the earth into plants and trees. However, this capacity to reduce entropy has an upper threshold, above which entropy and disorder can no longer be reduced.

According to Deutscher (2008), an order of magnitude for the maximum amount of energy that could be used without increasing excessively entropy is 4 Gigatonnes of carbon per year, which was produced by the total combustion of fossil fuels in 1975, since anthropogenic effects on the climate were not noticeable before that date. Thus, the objective to reduce overall energy consumption to the pre-1975 level seems in principle possible. Here the choice between producing even more energy than we are using now with renewable sources and reducing energy production at or below the level required to limit entropy production to a sustainable level is extremely important. The problem is whether this limit can be attained by means of a development path that does involve huge sacrifices for the whole world or a very uneven distribution of these sacrifices amongst different countries.

This constraint could be satisfied if we managed to produce a constant[13] level of services with a sufficiently reduced energy input. In Chapter 1 it was shown that all the production destined to consumers can be represented as production of *indirect* services, embodied in physical products, or as production of *direct* services, the two ways being partly substitutable. In both cases energy, raw materials, knowledge, physical and human capital are used. Energy, raw materials, and physical capital use can then be reduced by either (a) lowering the amount of these inputs used in the production of material goods supplying a constant level of services, or (b) switching from indirect to direct services whenever the latter involves lower consumption of energy, raw materials and physical capital. An example of this is given by car sharing, in which the stock of physical capital (cars) used to supply a given level of transport services is reduced by means of the coordination provided by ITC (see eResources, Chapter 8). In summary, reducing the environmental impact of existing technologies while preserving as much as possible the present level of services is more likely to be obtained by increasing energy efficiency than by indiscriminately increasing the amount of 'clean' energy we use. To increase energy efficiency, defined as the amount of energy required to produce a unit of services, is likely to be as important, if not more important, than to increase total energy production.

The maximum entropy criterion described above can be very useful in providing a simple guidance to the reduction of the environmental impact of human activities, but it can also help us to reduce many types of pollution. For example, how can we limit the pollution originated by plastics? Dispersing plastic bags in the EE increases disorder and entropy while collecting all these bags in one or few places increases order and reduces entropy.

Similarly, collecting all metals or valuable chemical elements in one or a few places, called secondary mines, reduces entropy and creates order and value. These two are just examples of the circular economy in which the concept of wastes disappears because all outputs from given processes, including wastes, become inputs to other processes. Of course, the circular economy is not beyond the corner. A large amount of search activities, as well as technological and institutional innovation, will be required to get there. Whatever strategy we choose, the transition path to a sustainable world SES is likely to require a lot of technological innovation and a lot of institutional innovation. Once more, we will need the coevolution of technology and institutions.

The transition towards a sustainable SES could not be achieved by substituting the present set of 'polluting' activities with an environmentally safe set producing the same services. Although some substitution processes will undoubtedly be part of the transition, we can expect the structure of the SES to be completely different, because the new processes introduced would need to change many, and possibly all, of their input-output links. The shift to renewable energy would need to use completely different inputs, be they wind, sun, tides or geothermal energy, the spatial distribution of which would be completely different with respect to fossil fuels. A similar change of input patterns would occur following a shift to the bioeconomy (Saviotti, 2017).[14] In both cases there would be huge changes in patterns of trade and in the relative economic position of different countries. Furthermore, the investment requirements of such a transition are almost impossible to calculate. As usual, these changes would create huge opportunities and considerable destruction. There will be winners and losers. The transition to a sustainable SES will have an intrinsically political nature. To facilitate such a transition, well-designed patterns of international collaboration would be more advisable than letting the market do it.

What has been written so far implies that we have damaged our natural environment and that we need to change the human activities we use, but that we can design a new, sustainable development path. The entropy criterion was cited as proof that by reducing our total energy consumption below a given threshold, we can in principle preserve a reasonably wide range of human activities and a satisfactory standard of living. A more pessimistic outlook can be derived from the recent report of the IPCC (2021). What the entropy criterion cannot help us with is the predicted increase in variance of the variables measuring the effects of climate change. Examples of these potentially extreme events (Hallegatte, 2007) are the level of seas and oceans or the strength of winds. It means that infrastructures, buildings and most man-made artefacts (MMAs) should be built to withstand the maximum value of the variables measuring extreme events. Unless we reverse the trend of climate change on time, the cost of damages caused by these extreme events could exceed the investment capabilities of individuals and countries. The problem is magnified by the increasing frequency of uninsurable events (ClimateWise, 2014). For example, if an extreme event destroyed someone's house, the cost of rebuilding the house could exceed the investment capabilities of the owner, the extreme event would be uninsurable, and the owner and his/her family would remain homeless. If this happened in only very few cases, society would be able to compensate the owners, but that could become impossible if the extreme event were to destroy a very high percentage, say 90%, of the existing stock of houses. The following general propositions can be derived from this discussion:

> We have so far lived in a very benevolent environment to which we have been able to adapt (ADTO) in a biological sense, and into which we have introduced modifications (ADOF) aimed at creating material wealth and at improving our standard of living. However we judge these achievements, and there are very good reasons to be critical of some of them, the path we followed is destabilizing our natural environment and risks destroying our civilization.
>
> There is an upper threshold to the investment required to correct the damages caused by climate induced extreme events of increasing intensity and frequency. Beyond this threshold the damage inflicted by uninsurable extreme events could become irreversible, or at least, the time required to reconstruct the system could be enormously longer than the time during which the destruction occurred. This could mean the end of human civilization as we know it.

As with the example of unemployment, the impact of human activities on the natural environment is likely to require a discontinuous transition lasting part of the XXIst century and involving a complex redesign of our production and innovation systems and of our welfare states. The task of analysing the underlying problems is probably beyond the scope of neoclassical economics with its assumptions of general equilibrium and rationality. Qualitative change, discontinuities, paradigms and trajectories, adaptive behaviour, efficiency and creativity, open and closed systems are likely to be more useful dealing with this type of phenomena. The policy implications discussed in this chapter are just examples of the possible applications of evolutionary economics. There are many more possible ones, such as the distribution of education and knowledge in a democratic system, migrations, and the institutions capable of providing adequate governance in a globalized system. The detailed discussion of these and other cases exceeds both the intended content and the space limits of this book. The detailed analysis of other examples is planned to be the content of a following book by Morris Teubal and Pier Paolo Saviotti.

At this point we cannot only differentiate evolutionary from neoclassical economics, but start to think what kind of evolutionary economics we want. To achieve the previous policy objectives, evolutionary economics needs to broaden its scope to include the study of such phenomena as education, employment, income distribution, trade, pensions, and migrations. The version of evolutionary economics required is not the existing one, but needs to be developed in part along the lines discussed in this book. As compared to the neoclassical type, evolutionary economics needs to be simultaneously humbler and more ambitious. Humbler, admitting that the limitations of human knowledge make us incapable of predicting accurately the consequences of our decisions, more ambitious in the sense that the boundaries of EVTH need to be much larger than those of Neo, considering the material basis of economics, the contributions of different disciplines and complexity science. It may seem excessive to define such a broad and apparently impossible to achieve objective for evolutionary economics. However, what I propose is a greater awareness of the interactivity of different components of our SESs and their EE, accompanied by a greater openness to other research traditions in economics, including the organization of joint events (conferences, workshops etc.). When each school of thought specializes in the study of a different subset of the EE or an SES, there is always the need to provide coordination and coherence in the whole edifice of knowledge. Although we are incapable of predicting accurately and completely the future effects of our innovations and policies, we need to keep exploring the possible scenarios to which such innovations are likely to give rise, not because such exploration can provide us with easy solutions to future problems but because better explorers are likely to be better adaptive improvers.

Notes

1 For a recent modelling approach to this combination see Dosi et al. (2010, 2013).
2 The concept of spontaneity can be extended to a completely self-organizing community without any central power. In more realistic terms, it can be interpreted as meaning a society in which the government carries out only some very basic functions, such as defence, police, and a minimum of education.
3 In this extended interpretation, the concept of compensation becomes equivalent to that of a fair distribution.
4 By quasi-full employment, we mean levels lower than 10%.
5 Often called Global Value Chains (GVC).
6 See the work by Saviotti and Pyka, by Saviotti, Pyka, Jun, and by Ciarli et al.
7 About the definitions of efficiency and creativity see Chapter 4.
8 Deep learning is an artificial intelligence (AI) function that imitates the workings of the human brain in processing data and creating patterns for use in decision-making. See for example: https://www.investopedia.com/terms/d/deep-learning.asp.
9 Best amongst the then existing forms of social organization.
10 This corresponds to what is often called guaranteed income.
11 A similar case exists in France for people active in shows (intermittants du spectacle) who receive a basic monthly allowance and are allowed to keep what they earn with their shows, concerts etc.
12 Recent reports by the IPCC (IPCC, 2021) and an updated versions of the report on 'Limits to Growth' of the MIT (Meadows et al., 1972) imply that the survival of our SES is at stake if we do not drastically reduce its impact on the natural environment before the year 2040. Furthermore, we are not now discussing a future crisis that can still be prevented, but an ongoing one that has not yet

reached its final state. What was expected to be a smooth transition towards a sustainable state is likely to be an abrupt one. The complex and interdependent nature of the world SES is such that the investment required to reduce its environmental impact is likely to be higher the faster the reduction envisaged. For example, the macroeconomic implications of reducing the impact of human activities on climate policy are likely to be very significant (Pisani-Ferry, 2021). It might very well be that the investment required to avoid a collapse of our global SES will impoverish us all.

13 Here the constant level of services is considered the one we are using now. This does not exclude the possibility to completely discard some types of services that are just wasteful.

14 In the bio-economy all inputs of a fossil nature would be replaced by renewable inputs coming from a modified agriculture.

References

Accenture (2017) Why is artificial intelligence important?

Acemoglu D., Autor D., Dorn D., H. Hanson G.H., and Price B. (2016) Import competition and the great US Employment Sag of the 2000s. *Journal of Labor Economics*, 34(S1): S141–S198.

Ayres R.U. (1998) The second law, recycling and limits to growth, Working paper, INSEAD Centre for Environmental Resources, 98/38/EPS/CMER.

Baldwin R. (2016) *The Great Convergence: Information Technology and the New Globalisation*, Cambridge, MA, Harvard University Press.

Baldwin R. (2018) A long view of globalisation in short: The New Globalisation, Part 5 of 5 Vox EU, 05 December 2018.

Bates Clark J. (1899) *The Distribution of Wealth: A Theory of Wages, Interests and Profits*, New York, Macmillan Company.

Beinhocker E.D. (2007) *The Origin of Wealth, The Radical Remaking of Economics and What It Means for Business and Society*, Boston, MA, Harvard Business School Press.

Bekker S., Mailand M. (2018) The European flexicurity concept and the Dutch and Danish flexicurity models: how have they managed the Great Recession? *Social Policy and Administration*, 53(1): 149–155.

Boulding K. (1966) The economics of the coming spaceship earth, in Jarrett H. (Ed.), *Environmental Quality in a Growing Economy*, Resources for the Future, Baltimore, MD, Johns Hopkins University Press, 3–14.

Brynjolfsson E., McAfee A. (2011) *Race against the Machine*, Lexington, MA, Digital Frontier Press.

Carsten H.P. (2011) The evolutionary approach to entropy: reconciling Georgescu-Roegen's natural philosophy with the maximum entropy framework. *Ecological Economics*, 70(4): 606–616.

ClimateWise (2014). Insurability in the face of climate change, University of Cambridge Institute for Sustainability Leadership and ClimateWise.

Copeland B.J. (2020) Artificial intelligence. *Encyclopedia Britannica*, https://www.britannica.com/technology/artificial-intelligence.

Daly H.E. (1977, 1991) *Steady-State Economics: Second Edition with New Essays*, Washington DC, Island Press.

Daly H.E. (1990) Commentary toward some operational principles of sustainable development. *Ecological Economics*, 2: 1-6.

Daly H.E. (2002) *Sustainable Development: Definitions, Principles, Policies, Invited Address, World Bank*, April 30, 2002, Washington, DC.

Daly H.E. (2007) *Ecological Economics and Sustainable Development: Selected Essays of Herman Daly*, Cheltenham, Edward Elgar.

Demaria F., Schneider F., Sekulova F., Martinez-Alier J. (2013) What is degrowth? From an activist slogan to a social movement, *Environmental Values*, 22: 191–215. https://doi.org/10.3197/096327113x13581561725194

Deutscher G. (2008) *The Entropy Crisis*, Singapore, London, World Scientific.

Dosi G., Fagiolo G., Napoletano M., Roventini A. (2013) Income Distribution, Credit and Fiscal Policies in an Agent-Based Keynesian Model, *Journal of Economic Dynamics and Control*, 37: 1598–1625.

Dosi, G., Fagiolo G. Roventini, A., (2010). Schumpeter meeting Keynes: a policy-friendly model of endogenous growth and business cycles. *Journal of Economic Dynamics and Control*, 34(9): 1748–1767, September.

Eurofound (2009) *Flexicurity and Industrial Relations*, European Foundation for the Improvement of Living and Working Conditions.

European Commission (2013) Flexicurity in Europe, Administrative Agreement, JRC N°31962-2010-11 NFP ISP - FLEXICURITY 2, Final Report.

Fagerberg J., Shrolec M. (2008) National innovation systems, capabilities and economic development. *Research Policy*, 37(9): 1417–1435.

Frenken K., van Oort F.G., Verburg T. (2007) Related variety, unrelated variety and regional economic growth. *Regional Studies*, 41(5): 685–697.

Frey C.B., Osborne M.A. (2013) *The Future of Employment: How Susceptible Are Jobs to Computerisation?* Oxford Martin School, Oxford University.

Frey C.B., Osborne M.A. (2017) The future of employment: how susceptible are jobs to computerisation?, *Technological Forecasting and Social Change*, 114(C): 254–280.

Georgescu Roegen N. (1971) *The Entropy Law and the Economic Process*, Cambridge, MA, Harvard University Press.

Gereffi G. (1999) International trade and industrial upgrading in the apparel commodity chain. *Journal of International Economics*, 48(1): 37–70.

Gowdy J. (1994) *Co-evolutionary Economics: The Economy, Society and the Environment*, Dordrecht, Kluwer Academics.

Hallegatte S., Hourcade J.C., Dumas P. Why economic dynamics matter in assessing climate change damages: illustration on extreme events. *Ecological Economics*, Elsevier, 2007, 62 (2), pp.330–340. 10.1016/j.ecolecon.2006.06.006. hal-00164626

Harari Y.N. (2011) *Sapiens: A Brief History of Humankind*, London, Penguin Random House.

Helpman E. (2016) Globalization and wage inequality, NBER working paper 22944.

Hidalgo C.A. (2015) *Why Information Grows, The Evolution of Order, from Atoms to Economies*, London, Penguin Random House.

Hidalgo C.A., Klinger B., Barabasi A.-L., Hausmann R. (2007) The product space conditions the development of nations. *Science*, 317: 482–487.

Hidalgo C.A., Hausmann R. (2009) The building blocks of economic complexity. *PNAS*, 106(26): 10575.

Hobsbawm E.J. (1968) *Industry and Empwere*, Harmondsworth, Penguin Books.

Huberman M., Minns C. (2007) The times they are not changin': Days and hours of work in Old and New Worlds, 1870–2000, *Explorations in Economic History*, 44: 538–567.

ILO (1976) *Employment, Growth and Basic Needs: A One World Problem*, Geneva, International Labor Office.

IPCC, 2021: Summary for Policymakers. In: Climate Change 2021: The Physical Science Basis. Contribution of Working Group I to the Sixth Assessment Report of the Intergovernmental Panel on Climate Change [Masson-Delmotte, V., P. Zhai,

A. Pirani, S. L. Connors, C. Péan, S. Berger, N. Caud, Y. Chen, L. Goldfarb, M. I. Gomis, M. Huang, K. Leitzell, E. Lonnoy, J. B. R. Matthews, T. K. Maycock, T. Waterfield, O. Yelekçi, R. Yu and B. Zhou (eds.)]. Cambridge University Press.

Lee K., Szapiro M., Mao Z. (2017) From Global Value Chains (GVC) to innovation systems for local value chains and knowledge creation. *The European Journal of Development Research*, 30(3): 424–441. https://doi.org/10.1057/s41287-017-0111–6. S2CID 158736538

Lovins A.B., Lovins L.H., Hawken P. (2000) *A Road Map for Natural Capitalism*, Boston, MA, Little Brown.

Lundvall B.A. (2002) *Innovation, Growth and Social Cohesion: The Danish Model*, Cheltenham, Edward Elgar.

Martínez-Alier J., Unai P., Franck-Dominique V., Zaccai E. (2010) Sustainable de-growth: Mapping the context, criticisms and future prospects of an emergent paradigm. *Ecological Economics*, 69: 1741–1747.

Marx K. (1867, 1954) *Capital*, London, Lawrence and Wishart.

Maslow A. (1943) A theory of human motivation. *Psychological Review*, 50: 370–396.

Mazzucato M. (2013) *The Entrepreneurial State: Debunking Public vs Private Sector Myths*, London, Anthem Press.

Meadows D.H., Meadows G., Jorgen Randers J., Behrens W.W.III. (1972) *The Limits to Growth*. New York, Universe Books. ISBN 0-87663-165-0

Metcalfe J.S. (1994) Evolutionary economics and technology policy, *The Economic Journal*, 104(425): 931–944.

Metcalfe J.S. (1998) *Evolutionary Economics and Creative Destruction*, London, Routledge.

Metcalfe J.S., Foster J., Ramlogan R. (2006) Adaptive economic growth, *Cambridge Journal of Economics*, 30: 7–32.

Milgrom P. Roberts J. (1992) *Economics, Organization and Management*, Englewood Cliffs, Prentice Hall.

Morrisson C., Murtin F. (2007) Education inequalities and the Kuznets curves: a global perspective since 1870. PSE Working Papers n2007–12. 2007. <halshs-00588085>HAL Id: halshs-00588085https://halshs.archives-ouvertes.fr/halshs-00588085

Morrisson C., Murtin F. (2009) The kuznets curve of education: a global perspective on education inequalities, in Morrisson C., Murtin F. (Eds.), London, Centre for the Economics of Education, London School of Economics June 2010 ISSN 2045-6557.

Nelson R., Winter S. (1982) *An Evolutionary Theory of Economic Change*, Cambridge, MA, Harvard University Press.

Newman K.S. (1999) *No Shame in My Game: The Working Poor in the Inner City*, New York, Vintage Books, Random House and Russel Sage Foundation.

Nussbaum, M. (2011) *Creating Capabilities*, Cambridge, MA: Harvard University Press.

OECD. (2007) Globalisation, Jobs and Wages, Policy Brief, Paris.

Pearce D. (1992) Economics, equity and sustainable development, pp. 69-76 in Ekins P., Max-Neef M. (Eds.), *Real-Life Economics*, London, Routledge.

Pearce D.W., Turner R.K. (1989). *Economics of Natural Resources and the Environment*. Baltimore, MD, Johns Hopkins University Press. ISBN 978-0801839870.

Pisani-Ferry J. (2021) *Climate Policy is Macroeconomic Policy, and the Implications Well Be Significant*, Policy Briefs PB 21-20, PIIE, Washington, DC, Peterson Institute for International Economics.

Ramlogan R., Metcalfe J.S. (2006) Restless capitalism: a complexity perspective on modern capitalist economies, in Garnsey E., McGlade J. (Eds.), *Complexity and Co-evolution*, Cheltenham, Edward Elgar, 115–146.

Ranis G., Stewart F., Samman E., (2005): *Human Development: Beyond the HDI*, Discussion Paper, No. 916, Yale University, Economic Growth Center, New Haven, CT.

Robert V., Yoguel G. (2022) Exploration of trending concepts in innovation policy. *Review of Evolutionary Political Economy.* https://doi.org/10.1007/s43253-022-00064-9

Rodrik D. (2011) *The Globalization Paradox: Why Global Markets, States and Democracy Can't Coexist*, Oxford, Oxford University Press.

Saez E., Zucman G. (2019) *The Triumph of Injustice*, Norton (Le Triomphe de l'Injustice: Richesse, Evasion Fiscale et Démocratie, Paris, Seuil (2020).

Sapir A. (2006) Globalization and the reform of European social models. *Journal of Common Market Studies*, 44(2): 369–390.

Saviotti P.P. (2018) Innovation and consumption in the evolution of capitalist societies, in Spinozzi P., Mazzanti M. (Eds.), *Cultures of Sustainability and Wellbeing. Theories, Histories and Policies*, London, Routledge, 72–84.

Saviotti P.P. (2017) Structural Change, Knowledge and the Bioeconomy, in Dabbert S., Lewandowski I., Pyka A., Weiss J. (Eds), *Knowledge-driven Developments in the Bioeconomy – Technological and Economic Perspectives*, Heidelberg, Springer, 17–32.

Saviotti P.P., Pyka A. (2004) Economic development by the creation of new sectors. *Journal of Evolutionary Economics*, 14(1): 1–35.

Saviotti P.P., Pyka A. (2008), Micro and macro dynamics: industry life cycles, inter-sector coordination and aggregate growth. *Journal of Evolutionary Economics*, 18: 167–182.

Saviotti P.P., Pyka A. (2013) From necessities to imaginary worlds: structural change, product quality and economic development. *Technological Forecasting & Social Change*, 80: 1499–1512.

Sen A. (1985) *Commodities and Capabilities*, Amsterdam, North-Holland.

Slaughter M.J., Swagel P. (1997) Does Globalization Lower Wages and Export Jobs? *IMF Economic Issues* N° 11 pp. 1–12

Stanton E. (2007) *The Human Development Index: A History*, Working Paper Number 127, Political Economy Research Institute, University of Massachusetts at Amherst.

Streeten P. with Burki S.J., ul Haq M., Hicks N., Stewart F. (1981) *First Things First: Meeting Basic Human Needs in the Developing Countries*, Published for the World Bank by Oxford University Press.

UNCTAD (2013) *Global Value Chains: Investment and Trade for Development.* World Investment Report 2013, United Nations, UNCTAD: New York & Geneva.

van den Bergh J.C., Gowdy J.M. (2000) Evolutionary theories in environmental and resource economics: approaches and applications. *Environmental and Resource Economics*, 17: 37–57. https://doi.org/10.1023/A:1008317920901

Vermeulen B., Kesselhut J., Pyka A., Saviotti P.P. (2018) The impact of automation on employment: just the usual structural change? *Sustainability*, 10: 1661.

WCED (Report of the World Commission on Environment and Development: Our Common Future (1987) The Brutland Report, Oxford, Oxford University Press.

Weinstein D. (2019) Herbert Spencer, *The Stanford Encyclopaedia of Philosophy* (Fall 2019 Edition), Edward N. Zalta (ed.), <https://plato.stanford.edu/archives/fall2019/entries/spencer/>.

Wills A., Goujon A. (1998) Diffusion of education in six world regions, 1960–1990. *Population and Development Review*, 24(2): 357–368.

Index